D1480805

The Nature of Executive Leadership

The Nature of **Executive Leadership**

A Conceptual and Empirical Analysis of Success

Stephen J. Zaccaro

American Psychological Association
Washington, DC

Published by
American Psychological Association
750 First Street, NE
Washington, DC 20002

Copies may be ordered from
APA Order Department
P.O. Box 92984
Washington, DC 20090-2984

In the U.K. and Europe, copies may be ordered from
American Psychological Association
3 Henrietta Street
Covent Garden, London
WC2E 8LU England

Typeset in Meridien by EPS Group Inc., Easton, MD

Printer: Data Reproductions Corp., Auburn Hills, MI
Cover Designer: Watermark Design Office, Alexandria, VA
Project Manager: Debbie K. Hardin, Charlottesville, VA

The opinions and statements published are the responsibility of the authors, and such opinions and statements do not necessarily represent the policies of the APA.

Library of Congress Cataloging-in-Publication Data

Zaccaro, Stephen J.
    The nature of executive leadership : a conceptual and empirical analysis of success / Stephen J. Zaccaro.
        p.   cm.
    Includes bibliographical references and index.
    ISBN 1-55798-732-7
        1. Executive ability.   2. Leadership.   I. Title.

HD38.2 .Z33 2000
658.4'092—dc21   00-060601

Printed in the United States of America
First Edition

Contents

List of Tables, Exhibits, and Figures

Tables

Exhibits

Figures

Acknowledgments

The work that went into writing this book was financially supported by the U.S. Army Research Institute for the Behavioral and Social Sciences (ARI). It is based on research done by the author and published by ARI in 1996 under contract with the Consortium of Universities. I gratefully acknowledge the significant support of Edgar Johnson, Robert Ruskin, and Michael Drillings during the course of that research project. I also would like to indicate my appreciation for the assistance, advice, reviews, and critical suggestions offered by several other individuals, including Richard Klimoski, Michelle Marks, Michael McGee, Lori Zukin, Donna Williams, Theodore Gessner, Julie Johnson, Vicki Threlfall, Edwin Fleishman, and Michael Mumford. In addition, Mary Lee Peterson provided invaluable assistance in the preparation of this book and its numerous tables and figures. Finally, I want to thank the staff and editors at the American Psychological Association for their advice and assistance in preparing the manuscript for publication.

The views, opinions, and findings in this book are not to be construed as official Department of the Army positions unless so designated by other authorized documents.

The Nature of Executive Leadership

Executive Leadership: An Introduction

1

The quality of an organization's top leaders is a critical influence on its overall effectiveness and continuing adaptability (Katz & Kahn, 1978). Senior leaders are expected to adopt a long-term perspective of the organization within its environment as well as develop short-term goals and strategies that are congruent with that perspective. In their planning and exertion of influence, senior leaders also are required to balance myriad, typically conflicting, constituencies, demands, goals, and requirements, both within and outside the organization. When leaders accomplish these tasks successfully, their organizations are likely to be performing well and in a position to adapt quickly to environmental dynamics. In other words, high-quality senior leaders contribute significantly to the success and vitality of their organizations.

Recently, there has been a significant increase in research on executive leadership; this increase has been fueled by a growing interest in explaining organizational effectiveness through the actions of top executives (Hambrick, 1989; Hambrick & Mason, 1984). Although popular books and seminars on successful leadership continue to proliferate, few of these are based on this research. And, although many promising new ideas have emerged in the scholarly literature from this research, they have not been reviewed and integrated into a meaningful framework for leadership researchers and practitioners. Thus, questions about (a) what is known about executive leadership, (b) how the actions of executive leaders contribute to effective organizations, (c) what attributes successful top leaders possess, and (d) how executive qualities can be assessed and developed remain unanswered from a firm conceptual and empirical foundation. Indeed, researchers still do not universally agree whether senior leaders are even important for organizational success. Such evidence must be established to justify the considerable effort being directed at understanding top organizational leadership.

This book, then, grew out of the need to aggregate, examine, and evaluate existing knowledge about executive leadership and to begin providing answers to these questions. Accordingly, its purpose is to review research on executive leadership from multiple domains. The objectives of this book are to (a) describe and critically analyze leading conceptual models of executive leadership according to several specific criteria; (b) synthesize existing empirical research to determine what is known about executive leadership; and, (c) identify necessary future directions for research. The intent is to offer an integrated basis for understanding executive leadership and thinking about its role in organizational effectiveness.

It is my hope that, on the basis of this integration, industrial psychologists, organizational consultants, and others who work with executive leaders will have an empirically grounded framework within which to develop ways of assessing, selecting, training, developing, and coaching executives. As will be shown, much of the existing research has been based on leaders at lower levels of the organization, and the characteristics that make for effective middle-level managers are distinctly different than those that make for successful executive leaders. It is critical that those working with executives become aware of the unique nature of executive leadership and the knowledge, skills, abilities, and other characteristics that define effective executive leadership.

In this book, I examine several leading conceptual models that focus on the nature and requisite qualities of executive leadership. These include conceptual complexity models, behavioral complexity models, strategic decision-making models, and visionary or inspirational leadership models. These conceptual models are reviewed, in part, using criteria proposed by Day and Lord (1988) for a systematic theory of executive leadership. These criteria will be described later in this chapter. Also, I review research that had as its goal the empirical testing of conceptual assumptions about executive leadership. The purpose of this review is to evaluate the conceptual frameworks developed regarding executive leadership, in particular, to ascertain what parts have received significant validation. However, given the recency of most executive leadership models, these empirical examinations are likely to be incomplete. Nonetheless, enough research is available to begin to evaluate the potential of the various models. Graduate students and other researchers will find in this book many empirical questions to address regarding the assessment, selection, training, and development of executives. I have made specific recommendations regarding the most pressing research questions. In addition, I have identified some of the methodological problems with previous research and made recommendations for avoiding these problems in future research.

The remainder of this chapter covers five topics. First, I provide a brief examination of qualitative differences in the nature of leadership across organizational levels. Second, I offer a working definition of *senior leadership*. All the conceptual models described in this book assert that senior leadership is qualitatively different from junior leadership. Therefore, I offer a description of the functions and nature of senior leadership as a starting point. Although this definition may be at variance with other approaches described elsewhere in this book, a significant degree of consensus does exist regarding the nature of such leadership. Third, I review briefly the evidence that senior leaders are critical contributors to organizational performance. Fourth, I describe the criteria used to evaluate both the existing conceptual models and their corresponding empirical bases. Fifth, I conclude the chapter with a brief description of the major conceptual approaches to senior leadership that are reviewed and analyzed in subsequent chapters.

Do Executive Leaders Really Matter?

Calder (1977) argued that the influence of leadership is exaggerated and a product of attributional biases and implicit theories people have of the supposed role of leaders in society. Meindl and his colleagues (Meindl, 1990; Meindl & Ehrlich, 1987; Meindl, Ehrlich, & Dukerich, 1985) have offered similar notions about the so-called "romance of leadership." There are two schools of thought on the limited effect of top executives in organizational performance within the strategic management literature. One of these perspectives argues that organizational performance is strictly a function of environmental characteristics and contingencies (Aldrich, 1979; Bourgeois, 1984; Hannan & Freeman, 1977; Lawrence & Lorsch, 1967; Romanelli & Tushman, 1986). The other perspective suggests that organizational strategies and decision making result not primarily from the characteristics and dispositions of top leaders, but rather from previous organizational actions and the existing or predominant organizational culture (Miles & Snow, 1978; Starbuck, 1983).

Two widely cited executive succession studies have been offered to support the argument that senior leaders are not truly influential for organizational performance. Lieberson and O'Connor (1972) examined the effects of executive succession in 167 corporations representing 13 industries and covering a 20-year time span. They compared executive succession with both immediate and 3-year changes in sales, earnings, and profit margins. The results of their analysis indicated that leadership accounted for 6.5% to 15.2% of the variance in immediate organizational outcomes and 6.3% to 31.7% of variance in outcomes after 3 years. Lieberson and O'Connor interpreted these percentages as showing that leaders contribute little to organizational performance beyond the effects of environmental factors. Salancik and Pfeffer (1977), who examined mayoral change in 30 cities over an 18-year time frame, reached a similar conclusion. After controlling for city and year, mayors explained between 5.6% and 10% of the variance in city income and expenditures. These percentages changed to between 4.9% and 24.2% when financial outcomes were computed relative to total city budget.

After reviewing these studies, Day and Lord (1988) argued that the authors' original interpretations were erroneous. Day and Lord noted that even the 7.5% variance in net income attributable to leadership reported by Lieberson and O'Connor (1972) represented a substantial amount for most organizations. Furthermore, when examining leadership effects over time (i.e., after a 3-year lag) and adjusting for effects of company size (i.e., by examining only profit margins as organizational outcomes), the variance attributable to leadership increased to 32%. Day and Lord noted a similar misinterpretation of the data from Salancik and Pfeffer (1977).

A number of other studies have provided convincing evidence of the effect of executive leaders on organizational performance. For example, Weiner and Mahoney (1981) examined executive succession effects in 193 companies across a 19-year time span. They reported that leadership accounted for approximately 44% of the variance in profit margins and 47% of the variance in stock prices. Barrick, Day, Lord, and Alexander (1991) used a linear decision-theoretic utility procedure to calculate the financial impact of leadership in 132 organizations over a 15-year period. Their results demonstrated that an average executive's tenure with an organization was responsible for substantial financial gain, with a utility point estimate of more than $25 million after taxes.

Hitt and Tyler (1991) examined the influence of three sets of variables on organizational performance: (a) industry characteristics, (b) objective environmental criteria, and (c) personal characteristics of top executives. The first two sets of variables were derived from strategic management theories that limit the effect of leaders on organizational performance (Aldrich, 1979; Bourgeois, 1984, Hannan & Freeman, 1977; Lawrence & Lorsch, 1967; Miles & Snow, 1978; Romanelli & Tushman, 1986; Starbuck, 1983), whereas the last set of variables was suggested by theories that argue for substantial influence of organization executives (Child, 1972; Hambrick, 1989; Hambrick & Mason, 1984). Hitt and Tyler reported that after controlling for the influence of industry and environmental characteristics, the characteristics of senior leaders still explained significant variances in acquisition decisions.

Taken together, these results argue for Hambrick and Mason's (1984) assertion that "top executives matter" (p. 194). Given an obvious and consistent interest in improving organizational performance, these results provide a compelling rationale for the systematic investigation of executive leadership, particularly the factors that enhance the facilitative effects of such leaders on organizations.

The Unique Nature of Executive Leadership

Leadership has been a major topic in organizational science for almost a century and has spawned literally thousands of empirical and conceptual studies. Surprisingly, however, relatively little of this research has focused explicitly on leadership at top organizational levels. Such leadership has been called "senior" leadership (Heller, 1972; Kimmel, 1981), "executive" leadership (Barnard, 1938; Carlson, 1951), or "strategic" leadership (Hambrick, 1989; Phillips & Hunt, 1992; U.S. Department of the Army, 1993). These terms are used interchangeably throughout this book. An annotated bibliography of senior leadership research prepared by Kimmel (1981) listed 135 entries from both the military and non-military literatures. Fewer than half, 64, of the studies were identified as empirical research. Although this number of studies is not insignificant, it is noteworthy that Stogdill's (1974) comprehensive *Handbook of Leadership: A Survey of the Literature* contained about 3000 references on leadership in general and Bass's (1990) third edition of this handbook listed approximately 7500 citations. An admittedly rough comparison of these numbers suggests, then, that only about 2% to 5% of the general literature on leadership has been directed specifically toward top organizational leaders. This observation was echoed by Day and Lord (1988), who stated, "The topic of executive leadership . . . has not been a major concern of leadership researchers or theorists. Their focus has been primarily lower-level leadership" (p. 458).

Why have leadership researchers generally neglected the topic of executive leadership? One reason may be that quality empirical research with such leaders is prohibitively difficult to accomplish. There are simply more junior leaders than senior leaders with whom to conduct research. One or two large organizations could likely provide a sample large enough for most empirical research requirements. A comparable sample of executive leaders, however, would require sampling from many organizations. It also is probable that executives are unable or unwilling to devote significant amounts of time to such research.

Identifying the consequences of senior leadership for organizational effectiveness requires the measurement of variables that often can be gained only through an archival or historical analysis of organizational performance (Day & Lord, 1988). Such analyses typically have been used in executive succession studies, in which the effects of executive leadership are examined on such variables as organizational change (e.g., Miller, 1993); returns on assets, sales, and equity (Dalton & Kesner, 1985; Haleblian & Finklestein, 1993; Zajac, 1990, respectively); and stockholder reactions (e.g., Lubatkin, Chung, Rogers, & Oers, 1989). However, this approach can be quite problematic when the researcher's intention is to associate such outcomes with measures of psychological constructs reflecting executive characteristics (e.g., personality, cognitive skills, motivational orientation). This is because these constructs are exceedingly difficult to assess from archival and historical records (see House, Spangler, & Woycke, 1991, as an example of this kind of research). Indeed, a 1994 review of 30 years of succession research reported very few, if any, multivariate studies that examined a range of psychological constructs in the context of executive succession (Kesner & Sebora, 1994).

Finally, the criteria for effective executive leadership are likely to be qualitatively different than those for lower-level leadership. Whereas the effects of lower-level leadership often can be assessed fairly directly with measures of unit performance, subordinate attitudes, and leader promotion rate, the outcomes of executive leadership frequently are manifested at a point in time more remote from the leader's actions than at lower organizational levels (Jacobs & Jaques, 1987). Thus, the association between action and consequence at the top of an organization is likely to be more indirect or ambiguous and therefore more difficult to observe. This fact constrains, for example, a demonstration that certain constellations of executive skills are significantly associated with indices of executive performance.

Nevertheless, as shown by Kimmel (1981), these obstacles have not precluded at least some research on senior leadership. That the primary focus of earlier leadership theories was lower-level leadership may be attributed to the possibility that such theories have implicitly assumed that explanations and causal models of junior leadership pertain equally well to senior leadership. However, as Day and Lord (1988) argued, "applying leadership theories developed at lower levels to explain leadership at upper levels assumes a construct isomorphism across levels that is probably not true" (p. 459).

QUALITATIVE DIFFERENCES IN ORGANIZATIONAL LEADERSHIP

Accordingly, several leadership theorists have proposed that there are qualitative differences in the nature of leadership across organizational levels. For example, Katz and Kahn (1978) specified three distinct patterns of organizational leadership. The first pattern concerns the administrative use of existing organizational structures to maintain effective organizational operations. If problems develop to disrupt these operations, existing organizational mechanisms and procedures are used to resolve them. Indeed, Katz and Kahn noted that "such acts are often seen as so institutionalized as to require little if any leadership" (p. 537). This leadership pattern occurs at lower organizational levels. It requires technical knowledge; understanding of organizational rules, policies, and procedures; and equitable use of coercive and reward power. The second leadership pattern involves the embellishment and operationalization of formal structural elements. Such actions are the province of middle-level leaders and require that leaders possess a two-way orientation (i.e., toward both superiors and subordinates) as well as significant human relations skills. The third pattern of organizational leadership concerns structural origination or change in the organization as a reflection of the formulation of new policy. Katz and Kahn argued that this leadership pattern occurs at the top levels of the organization and, in terms of leader abilities and skills, requires a system-wide perspective and a high level of personal charisma. This distribution of separate leadership patterns across organizational levels suggests that there are significant qualitative differences in the nature of junior and senior leadership.

Such qualitative differences between upper- and lower-level organizational leaders were also proposed in separate theoretical formulations by Jaques and Jacobs (1987); Mumford, Zaccaro, Harding, Fleishman, and Reiter-Palmon (1993); and Bentz (1987). Jaques and Jacobs theorized that the nature of leadership works changes across organizational levels such that senior leaders are more responsible for institutional adaptation within the broader organizational environment and operate with longer work or task time frames and greater individual discretion. Mumford, Zaccaro, et al. proposed that as individuals ascend organizational levels the number of groups and subsystems they are responsible for increases; accordingly, they must take into account more organizational units when solving organizational problems. Furthermore, at higher organizational levels, the problems confronting leaders become more ill-defined and more susceptible to effects from the organization's environment. Thus, according to Mumford, Zaccaro, et al., the nature of leader problem solving and the requisite influence patterns change significantly across organizational levels. Along similar lines, Bentz argued that the breadth of business units that must be managed and coordinated (i.e., "scope") as well as the "internal complexity, diversity, and ambiguity of functions within and across units managed, within and across varieties of personal relations, and across decisions made" (i.e., "scale," pp. 1–2) increase dramatically for executive leaders.

Most current theories of leadership either propose generic conceptual models that apply across organizational levels or restrict their focus to lower-level leadership. The changes in leader performance described by these theorists and researchers indicate that the current approaches are limited at best and highly misleading at worst. More systematic theories of executive leadership that recognize these qualitative differences are needed. Indeed, Day and Lord (1988) wrote,

> We strongly urge researchers and theorists interested in leadership to consider upper levels of management as an important practical domain that needs theoretical and research attention. We believe the opportunity exists for the development of innovative and practically relevant leadership theory and research (pp. 458–459).

RECENT TRENDS

Recent trends in the leadership literature indicate that greater attention is indeed being directed toward understanding the unique properties of senior organizational leadership. For example, a major topic of leadership research in the 1980s and 1990s was charismatic or transformational leadership. Although some researchers have argued that such leadership can occur at all organizational levels (Bass, 1985), the focus of various conceptual models of visionary or inspirational leadership has clearly been the individuals at the top of the organization (e.g., House, 1977; Sashkin, 1988; Tichy & Devanna, 1990). Another major research topic that has emerged in the past 10 to 15 years is the characteristics and influence of top management teams (e.g., Finklestein, 1992; Finklestein & Hambrick, 1990; Hambrick, 1994; Hambrick & Mason, 1984; Smith, Smith, Olian, & Sims, 1994; Sutcliffe, 1994; Wiersema & Bantel, 1992). How the demography and processes of top management teams influence organizational climate, strategies, and performance is being researched. Finally, this increased interest in top organizational leadership is shown in Yukl's 1994 edition of his leadership textbook, *Leadership in Organizations*. In particular, a new chapter summarizing research on "strategic leadership by top executives" was added. This increased attention supports the premise that there is something different about executive leadership, prompting the question, What is the nature of executive leadership?

What Is Executive Leadership?

One of the earliest treatises on the definition and nature of senior leadership was offered by Barnard (1938), who described the functions of organization executives. Barnard argued that organizations emerged when individuals agreed to coordinate their activities in a collective effort to achieve a common purpose. Organizations derived their success and vitality from their members' willingness to cooperate for a collective purpose and from the quality of communication among participants that furthered this cooperation. This collective purpose provided the "coordinating and unifying principle" (p. 95) for the organization. From this theory of formal organization, Barnard articulated that the functions of executives were related to "all the work essential to the vitality and endurance of an organization, so far, at least, as it must be accomplished through formal coordination" (p. 215).

A prominent element of this definition is the executive's responsibility to ensure that the organization "works" correctly in the accomplishment of its purpose. Accordingly, Barnard (1938) noted that "executive work is not that *of* the organization, but the specialized work of *maintaining* the organization in operation" (p. 215). Because organizations are grounded in interpersonal cooperation around a collective purpose as well as in communication systems that further this cooperation, specific executive functions become (a) the definition of organizational purpose, (b) the identification of personnel willing to cooperate in accomplishing this purpose, and (c) the development of a communication system fostering organizational cooperation. Executives are placed by their responsibility at the critical nexus of this communication system.

Barnard's (1938) description of executive leadership provided two major elements that have become consistent themes in subsequent conceptual models distinguishing executive leadership from junior leadership. First, senior leadership involves the coordination and maintenance of the organization as a whole, including all of its subcomponents. Barnard's overarching theme of coordination around a collective purpose maintains that executive leaders are responsible for orchestrating and managing the integration of these multiple subcomponents so that they work in synchrony to move the organization in the direction established by the executive.

Second, executives establish purpose, which is then implemented through the various levels of the organization. At each descending level, this purpose becomes operationalized in terms of more specific goals and tasks that operate within increasingly shorter time frames. This collective arrangement follows from the subordinates' commitment to the executive's formulated direction and from their cooperation in instituting that direction. This aspect of executive leadership (i.e., the definition and institution of organizational purpose), together with the role of organization-wide management, has remained central to most, if not all, conceptions of senior leadership.

Barnard's (1938) emphasis regarding executive leadership functions was predominantly on the executive's internal maintenance and directional focus of the organization. A theme regarding senior leadership that has emerged since Barnard's work is boundary spanning as a critical leadership function. This concept was articulated most clearly by Katz and Kahn (1966, 1978), who viewed organizations as open systems inextricably connected with their environments through their acquisition of required organizational resources and the distribution of finished organizational products. Indeed, an organization's survival depends in large part on how well its structure is able to adapt to the characteristics of the embedding environment. Furthermore, several organizational subsystems, such as marketing, sales, and research and development, exist primarily for the purpose of facilitating the organization's interaction with and adaptation to its environment. Although Katz and Kahn agreed with Barnard that a major role of senior leadership is to maintain and enhance the internal and interpersonal dynamics of an organization, they also argued that "leadership emerges as individuals take charge of relating a unit or subsystem to the external structure or environment" (Katz & Kahn, 1978, p. 532). That is, leaders are responsible for maintaining and managing organizational boundaries, particularly the organization's external dynamics and interactions (Gilmore, 1992). Such responsibilities are also referred to as *boundary-spanning activities.*

Katz and Kahn (1978) did not limit such boundary management to senior leaders, however. At lower organizational levels, junior leaders manage the boundary between their units and the larger organizational system. What, then, is different about senior leadership? First, the boundary management activities of senior leaders, compared with those of junior leaders, incorporate the interactions of the organization as a whole with its external environment. This introduces a qualitative difference in complexity. External environments typically are more dynamic and characterized by more novelty than what is likely to be found in most internal organizational environments. Furthermore, in their interactions within larger environments, senior leaders are faced with balancing the demands and requirements of multiple organizational constituencies, whereas junior leaders typically are concerned only with the requirements of single units. For example, the university president who must lobby a state legislature for annual appropriations has to prioritize the demands of several university groups. Within the university, however, department leaders are concerned only with the needs of their specific units.

Katz and Kahn (1978) noted that the senior leader's external focus is also characterized by an orientation toward environmental opportunities that may allow the organization to enhance its position and viability within its environment. Accordingly, a major senior leadership function that emerges from the leader's external boundary management activities is the introduction of organization-wide policies and structural changes intended to increase the organization's ability to adapt to its environment. Indeed, Katz and Kahn argued that "except in democratically constituted systems, only the top echelons of line and staff officers are really in a position to introduce changes in structure" (p. 537). Note that although these activities of internal change, development, and incorporation of organizational structure resemble Barnard's (1938) executive functions, Katz and Kahn derived them from the senior leader's primary responsibility for management of the boundary between the organization and its environment. That is, contingencies, demands, and opportunities within the organization's environment drive the development and constitution of the organization's structure.

Most current models of senior leadership assume these two executive functions of boundary management and organization-wide coordination. For example, strategic decision-making and management theories define top leadership as involving the establishment of organizational strategy in accordance with environmental conditions and the implementation of strategy within the organization (Hambrick, 1989; Hambrick & Mason, 1984). Charismatic and transformational leadership theories emphasize the organization and motivation of subordinates' efforts in line with established purposes and direction (Bass, 1985; House, 1977). Conceptual complexity theories describe the articulation of organizational purpose within increasingly greater time spans regarding the organization and its environment (Jacobs & Jaques, 1987, 1990, 1991). Finally, behavioral complexity theories emphasize the need for senior leaders to coordinate the demands and requirements of multiple constituencies in accordance with the organizational purpose (Hart & Quinn, 1993; Quinn, 1984, 1988; Tsui, 1984a, 1984b).

Considered together, these various models suggest that there is some consensus regarding the definition and nature of executive leadership. Accordingly, for the purposes of this book, executive leadership is defined as follows:

> That set of activities directed toward the development and management of the organization as a whole, including all of its subcomponents, to reflect long-range policies and purposes that have emerged from the senior leader's interactions within the organization and his or her interpretations of the organization's external environment.

This definition specifies both the internal and external systematic perspectives advocated by Katz and Kahn (1978) for upper-level organizational leaders. It also assumes that top leaders are responsible for maintaining the vitality and adaptability of their organizations in the context of shifting environmental demands and contingencies. This does not mean that executives merely adjust or react to environmental forces. Successful executives often create their own operating environments. Thus, senior leaders can be viewed as critical determinants of organizational effectiveness.

Key Questions Regarding Executive Leadership Research

Day and Lord (1988) offered several prescriptions and suggestions for evaluating systematic theories of executive leadership. First, a theory of executive leadership should specify the means and mechanisms by which executive leaders influence organizational effectiveness. In line with Barnard (1938) and Katz and Kahn (1966, 1978), Day and Lord proposed, for example, that leaders affect organizational performance by (a) influencing the external environment of the organization, (b) adapting the organization to environmental contingencies, and (c) shaping and managing the organization to increase its efficiency and adaptability. Each mode of influence can involve direct leadership influence methods such as political lobbying, strategic planning, and organizational role specification as well as indirect tactics such as organizational image building, envisioning, and production norm setting. These suggestions indicate that executive leadership theories should specify the nature of executive influences on organizational processes to explain the unique contributions of the activities of top organizational leaders. That is, a conceptual framework of senior leadership should provide answers to the following key questions regarding the nature of senior leadership work and its influence on organizational performance:

- How do the requirements for executive leadership performance differ from those requirements at lower organizational levels?
- At what organizational level do performance requirements shift in quality?
- How are leader effectiveness and influence defined and operationalized at different organizational levels?
- What is the relationship between the accomplishment of executive leadership performance requirements and organizational effectiveness?

The specification of the unique qualities of executive leadership facilitates the delineation of the corresponding knowledge, skills, abilities, and other characteristics that enhance effective accomplishment of such work. Accordingly, Day and Lord (1988) noted that executive leadership theories need to describe the individual characteristics that are associated with successful executive leadership. Specifically, two key points need to be addressed. First, such theories should denote the knowledge, skills, abilities, and other characteristics that distinguish senior leaders from junior leaders. These variables should be associated with promotions to upper-level leadership positions. Second, senior leadership models need to specify what individual qualities are associated with success at the executive level. Because the nature of leadership changes as one ascends the organizational hierarchy, the variables that predict success at lower levels and those that predict leadership promotion will be different from the critical individual constructs that predict effectiveness in senior leadership roles. These points suggest the following questions regarding the nature of critical executive leader knowledge, skills, abilities, and other characteristics:

- What individual characteristics distinguish executive leaders from lower-level leaders?
- What individual characteristics distinguish successful executive leaders from unsuccessful executive leaders?

Several particular measurement and methodological issues are critical to the study of senior leadership. Both sampling issues and the nature of relevant dependent variables change considerably when leadership is examined at different organizational levels. For example, the influence of successful senior leadership is likely to be manifested over longer time frames than junior leadership. For this reason, Day and Lord (1988) suggested more historical analyses that examine leader influence on organizational performance. Also, although measures of individual and single-unit performance are appropriate as criteria at lower organizational levels, organization-wide outcomes such as profitability, market share, and sales growth are more appropriate criteria for the assessment of senior leaders. Thus, the empirical examination of hypotheses about such leadership should not depend solely on criteria that are more applicable to junior leadership. Finally, theories and models that specify the unique nature of senior leadership work, as well as particular senior leader skills and competencies, should also offer appropriate and psychometrically sound strategies for assessing these constructs. These issues raise the following questions:

- What are the psychometric qualities of measures that assess executive leadership characteristics and skills?
- What is the quality of the research methodologies and criteria being used to assess theories and models of executive leadership?

Well-specified models of senior leadership should also provide the basis for the effective training and development of such leaders. Senior leader development is tied to progress in career and adult development, particularly in terms of the emergence of certain senior leader competencies. For example, Mumford, Zaccaro, et al. (1993) proposed that wisdom or complex social judgment skills are critical determinants of successful senior leader problem solving. The development of wisdom may be associated with the emergence of other complex thinking skills as with an array of early career experiences. Senior leader development may be inextricably tied to adult and career development patterns. Thus, effective theories of senior leadership should specify the framework of developmental interventions that correspond to their key conceptual variables. This suggests a final question:

- What developmental interventions have emerged from conceptual models of senior leadership and have been validated by empirical research?

Exhibit 1-1 summarizes these key questions that guided the review and critical analysis of executive leadership research contained in this book. This research reflects several conceptual perspectives that are introduced in the final section of the chapter.

EXHIBIT 1-1

Key Questions and Criteria for a Critical Analysis of Senior Leadership Research

- How do the requirements for executive leadership performance differ from those at lower organizational levels?
- At what organizational level do these performance requirements shift?
- How are leader effectiveness and influence defined and operationalized at different organizational levels?
- What is the relationship between the accomplishment of executive leadership performance requirements and organizational effectiveness?
- What individual characteristics distinguish executive leaders from lower-level leaders?
- What individual characteristics distinguish successful executive leaders from unsuccessful executive leaders?
- What are the psychometric qualities of measures that assess executive leadership characteristics and skills?
- What is the quality of the research methodologies and criteria being used to assess theories and models of executive leadership?
- What developmental interventions have emerged from conceptual models of executive leadership and been validated by empirical research?

Conceptual Perspectives of Executive Leadership: An Overview

A survey of leadership research from different disciplines (e.g., psychology, public administration, strategic management) identified four major conceptual perspectives of executive leadership: (a) conceptual complexity models; (b) behavioral complexity models; (c) strategic decision-making models; and (4) visionary or inspirational leadership. Each approach, with its corresponding empirical research base, is reviewed.

Conceptual complexity models of executive leadership proceed from the premise that organizations operate within increasingly complex environments. This environmental complexity results in the stratification of organizations, wherein higher levels of leadership are characterized by greater information-processing demands and by the need to solve more ill-defined, novel, and complex organizational problems. To thrive, executive leaders require significant conceptual capacities that allow them to make sense of and navigate successfully within such complex environments. Thus, models that follow from these premises (e.g., (Jacobs & Jaques, 1987, 1990; Jaques, 1986; Lewis & Jacobs, 1992; Markessini, 1991; Mumford, Zaccaro, Harding, et al., 1993; Streufert & Swezey, 1986) emphasize the complex nature of senior organizational leadership and the correspondingly complex conceptual capacities required of such leaders.

Behavioral complexity theories emphasize the multiple roles and corresponding behavioral patterns required of senior leaders. They argue that because senior leaders deal with multiple constituencies with different demands they need to display different behaviors to be effective in a variety of organizational situations. These requirements also can result in senior leaders having to balance competing behavioral patterns, such as mentoring and developing subordinates while at the same time being task focused and directive regarding organizational production. Examples of behavioral complexity models of leadership include Mintzberg's (1973, 1975) classification of managerial roles, Tsui's (1984a, 1984b) multiple constituency framework, and Quinn's (1984, 1988) competing values framework.

Strategic decision-making models of executive leadership argue that organizational effectiveness emerges from an appropriate fit between the organization and its environment and that the role of senior organizational leaders is the analysis, creation, and management of this fit (Bourgeois, 1985; Lawrence & Lorsch, 1967; Thompson, 1967; Wortman, 1982). The strategic management functions of executives include scanning the organization's environment and subsequent analysis of problems and opportunities, forming policies and strategies from this analysis, implementing and interpreting these policies within the organization, and evaluating policy consequences given organizational conditions (Wortman, 1982). Characteristics that influence the quality of strategic policy making include cognitive abilities, functional expertise and knowledge, motivational characteristics such as self-efficacy and need for achievement, and personality characteristics such as locus of control and risk propensity.

Theories of visionary or inspirational leadership subsume a number of different approaches related to charismatic, transformational, and visionary leadership. These theories argue in common, though, that leaders develop a vision that is used to structure and motivate collective action. Furthermore, considerable emphasis is placed on the empowerment and development of subordinates (Bass, 1985). The various theories of visionary or inspirational leadership differ regarding the role of vision, external versus internal focus, and empowerment, but they share an emphasis on inspiring followers in accordance with a specified organizational direction. Visionary models of leadership have offered a number of individual characteristics that enhance a leader's capacity to formulate and implement an organizational vision. These include cognitive abilities (i.e., creativity, reasoning skills, intelligence, verbal ability, cognitive complexity), self-confidence, socialized power motives, propensity for risk, and social and nurturance skills.

Although these approaches are presented as different conceptual frameworks, they overlap in several critical ways. For example, conceptual complexity theories emphasize the role of senior leaders in organizational planning from a 5- to 20-year time frame. Behavioral complexity theories specify two of the key roles of executive leaders to be those of mentor and visionary. Both roles are similar to those offered in several visionary or inspirational leadership models. Furthermore, leader visions are expected to reflect a congruence between the organization and its environment at some future point in time, a premise that is reflected in several strategic decision-making models. These observations indicate that the four conceptual approaches described emphasize the general responsibility of senior leaders to establish the long-term purpose and direction of the organization.

The boundary management requirement of senior leaders is another constant theme across all four conceptual approaches. Conceptual complexity theories argue that the complex problem-solving skills required for effective executive leadership are derived from the informational complexity of the environment the senior leader must confront as a representative of his or her organization. Behavioral complexity theories cite that top leaders must balance the roles of liaison and ambassador for the organization along with other key roles. Strategic decision-making theories regard strategic thinking as involving leaders' efforts to develop and maintain congruence between organizational and environmental conditions. Finally, visionary leadership theories note that effective executive visions are idealized representations of how organizations should fit within a dynamic environment at a future point in time.

Thus, although these conceptual frameworks emphasize somewhat different factors regarding the nature of executive leadership and key executive leadership competencies, they share the major characteristics described by Barnard (1938) and Katz and Kahn (1966, 1978)—organizational direction setting and environmental boundary management. In this book, each conceptual approach is the subject of two chapters. In one chapter, the conceptual model is described in detail, then evaluated according to the applicable questions listed in Exhibit 1-1. In another chapter, the empirical research completed under the rubric of each conceptual approach is reviewed and then critically analyzed, again according to criteria derived from the questions in Exhibit 1-1. The final chapter integrates these reviews and analyses into a general framework that suggests what is known about top organizational leadership. A number of recommendations and suggestions are offered regarding future directions in executive leadership research.

Conceptual Complexity Theories of Executive Leadership: Conceptual Review and Evaluation

2

ew people, whether upper-level executives or lower-level managers, would deny that the contemporary workplace has become quite complex. The work environment has changed significantly, and relationships and responsibilities are no longer clear-cut. Indeed, the environment within which senior organizational leaders now must operate is of such complexity that leader success has become predicated on the possession and application of higher order cognitive abilities and skills. This point reflects a basic premise in cognitive science that task or problem complexity requires that the problem solver possess corresponding cognitive complexity (Jaques, 1990a). Davidson, Deuser, and Sternberg (1994) argued, for example, that as problems become more ill defined and unstructured or require insight and creativity, problem solvers need to apply higher order and metacognitive problem-solving skills to address them effectively. Holyoak (1984) suggested that novel problems require more analogical reasoning strategies, whereby mental models from related domains are applied to a target domain to generate a workable solution. Schroder, Driver, and Streufert (1967) provided the most direct evidence of this correspondence, demonstrating that task performance declined when individuals possessed insufficient cognitive complexity to complete a task with high information-processing requirements (see also Streufert & Streufert, 1978).

Task and Cognitive Complexity

For executive leaders, what produces this operational complexity? The primary culprit is information-processing demands that increase in magnitude at higher organizational levels. The complexity of executive information processing follows from the data that executive leaders must assimilate and the cognitive structures they require for a fully integrated representation of diverse organization-related information. Analyses by Campbell (1988) and Schroder et al. (1967) described three information dimensions that define task complexity: (a) information load, (b) information diversity, and (c) rate of information change. *Information load* refers to the number of information sources and dimensions requiring attention (Campbell, 1988, p. 43). *Information diversity* is defined by the number of alternatives associated with each information source. *Rate of information change* reflects the dynamic and uncertain character of information sources.

The work of executive leaders is characterized by each of these dimensions. Campbell (1988) argued that multiple possible solution paths increase overall information load. Executive leaders are responsible to a variety of different internal and external stakeholders. Furthermore, a wide range of dynamic environmental forces and influences (e.g., economic, political, legal, technological; Hall, 1991; Katz & Kahn, 1978) continuously affect the organization. These factors virtually guarantee that executive leaders will have to generate, attend to, and choose from multiple solution paths. Furthermore, the diversity within and between constituencies and the fluid nature of most organizational environments create multiple outcome possibilities, conflicting or interconnected solution paths, and ambiguous associations between defined solution paths and outcomes (i.e., high information diversity and rate of change). Each of these characteristics contributes to high information-processing demands and, hence, greater task complexity (Campbell, 1988).

Mumford, Zaccaro, Harding, Fleishman, and Reiter-Palmon (1993) reported that both the novelty of and lack of definition in most of the problems executive leaders confront also contribute to operational complexity. At times, senior leaders need to work with "problem spaces" that are ill-defined and outside of their comfortable frames of reference. Anderson (1990; see also Newell & Simon, 1972) defined a *problem space* as containing the initial situation and parameters confronting the problem solver (*initial state*), the multiple paths to potential solutions (*intermediate states*), and the desired solution or goal (*goal state*). A problem is considered to be well-defined when its space contains clearly specified initial, intermediate, and goal states. In such cases, the problem solver proceeds through a series of steps until a solution is generated; success is determined by the solver's knowledge of this progression and the specific steps to the appropriate solution.

Ill-defined problems, however, are those for which the starting parameters, the permissible solution paths, and the solution goals are ambiguous and unspecified (Holyoak, 1984). In such cases, the problem solver must identify the problem, search for acceptable solution paths, and select a goal state. It is important to note that any chosen goal state may not generate consensus regarding its appropriateness. These tasks increase the complexity of problem solving for the solver. Mumford, Zaccaro, Harding, et al. (1993) suggested that the proportion of ill-defined problems characterizing the work of leaders increases as one ascends the organizational hierarchy. Thus, in addition to high information-processing demands, the complexity of executive leaders' work increases as a result of the relatively large proportion of ill-defined problems they must confront.

Jaques (1978, 1986, 1990) defined work complexity in part as the longest time span associated with the completion of any required work. Time spans range from immediate at the lowest levels of an organization to 20 to 50 years for top executive leaders. Operational time spans that extend far in the future obviously contain significant information load, diversity, and ambiguity. In addition, environmental dynamics and uncertainty clearly render such long-term problems ill-defined. Therefore, the nature and complexity of executive work can perhaps be grounded most directly in the extended time spans required for its completion.

The premise of requisite correspondence between the complexity of leaders' operating environments and their cognitive capacities serves as the basis for two theoretical approaches to executive leadership described in this chapter. Each of these conceptual frameworks emphasizes cognitive capacities beyond intelligence; therefore, they are labeled *conceptual complexity theories*. The more prominent of these is stratified systems theory (SST; Jacobs & Jaques, 1987, 1990, 1991; Jacobs & Lewis, 1992; Jaques, 1976, 1986, 1989; Jaques & Clement, 1991); it will be described first. The second framework to be discussed is Streufert's interactive complexity theory (ICT; Streufert & Nogami, 1989; Streufert & Swezey, 1986).

The presentation of these conceptual complexity theories of executive leadership is organized according to the four major themes identified in chapter 1: (a) nature of organizational leadership, (b) requisite leader characteristics, (c) measurement tools, and (d) leader development. The descriptions of both theories around each theme are then followed by an evaluation of how they address the questions and criteria outlined in chapter 1 (see Exhibit 1-1).

Nature of Organizational Leadership: Stratified Systems Theory

According to SST organizational work varies in complexity across levels, yet the fundamental purpose of leadership remains the same. In the following section, this overall purpose is discussed first, following by the stratification of work proposed by this theory.

DEFINITION OF LEADERSHIP

According to Jacobs and Jaques (1990), "leadership is a process of giving purpose [meaningful direction] to collective effort, and causing willing effort to be expended to achieve purpose" (p. 282). This definition of leadership applies within and across organizational levels, although leader performance requirements are differentiated by level. For example, a critical role of leadership is providing a purpose for collective, organized action. At lower organizational levels this role may translate to direction setting for individuals or small units. At upper levels, however, leadership involves the establishment of direction, in the form of vision or strategy for the organization as a whole.

Jacobs and Jaques's (1990) definition specifies the mobilization and coordination of collective effort as an essential component of the leadership process. At lower organizational levels, this involves such activities as specifying tasks, monitoring performance, translating goals and plans established at upper levels into day-to-day production activities, and motivating subordinates to accomplish these goals and plans. At the top of the organization, this involves the generation of resources from the larger environment, the allocation of resources within and across organizational subsystems, and the empowerment of the organization as a whole (Bass, 1985).

Jacobs and Jaques (1987, 1990) specified several important elements of their definition of leadership that shape the remainder of their conceptual framework. First, the process of leadership involves decision discretion. That is, leadership occurs when the individual occupying a position is able to make choices about decision alternatives and problem solutions. Jacobs and Jaques (1990, p. 282) argued, in fact, that without the possibility of choice and discretion, there is no opportunity for leadership. Mumford and his colleagues (Fleishman et al., 1991; Mumford, 1986; Mumford, Zaccaro, Harding, et al., 1993) made essentially the same argument. The presence of this element in the definition of leadership suggests that leadership processes include the specification of a problem, the delineation of choices, and the evaluation and selection of the most appropriate choice or choices. These decision functions essentially mean that leadership in large part reflects a cognitive, or problem-solving process (Jacobs & Jaques, 1987; Mumford, Zaccaro et al., 1993). Furthermore, as previously described, problem types and decision choices become more ambiguous, less structured, more novel, and more differentiated at higher organizational levels. Thus, the cognitive process of leadership becomes correspondingly more complex.

A second element of leadership states that the consequential adaptiveness of an organization determines the effectiveness of a leader's direction-setting efforts. That is, the choices made through the process of leadership are validated by how well the organization subsequently adapts to environmental contingencies. Jacobs and Jaques (1987) describe this critical leadership element as follows:

> Viewed as open systems, organizations are entities, acting within an environment that is generally competitive and sometimes hostile. They are dependent on the external environment for resources (information, matter, and energy) and must maintain no less than parity between resources acquisition and resources utilization or eventually die. . . . The most fundamental organizational issue is continued survival, and the key leadership task at any given level is to contribute to survival by whatever means is appropriate for the level or system or subsystem at which leadership is being exerted. (p. 14)

At lower organizational levels, this requirement often translates to ensuring that unit goals, tasks, and resources are congruent with the strategies and purposes established at upper levels. Indeed, Ancona (1987) and Ancona and Caldwell (1992) defined a number of boundary management functions in organizational groups that facilitate such congruence. However, at the top of the organization, adaptation requires that executive leaders act and interact increasingly within the external environment to stabilize existing resources and acquire new ones. The complexity of the organization–environment interaction is such that although some of the forces and influences generated by the organization or within the environment will have immediate or short-term consequences, most effects will be manifested over a much longer period. Thus, organizational adaptation at the executive level requires more proactivity and planning within longer time frames. This requirement adds to the cognitive demands confronting senior leaders.

One of the most critical elements of organizational leadership specified by SST is the provision by the leader of a frame of reference for collective action. This frame of reference, also called a causal map or conceptual model by Jacobs and Jaques (1987, 1990), is a cognitive representation of the elements and events that comprise the operational environment within which leadership occurs. That is, such a map or model contains the pattern of causal (antecedental and consequential), categorical, or incidental relationships among these elements and events. A causal frame of reference provides the basis for a leader's understanding and interpretation of information and events encountered in the organization's operational environment. It also provides meaning for organizational direction and purpose established through the leadership process. That is, the logic and rationale for an articulated direction presumably is grounded in the causal relationships interpreted by an executive leader as existing among the critical events affecting the organization.

Jacobs and Jaques (1987; Jacobs & Lewis, 1992), relying on the notion of requisite variety (Ashby, 1952), argued that the complexity of a causal map must correspond to the complexity of the operating environment being patterned. Therefore, the frames of reference or causal maps developed by senior leaders must be more complex than those of leaders at lower organizational levels. This required difference results because (a) executive leaders' maps must accommodate many more causal elements; (b) these elements have more complex interconnections and associations; (c) multiple causal chains may be occurring simultaneously, requiring both differentiation and integration; (d) antecedental events occur over longer time frames at higher organizational levels, greatly increasing the difficulty of perceiving and integrating them into a comprehensive causal map; and (e) executives who are operating within the external environment also need to factor into their frames of reference the strategies and purposes of executives of other co-acting and competing organizations (Jacobs & Jaques, 1987). The requirement of increasingly complex models and causal maps at upper organizational levels dictates the need, then, for higher order cognitive skills and capabilities at those levels.

Organizational Stratification

The points raised thus far suggest that understanding organizational leadership requires a model that specifies how performance demands change qualitatively at particular points in the organizational structure. SST specifies such a model. This model, illustrated in Figure 2-1 (from Lucas & Markessini, 1993, p. 6; see also Jacobs & Jaques, 1987; Jacobs & Lewis, 1992), contains three layers that reflect three functional domains. These layers incorporate seven strata. Each successive layer and stratum represents an increasingly complex operating environment with a longer time span for the conduct of leadership processes. *Time span* refers to the maximum time horizon for tasks that require leadership at any particular organizational level. Figure 2-1 displays time spans, general task requirements, and corresponding organizational examples (e.g., from the U.S. Army, civil service, and private industry and commerce) for each of the seven strata.

The lowest functional domain is the *production or command* domain, composed of Strata I-III. Here, leadership is characterized as involving direct and small-group interaction, and tasks are fairly concrete and accomplished usually within relatively small time frames (ranging from 1

FIGURE 2-1

Levels of Organizational Stratification Proposed by Stratified Systems Theory

Stratum	Domain	TOE grade	Type of unit supervised with civil service and industrial correlates (U.S. Army)	(Civil service)	(Industry & commerce)	Task requirements and characteristics — Systems, resource, and policy task requirements	Scope of work — Representative no. of subordinates	Sphere of influence	SST postulated time span of work
VII	INDIRECT / Strategic/systems	General	Unified or specified command or field armament	Cabinet secretary	Corporation	Create and integrate complex systems; organize acquisition of major resources; create policy.	500,000–1,000,000	Continental	20+ years
VI		Lieutenant general	Corps	Deputy secretary	Group	Oversee direct operation of subordinate divisions; allocate resources; apply policy.	50,000–60,000	National	10–20 years
V	Organizational	Major general	Division or TA organization	Under secretary	Full DMS	Direct operation of complex systems; allocate assigned resources; implement policy.	11,000–12,000	Regional	5–10 years
IV		Brigadier general	Separate brigade	Assistant secretary	Medium-size business	Direct operation of systems; organize resource allocations to interdependent subordinate programs and subsystems; implement policy.	5,000	Sector	4–7 years
		Colonel	Divisional brigade				2,500	10–15 KM	
III	DIRECT / Command	Lieutenant colonel/sergeant major	Battalion	Principal staff	One-man business or unit	Develop and execute plans and tasks; organize subsystems; prioritize resources; translate and implement policy and assigned missions.	500–600	4,000–5,000 M	1+ years
		Major	Battalion ORT level						
II		CPT/first sergeant	Company platoon	Assistant principal	Section	Supervise direct performance of subsystems; anticipate/solve real-time problems; shift resources; translate and implement policy.	100–200	1500 M	3+ months
I		Lieutenant/NCO	NOCs and ORs	Clerical and office supervisor	Supervisor and shop and office floor	Direct performance of work; use practical judgment to solve ongoing problems.	3–40	400 M	<3 months

From *Senior Leadership in a Changing World Order: Requisite Skills for U.S. Army One- and Two-Star Assignments* (p. 6), by K. W. Lucas and J. Markessini, 1993 (ARI Technical Report No. 976). Alexandria, VA: U.S. Army Research Institute for the Behavioral Sciences. Reprinted with permission on.

day to 2 years). Stratum I managers implement very-well-specified tasks, whereas Stratum II managers are required to anticipate problems and begin to meet personnel development needs. Stratum III managers typically develop plans to implement strategy and policy directives established at upper levels. Accordingly, they need to balance immediate production demands with future resource requirements.

The next functional domain is the organizational domain, composed of Strata IV and V. *Organizational* domain leadership requires the provision of a comprehensive frame of reference that begins to pattern elements of the external environment for the organization as a whole. Leaders also coordinate and integrate the activities of multiple subsystems. Stratum IV leadership involves indirect management of subordinates in the production subsystem. Leaders at this level establish production goals, strategies, and time frames to be implemented by others. Furthermore, at this stratum, leaders coordinate the demands and activities of more than one production unit. The time span of Stratum IV work is typically 4 to 7 years.

Stratum V is the first level at which leadership responsibility can extend to either a single organization with no buffer from the external environment or to a component of a corporation or business conglomerate. Direct boundary management with the external environment represents a larger proportion of requisite leadership work. Stratum V managers make strategic and policy decisions that can result in substantial alterations in the structure and climate of the organization. Furthermore, they provide a frame of reference for the organization as a whole within its external operating environment. Accordingly, they operate within a 5- to 10-year time span.

Jacobs and Jaques (1987) defined senior leader or executive work as occurring in the strategic or systems functional domain. They described such work as involving the development and nurturance of new business units (i.e., structural change) and the formation of national and international networks. Such networks facilitate the extensive environmental scanning activities required of executive leaders. Thus, Jacobs and Jaques noted that for such leaders,

> the primary business at the systems level lies in two areas. One is interaction with [the] external environment, both impacting on it and getting and interpreting information from it to produce a more rational (stable) environment within which subordinate companies can operate. The second is creating critical resources masses, that is, fiscal, raw materials, personnel, technological, and favorable public and/or political opinion, for future ventures. (p. 25)

Stratum VI work involves the integration of various business units and formulation of strategies and policies to be applied either generically or differentially to them. Leaders at this level provide a frame of refer-ence, developed substantially with Stratum VII leaders, to subordinate units that charts the direction of the organization as a whole. Accord-ingly, their operational time frame is 10 to 20 years. Stratum VII leaders typically are organization heads, chief executive officers, and, in the case of the U.S. Army, four-star generals. Their work requirements involve extensive interaction outside of the organization to create new subsid-iary business units and acquire the resources necessary to sustain these and existing units. Furthermore, responsibility for the creation and change of organizational climate as well as the establishment of orga-nizational values resides at this level. The time span for this work is 20 years and beyond.

In defining the work of executive-level leaders, SST appears to em-phasize the leader's external systemic perspective in relation to his or her internal systemic perspective (Gardner & Schermerhorn, 1992). In fact, Jacobs and Jaques (1987) noted that the consistencies at the ex-ecutive leadership level "stem from the location of the corporate head-quarters, essentially outside their subordinate systems and within the external environment—political, economic, social, technological, and intellectual (ideas)" (p. 25). This suggests that the sphere and modes of influence of senior leaders are directed more toward the organization's external environment than toward its internal operations. Other per-spectives of senior leadership described later in this book contain a more even balance between external and internal functions. For example, behavioral complexity theories maintain that effective leadership re-quires equal time be given to these somewhat competing orientations (see chapter 4).

Although SST emphasizes the executive leader's orientation to the external environment, it does not entirely neglect the proposed opera-tional responsibilities of executive leaders. Jacob and Jaques (1987) noted that the primary responsibility of leaders in Stratum VII is the creation of new organizational units. They accomplish this by develop-ing consensus among Stratum VI leaders to support their initiatives and commit their immediate subordinates to the operational implementation of new policies and plans. Furthermore, an executive leader must create an organizational culture that supports the implementation of his or her vision. Thus, senior leaders are not only engaged in organizational man-agement, but they also use both structural and climatic means of or-ganizational change to implement their formulated direction.

Nonetheless, the primary orientation of the executive leader re-mains decidedly outward. For example, Jacobs and Jaques (1987) noted that although senior leaders engage in consensus building among or-ganizational members to implement decisions, operational details are left to subordinates' discretion. They focus their energy, instead, on the creation and acquisition of critical resources needed for new organizational units. Furthermore, an executive's efforts to change the psychological climate of an organization are primarily initiated to ensure "that the corporate culture and value system are 'like' the culture and value system of the encompassing society" (p. 25). The purpose of developing this fit is to increase the likelihood that new business units will be accepted within the larger organizational environment.

SST provides a clear delineation of leadership work and role requirements that differ qualitatively across organizational levels. In essence, as leaders move to higher levels of the organization, they are required to plan and think within longer time spans and incorporate more influences from outside the organization into their perspective. Furthermore, requisite social influence patterns change from primarily unidirectionally downward to more consensual and persuasive. Both of these requirements suggest the need for extensive network building to provide additional information conduits, as well as facilitate the more informal influence process of consensus building.

Nature of Organizational Leadership: Interactive Complexity Theory

Although interactive complexity theory (ICT) was introduced more than 30 years ago (e.g., Driver & Streufert, 1966; Schroder et al., 1967; Streufert & Driver, 1967), it has been applied to organizational leadership only within the past 10 to 15 years (e.g., Streufert & Nogami, 1989; Streufert & Swezey, 1986).

ICT, as it applies to organizational leadership, is concerned with the structure, rather than the content, of information processing by organizational leaders. ICT proposes that, in essence, "optimal functioning of individuals is viewed as an interactive effect of two variables, one concerned with individual differences, the other with environmental conditions" (Streufert & Swezey, 1986, p. 25). The term *individual differences* refers to an individual's ability and inclination to differentiate and integrate multiple information sources. Organizational structures and their operating environments also can be fairly unidimensional, highly differentiated, or somewhere in between. Streufert and Swezey argued that success in an organization occurs when the cognitive complexity of an individual matches the level of organizational or environmental complexity. This argument is consistent with the requisite variety premise of SST.

Unlike SST, however, ICT, as applied to organizational systems, does not provide a systematic classification of differences in environmental complexity across organizational levels. Nonetheless, Streufert and Swezey (1986) offered several broad differences in complexity between lower and upper organizational levels. First, an essential component of organizational complexity is information load, or the amount of information flowing into the organization as well as information exchanges among segments of the organization. At upper organizational levels, there typically are more sources of information flow; therefore, more information must be differentiated and integrated by leaders at these levels than at lower organizational levels. Also, upper-level leaders are responsible for differentiating and integrating the needs, demands, and climates of more organizational segments than lower-level managers. Lower-level managers generally can operate successfully from the perspective of their subordinate unit (i.e., using a unidimensional cognitive space); upper-level leaders need to operate within multiple perspectives from diverse organizational components.

A third element of differential complexity across organizational levels, as identified by ICT, is that individual organizational units often will have only one, possibly two, goals. For example, managers of a production unit may be guided by the goal of maximizing product output and perhaps that of personnel development. Managers of a sales department may be guided by the single goal of maximizing monthly sales orders. At the top of the organization, however, multiple goals are operative, including profit, investments, organizational change, and best positioning of the organization relative to its environment. Furthermore, some goals are short-term whereas others are long-term. Both the number of goal dimensions and the corresponding time frame for each need to be integrated by top managers for an organization to be successful.

Fourth, ICT gauges the degree of fluidity and turbulence characterizing the external environment as an element of organizational complexity. The optimal level of individual complexity depends on the degree of environmental complexity present. Several theories have postulated that organizational environments have multiple components (e.g., political, technological, legal, economic) and that each component may vary from (a) stable to turbulent, (b) uniform to diverse, and (c) organized to random (Emery & Trist, 1965; Hall, 1991; Katz & Kahn, 1978). Thus, an organization's environment can range from fairly simple in all of its components, to complex in some of its components but not others, to complex in all of its components. If an organization's environment is simple or only moderately complex, then high levels of individual complexity are not necessary and actually may be counterproductive (Streufert & Swezey, 1986). However, given the rapid rate of change in today's world, the operating environment for most organizations is likely to be decidedly complex. Because executives have primary responsibility for boundary management with the external environment, they need to be able to respond to the resultant complexity.

Although ICT does not offer the formal stratification model of organizational work that SST provides, it does reflect in broader strokes the qualitative changes in organizational leadership requirements that are specified by SST. Streufert and Swezey (1986), however, did leave open the possibility that, under certain conditions of environmental stability and relative uniformity, high levels of cognitive complexity may be counterproductive, a point not highlighted by SST. Streufert and Swezey noted, for example, that

> a cognitively complex executive is likely to be a superior planner
> who is able to actively consider a large number of contingencies
> and their implications. Is such a person consequently a better
> executive? The answer is not necessarily "yes." Under some
> conditions, "overplanning" can be just as detrimental as
> underplanning. In some cases, a simple, straightforward decision
> might be preferable to a well-considered strategic decision. (p. 71)

SST does not appear to consider the moderating role of environmental factors on executive cognitive requirements. Instead, it assumes that at the systems level (i.e., Strata VI and VII), organizational environments will be turbulent, diverse, and ambiguous. ICT accepts such conditions as the norm but argues for the need to consider variance in the nature of organizational environments.

Streufert and Swezey (1986) argued more forcefully against the time span notions postulated by SST. They did not disagree that longer time spans are associated with the need for greater cognitive complexity. They did suggest, however, that planning over a long time span is productive primarily in stable environments in which rapid and contingency-based or sequential decision-making is not required. They argued that long-term planning under conditions of environmental fluidity and uncertainty would represent counterproductive overplanning. This led them to conclude that "time span is not a primary component of executive planning styles" (p. 78). They even suggested that 5-year strategic plans are not productive because they tend to be inflexible and based on premises that rapidly become outmoded.

These differences between SST and ICT may not be as significant as Streufert and Swezey (1986) suggested. Jacobs and Jaques (1987) proposed that time span represents the maximum horizon for possible executive work, not the horizon for the typical executive task. Thus, much executive work, even in Stratum VII, may be completed in relatively short time spans. SST does not explicitly provide that an executive leader's frame of reference (or cognitive map) must be flexible. However, the usefulness or effectiveness of these maps is grounded in the degree to which they create adaptive responses by the organization. This criterion of adaptability suggests a degree of flexibility in these conceptualizations. Nonetheless, the uniformly strong emphasis on complex planning and reflection by SST at the executive organizational level is a characteristic that is disputed by several executive leadership models in addition to ICT (e.g., Mintzberg, 1973, 1975). Furthermore, SST's focus on long-term planning raises a question of applicability to some executive leaders, such as those in the military, who typically have relatively short tours of duty (e.g., 2 years) in most strategy-making or policy-setting positions. Perhaps planning responsibilities, and particularly the organizational structure changes that are defined by SST as the province of senior executive leaders, differ qualitatively for military versus nonmilitary leaders, for whom position tenure may be considerably longer.

SUMMARY AND CONCEPTUAL EVALUATION

In their exhortation for a systematic theory of executive leadership, Day and Lord (1988) argued that such a theory should (a) clearly specify the qualitative differences between upper- and lower-level leadership; (b) be grounded in organizational theory; and (c) describe the mechanisms through which executive leaders influence organizational performance. The descriptions of senior leadership work offered by the two theories in this section, particularly that of SST, reflect Day and Lord's (1988) suggestions for an appropriate and systematic executive leadership theory. Each theory specifies clear and qualitative differences between upper-, middle-, and lower-level leader performance requirements. SST provides a fairly precise index of these differences in terms of specific critical tasks and work time spans. These two operational definitions of changing work complexity are also used to delineate particular qualitative shifts in work across organizational levels. ICT defines these qualitative differences in terms of changes in information-processing requirements. Within each model, the postulated work performance differences across organizational levels provide the framework for specifying separate requisite leader characteristics for each level of leadership.

SST is intrinsically imbedded in the open systems theory of organizations (Katz & Kahn, 1978). As such, it provides an illustration of the integration of leadership and organization theory called for by Day and Lord (1988). ICT extends a model of individual and environmental complexity to organizational action; thus, it represents a different perspective. Nonetheless, the definition of organizational complexity offered by Streufert and Swezey (1986) and their description of the complexity confronting executives are congruent with several models of organizational decision making. Indeed, by applying a taxonomic classification of organizational systems (Swezey, Streufert, & Mietus, 1983), Streufert and Swezey demonstrated the extensive use of complexity theory terminology in organizational and systems theories.

SST is more specific than ICT in terms of how leader effectiveness is defined and how executive work performance influences organizational success. Such success is defined by how adaptive an organization is within its larger environment. Accordingly, leader effectiveness is defined ultimately as how well the supervised unit fits within its larger environment. The nicety of this criterion is its applicability across all levels of an organization. The leader's role is to provide direction for a unit (ranging in size from a small group to an entire organization) that is adaptive within a larger set of requirements. However, these requirements become more diffuse and uncertain at upper levels as leaders begin to position the organization as a whole within its external environment.

This direction-making process is also the means by which executive leaders influence organizational performance. SST argues that organizations succeed when their structures and subsystems are congruent with dynamic environmental conditions. The mechanism that guides the selection of actions regarding organizational adjustment and change is the frame of reference or cognitive map that is formed by the executive leader and represents the actual and potential causal forces operating on the organization. The quality of organizational adaptation, and therefore performance, is grounded in the quality and accuracy of the executive's mental model that is formed and communicated to the rest of the organization. Along these lines, Jacobs and Jaques (1991) noted:

> Executive leaders "add value" to their organizations in large part by giving a sense of understanding and purpose to the overall activities of the organization. In excellent organizations, there almost always is a feeling that the "boss" knows what he is doing, that he has shared this information downward, that it makes sense, and that it is going to work. (p. 434)

This approach emphasizes information-processing and structured problem-solving activities as critical to effective executive leadership. Two caveats mitigate this, however. First, in most instances executive leaders are experts in their domains and as such do not need to conduct a full range of information-processing activities to solve well-defined and simple organizational problems. Instead, they use highly developed and domain-specific knowledge structures to interpret problem spaces and derive solutions (Lord & Maher, 1993). The second caveat reflects expert executives' approach in novel or ill-defined situations in which existing knowledge structures and simple information-processing activities are inadequate for successful problem solving. Expertise based on well-developed knowledge structures actually may constrain how executives respond to new situations. Thus, they need to be open to alternate problem-solving approaches and ways of thinking. For example, Lord and Maher (1993) discussed executive information processing during periods of substantial organizational change when existing schemas no longer apply. They noted that "substantial change requires sensitivity to new types of information and the capacity to use both information and *different types of information processing* in order to develop new problem solutions and organizational responses" (p. 252).

In summary, regarding their descriptions of the nature of executive work and its impact, the two conceptual complexity theories, SST and ICT, appear to satisfy several of the criteria for a well-formed conceptual framework of executive leadership. However, as noted by Day and Lord (1988), a critical component of such a framework is the delineation of requisite leader characteristics. The next section describes the contributions of each of these theories in this area.

Requisite Leader Characteristics: Stratified Systems Theory

Jacobs and Jaques (1987) proposed three sets of leadership skills that are present across organizational levels, although each set is more or less influential at different levels. Using the work of Katz (1955), Mann (1965), and Katz and Kahn (1966, 1978), they identified these sets as including technical, interpersonal, and conceptual skills. Whereas technical skills are more important at lower organizational levels, conceptual skills are proportionately more important as determinants of leader effectiveness at upper organizational levels. Jacobs and Jaques used a conceptual framework of leader skills developed by Clements and Ayers (1976) to elaborate these three sets and describe how leader skills change in focus across organizational levels. Clements and Ayers identified nine skill dimensions: technical, management science, communication, human relations, counseling, supervision, decision making, planning, and ethics. Table 2-1 presents Jacobs and Jaques's (1987, p. 31) integration of Clements and Ayres's formulation within the framework of SST.

At production levels of leadership (i.e., Strata II and III), primary leadership skills include an understanding of the technical requirements of the work and the knowledge to meet those requirements. They also include human relations and communication skills that facilitate the motivation and use of personnel to complete production tasks within requisite time frames. Because the work at these levels is concrete and

TABLE 2-1

Leader Skill Requirements by Organizational Level

Production level	Organizational level	Systems level
Concepual		
Planning—Establishes intermediate general objectives and organizes short-term programs; schedules work, maintenance, and short-term production goals.	*Planning*—Develops plans; makes forecasts; analyzes organizational progress within long time frames; defines and interprets policy; allocates resources.	*Planning*—Develops a flexible change posture; interprets ambiguity; originates structure; synthesizes economic principles; synthesizes social and cultural influences.
Decision making—Makes decisions on operational procedures; carries out decisions dealing with structured content; follows standardized procedures and decision-making processes with regard to specific work-unit functioning; assigns workers and groups of workers to specific jobs.	*Decision making*—Establishes effective decision-making climate; decides whether to seek to obtain capital resources.	*Decision making*—Synthesizes abstract content; plans decisions within long-term perspective; chooses whether or not to procure resources.
Ethics—Focuses on product improvement and service quality; deals with client complaints.	*Ethics*—Is responsible for reputation of products/services; is responsive to social and community needs; is concerned with public relations.	*Ethics*—Articulates appropriate organizational value system; focuses on company integrity and reputation; formulates plans for maintaining the good will of the organization; develops ethical framework consistent with corporate goals and policies; synthesizes and responds to environmental issues.

Interpersonal

Communication—Employs organizational feedback techniques; provides interpersonal and performance feedback; provides daily production information.

Human relations—Works to create supportive work atmosphere; maps interpersonal relations within small work group and between work groups; maintains equity within workforce.

Counseling—Establishes yardsticks to evaluate individual and group performance; provides and receives unit performance feedback.

Supervision—Focuses on efficiency of operations; performs linking-pin tasks; establishes procedural and quality-control checks; reviews production results; organizes use of equipment and develops workforce cohesion; assigns individuals to tasks; orients and trains new people; assures safe operation of equipment.

Communication—Establishes information networks; facilitates organizational communication.

Human relations—Creates a supportive environment and an effective working climate within the organization.

Counseling—Evaluates performance appraisal systems; identifies colleagues who have personal problems that might adversely affect organizational well-being.

Supervision—Reinforces the motivational climate; coordinates sub-unit objectives; establishes organizational structure.

Communication—Communicates extraorganizationally with government officials, pressure groups, etc.; represents the organization's viewpoint to the public; relies on organizational channels for internal communication.

Human relations—Develops the organization's relations with those outside organization.

Counseling—Establishes conducive climate.

Supervision—Focuses on executive development programs; develops an effective motivational climate; maintains total organizational perspective.

Note. From "Leadership in Complex Systems," by T. O. Jacobs and E. Jcques, in *Human Productivity Enhancement* (p. 31), by J. Zeidner (Ed.), 1987, New York: Praeger. Copyright © 1987 by Joseph Zeidner. Reprinted with permission.

almost completely prescribed by higher level strategies and assignments as well as by existing rules and regulations, necessary cognitive skills are limited to short-term planning, goal setting, and task structuring as well as resolving immediate and direct production problems.

Skills for organizational levels of leadership (i.e., Strata IV and V) include the interpersonal skills necessary at the production level as well as skills oriented toward consensus building, the establishment of communication and information networks, and the development of subordinate capabilities (Jacobs & Jaques, 1987). Technical skills become relatively less important, although organizational-level managers need to understand organizational systems and how various subsystems are integrated. Conceptual skills include long-term planning, balancing and integration of multiple business strategies, and environmental analysis and interpretation.

Systems-level leadership (i.e., Strata VI and VII) requires interpersonal skills that facilitate communication with a diverse set of external constituencies, representation of the organization to external agencies, and development of a corporate climate that is reflective of executive values and policies. Skills promoting collective strategic thinking and consensus building among other systems-level leaders representing diverse internal and external groups are also necessary. Technical skills are proportionally least influential at this level. Instead, the most critical executive skill is the conceptual complexity or cognitive capacity that allows the senior leader to develop a frame of reference that appropriately maps the complexity of the organizational operating environment. According to STT, this skill is perhaps the most important executive leadership attribute. Lewis and Jacobs (1992) argued that

> the fundamental individual difference variable that most often distinguishes successful strategic leaders from unsuccessful ones is the extent to which leaders' conceptual capacity meets or exceeds the conceptual demands inherent in their work. Those promoted to strategic leadership typically already possess the requisite interpersonal and technical skills needed to be successful. These skills and the motivation to lead will usually already have been amply demonstrated at lower managerial levels. (p. 136)

Lewis and Jacobs (1992) suggested that a leader's effectiveness at the top of the organization is likely to be a function of cognitive abilities rather than interpersonal competencies, technical skills, or even motivational and personality differences. These latter variables, along with cognitive skills, predict differences between junior and senior leaders. However, executive leaders presumably already possess these requisite correlates of success. Accordingly, successful and unsuccessful executive leaders are distinguished by differences in their conceptual capacities.

CONCEPTUAL CAPACITY

According to SST, leader effectiveness is in part a function of how well a frame of reference provided by the leader patterns the causal and other mechanisms in the environment operating at any particular organizational level. Causal factors increase in magnitude and in the intricacies of their interrelationships at upper organizational levels, and leaders' cognitive maps need to be correspondingly more complex. *Conceptual capacity* is defined as the extent of an individual's ability to think about and organize his or her experiences (Jacobs & Lewis, 1992, p. 124). It includes the element of *time horizon*, which was defined by Jaques and Clement (1991, p. 50) as "the longest period into the future within which a person is capable of organizing and carrying through given tasks or projects, handling them as they arise on the way, and reaching the eventual goal" (p. 50).

Conceptual capacity is reflected in the complexity of the pattern or map an individual is capable of constructing to cognitively represent work experiences. As these experiences become increasingly complex, with more obscure cause-and-effect relationships, individuals require more abstract thinking abilities to develop the requisite cognitive maps. At lower levels of complexity (e.g., those that characterize the operating environment in the production domain), categorical and causal relationships are fairly simple and concrete; accordingly, information-processing requirements and the cognitive maps necessary to perform them effectively are relatively simple. Conceptual capacity demands are therefore limited at this level (Jacobs & Jaques, 1987).

For middle-level managers in the organizational domain, patterns of influence in the operating environment become more complex. At this level, it is necessary to construct a map of the external environment as well as the place of the organization within the environment. This construction process requires more abstract and analytical thinking skills because fewer concrete referents exist for concepts and ideas that become active at this level (Jacobs & Lewis, 1992; Lewis & Jacobs, 1992). Furthermore, more causal and categorical dimensions are operative in organizational domains, requiring the capacity to simultaneously consider and differentiate among these dimensions (Jacobs & Lewis, 1992).

Executive leaders operating in the systems domain are required to understand more complex forms of organization (e.g., multi-company corporations) within environments with a greater number of and more far-reaching influential constituents. They need to extrapolate these connections over a relatively long time span (Jaques, 1986). Furthermore, executive leaders have the responsibility of developing new business units (i.e., Stratum V units) that must fit adaptively within the existing and dynamic system arrangements. To accomplish these tasks, they need to perceive and construct a conceptual pattern that (a) provides a basis for the selection of organizational actions within this very complex operating environment and (b) provides the terms and language for the interpretation and explanation of these actions to managers acting at lower organizational levels. SST proposes that cognitive abilities related to abstract synthesis and integration are necessary to construct the frames of reference necessary in this domain.

Jaques (1986, 1989) argued that conceptual capacity or to use his term, "cognitive power" can be charted at a particular point in an individual's working life. This represents "the maximum time span at which a person can work at a given point in time" (Jaques, 1986, p. 374). Jaques then proposed a series of maturation or growth curves that represent predictable increases in an individual's cognitive power over his or her life span. Figure 2-2 displays Jaques's maturation curves.

Jaques (1986) proposed eight modes representing different levels of cognitive power. Each mode is reflected at some point along the organizational strata described earlier in this chapter. Note that the highest level of cognitive power that can be achieved early in one's working life (i.e., 20–25 years in age) allows a time horizon of no more than 2 to 4 years and reflects potential for Strata IV work. The lowest levels of cognitive power reflect an immediate time horizon and work at the bottom of Strata I. However, differences between cognitive modes in terms of time span potential become greater over time. For example, individuals capable of Mode I or II cognitive processes in their 20s begin at Stratum I, and subsequent increases in their cognitive power match them with no higher than Stratum II work. However, individuals at the levels of Modes VI, VII, and VIII are capable of Stratum III work early in their careers and of moving to Strata VI and VII work later in their lives.

Jaques's maturation curves, then, indicate that the higher an individual's cognitive power early in life, the greater number of work strata he or she is able to cross during his or her career. However, Jaques also noted that individuals may not move into different maturation bands. For example, no number of developmental interventions can help an individual who is capable of, at best, Mode IV cognition lead effectively at any organizational level higher than mid-Strata IV. If confirmed, these maturation bands have significant implications for the selection and development of senior leaders. In essence, they suggest a native or innate component of the set of requisite executive skills.

PROCLIVITY

Jacobs and Jaques (1990) pointed out that the development of frames of reference or cognitive maps is effortful work. Accordingly, the potential afforded by an individual's cognitive power needs to be accompanied

FIGURE 2-2

Jaques's Cognitive Power Maturation Curves

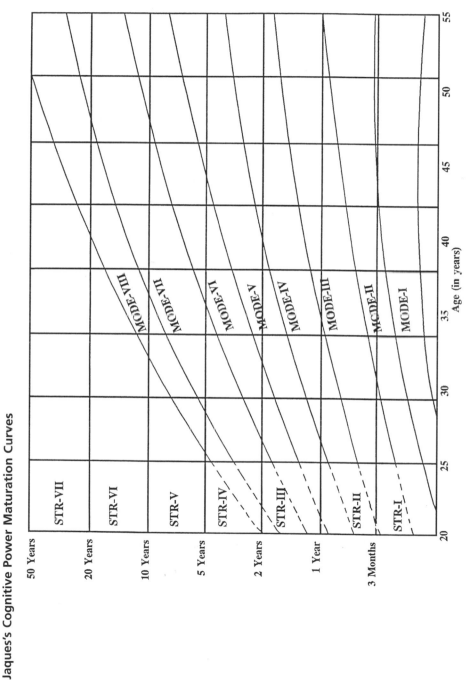

STR = stratum. From "The Development of Intellectual Capability: A Discussion of Stratified Systems Theory," by E. Jaques, 1986, *Journal of Applied Behavioral Science,* 22, p. 375. Copyright 1986 by Sage Publications. Adapted with permission.

by a temperament characteristic that reflects his or her desire or inclination to engage in reflective thinking or cognitive model building. Jacobs and Jaques labeled this inclination *proclivity* and argued that it reflects the degree to which an individual is intrinsically rewarded by the cognitive activity of organizing complex experiences. They suggested that such proclivity may be operationalized by the Myers-Briggs Type Indicator, specifically the NT (intuitive–thinking) profile. Church and Alie (1986) offered the following descriptions of intuitive and thinking individuals:

> *Intuitive Individuals*: These individuals gather information primarily through associating new information and ideas with previously acquired information. . . . Intuitives dislike structure, details, and routine, and enjoy new problems and situations. . . . They also exhibit the conceptual ability to perceive environments as wholes and problems or events as parts of wholes. This is an attribute seen as desirable in strategic-level managers.

> *Thinking Individuals*: Thinkers prefer to evaluate information and make decisions on the basis of logic. They tend to take a rational, systematic approach to problem solving and order people, situations, and information in a structured framework without considerations for the feelings of others. Thinking individuals tend to rely on cognitive processes for dealing with environments and people. (p. 33)

Individuals who are inclined toward an NT cognitive style can be characterized as reflective thinkers interested in building mental models and conceptualizations of their experiences. Accordingly, Jacobs and Jaques (1990) suggested that the proportion of NTs relative to other styles might increase at higher organizational levels.

U.S. ARMY EXECUTIVE LEADERSHIP RESEARCH

The U.S. Army Research Institute (ARI) has undertaken several other research projects into the nature of executive thinking and corresponding executive skills (Geiwitz, 1993; Laskey, Leddo, & Bresnick, 1990; Markessini, 1991; Mumford, Zaccaro, Harding, et al., 1993). Each of these projects is conceptually related to or congruent with SST. The premise that executive thinking requires high-level metacognition and particular metacognitive skills is common to all of them.

Perhaps the most prevalent definition of *metacognition* is one's "knowledge and cognition about cognitive phenomena" (Flavell, 1979, p. 906). Garofalo and Lester (1985) distinguished between cognition and metacognition by noting that "cognition is involved in doing, whereas metacognition is involved in choosing and planning what to do and monitoring what is being done" (p. 164). Although several conceptualizations of metacognition exist in the literature, the one most applicable to the ARI research on executive leadership emphasizes the role of metacognitive processes and skills in complex problem solving (Brown, 1978; Davidson et al., 1994; Gagné, 1985; Geiwitz, 1993; Sternberg, 1985). *Metacognitive processes* are defined as executive functions that control the application and operation of cognitive abilities and skills.

Table 2-2 presents the metacognitive and complex thinking skills proposed by four ARI-sponsored research programs. Although each program proposed a different set of metacognitive processes and skills, four general skill-related processes can be identified from these and other

TABLE 2-2

Executive Leadership and Proposed Metacognitive Skills

Study	Proposed metacognitive skills
Geiwitz (1993)	Problem detection
	Problem representation
	Selection of problem-solving method
	Strategic application of problem-solving method
	Evaluation of solution choices
	Recognition of errors
	Resource allocation
	Temporal monitoring
	Social monitoring
	Executive monitoring
Laskey, Leddo, & Bresnick (1990)	Metagoal and causal map formation
	Metaplan for building plans
	Metaplan for evaluating plans and projecting consequences
Markessini (1991)	Awareness of
	independent cognitive processes
	cognitive style (e.g., Myers-Briggs Type Indicator)
	how cognitive characteristics interact with situation
	Executive functions—use of
	self-management of learning process
	reflection on experience
	Executive functions—strategic control
Mumford, Zaccaro, Harding, Fleishman, & Reiter-Palmon (1993)	Problem construction
	Information encoding
	Category search
	Category specification
	Combination and reorganization of best-fitting categories
	Idea evaluation
	Implementation
	Monitoring

investigations of metacognition (Brown, 1978; Davidson et al., 1994; Gagné, 1985; Sternberg, 1985). The first process is defining the nature of the problem to be solved. This includes the awareness that a problem exists, the identification and definition of the problem, and the construction of the problem's parameters. Problem solvers may use an array of cognitive abilities, such as verbal and written comprehension, memory skills, and inductive and deductive reasoning (Fleishman 1975; Fleishman & Quaintance, 1984) to interpret information regarding the nature of a particular problem. The second process is specifying the most appropriate solution paths. This specification may proceed from the application of convergent thinking, divergent thinking, or logical reasoning skills to information derived from the construction and representation of the problem. The third and fourth processes are implementing the chosen solution and monitoring and evaluating of the solution and its consequences, respectively. Because leaders implement solutions within complex social environments, they need to apply a variety of cognitive and social competencies that promote solution implementation and the acquisition of information needed for effective monitoring and evaluation.

Metacognitive skills include not only particular cognitive abilities (e.g., oral, written comprehension, verbal reasoning) but also the awareness and regulation of the application of those abilities in understanding a problem, specifying a solution, and implementing and evaluating best-fitting strategies. That is, for each of the aforementioned processes, metacognitive problem-solving skills reflect an expertise in knowing what cognitive abilities are applicable in particular problem domains and in evaluating the products of their application. For example, regarding problem definition or construction, cognitive reasoning skills (e.g., deductive reasoning) are used to generate a particular understanding of a problem from available information. The addition of metacognitive skills help the problem solver to evaluate the constructed problem both in terms of the processes that led to its derivation and of its fit to the extant problem domain (e.g., Is this the "correct" or best way to construct this problem?). The value of metacognitive skills then is to facilitate flexibility in creative problem solving, particularly in how information is used and in the selection of solution strategies that correspond to different types of problems (Davidson et al., 1994; Jausovec, 1994b).

The studies cited in Table 2-2 on executive metacognition complement other work on SST initiated by ARI (e.g., Jacobs & Jaques, 1987, 1990, 1991; Jaques, Clement, Rigby, & Jacobs, 1986). The table represents an important extension regarding the specific thinking skills required by executives to build the frames of reference necessary for successful organizational action. Each research program, however, represents a preliminary stage in theory and conceptual development, and further integrative work is necessary.

Requisite Leader Characteristics: Interactive Complexity Theory

The major leader characteristic described by ICT is the structural properties of an individual's information-processing orientation, or his or her degree of cognitive complexity. To understand Streufert's concept of cognitive complexity and its application to leadership, several components of information-processing structure need to be defined. The most elemental of these is *dimension*, which is defined as "a bipolar scale having two or more points of discrimination among stimuli" (Streufert & Swezey, 1986, p. 16). Organizational examples of possible managerial dimensions are profit and productivity. A second structural component is *discrimination*, or "the process of dividing (or the degree to which division has been accomplished) a cognitive bipolar dimension into subsections for the placement of stimuli that have relevance to the endpoints of that dimension" (Streufert & Swezey, 1986, p. 16). Thus, for example, the division of a cognitive space representing productivity into different degrees from very low or very poor to very high or excellent reflects the process of discrimination. This process also represents a basic conceptualization of the environment, containing both elemental differentiation (i.e., multiple dimension points) and integration (i.e., a conceptual meaning uniting these points).

The next two components of information-processing structure, differentiation and integration, represent the basic factors in cognitive complexity. *Differentiation* is defined as "the process of dividing a cognitive or conceptual space . . . into two or more orthogonal or oblique (but nearly orthogonal) bipolar dimensions, systems, or subsystems" (Streufert & Swezey, 1986, pp. 16–17). In differentiating, an individual begins to conceptualize the environment using multiple dimensions. Thus, a manager who understands his or her work in terms of production and personnel development has specified two separate work dimensions and has displayed some differentiation. The process of combining or relating these dimensions into a single comprehensive perspective—that is, "to produce an outcome that is determined by the *joint* (weighted or unweighted) demands of each dimension, system, or subsystem involved" (Streufert & Swezey, 1986, p. 17)—*is integration.* Note that integration cannot occur without some degree of a priori differentiation.

Cognitive complexity represents the level of both differentiation and integration applied by an individual to one or more conceptual domains. A person who is high in cognitive complexity possesses a highly differentiated and integrated cognitive space; a person with low cognitive complexity is likely to operate with fewer dimensions (perhaps even unidimensionally), with little differentiation and integration.

Streufert and Swezey (1986) made a distinction between hierarchical and flexible integration that is critical for understanding effective executive leader thinking. Hierarchical integration represents a differentiated and integrated cognitive space in which the established relationships among the dimensions are stable. In essence, such integration represents a fixed, albeit complex, view of the world. Flexible integration occurs when the relationships among differentiated and integrated dimensions in cognitive space are perceived as varying in response to environmental dynamics.

Streufert and Swezey (1986) argued that strategic thinking involves a high level of flexible, integrative thinking. Executives who use such thinking bring multiple dimensions of the organizational space together into a coherent whole that remains adaptive to significant environmental changes. Thus, such executives develop an understanding that incorporates various elements of their organizations, their competitors, present environmental influences, and future trends related to their stakeholders. This understanding remains flexible to accommodate significant conceptual changes in any or all of the dimensions in the conceptual model.

This skill is fairly compatible with the conceptual capacity notion proposed by SST. In fact, Jacobs and Jaques (1991) used the terminology of ICT to describe changes in leader thinking across organizational levels. However, Streufert and Swezey (1986) offered two other distinctions that are not made explicit by SST. First, complexity in leadership is not synonymous with complexity in decision making. *Leadership complexity* refers to differentiation and integration regarding different leader styles (e.g., initiating structure, consideration, production emphasis, persuasiveness), whereas *decision-making complexity* refers to the use of differentiation and integration in strategy formation and planning. Leaders can be complex in terms of different styles, but not necessarily in terms of decision making. The reverse also can be true. Streufert and Swezey proposed that successful upper-level executives should be cognitively complex in both of these areas.

A second distinction concerns the down side of high flexible integration. High integration is not possible without a significant degree of differentiation. However, a high degree of flexibility could result in an individual continually adjusting his or her conceptual model in response to relatively minor environmental variations. Accordingly, Streufert and Swezey (1986) pointed out that individuals using higher levels of flexibility and integration in their decision making may inhibit their reaching a closure point, even a temporary one. They implied (although they did not explicitly state) that for effective executive thinking, a high level of flexible integrative complexity is combined with a significant degree of self-discipline that forces decision closure when warranted by environmental exigencies.

Summary and Evaluation

Both SST and ICT follow Day and Lord's (1988) suggestion that a systematic theory of executive leadership should specify individual differences in leader ability. Both theories also emphasize substance over style in terms of leadership. Day and Lord argued that executive leadership theories need to go beyond a focus on leadership styles (e.g., consideration and initiation of structure) to emphasize more cognitive factors such as analytic and perceptual abilities as well as skill in decision making. This is precisely the orientation of both SST and ICT (e.g., see Lewis & Jacobs, 1992, pp. 122–126, on leader style versus conceptual capacity).

The range in cognitive abilities among executive leaders typically is expected to be more restricted than may actually be the case. That is, most executive leaders are assumed to be intelligent, and derailment is attributed to low levels of other attributes such as personality and social skills (Lombardo & McCauley, 1988; McCall & Lombardo, 1983). However, Levinson (1994) noted the following:

> A major issue that is getting practically no attention in the management literature is the reality that in many cases the chief executive officer does not have the conceptual capacity to grasp the degree of complexity that he or she must confront. In short, they simply do not know what they are really up against, and what is happening to them and to their organizations, let alone knowing what to do about it. They simply cannot absorb the range of information they should and organize it from its multiple sources and focus it on the organizations' problems in a way that would both become vision and strategy.

The models reviewed in this chapter provide the conceptual base for understanding the role of such capacities in executive performance.

SST specifies a set of technical, interpersonal, and conceptual skills that separate lower-level from executive leaders (see Table 2-1). ICT focuses on a single differentiating factor-cognitive complexity. Both theories are congruent in that effective executive leadership is determined primarily by the degree of cognitive conceptualization skill possessed by the executive leader. SST is rather explicit in placing less importance on personality and motivational factors (Sashkin, 1992). That is not to say that these factors are irrelevant to executive performance. Lewis and

Jacobs (1992) argued, however, that all executives will have already demonstrated the requisite motivational and dispositional qualities; conceptual capacity is proposed to explain the most variance in executive leader performance. Although this is consistent with the major task assigned to executive leaders to facilitate organizational performance (i.e., the construction of a comprehensive and integrated frame of reference or cognitive map to guide collective action), other senior leadership theories stress a broader constellation of individual qualities as determinants of such variance. For example, ICT suggests that cognitive complexity needs to be combined with a dispositional orientation that facilitates decision closure at the appropriate time for effective decision making.

Likewise, information processing during periods of organizational ferment and change, when existing ways of thinking no longer apply, requires other characteristics such as adaptability, tolerance for ambiguity, and openness to new experiences. Otherwise, executive leaders may react to such a period with considerable resistance and fail to make the kinds of cognitive reorientations necessary for organizational survival and effectiveness.

The differences between these two theories are, of course, empirical questions. They should not detract from the observation that each theory provides a level of conceptual sophistication in its specification of executive leader skills and capabilities. Two remaining issues for these theories of executive leadership, the measurement and development of these capabilities, are addressed in the next section.

Measurement of Executive Conceptual Complexity: Stratified Systems Theory

Given the importance of conceptual complexity for senior leadership work, a central concern is the measurement of such capacities. Indeed, some criticism of SST has focused on the relative inattention paid to the measurement of cognitive capacity (Streufert & Swezey, 1986). The measurement of this capacity is not likely to be amenable to traditional survey or multiple-choice methods (Jacobs & Jaques, 1990; Streufert & Swezey, 1986). Instead, the more appropriate measurement format may be one that includes *constructed response tasks*, defined by Bennett (1993b) as "task[s] for which the space of examinee responses is not limited to a small set of presented options. As such, the examinee is forced to formulate, rather than recognize, an answer" (p. 100). Several researchers have argued that such measures provide more effective assessments of higher order cognitive skills, such as conceptual capacity, than multiple-choice measures (Ackerman & Smith, 1988; Birenbaum & Tatsuoka, 1987; Sebrechts, Bennett, & Rock, 1991; Ward, Frederickson, & Carlson, 1980). Stamp (1988) developed a measure of cognitive power, called the Career Path Appreciation technique (CPA), that combines constructed response tasks with extensive interviews. The ARI sponsored research on the development of the Strategic Leadership Development Inventory (SLDI; Industrial College of the Armed Forces, 1994; Stewart, Kilcullen, & Hopkins, 1993), which uses a multiple-choice format but has the advantage of including the perspective of the rated leader as well as those of the leader's peers, superiors, and subordinates. The SLDI assesses attributes in addition to cognitive conceptualization skills. The characteristics and structure of both measures are described in this section. Evidence regarding their psychometric properties is presented in chapter 3.

CAREER PATH APPRECIATION MEASURE

The CPA uses an interview methodology that combines three separate assessment tasks to identify an individual's current level of conceptual capacity. Then, on the basis of this score, the assessee's age, and Jaques's (1986) maturation curves, the individual's maximum attainable level of cognitive capacity and work level are predicted. Thus, the CPA produces an index of both current and potential cognitive work capacity.

Three tasks make up the CPA. One is the phrase-selection task. The assessee is given nine sets of six cards. Each card describes an approach to solving a problem or completing a work assignment. Each set reflects six work levels proposed by SST. For example, one set contains the following phrases (Lewis, 1995, p. 15; from Stamp, 1986):

- Work to a complete set of instructions (Level I),
- Work within a given framework (Level II),
- Work with connections even if particular links are unclear (Level III),
- Work in abstracts and concepts (Level IV),
- Work with a minimum of preconceptions (Level V),
- Define the horizons of the work (Level VI).

The assessee is required to select the cards that reflect his or her most and least comfortable approaches to work; he or she is then asked to explain and discuss his or her choices. The choices, and particularly the corresponding discussions, provide information used to determine the assessee's current conceptual capacity.

Another CPA task is the symbol sort task (Bruner, 1966), in which an assessee is presented with four target cards, three with geometric symbols on them and the fourth blank. The assessee is then given a pack of symbol cards and asked to sort them under the four target cards according to self-developed sorting rules. Feedback is given by the assessor throughout the task regarding the correct (or incorrect) placement of symbols under the three symbol target cards but not for any sorts to the blank card. Success on this task requires abstracting and conceptualizing appropriate sorting rules.

The third part of the CPA is a work history interview, in which the assessee provides information regarding his or her previous and current work positions and assignments. The assessee is asked to indicate the maximum time spans and work challenge for each position. This information is considered useful not only in assigning current capacity values, but also for predicting the growth in these values over time (Lewis, 1995).

Scoring of the CPA requires a strong understanding of SST. The results from the three tasks are analyzed to place the assessee in one of seven levels, each having categories of high, medium, and low; thus, the range of possible scores on the CPA is 1 to 21. CPA data also can be used in combination with Jaques's (1986) maturation curves to determine future potential conceptual capacity.

STRATEGIC LEADER DEVELOPMENT INVENTORY

The SLDI is based not only on SST, but also on Kegan's (1982) stage theory and on work by Hogan, Raskin, and Fazzini (1990) on the attributes of ineffective leaders. The SLDI contains attributes derived from SST that facilitate long-term envisioning, consensus building, and team building. SLDI attributes derived from Kegan's theory reflect high levels of adult maturity. Stage theory proposes four stages of gaining maturity that are defined in terms of developing a broader, more realistic, and objective personal and world perspective. Stage 4, which is presumably characteristic of the successful strategic thinker, includes individuals who "have the capacity to operate their own judgmental processes unconstrained by the standards, values, or points of view of others" (Lewis & Jacobs, 1992, p. 128).

The SLDI contains an assessment of negative attributes derived from research on managerial derailment (Hogan et al., 1990; Lombardo, Ruderman, & McCauley, 1987; McCall & Lombardo, 1983). Hogan et al. (1990) defined three personality profiles of flawed or ineffectual managers. The first is the high likeability floater, who has high social skills, is congenial and easy to get along with, and almost never causes disruptions. However, because such an individual has low ambition and no direction, he or she (and the units he or she manages) do not perform well. The second profile is the *hommes de ressentiment*, or the manager who is outwardly charming and competent but who harbors deep resentment toward others and seeks avenues of revenge. The third profile is the narcissist. Managers with this profile are intolerant of criticism, resist accepting suggestions from others, take disproportionate credit for success, avoid responsibility for failure, and are overconfident in their judgments (Hogan et al., 1990). Each of these profiles limits movement to and performance in strategic leadership positions.

The SLDI is a 360-degree assessment inventory—that is, the target leader completes the inventory, as do four of his or her subordinates, three peers, and three superiors. Certain attributes are rated only by a subset of raters (i.e., by self, peer, subordinate, or superior), whereas all raters evaluate other attributes. This assessment approach assumes that each of these constituencies will have overlapping as well as differing perspectives of the target leader, thus producing a complete picture of the leader's strength and weaknesses. Table 2-3 presents the attributes assessed by the SLDI, with corresponding definitions and rating source.

TABLE 2-3

Strategic Leadership Development Inventory: Attributes

Factor	Source
Conceptual skills and attributes	
Conceptual flexibility	Superiors, peers, self
Political sensibility	Superiors, peers, self
Long-term perspective	Superiors
Quick study/perception	Peers
Complex understanding	Subordinates
Positive attributes	
Empowers subordinates	All
Has strong work ethic	Superiors, self
Is personally objective	Subordinates, self
Displays professional maturity	Superiors
Facilitates team performance	Peers
Negative attributes	
Technically incompetent	All
Explosive, abusive	All
Arrogant, self-serving, unethical	All
Rigid, given to micromanaging	Superiors, peers, self
Inaccessible	Subordinates

Adapted from *A Guide to the Strategic Leader Development Inventory*, 1994, Washington, DC: Defense University, Industrial College of the Armed Forces.

Measurement of Executive Conceptual Complexity: Interactive Complexity Theory

Streufert and Swezey (1986) described a number of measures developed to assess flexible integrative complexity. These include the Sentence Completion Test (Schroder & Streufert, 1962), the Impression Formation Test (Streufert & Driver, 1967), and Textual Analysis (Suedfield & Rank, 1976), as well as methods reflecting post hoc analysis of decision-making structure (e.g., time–event matrices, post-decision interviews, experimental simulations). A full description of all of these measures is beyond the scope and intent of this book. Also, with a few published exceptions (Streufert, 1983, 1984; Suedfield, Corteen, & McCormick, 1986), these measurement strategies have not been used to assess cognitive complexity in executive leaders. Accordingly, only very brief descriptions of these measures are provided. Interested readers are referred to Streufert and Streufert (1978) and Streufert and Swezey (1986), as well as to original sources, for more in-depth descriptions.

The Sentence Completion Test presents respondents with sentence stems ("When I am criticized . . .") and requires them to generate additional sentences to complete each stem. Expert judges then rate responses for degree of cognitive complexity. Exhibit 2-1 presents sample responses provided by Streufert and Swezey (1986) that reflect low cognitive complexity, differentiation, and integration. The Impression Formation Test, based on Asch's (1946) classic study, requires respondents to write descriptions of three persons. The first has the characteristics of "intelligent," "industrious," and "impulsive." The second has the characteristics of "critical," "stubborn," and "envious." The third is described with all six characteristics. Cognitive complexity is defined by how completely a respondent integrates these qualities that differ in affective tone into a coherent portrait of a single person. Individuals with low cognitive complexity may deny the possibility of integration. Exhibit 2-2 presents sample differentiated and integrated responses. Textual Analysis is an adaptation of the Sentence Completion Test that is used to estimate differentiation and integration from archival and written material. For example, Suedfield et al. (1986) derived estimates of the cognitive complexity scores of six Civil War generals (Burnside, Grant, Hooker, Lee, McClellan, and Meade) from official dispatches, battle orders, and published letters from Civil War archives.

These measures of integrative complexity require expert raters to make substantial subjective interpretation of either cued or uncued written material. Streufert and Swezey (1986) described other techniques

---

EXHIBIT 2-1

Sample Sentence Completion Test Responses Illustrating Levels of Integrative Cognitive Complexity

Sentence Completion Test fragment
"When I am criticized . . ."
Low cognitive complexity response
When I am criticized, I am usually wrong. I appreciate criticism because I learn from it. Most of the time people who criticize me have my welfare in mind. Particularly when the criticism comes from an authority I will change my ways.
Differentiated response
When I am criticized, it typically means that the other person has a different view of thinking than I do. Maybe he grew up in a different environment and learned to think differently. Probably his way of thinking is okay—but so is mine. Most of the time I ignore that criticism.
Integrated response
When someone criticizes me, I listen carefully. I don't necessarily agree with all that person may say, but there are parts of these views that may be relevant to what I am doing or thinking. Sometimes I combine some of their views with mine.

Adapted from "The Measurement of Differentiative and Integrative Complexity: Measuring Individual, Team, and Organizational Performance," in *Complexity, Managers, and Organizations* (pp. 144–147), by S. Streufert and R. W. Swezey. Copyright 1986 by Academic Press. Adapted with permission.

that involve the analysis of decision making to derive scores of integrative complexity. These procedures involve individuals engaged in decision making in either a real-time setting or a computerized experimental simulation (Swezey, Streufert, Criswell, Unger, & van Rijn, 1984). Data from post hoc interviews or analysis of the alternatives selected at var-

---

EXHIBIT 2-2

Sample Impression Formation Test Responses Illustrating Levels of Integrative Cognitive Complexity

Impression Formation Test instruction
"Describe a person with the following attributes: intelligent, industrious, impulsive, critical, stubborn, envious."
Differentiated response
This person is a good worker who makes quick decisions, and everyone at work likes him. But when he comes home to his wife and children, he can be very nasty.
Integrated response
Such a person makes quick decisions. They are usually quality decisions because she is bright and has gained much experience. She is critical of those who work for her because she is jealous of her superiors because she wants to advance quickly—a goal she pursues relentlessly and with great effort.

Adapted from "The Measurement of Differentiative and Integrative Complexity: Measuring Individual, Team, and Organizational Performance," in *Complexity, Managers, and Organizations* (pp. 144–147), by S. Streufert and R. W. Swezey. Copyright 1986 by Academic Press. Adapted with permission.

ious points in a decision-making process are then used to derive a time–event matrix. This matrix is a representation of action sequences plotted along the dimensions of time and decision type. *Decision type* refers to different categories of actions that can be selected in the course of a problem. Examples of military decision types include troop-movement decisions and air-support decisions (Streufert & Swezey, 1986, p. 152). Researchers plot the structure of decision making by indicating the actions (denoting particular decision types) selected at particular points in time. Arrows connect a decision at one point in time that is considered to be related to a decision at another point in time; diagonal arrows in the matrix represent connections between different decision types. A cognitively complex response is reflected in proactive strategy-based decision making (i.e., interrelated and sequentially planned decisions), whereas low complexity is reflected in reactive decision-making with fewer connections among decisions of one type or among different decision types. Sample matrices provided by Streufert and Swezey (pp. 158, 193) depicting low and high integrative complexity are illustrated in Figure 2-3.

Summary and Evaluation

Researchers in both SST and ICT have in common their use of constructed response tasks to measure leader attributes. Such tasks require that respondents generate responses to a stimulus rather than select responses from a predetermined set. Studies on the measurement of complex cognitive abilities and skills have reported that constructed response tasks resemble actual problem solving more closely and are more effective for such assessment than multiple-choice or inventory tasks (Ackerman & Smith, 1988; Bennett, 1993b; Bennett et al., 1990; Birenbaum & Tatsuoka, 1987; Sebrechtset et al., 1991; Ward et al., 1980). However, such measures are burdened with considerable administrative costs as well as significant potential for error. Several of the measures described are fairly time-consuming, requiring several hours of assessment per individual (e.g., CPA, derivation of decision-making time–event matrices). Also, almost all of the measures described require some judgment and evaluation by expert raters. Indeed, Jacobs and Jaques (1991) stated that the assessment of responses to the CPA requires thorough knowledge of SST and a conceptual capacity of Level IV or higher in Jaques's (1986) classification. This significantly limits the widespread use of this measure as an executive assessment tool. The same concern applies to a lesser degree to Streufert's cognitive complexity measures.

Another concern with measures using constructed response tasks is their construct validity (Bennett, 1993a, 1993b). When tasks require the

FIGURE 2-3

Sample Time–Event Matrixes Illustrating (A) Low and (B) High Integrative Complexity

(A) Low Integrative Complexity

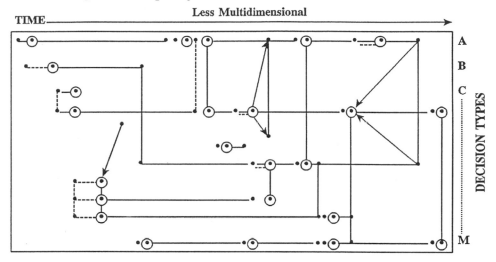

(B) High Integrative Complexity

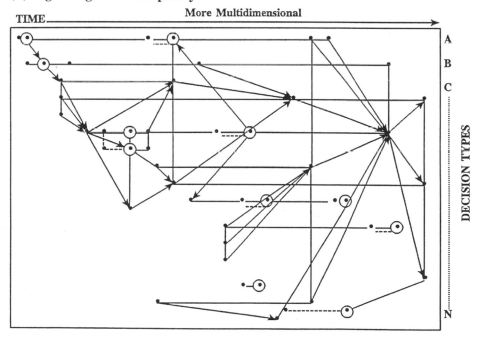

Adapted from "The Measurement of Differentiative and Integrative Complexity: Measuring Individual, Team, and Organizational Performance," in *Complexity, Managers, and Organizations* (pp. 144–147), by S. Streufert and R. W. Swezey. Copyright 1986 by Academic Press. Adapted with permission.

generation of a complex series of responses, they may reflect the influence of other motivational and dispositional variables—that is, they may assess variables in addition to complex cognitive skill. For example, the CPA includes a work history interview that is designed to assess an interviewee's degree of comfort in the level of work complexity required of previous positions. Responses to such prompts may reflect a number of qualities in addition to conceptual skill, such as mastery and achievement motives as well as dispositional flexibility and tolerance of uncertainty. Likewise, the coding guidelines of the phrase-selection task describe personal preferences in problem solving as part of the definition of each level of functional capacity (McIntyre, Jordan, Mergen, Hamill, & Jacobs, 1993). Again, this suggests that responses may include not only conceptual skill, but also other dispositional, stylistic, and value-orientation qualities. However, this is a validation question and therefore an empirical one; indeed, several studies have provided some psychometric evidence regarding the CPA (Lewis, 1993, 1995; McIntyre et al., 1993; Stamp, 1988).

The time–event matrix raises different validity concerns. Cognitive complexity appears to be defined in terms of how integrated a decision maker's strategic plan is in a series of problem domains. That is, structural differences in decision making are used to denote differentiation and integrative complexity. The problem with this technique, however, is one of circularity—cognitive complexity is defined (or operationalized) as integrated strategic planning, which is hypothesized as a consequence of complex thinking skills. Careful attention needs to be directed at the use of this technique in the context of executive skill assessment.

These concerns notwithstanding, the measures described provide a potentially strong methodological basis for the evaluation of executive performance and skill requirements proposed by conceptual complexity theories of executive leadership. Furthermore, to the degree these measures demonstrate predictive validity, they may serve as part of an effective executive assessment and development program.

An effective theory of executive leadership should provide prescriptions for the development and training of budding executives. Some of the developmental issues and ideas raised by SST and ICT are described in the final section of this chapter.

Leader Development: Stratified Systems Theory

Jaques, Clement, Rigby, and Jacobs (1986) provided the following formula for defining an individual's level of work capability (LoC)

$$\text{LoC} = (\text{PE} * \text{CP} * \text{O}),$$

where PE represents psychological equipment and includes the knowledge, skills, values, and temperament required for work completion; CP represents cognitive power; and O represents the opportunities and developmental experiences an individual has had to acquire requisite skills and knowledge. This formula, together with other statements by SST theorists (Jacobs & Jaques, 1990; Jaques, 1986; Lewis & Jacobs, 1992) suggests several important points regarding leader development. One of these, mentioned earlier in this chapter, is the relative immutability of potential and actualized cognitive power. Thus, Jaques et al. (1986) noted that "a person's cognitive power sets the maximum level of work of any kind that he/she would be capable of *even with maximum opportunities for the development of the necessary [psychological] equipment*" (p. 23, italics added). This means that without sufficient constitutional equipment, no amount of development effort can help lower-level organizational leaders rise or be promoted into executive leadership positions. This argument puts significant weight on executive selection relative to executive development. Or, at least, selection needs to precede developmental efforts at various points in a leader's career. Selection criteria should focus primarily on the level of displayed and potential conceptual capacity (Lewis & Jacobs, 1992).

Although potential conceptual capacity is fixed, according to Jaques's (1986) growth curves, it does mature over an individual's life span. Jacobs and Jaques (1990) argued that executive development interventions should focus primarily on conceptual skill development. However, individuals with high potential may not be offered sufficient, if any, opportunities for using their conceptual capacities early in their careers. Organizational work at the levels likely to be occupied at early career points will not require the conceptual skills such individuals possess. In fact, the use of these skills at these early levels may actually be counterproductive (Streufert & Swezey, 1986). This is where proclivity, or an individual's inclination toward mental model building, plays an important role. Junior leaders with high conceptual proclivity are likely to be engaging in such activities early in their careers even in the absence of extrinsic rewards for doing so (Jacobs & Jaques, 1990). According to SST, this proclivity, then, is likely to be influential for a leader's progress along predicted conceptual maturation paths.

Lewis and Jacobs (1992) also argued that the development of conceptual capacity proceeds slowly, with milestones occurring when individuals reach the limitations of their current constructed models of experience. When current models are insufficient, leaders will attempt to reconceptualize their more complex operating environment, developing new frames of reference that reflect higher levels of cognitive power. This argument suggests that effective developmental experiences are likely to be those that push leaders to the limit of and beyond their current frames of reference. Along these lines, Lewis and Jacobs (1992) suggested the following:

> The heart of managerial development, therefore, should be the planned assignment of high-potential leaders and managers to successively more challenging work roles where a mentor is present who can help the individual better understand the new, more complicated world in which the new manager must now operate. (p. 136)

Developmental efforts, then, need to be targeted to the psychological equipment required by leaders advancing to the next organizational level. This recommendation, together with those for the maturation of conceptual capacity, implies that leader development is a career-long endeavor that should feature (a) specific instructional interventions linked to skill development and knowledge acquisition at particular organizational levels; (b) opportunities for the practice of newly acquired skills and knowledge; and (c) the assignment of developing leaders into work roles that force them to continuously revise their cognitive maps and models of their operating environment. Taken together, these development opportunities appear to be the most appropriate for the variables linked by SST to executive effectiveness.

Leader Development: Interactive Complexity Theory

Streufert and Swezey (1986) did not offer a set of prescriptions or a model for executive leader development. They suggested that cognitive complexity could be trained by presenting individuals with evidence of multidimensionality in a conceptual domain. This suggestion resembles Jacobs and Lewis's (1992) prescription that leader development include the role of a mentor to encourage a broader perspective. Complexity in a specific domain may also be trained if other conceptual domains constructed by an individual are already differentiated and integrated. In such circumstances, a form of analogical reasoning can be used to foster the discovery of dimensions in a previously undifferentiated conceptual space. However, little, if any, empirical research has been completed to evaluate the effects of these training strategies on the development of integrative complexity, the requisite capacity for executive work. Thus, these strategies are, at best, speculative at this point.

LEADER DEVELOPMENT: SUMMARY AND EVALUATION

A central issue in conceptual complexity theories of leadership is whether requisite cognitive capabilities can be developed. And, if they can, there is the question of whether the investment costs of such training are so prohibitive that primary emphasis should be placed on selection. SST adopts the position that potential conceptual capacity is fixed early. However, this framework provides a substantial rationale for executive development interventions by arguing that career-long efforts are necessary to actualize this potential. Furthermore, SST argues that other requisite leader skills are not fixed and therefore benefit from targeted training and development.

This theory then complements its postulates on the nature of executive performance requirements and requisite executive skills with corresponding prescriptions for executive development. The result is a well-rounded and coherent conceptual model of executive leadership.

CONCEPTUAL COMPLEXITY THEORIES: SUMMARY

A conceptual evaluation of the models described in this chapter, particularly SST, indicates that they contain several of the elements prescribed by Day and Lord (1988) for a theory of executive leadership. SST provides a comprehensive conceptual framework for understanding the nature of executive leadership and the individual characteristics required for such work. Its model of leader performance requirements specifies qualitative shifts in these requirements across organizational levels. Thus, executive leadership cannot be explained using a framework for understanding lower-level leadership. Furthermore, the requisite leadership skills differentiate not only between lower- and upper-level organizational leaders, but also between those leaders who are effective at the top of the organization and those who are not. SST also provides a model and set of prescriptions for the development of key executive leader capabilities. Finally, studies by Stamp (1988) and by the ARI have produced measurement strategies for the assessment of these capabilities. Accordingly, this theory provides an elegant and testable framework for understanding executive leadership. ICT is a more narrow approach, but it also provides testable propositions regarding executive performance requirements and requisite skills. Chapter 3 presents a summary and evaluation of empirical studies that provide evidence regarding these theories.

Conceptual Complexity Theories of Executive Leadership: Empirical Review and Evaluation

3

Chapter 2 presented a theoretical review and evaluation of two conceptual complexity theories of executive leadership: stratified systems theory (SST) and interactive complexity theory (ICT). This chapter examines empirical research that either directly tested those theories or provides data that are indirectly relevant to them. Although first developed 30 to 45 years ago (Jaques, 1956, 1964; see also Jaques, 1976), SST has not yet been the subject of comprehensive review and evaluation. ICT has only recently been extended to executive leadership, and thus has generated less research in this domain. For this reason, the primary focus of this chapter is on SST.

This chapter organizes the empirical research on these models around the following themes: (a) executive leader performance requirements; (b) requisite executive leader characteristics; (c) measurement of conceptual complexity; and (d) leader development targeting cognitive skills. The U.S. Army has sponsored a significant number of studies based on SST. Accordingly, this chapter reviews both military and nonmilitary studies to determine the generalizability of particular findings across domains.

Figure 3-1 presents a research model that integrates several critical elements of executive leadership. This model represents a conceptual framework describing the particular relationships and linkages that should be the focus of empirical research on executive leadership. The model also includes executive leader performance requirements and competencies proposed by SST and ICT. The studies reviewed in this chapter are considered in the context of this model and in terms of whether they contribute valid evidence for (a) the proposed contents represented in each box (e.g., Do the executive leader performance requirements represented accurately reflect actual executive-level functioning?) and (b) the relationships proposed between the elements of

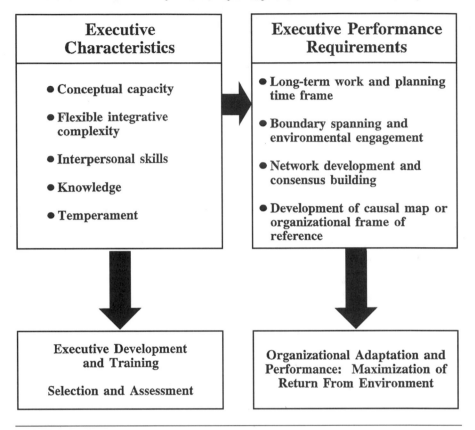

FIGURE 3-1

Research Model of Conceptual Complexity and Executive Leadership

Executive Characteristics	Executive Performance Requirements
• Conceptual capacity • Flexible integrative complexity • Interpersonal skills • Knowledge • Temperament	• Long-term work and planning time frame • Boundary spanning and environmental engagement • Network development and consensus building • Development of causal map or organizational frame of reference
Executive Development and Training Selection and Assessment	Organizational Adaptation and Performance: Maximization of Return From Environment

the model (e.g., Is the accomplishment of executive leader performance requirements significantly associated with organizational gain?).

As shown in the model, when executive leaders successfully accomplish their work requirements, the organization as a whole should gain value in the form of better performance and adaptation to environmental contingencies. SST is grounded in an open systems perspective of organizations that suggests "that organizations survive only as long as they are able to maintain *negentropy*, that is, import in all forms greater amounts of energy than they return to the environment as product" (Katz & Kahn, 1978, p. 226). Accordingly, research on executive leadership needs to demonstrate (a) critical executive leader performance requirements and (b) the association between the accomplishment of these requirements and organizational gain.

The model in Figure 3-1 indicates four executive leader performance requirements that are identified in the conceptual complexity theories of executive leadership. These are (a) long-term work and planning time span, (b) boundary management and environmental engagement, (c) network development and consensus building, and (d) development of an organizational causal map or frame of reference. These are presumably the means by which the executive leader adds value to the organization (Jacobs & Jaques, 1987, 1990, 1991; cf. Day & Lord, 1988). Therefore, their successful accomplishment should be empirically associated with indices of organizational adaptation and performance.

Conceptual capacity, or flexible integrative complexity, as well as other individual executive leader characteristics (e.g., interpersonal skills, knowledge, temperament) are the basis for the development of executive leader assessment tools and developmental interventions. Executive leadership research should focus on (a) the reliability and validity of such tools and (b) the validity and effectiveness of training and development interventions. The validity of such interventions should be defined in terms of gains in executive leader competencies, as measured with validated assessment tools.

The model in Figure 3-1 raises a number of research questions that serve as the focus of the empirical review in this chapter. These questions concern (a) the differences between lower- and executive-level work; (b) the relationship between executive leader work and organizational effectiveness; and (c) the specification, measurement, and development of individual characteristics that promote executive leader performance. Specific propositions are outlined to guide the review of relevant empirical research.

Executive Leader Performance Requirements

According to conceptual complexity theories regarding executive leadership performance requirements, information-processing demands increase significantly as one ascends the organizational hierarchy. This increase is attributed in part to the need for planning within longer timespans. Executive leaders' boundary management or boundary-spanning activities with the external environment and coordination of multiple organizational units contribute additional information-processing demands. These include (a) the need to develop comprehensive worldwide strategies and develop new business units (b) the need for continual environmental scanning; and (c) the need to examine, understand, and control how changes in one part of the organization affect other parts (Jacobs & Jaques, 1987; Jaques, 1989). Thus, the effective executive leader develops an integrated and flexible map of the causal and system factors operating within the organization and in its environment. Finally, to plan effectively and institute organizational change, executive leaders need to (a) develop effective information sources; (b) acquire the resources necessary for proposed changes; and (c) convince organizational constituencies of the appropriateness of specific planned changes. Another executive leadership requirement, then, is information network development and consensus building.

These theoretical statements from conceptual complexity theories of executive leadership lead to several specific propositions. The first set, presented next, addresses qualitative differences across organizational levels in four executive leader role or performance requirements:

1. Executive leaders engage in planning and policy creation within longer time horizons than lower-level leaders.
2. Executive leaders interact more frequently with external organizational constituencies than lower-level leaders.
3. Executive leaders engage in more network development and consensus-building activities than lower-level leaders.
4. Executive leaders develop a broader and more comprehensive cognitive map or frame of reference of the organization and its environment than lower-level leaders.

The successful accomplishment of executive leader performance requirements adds value to the organization as a whole. Therefore, each of the requirements listed previously is hypothesized to significantly improve organizational performance and effectiveness. This is derived from Day and Lord's (1988) notion that a systematic executive leadership theory should describe how executive leader performance influences organizational performance. Accordingly, the following are also proposed:

5. Long-term planning by executive leaders is positively associated with organizational effectiveness.
6. Boundary management activities by executive leaders are positively associated with organizational effectiveness.
7. Network development and consensus-building activities by executive leaders are positively associated with organizational effectiveness.
8. The quality of an executive leader's cognitive map or frame of reference is associated with organizational effectiveness.

These propositions were used to guide the empirical review of SST and ICT in this chapter, However, the theories differ regarding the definition and importance of some of them. For example, although, each theory addresses the issue of long-term planning, ICT places less importance on this issue than SST. Streufert and Swezey (1986) argued that "time span is not a primary component of executive planning styles" (p. 78), and they questioned whether long-term planning is connected with organizational effectiveness (see also Mintzberg, 1973, 1975, 1994). Therefore, the predictions regarding the frequency and efficacy of long executive leader planning time spans are more particular to SST. SST also articulates a greater range of differences in leadership performance requirements across organizational levels than most other theories (Hunt, 1991; Katz & Kahn, 1978). Whereas most theories describe three levels of organizational leadership, SST proposes seven levels subsumed under three domains (see Table 2-1).

Some of these propositions may apply equally to other models of executive leadership described in subsequent chapters of this book (e.g., behavioral complexity models, strategic decision-making theories). Nonetheless, they represent the more critical elements of the conceptual complexity theories. Even when there is overlap with other models, the variables delineated here are proposed as influencing executive leader and organizational performance through different mediating mechanisms. That is, boundary management, network development, and consensus-building activities are associated with the construction and communication of complex cognitive models of the organization and its environment. Thus, the means by which executive leaders add value to the organization are different in conceptual complexity models of executive leadership even though some of the antecedent conditions may be the same, as in, for example, behavioral complexity models.

Researchers associated with the U.S. Army Research Institute (ARI) have completed many studies investigating conceptual complexity models of executive leadership, particularly SST. Not surprisingly, much of this research used military samples. It is useful to document empirical evidence for conceptual complexity models broadly by sample. Accordingly, examination of these propositions, as well as other aspects of the conceptual complexity theories, is divided within this chapter according to research conducted in military and nonmilitary domains.

MILITARY STUDIES

Table 3-1 summarizes empirical studies using military samples that provide data relevant for the executive leader performance requirements listed previously. The majority of these studies used the interview method. Although this approach is common in executive leadership research (e.g., Isenberg, 1984; Kaplan, 1986; Kotter, 1982a, 1982b; Levinson & Rosenthal, 1984; Mintzberg, 1973), it is subject to criticism regarding the internal validity of its conclusions. Also, the sample sizes in

TABLE 3-1

Summary of Empirical Studies Examining Military Executive Leader Performance Requirements

Study	Participants	Study type	Findings
Harris & Lucas (1991)	8 four-star general officers, 33 three-star general officers	Structured interviews	Four-star officers reported longer work time spans and more boundary management requirements than three-star officers. Both groups cited comparable role requirements for network development, consensus building, and complex frame of reference.
Lucas & Markessini (1993)	48 one-star general officers, 26 two-star general officers; compared with sample from Harris & Lucas (1991)	Structured interviews	Recoded data from Harris and Lucas (1991) and found that one-, two-, and three-star officers reported similar task, planning, and maximum planning time spans. Maximum planning times for four-star officers were higher. One- and two-star officers also reported fewer boundary management requirements; similar requirements for network building and consensus development, and greater need for knowledge of total Army system than upper-level officers.
Markessini, Lucas, Chandler, & Jacobs (1994)	27 executive service and senior executive service members	Structured interviews	Civilian executives reported executive performance requirements of relatively long work time spans; boundary management, network development, and consensus-building activities; development of broad organizational and environmental understanding. Work requirements were reported as comparable to uniformed counterparts.
Rigby & Harris (1987)	61 military and civilian leaders from program management offices and major subordinate commands	Structured interviews	Major subordinate command leaders operated within longer time spans and engaged in more boundary management activities than subordinate leaders.
Stamp (1986)	168 female managers in business, government, nursing, and U.S. military at multiple organizational levels	Structured interviews	Described institutional barriers to career paths for women and as they move into organizational strata requiring higher cognitive power.
Steinberg & Leaman (1990b)	5,033 commissioned officers from second lieutenant to colonel	Survey	Colonels were more likely than lower-ranking officers to be involved in short- and long-term goal setting, planning, and policy making; developing contacts with organizations outside the Army; and working with civilian managers.

most of these studies were too small to allow the application of inferential statistics; thus, their conclusions are based on descriptive analyses. These limitations and their implications are discussed later in this chapter.

Harris and Lucas (1991; also summarized in Jaques, Clement, Rigby, & Jacobs, 1986) and Lucas and Markessini (1993) examined military general officers at the top four organizational strata defined by SST. Markessini, Lucas, Chandler, and Jacobs (1994) examined 27 U.S. Army civilian executives who were members of the executive service (ES) and senior executive service (SES; corresponding to SST Strata VI and VII leaders). The executives in each sample participated in structured interviews to determine (a) the nature of performance requirements at their respective organizational levels and (b) the skills necessary to complete these requirements. The differences in reported role and performance requirements across levels are of particular interest.

Other studies that focused on military leadership performance requirements include Stamp (1986), Rigby and Harris (1987), and Steinberg and Leaman (1990a, 1990b). These studies investigated leaders across all seven strata (Stamp, 1986), leaders primarily in the organizational domain (Rigby & Harris, 1987), and leaders ranging from the production to the organizational domains (i.e., lieutenant to colonel). Accordingly, they provide data on trends in performance requirements across levels that can be evaluated regarding the predictions of SST.

Long-Term Planning

SST proposes that planning time spans become longer at higher organizational levels, with Strata VII executive leaders operating within 20+ year time spans. Lucas and Markessini (1993) reported that the percentage of general officers who stated that long-term planning was important in their work rose from 25% for one-star officers to 40% for two-star officers to 63.6% for three-star officers to 87.5% for four-star officers. Content analyses of these interviews were used to uncover the specific range of work time span for each level. Revising the protocols used by Harris and Lucas (1991), Lucas and Markessini scored each general officer according to (a) task planning time span and (b) time horizon the officer could envision future events (labeled *performance capability*). Means for the first measure were in the 5- to 7-year time span for all four ranks. Means for the second measure were longer, with four-star general officers averaging a 19-year time horizon. However, the maximum horizons for the one-, two-, and three-star officers were all in the range of 9 to11.5 years. This is within the lower and upper time spans proposed by SST for two- and three-star officers, respectively, but it is longer than the time span proposed for one star officers.

Markessini et al. (1994) reported an even more fine-grained analysis of work time span for executive service (ES) and senior executive service (SES) civilian executives. They coded interview content using the following definitions of three different time spans:

Time span of work: a time period to formulate, prepare for, execute, and complete a specific job task, or set of tasks, that is self-determined or actively undertaken rather then institutionally defined.

Planning time frame: a time period for a mental construction that features a vision of the future, goals related to that vision, and a means to attain that future aspect.

Envisioning horizon: a time period for a particular vision of the future not necessarily tied to any articulated sense of a planning process. (p. A-1)

Table 3-2 displays the scores for these measures for the civilian executives and, where possible, for the general officers. The mean scores reported by the civilian executives were 4.5 years, 8.5 years, and 16.8 years for work time span, planning time span, and envisioning horizon, respectively. Markessini et al. also indicated modal scores of work time spans derived from the general officer interviews. (These scores are shown in Table 3-2; mean scores for this index were not provided. Also,

TABLE 3-2

Reported Mean Time Span Scores (in Years) for Civilian Military Executives and General Officers (GOs)

| | Time span measure | | | |
Sample	Typical task	Typical planning	Maximum planning (performance capability)	Envisioning horizon[a]
ES/SES	4.5	8.5	13.6	16.8
4-star GO	5–9[b]	7.0	19.0	—
3-star GO	0–4[b]	6.6	11.5	—
2-star GO	0–4[b]	4.7	8.6	—
1-star GO	0–4[b]	6.7	11.2	—

Note. ES = executive service; SES = senior executive service. Data adapted from *Senior Leadership in a Changing World Order: Requisite Skills for U.S. Army One- and Two-Star Generals* (ARI Tech. Rep. No. 976, pp. 33, 35), by K. W. Lucas and J. Markessini, 1993, Alexandria, VA: U.S. Army Research Institute for the Behavioral and Social Sciences, and from *Executive Leadership: Requisite Skills and Developmental Processes for the U.S. Army's Civilian Executives* (ARI Research Note 94-26, pp. 10–11, 13), by J. Markessini, K. W. Lucas, N. Chandler, and T. O. Jacobs, 1994, Alexandria, VA: U.S. Army Research Institute for the Behavioral and Social Sciences. Adapted with permission.
[a]Envisioning horizon scores were not provided for GOs.
[b]Only modal task time spans were provided for GOs.

no envisioning horizon scores were reported for general officers.) One-, two-, and three-star officers reported modal work time spans of 0 to 4 years, whereas the four-star officers reported a modal work time span of 5 to 9 years. Civilian executive leader modal responses were in the 0- to 4-year time span.

The conceptual distinctions among these measures are important. Responses on the work time span measure do not support the cross-level differences proposed by SST. In addition, these data suggest no real differences in average task planning time spans across the general officers. However, the maximum planning times, or performance capability scores, do support a difference between top military executives and those at lower levels. Also, the performance capability and envisioning horizon scores were within the time spans predicted by SST. Two significant caveats are in order, however, regarding interpretation of these data. First, time span responses were not specifically primed by the structured interview questions. Therefore, not all executives reported a planning time span. The percentage responding was 50%, 70%, 71%, 63%, and 70% for each of the general officer groups (from one-star to four-star) and the civilian executive leaders, respectively. Also, only 19% of the civilian executives reported an envisioning horizon time span. Therefore, some of the reported means may not be representative of each sample, particularly at the one-star level and for the civilian executives. Second, the number of four-star general officers in the sample was very low ($n = 8$). Although this sample represented 61.5% of the position incumbents at the time of the interviews, it was too low for any but descriptive analyses.

The conceptual distinctions in executive leader time spans made by Markessini et al. (1994) can be a useful refinement of SST. Indeed, they may represent an effective response to critics of this theory who have argued that executive leaders work within the long time spans proposed is atypical and often counterproductive (e.g., Mintzberg, 1973, 1975, 1990, 1994; Streufert & Swezey, 1986). The data from these three studies suggest relatively short work time spans and are consistent with the arguments of other executive leadership theorists. These data do suggest that executive leaders may have the capability to plan and envision over longer spans. Nonetheless, these studies provide evidence comparing variance in any of these time span measures to variance in individual and organizational performance outcomes. This leaves unresolved the questions of (a) whether any measure of time span is associated with organizational effectiveness and, more specifically, (b) whether the three measures of executive leadership time spans exhibit differential predictive validity regarding performance.

These studies described leadership time span requirements at the top of the organizational domain and in the systems domain of the stratification suggested by SST. Other military studies examined time span and policy-making requirements for leaders ranging across the production and organizational domains (Rigby & Harris, 1987; Steinberg & Leaman, 1990b). Jacobs and Jaques (1990) reported survey data from the professional development of officers study that is summarized in Figure 3-2. These data document longest assignment time spans for each military rank from second lieutenant to four-star general (unfortunately, no other reference or information about sample size and data collection was provided). These data show that, as expected, time spans increased steadily until the general officer ranks, at which point reported time spans were in the 5- to 10-year range. The data from general officers were consistent with the work and typical planning time span scores reported from the interview studies. However, the time spans for top executive leaders (three- and four-star officers) were lower than those predicted by SST.

Rigby and Harris (1987) examined the time spans for operations in U.S. Army program management offices (PMOs; Stratum IV leaders) and in major subordinate commands (MSCs; Stratum V leaders). The PMOs were found to operate within the 2- to 5-year time span predicted by SST, and the MSCs operated within the predicted 5- to 7-year time span. Steinberg and Leaman (1990b) administered an extensive task analysis instrument to 5033 commissioned officers ranging in rank from second lieutenant to colonel. They found that colonels (i.e., Strata IV leaders) were more likely than their lower-level counterparts to be involved in setting short-term and long-term unit/element goals and in making policy decisions. Compared with the data from general officers, the descriptive data from these studies indicate that planning or work time horizons are somewhat shorter in the organizational domain than in the systems domain but longer than in the production domain.

Boundary-Spanning Activities

According to conceptual complexity theories, the information-processing demands of executive leaders result not only from their need to operate within longer time spans but also from the requirement that they interact with multiple external constituencies. They also need to integrate the information contributed by different groups into a coherent frame of reference for the organization. Harris and Lucas (1991) reported that 75% of the four-star officers and 54.5% of the three-star officers described joint/unified command as part of their performance requirements. Such commands require interactions with subordinates from different components of the military opposed to within-Army command. Also, the four-star officers indicated that they reported to at least one external, nonmilitary constituency (e.g., U.S. or non-U.S. government

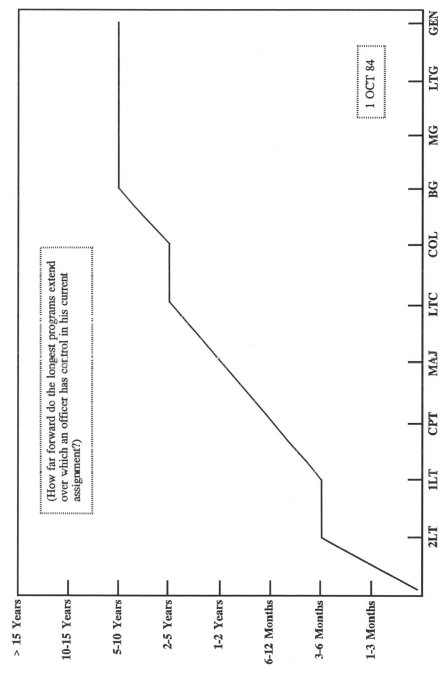

FIGURE 3-2

Median Program/Project Time Span (in years) by Rank

(How far forward do the longest programs extend over which an officer has control in his current assignment?)

1 OCT 84

> 15 Years

10-15 Years

5-10 Years

2-5 Years

1-2 Years

6-12 Months

3-6 Months

1-3 Months

2LT 1LT CPT MAJ LTC COL BG MG LTG GEN

representatives), whereas no three-star officers indicated such requirements. Finally, 87.5% of the four-star and 60.6% of the three-star officers reported that their work required a significant international focus. These descriptions support the premise of significant boundary-spanning requirements at the military executive leader level.

The content-coding categories for Lucas and Markessini's (1993) study of one- and two-star general officers were not identical to those of Harris and Lucas (1991), thus limiting direct comparison of general officers at the four ranks. However, one- and two-star officers reported fewer joint/unified command assignments than their strategic-level counterparts and no reporting channels outside the military.

Only 33% of the civilian executive leaders examined by Markessini et al. (1994) reported that an international focus was important in their work, a figure that is lower than that reported by their military counterparts. However, approximately 78% of these executive leaders stated that working across service boundaries was an important performance requirement.

As proposed by SST, studies of officers in the production and organizational domains have identified few or no external boundary-spanning activities by officers below the rank of general office or colonel. For example, Rigby and Harris (1987) reported that although MSC commanders (i.e., Stratum V leaders) were primarily responsible for exchanges between PMOs and external environment, the work of PMOs (i.e., Stratum IV leaders) was primarily internally focused. Furthermore, Steinberg and Leaman (1990b) found that the degree to which (a) developing contacts with organizations outside of the Army and (b) interacting with civilian managers was part of an officer's position requirements decreased substantially from the grade of colonel to lieutenant.

Network Development and Consensus Building

Most of the upper-level military and civilian executive leaders examined by Harris and Lucas (1991) and Markessini et al. (1994), respectively, highlighted the importance of social network development and consensus building as necessary parts of their work (percentages of executive leaders reporting this requirement ranged from 87.5% to 92.6%). Lucas and Markessini (1993) treated these variables separately in their study of one- and two-star officers and reported similarly high scores for network development (one-star officers, 85%; two-star officers, 95%). The percentages were somewhat smaller for the importance of consensus development (one-star officers, 65%; two-star officers, 80%).

Analyses of leadership requirements at Army ranks below general officer do not mention network development and consensus-building activities. Instead, the emphasis is, as expected, on directive leadership.

For example, Steinberg and Leaman (1990b) aggregated tasks on their executive leader requirements survey into the global duties of (a) train, teach, and develop leaders; (b) motivate personnel; (c) manage resources; and (d) provide direction. These kinds of leader requirements are consistent with those proposed for leaders in the production domain. Furthermore, they fit with the more directive and less collegial leadership orientation that is expected of more senior leaders.

Frame of Reference

According to Jacobs and Jaques (1987, 1990, 1991), a critical mechanism mediating executive leadership influence on organizational performance is the complexity of the cognitive maps executive leaders form of the short- and long-term and direct and indirect causal processes operating within and outside the organization. The military and civilian executive leaders examined by Harris and Lucas (1991), Lucas and Markessini (1993), and Markessini et al. (1994) all reported that such complex mental models are indeed required for executive leader performance, with requisite maps of greater complexity being reported at higher executive leader levels. For example, the general officers indicated a greater need to understand the external environment and how it affects organizational operations and requirements. Indeed, boundary-spanning activities require greater knowledge of multinational politics, international conditions, and differing cultures. Furthermore, understanding the dynamics of the other armed services within the context of joint and unified command was also reported as more critical at these levels. Executive leader strategic thinking and decision making envelops the entire Army within the broader defense, national, and international realms. Responses from these interviews indicate that military executive leader cognitive maps do include such knowledge.

SST places more emphasis on the external systemic orientation of top executive leaders than other executive leadership theories (cf. Katz & Kahn, 1978). In line with this argument, only 42.4% and 37.5% of the three- and four-star officers, respectively, indicated that an understanding of the internal Army system was important for their work. These percentages increased to more than 80% for the one- and two-star officers. The civilian executive leaders (78%) also attributed high importance to understanding "the interdependencies of the systems that comprise the Army" (Markessini et al., 1994, p. 14). The perspective of military executive leaders appears to shift from predominantly internal to predominantly external as they move from the organizational domain to the systems domain.

These findings are cited by Jacobs and Jaques (1990, 1991) and by the authors of each research report as evidence that executive leaders require more complex mental maps or frames of reference. However, these data reflect the content of these maps, not their structure. The complexity of executive leader frames of reference are grounded not only in their content but also in the intricacies of the linkages and associations among conceptual nodes represented in such cognitive systems. A cognitive map with a significant amount of knowledge content may be highly differentiated but display little or no integration. Yet, both SST and ICT argue that it is the integration of this knowledge into a meaningful pattern that is necessary for executive leader work. Unfortunately, the methods used and the data collected to date by various researchers do not provide sufficient grounds for making inferences about the explicit structure of requisite leader knowledge.

Evaluation

Most of the studies described explicitly addressed the variables in the form of testable predictions derived from SST. The development of testable predictions is most evident regarding executive leader planning. Most theories argued for three levels or domains of organizational leadership requirements (e.g., Katz & Kahn, 1978). SST incorporates seven strata within three levels. Differences among the levels are operationalized most directly in requisite planning and work time spans. Also, systems leaders were defined as being more externally focused than organizational leaders. The cross-section of data presented in the various military studies suggested only limited support for the seven discrete levels of organizational leadership defined by SST. As shown in Table 3-2, work time spans generally were comparable across brigadier, major, and lieutenant general officer levels, but somewhat higher for four-star officers. Also, Figure 3-2 indicates little or no difference across these levels, although greater differences were observed for production and organizational domain leaders. The data indicated that systems-level leaders operate from somewhat longer time spans (e.g., 6 to 9 years for three- and four-star generals and civilian executive leaders) than leaders at the organizational level (e.g., 2 to 6 years for one- and two-star generals and MSC and PMO leaders). Furthermore, systems leaders described interactions outside Army boundaries as a greater part of their work than organizational leaders. Consequently, knowledge of systems outside the Army was cited as more important by systems leaders than by organizational leaders.

These differences suggest significant qualitative shifts in performance requirements between organizational and systems domain leaders. Although there is some indication of finer gradations within these domains, the data as a whole do not consistently demonstrate the degree of differences in time span of work proposed by SST. Furthermore, the boundary between systems and organizational leadership is not precisely delineated, at least regarding work and planning time spans. Although the predictions of SST for Strata IV and V leaders appear to be supported, systems leaders demonstrate some compression in predicted time spans. Differences appear only when *work time span* is defined in terms of performance capability or envisioning horizon.

The different operationalizations of work time spans create another concern. Multiple definitions of work time spans prompts the question of which is the most pertinent or key executive leader performance requirement. This is important because critics of SST have argued that long operational time spans are dysfunctional, particularly within dynamic and fluid environments (Streufert & Swezey, 1986). Long-term planning can produce inflexible products that are not responsive to changing conditions. Flexible plans are likely to be those that reflect a relatively short (3 to 7 years) time span. The distinctions in work time spans made by Lucas and Markessini (1993) and particularly by Markessini et al. (1994) suggested that executive leader operational time spans are within this range. They also described executive leaders as capable of a longer time span. However, there is little evidence that executive leader thinking incorporating such longer time spans is necessary for effective executive leader performance.

In summary, the military studies suggested some initial support for increased information-processing demands at higher organizational levels. In support of Propositions 1–4, they indicated that upper-level leaders are required to (a) operate within relatively longer time spans, (b) be more involved in organizational policy making, (c) interact more frequently with external constituencies, (d) engage in more network development and consensus building, and (e) develop more complex cognitive maps than lower-level leaders. However, these observations and conclusions need to be tempered by several methodological concerns. First, the bulk of the research reported in Table 3-2 used structured interviews to gather data. Although such a strategy may at times be the only feasible way to study executive leadership, it is subject to a number of biases and validity issues that prevent definitive conclusions. This problem is compounded by the relatively small sample sizes in these studies (particularly at the top executive leader levels) that precluded the calculation of inferential statistics. Accordingly, such multivariate issues as (a) which definition of *time span* is most characteristic of executive leader work or contributes most to organizational effectiveness and (b) which executive leader performance requirement is most crucial for organizational performance could not be investigated. Therefore, the question remains, which role requirement is the most important means by which executive leaders add value to their organization? Or, are all specified executive leadership requirements of equal importance? These issues are critical for appropriate and comprehensive testing of both SST and ICT.

Resolving these questions requires not only a multivariate approach, but also the development of organizational effectiveness criteria. For example, Day and Lord (1988) recommended that a systematic theory of executive leadership describe "what top-level leaders do that impacts on performance" (p. 458). SST offers at least four mechanisms of executive leader impact: (a) long-term planning, (b) boundary management, network development and consensus building, and integrated cognitive map or frame of reference development. However, none of the studies described provided empirical support that any of these executive leadership functions actually add value to the organization. That is, none of these functions is tied to an organizational effectiveness criterion. As suggested in Figure 3-1, establishing this link is an important part of validating a model of executive leadership.

The approach reflected in the interview studies, particularly in the interview scripts and content-coding categories, was to describe the presumed determinants of more complex information processing, not the precise nature of executive leader information processing. The interview protocols could have been coded more specifically, for example, regarding how often executive leaders mentioned the need to handle greater quantities of information that is derived from a diverse set of sources, that often is incomplete, and that requires substantial reflection and interpretation. Such data would more directly assess hierarchical differences in organizational information-processing demands.

Some executive leader performance requirements inherently reflect more complex information-processing demands (e.g., long-range planning, building complex cognitive maps or frames of reference). However, executive leader requirements such as boundary management and network development and consensus building have been hypothesized by other models of executive leadership to reflect greater social complexity. (For examples, see the descriptions of behavioral complexity models in chapter 4.) These models propose a different (or at least an additional) mediating mechanism that suggests requisite executive leader capabilities other than cognitive complexity. Of course, it is likely that upper-level organizational performance requirements reflect both information-processing demands and social complexity These conceptual linkages need to be examined more precisely.

NONMILITARY STUDIES

Table 3-3 summarizes studies using nonmilitary samples that provide data on the propositions regarding executive leader performance requirements. Unlike the military studies described, few of the studies reported in this table proceeded from any a priori conceptual framework, much less the one provided by conceptual complexity theories of executive leadership. Therefore, these data can be interpreted as supporting multiple conceptual models (in fact, some of the studies cited provide data also relevant for behavioral complexity models; see chapter 5). Nonetheless, these studies provide some evidence for the specific questions addressed in this chapter and are examined from the perspective of conceptual complexity models.

As a group, the nonmilitary studies of executive leader performance requirements described in Table 3-3 used a greater variety of research methods than the military studies discussed in Tables 3-1 and 3-2. These include case studies and interviews, participant observation, descriptive surveys, work-oriented job analyses, and correlational survey studies. On the other hand, because most of the studies were not designed from a particular theoretical model, they did not address specific distinctions made by the conceptual complexity theories of executive leadership. For example, whereas SST postulates precise time spans for seven organizational levels, few if any of the following studies sought such information (see Goodman, 1967, as an exception). Instead executive leaders often were queried merely about their degree of long-term planning rather than its time span or time horizon. Such data reflect the general emphasis of SST but not its specific hypotheses. Similarly, of critical importance to both of the conceptual complexity theories is the premise that executive leaders must work with more complex information. However, few of the nonmilitary studies denoted systematically the nature of executive leader information requirements. Again, the data from these studies supported the theories' general emphasis but not their particulars.

Nonetheless, the variety of methodological approaches and the diversity of samples do provide the opportunity to investigate the degree to which findings from nonmilitary executive leaders present a picture of executive leader work requirements that is similar to that of military executive leaders.

Long-Term Planning

The results of the various studies described in Table 3-3 regarding leader planning suggest that

- Upper-level organizational leaders engage in more planning than lower-level leaders;
- Executive leader planning generally reflects a long-term perspective, although medium- and short-term perspectives are also prominent;
- Executive leader planning is associated with organization effectiveness.

TABLE 3-3

Summary of Empirical Studies Examining Executive Nonmilitary Leader Performance Requirements

Study	Participants	Study type	Findings
Baehr (1992)	1,358 managers at multiple organizational levels in companies from four industries (manufacturing, sales, professional, and technical)	Survey/ correlational	Executives in all industries but professional ones were more involved in long-range planning and objective setting than lower- or middle-level managers. Major functions of executive work were planning and employee development, followed by community relations.
Barr, Stimpert, & Huff (1992)	Top managers in two regional railroad companies over 25-year period. One company was successful; one declared bankruptcy shortly after study	Case study	Causal maps of top executives (derived from annual reports) of successful company were more responsive to environmental changes than those of unsuccessful company.
Calori, Johnson, & Sarnin (1994)	24 CEOs and 2 general managing directors from companies in four industries (brewing, car manufacturing, retail banking, and book publishing)	Interview	Complexity of CEO cognitive maps of industry was related to geographic and multinational scope of firm, but not to diversity of business portfolio.
Dollinger (1984)	82 owner/operators of retail and manufacturing companies (food and apparel industries)	Survey/ correlational	Intensity (proportion of executive's time) of executive boundary-spanning activities was significantly associated with two indices of organizational performance. Extensive boundary spanning (number of external contacts made) was not associated with any measures of performance.
Fahey & Narayanan (1989)	Top executive leaders in single corporation over 20-year period	Case study	Demonstrated nature of executive causal maps in context of environmental change. Executives' causal maps (derived from annual reports and public statements) evolved over time and were influenced by environmental changes. However, at different times, causal maps either failed to reflect critical environmental elements or included too many influences.

Fleishman & Friedman (1994)	Survey/correlational	117 managers at three levels in nine R&D companies	Upper-level leaders allocated substantially more time to strategic planning than middle-level or first-line managers. They also spent more time on personnel supervision, but comparable times on project management activities.
Goodman (1967)	Survey/correlational	169 managers across multiple organizational levels of single company	Measures of work time span displayed small to moderate correlations (.10 to .47) with hierarchical level.
Haas, Porat, & Vaughan (1969)	Survey/descriptive	355 managers at all organizational levels of large, metropolitan-area bank	Differences across three organizational levels in reported time spent planning were small. Also, top managers spent more time negotiating, coordinating, and supervising than planning.
Hambrick (1981b)	Survey/correlational	195 top, second-level, and third-level executives in colleges, hospitals, and insurance firms	Different measures of environmental scanning (i.e., output, throughput, administrative, regulatory, and total scanning) were correlated with hierarchical level in colleges and insurance firms, but not in hospitals. Amount of scanning was not consistently related to functional area.
Hemphill (1959)	Survey/descriptive	93 managers at three hierarchical levels in five companies	Comparison of managerial position descriptions across hierarchical levels indicated that as one moved from lower- to middle-level management, position responsibilities shifted away from direct personnel supervision to more planning and broad organizational control. At top executive levels, responsibilities shifted to concerns with reputation of company in environment and preservation of company assets.
Isenberg (1984)	Interview/observation	12 top senior company managers	Top executives devote significant proportion of time to strategy implementation rather than formulation. Thinking of senior managers is characterized as mix of intuition and disciplined analysis. They also work on multiple interrelated problems simultaneously, rather than one at a time.

(continued)

TABLE 3-3 continued

Study	Participants	Study type	Findings
Judge & Spitzfaden (1995)	CEO and senior R&D managers from eight biotechnology firms	Interview/survey/descriptive	Average time horizons across firms ranged from 5.0 to 8.5 years. Diversity of time horizons in strategic portfolio, but not average length of horizon, was associated with organizational financial performance. The four firms exhibiting high performance had more diversity than the four firms reporting relatively lower performance.
Kaplan (1986)	25 top executives and GMs	Interview	Author concluded from interviews that top executives are required to operate strategically (setting long-term direction, keeping eye on big picture), operate tactically (dealing constantly with problem solving), think multidimensionally, develop and use large social networks, and manage organizations of large scope.
Kotter (1982a, 1982b)	15 corporate GMs	Interview/observation	Two major aspects of GM job are agenda setting and network building. Time frames of typical GM agendas range from short-term (0–12 months) to long-term (5–20 years), although long-term agendas represent "vague notions" about financial, business, and organizational issues. GM networks can incorporate hundreds or thousands of individuals from within and outside the company. Networks are developed to update and implement managerial agendas.
Kraut, Pedigo, McKenna, & Dunnette (1989)	1,412 managers at multiple organizational levels of large U.S. business enterprise (658 first-line supervisors, 553 middle-level managers, 201 executives)	Survey/descriptive	Executives attached greater importance to monitoring business environment as part of job than middle-level managers or supervisors. Supervisors rated supervising individuals as more important than middle-level managers or executives. Planning was rated as similarly important by middle-level managers and executives.

Study	Sample	Method	Findings
Levinson & Rosenthal (1984)	6 corporate CEOs	Interview	Performance requirements of corporate CEOs involve long-range envisioning as well as action orientation. They also must interact with multiple external constituencies.
Luthans, Rosenkrantz, & Hennessey (1985)	52 managers from multiple organizational levels in state department of revenue, campus police department, and manufacturing company	Observation	Top-level managers displayed more planning and co-ordinating behaviors than lower- or middle-level managers. Also, degree to which manager interacted with constituencies outside organization was significantly associated with individual promotion rate.
Mahoney, Jerdee, & Carroll (1965)	452 managers at multiple organizational levels in 13 companies (manufacturing, finance, insurance, agricultural products, public utilities, and wholesale trade)	Survey/descriptive	Planning activities increased in frequency from lower to upper levels of management. Proportion of top manager activities was highest for planning, followed by supervising.
C. C. Miller & Cardinal (1994)	Not applicable	Meta-analysis of 26 studies of strategic planning and firm performance	Strategic planning was positively associated with two measures of organizational performance. Relationship between planning and profitability was stronger under conditions of environmental turbulence.
Tornow & Pinto (1976)	489 managers at three hierarchical levels in six diverse companies within parent corporation	Survey/descriptive	Upper-level executives exhibited substantially higher scores on long-range thinking and planning than middle-level or beginning managers. They also indicated less responsibility for direct supervision than beginning managers and less responsibility for coordination or organizational units than middle-level managers.

Note. CEOs = chief executive officers; R&D = research and development; GMs = general managers.

These results are generally consistent across different methodologies. Kotter (1982a, 1982b) interviewed 15 corporate general managers whose responsibilities ranged from business unit management (i.e., Stratum V) to multidivisional or corporate chief executive officer (CEO; i.e., Stratum VII). The latter were described as having more demanding long-term responsibilities than the former. Furthermore, Kotter abstracted a typical strategic agenda constructed by the general managers within their first year in their position. This agenda is shown in Figure 3-3. As suggested by SST, time spans for these leaders can range up to 20 years. However, in line with ICT, these plans are very vague and suggest a significant degree of flexibility. Furthermore, a significant part of executive leader planning is reflected in short- and medium-term time spans, in which plans are more detailed and presumably more fixed.

Kaplan (1986) and Levinson and Rosenthal (1984) offered similar abstractions from executive leader interviews. However, Isenberg (1984) noted from his case studies that "even very senior managers devote most of their attention to the tactics of implementation rather than the formulation of strategy" (p. 84). This observation is congruent with those of Mintzberg (1973, 1975) and portrays the executive leader as action oriented rather than reflective. It also is consistent with Peters and Waterman's (1982) observations of excellent companies. This reflection-versus-action debate has resonated through a significant portion of the executive leadership literature and was the basis for some of the behavioral complexity models described in chapter 4.

These case studies and interviews present an impressionistic portrayal of executive leader planning requirements. Several other studies provided more systematic and quantitative data. Luthans, Rosencrantz, and Hennessey (1985) observed 52 managers at multiple levels of three organizations. They reported that upper-level managers exhibited more planning and coordinating behaviors than middle- or lower-level managers did; however, the level of top management and the time span of planning were not specified. Mahoney, Jerdee, and Carroll (1965) surveyed 452 managers ranging from first-line supervisor to company president and found that the percentage of managers who were characterized as "planners" was highest among top-level managers. However, Haas, Porat, and Vaughan (1969) reported smaller differences in planning across organizational levels, whereas Kraut, Pedigo, McKenna, and Dunnette (1989) found that the number of leaders who said that planning and resource allocation were of "utmost" or "considerable" importance actually declined from middle to executive leader levels (however, both groups cited these activities as important in their jobs). It should be noted that SST would argue that planning is more the province of executive leaders whereas resource allocation is more likely to be the

FIGURE 3-3

Typical Executive Leader Planning Agenda

Key Issues

Time Frame	Financial	Business (Products/Market)	Organizational (People)
Long-run (5-20 years)	Usually contains only a vague notion of revenues or ROI desired in ten or twenty years.	Usually only a vague notion of what kind of business (products and markets) the GM wants to develop.	Usually vague. Sometimes includes notion about the "type" of company the GM wants and the caliber of management that will be needed.
Medium-run (1-5 years)	Typically includes a fairly specific set of goals for sales and income and ROI for the next five years.	Typically includes some goals and plans for growing the business, such as: • see that three new products are introduced before 1981 • explore acquisition possibilities in the area of . . .	Usually includes a short list of items, such as: • by 1982, will need a major reorganization • before 1981, I need a replacement for Corey
Short-run (1-12 months)	Typically includes a very detailed list of financial objectives for the quarter and the year in all financial areas: sales, expenses, income, ROI, etc.	Usually includes a set of general objectives and plans aimed at such things as: • the market share for various products • the inventory levels of various lines	Typically includes a list of items, such as: • find a replacement for Smith soon • get Jones to commit himself to a more aggressive set of five-year objectives

ROI = return on investment; GM = general manager. From *The General Managers* (p. 62), by J. P. Kotter, 1982, New York: Free Press. Copyright 1982 by The Free Press, a division of Simon & Schuster. Adapted with permission.

concern of managers below the executive level (i.e., executive leaders are concerned with resource acquisition). Two different managerial activities appear to be confounded in this finding.

These studies provided mixed results regarding the proposition that senior leaders engage in more planning than their lower-level counterparts. Moreover, none of the studies clearly specified long-term planning versus short- or medium-term planning in their queries. Three studies that used survey methodologies to complete work-content analyses of managerial jobs at different organizational levels examined planning from a specifically stated long-range perspective. For example, Tornow and Pinto (1976) developed the Management Position Description Questionnaire, which included as one of its factors *product, marketing, and financial strategy planning*. This factor was defined as indicating "long-range thinking and planning" (p. 414). Tornow and Pinto reported that upper-level executive leaders exhibited standardized scores on this factor that were more than one standard deviation above the mean, whereas standardized scores for middle- and lower-level leaders were more than one half standard deviation below the mean. No other job factor in this study exhibited this magnitude of difference between executive leaders and both groups of lower-level managers.

Hemphill (1959) administered the Executive Position Description Questionnaire to 93 managers across three executive levels from five organizations. One of the dimensions of this survey was *long-range planning*, which was defined as follows:

> systematic long-range thinking and planning. The concerns of the incumbent are broad and are oriented toward the future of the company. These concerns extend to industrial relations, development of management, long-range objectives of the organization, solvency of the company, pilot projects, the business activities the company should engage in, existing or proposed legislation that might affect the company, and the evaluation of new ideas. (p. 59)

Note that Hemphill's description captures not only the temporal aspects of planning but also the scope and expanse of topics covered in executive leader planning. In this way, it incorporates many of the elements of systems-level leadership identified by SST. Hemphill does not report mean differences on this dimension among executive leaders. However, he noted from his data that upper-level executive leaders scored higher on this dimension than lower-level executive leaders.

Baehr (1992) developed and administered a job-oriented job analysis instrument similar to that used by Tornow and Pinto (1976) to 1358 managers at different organizational levels in manufacturing, sales, professional, and technical organizations. One of the job functions included in the survey was setting organizational objectives, which involved formulating the overall organizational mission and establishing short- and long-term objectives. Baehr found that this function was unique to executives in all types of industries except professional organizations.

Taken together, these studies demonstrate support for Proposition 1 —that planning, particularly long-term planning, is more likely to be a part of leadership requirements at the top of the organization than at any other level. Furthermore, the general pattern reported from these nonmilitary studies is congruent with the pattern reported from the military studies described earlier. These studies, however, did not examine the more fine-grained distinctions in planning time spans proposed by SST. A study by Goodman (1967), using a nonmilitary sample, was designed specifically to test Jaques's (1956, 1964) distinctions. Goodman surveyed 169 managers from six strata in a single company and gathered four measures of work time spans:

- *Individual time extension*: The length of future time, which is conceptualized by the individual.
- *Time value orientation*: The value a person gives to living for the future relative to the present.
- *Time span of multiple tasks*: How far in time does the job permit the incumbent to plan ahead?
- *Level of abstraction*: What percentage of time on the job is spent on planning activities? (pp. 160–162)

Goodman reported that a manager's time value orientation was not correlated with managerial level. The range of correlations for the remaining measures was .20–.47. Although these correlations were statistically significant, Goodman did not consider them to be of sufficient magnitude to support the level of distinction proposed by Jaques. These data suggest broad differences in time span of work across organizational levels but not necessarily the number of differences suggested by SST.

An extension of the time span notion was provided by Judge and Spitzfaden (1995), who examined both the average time span of executive work as well as the diversity or dispersion of time horizon spans across different strategic projects. That is, some projects had relatively short time spans, whereas others had longer horizons. Although SST discusses only the length of executive leader time horizons, Judge and Spitzfaden argued that "firms operating in complex and dynamic environments may need a *diverse* set of time horizons at the strategic level to cope with environmental uncertainty" (p. 180). They examined these measures in eight companies by interviewing company CEOs and senior research and development (R&D) managers. They also obtained measures of organization performance (stock returns and cash flow on investments). They found that time spans across the eight companies ranged from 5.0 to 8.5 years and that the companies varied in the dispersion of their time spans. When Judge and Spitzfaden divided the companies into two groups according to time span dispersion (high versus low), the performances of the four companies with greater dispersion in their strategic portfolio were higher than the performances of the four companies with less dispersion. No association was observed between average length of time span and company performance.

Judge and Spitzfaden (1995) offered some evidence for the importance of diversity, rather than length, in the time spans of an executive leader's strategic projects. However, the size of their sample allowed only descriptive analysis. The question then remains, Does planning, particularly long-term planning, produce better organizational performance? Previous studies and empirical reviews of this relationship have produced mixed and inconsistent results (Boyd, 1991; Mintzberg, 1990; Pearce, Robbins, & Robinson, 1987; Starbuck, 1985; Thune & House, 1970). A 1994 meta-analysis of 26 planning and performance studies by C. C. Miller and Cardinal (1994) sought to address these inconsistencies by statistically controlling for such moderating influences as firm size, capital intensity, and degree of environmental turbulence. They also corrected for five methodological variables, including whether planning was measured only as formalized planning or incorporated multiple forms of strategic planning. Performance indices were categorized into growth outcomes (sales, earnings, and deposit growth) and profitability outcomes (returns on assets, equity, sales, and total invested capital). C. C. Miller and Cardinal found that after controlling for several methodological contingencies, planning was significantly associated with both growth and profitability (expected correlations, controlling for relevant contingencies, were .50 and .43, respectively). Even more interesting was their finding that the correlation between planning and profitability was significantly moderated by environmental turbulence—this relationship was stronger in conditions of high turbulence. This finding is important because turbulent external environments mean higher and more complex information-processing demands. C. C. Miller and Cardinal's data support the proposition by conceptual complexity theories that, in the face of such demands, the application of conceptual mapping in the form of planning appears to increase organizational effectiveness.

C. C. Miller and Cardinal's (1994) meta-analytic findings suggest support for the idea that executive leader planning activities appear to add value to the organization. Although C. C. Miller and Cardinal did not clearly specify the temporal focus of organizational planning, these activities likely reflected a medium- or long-term perspective. It also is likely that top executive leaders were the instrumental planners in the sampled organizations. Although these are reasonable assumptions, their disconfirmation would diminish the support demonstrated for Proposition 5.

Boundary-Spanning Activities

The nonmilitary studies generally confirmed the proposed boundary management performance requirements of executive leaders. For example, Kraut et al. (1989) asked managers at multiple organizational levels to rate the importance of several tasks for the performance of their job requirements. They observed that tasks related to monitoring the business environment and being aware of sales, business, economic, and social trends demonstrated a significant shift toward higher importance at the executive leader levels. In fact, they reported that "for managers below the executive ranks, these tasks rate the lowest in importance" (p. 289). Studies using interview and case study methods also confirmed the predicted stronger emphasis on the external environment by organizational executive leaders (e.g., Kotter, 1982a, 1982b; Levinson & Rosenthal, 1984). However, mixed evidence is provided by Hambrick (1981b), who examined environmental scanning activities across multiple organization levels in college, hospital, and insurance executive leaders. He reported that different measures of scanning were significantly correlated with hierarchical level in the college and insurance samples, but not the hospital sample.

Studies by Dollinger (1984) and Luthans et al. (1985) associated boundary-spanning activities with indices of personal and organizational effectiveness. Luthans et al. defined managerial success in terms of individual promotion rate and found that increased interactions with outside constituencies was associated with more rapid promotion rates. Although this finding is suggestive, it raises questions of reverse association or causality—that is, rapid promotion may have put these managers in positions requiring greater boundary management. Also, Luthans (1988) contrasted successful managers (i.e., defined by high promotion rate) with effective managers (i.e., defined by unit performance and subordinate motivation). Boundary management was not as readily associated with effectiveness as it was with personal success. Finally, the level of management examined by Luthans et al. was not exclusively top management; thus, the nature of boundary-spanning activities may have differed significantly for different groups or levels of managers.

Dollinger (1984) conducted an analysis of boundary management and organizational effectiveness that resolved several of these issues. His sample consisted of 82 company owners/operators. Therefore, they represented the top level of management in their respective organizations.

Performance was assessed through retained earnings, sales, and economic benefits accruing to the owner. Boundary spanning was measured by the intensiveness (proportion of total work time) and extensiveness (number of contacts made) of interactions with external constituencies. To focus only on owner boundary-spanning activities and their effect on performance, Dollinger measured and controlled for total boundary-spanning activities performed by other organizational members. He found that intensive boundary spanning was associated with sales and accrued gross, even after controlling for several contextual variables (company age, number of employees, type of business, and total organizational boundary spanning). Extensive boundary spanning, however, was not associated with organizational performance. This study demonstrated that the percentage of time top organizational executive leaders (not the organization as a whole) interacted with external constituencies was linked to greater organizational effectiveness.

These studies support Propositions 2 and 6 that (a) there is a decided shift toward a more external systemic perspective as a manager moves from lower and middle organizational levels to the executive ranks, and (b) the effective accomplishment of boundary-spanning performance requirements is associated with greater organizational effectiveness. However, top military leaders in the study by Harris and Lucas (1991) displayed a greater external than internal perspective—that is, they were oriented to a greater extent outside than inside the organization. This orientation is predicted by SST, which suggests that top executive leaders are almost exclusively externally focused. Research with executive leaders in nonmilitary settings, however, has suggested a more evenly balanced perspective. For example, on the basis of intensive interviews of 15 general managers, Kotter (1982a, 1982b) described a large proportion of their work as internally focused. Also, the work-oriented job analysis Baehr (1992) completed on 1358 managers yielded the following summary of executive leader performance functions:

> In general, top level executives perform at least three different types of functions: *the major emphasis* is on the steering and operational functions such as Objective Setting and Decision Making, followed by functions that deal specifically with the development of the work force, such as Developing Employee Potential and Developing Teamwork and, *at a somewhat lower level of importance*, functions that involve the community outside of the work place, such as Community/Organization Relations and Dealing with Outside Contacts. (p. 47, italics added)

Other studies using survey and observation methods have also confirmed the significant internal systemic focus of top managers (e.g., Haas et al., 1969; Mahoney et al., 1965; Morse & Wagner, 1978, Tornow & Pinto, 1976). Simply put, such executive leaders, although certainly more externally oriented than their subordinates, focus a significant amount of time, energy, and attention on internal organizational and operational management. This pattern differs from that suggested by Harris and Lucas (1991) and Lucas and Markessini (1993) from their interviews with top Army executive leaders (i.e., four-star general officers).

Three factors may explain these differences between military and nonmilitary executive leaders. First, different methods were used for each set of studies; the military samples were examined using structured interviews, whereas the nonmilitary studies used a variety of methods, including time-on-task analyses, participant observations, and job and task inventories. The latter approaches are more systematic than the interview approach. Surveys and inventories, for example, reflect many different aspects of executive leader work, whereas the interview method in the military studies used an open-ended format that did not necessarily cue the full range of work functions. This may have resulted in overrepresentation of externally oriented functions in the interview data because such functions may be less routine and therefore more interesting to both the interviewee and the interviewer, who are then more likely to discuss them.

A second difference between the military and nonmilitary studies is their specification of executive leaders. The military studies used a more precise delineation of executive ranks, essentially separating the top levels (four- and three-star officers) from the next-lower levels (one- and two-star officers). In most of the nonmilitary studies, executive leaders typically were combined into a single group identified as upper-level managers or leaders. For example, several of the participants in Kotter's (1982a, 1982b) study would not likely be categorized as Strata VI or VII leaders. Likewise, although Baehr's (1992) sample of upper-level leaders included those with titles such as chief operating officer and executive vice president, others were identified as vice presidents, general managers, and divisional heads, none of which would likely reflect systems-level work. This distinction is important because the external systemic focus was attributed most strongly for Stratum VII leaders, slightly less so for Stratum VI leaders, and much less so for Strata IV and V leaders. Combining these different leaders into a single group, as was typical in the nonmilitary studies, would have resulted in a distorted, more internally focused perspective being ascribed to them.

Another factor explaining the observed difference between these two sets of samples simply may be that military leaders are required to be more externally focused than their nonmilitary counterparts. This, of course, violates a premise of SST, that it is generalizable across many different types of executive leadership (Jacobs & Jaques, 1987, 1991). Nonetheless, there are significant differences between military and nonmilitary organizations that could have implications for executive leader boundary management functions. For example, each military service participates in several joint arrangements (e.g., Joint Chiefs of Staff; joint/unified commands) that are peculiar to this organization type. Although nonmilitary organizations may engage in joint ventures, such arrangements are not as formalized as in the military. In addition, each military service reports to other civilian authorities (e.g., the president, secretary of defense, Congress). Furthermore, formal relationships may be established with other government and international organizations (e.g., United Nations, NATO). Nonmilitary organizations may have similar kinds of arrangements, but they rarely are as pervasive and formal as in military organizations. Thus, the difference in external systemic focus observed between military and nonmilitary top executive leaders may reflect a very real difference in required performance functions.

Network Development and Consensus Building

Fewer nonmilitary studies have specifically documented network development and consensus building as key executive leader performance requirements. Some surveys and observational studies have cited somewhat related functions such as communications (Baehr, 1992), information handling (Morse & Wagner, 1978), and interacting with others (Luthans et al., 1985), whereas others did not mention such functions as important to managerial work. However, in the latter case, exclusion of these functions from work inventories may have reflected an a priori research bias. That is, several studies (e.g., Haas et al., 1969; Kraut et al., 1989; Mahoney et al., 1965; Tornow & Pinto, 1976) chose not to include network development and consensus building in their surveys of executive leader functions administered to top managers.

Alternatively, two interview-based studies do provide a strong picture of network development and consensus building as executive leader performance requirements (Kaplan, 1986; Kotter, 1982a, 1982b). On the basis of interviews of 15 general managers, Kotter observed that they established elaborate networks that "often included hundreds or thousands of individuals" (1982a, p. 67). These networks included constituencies such as financial sources; customers, suppliers; government and media contacts; and organizational peers, superiors, and subordinates. Kaplan's interviews with 25 executive leaders confirmed similar networks. As suggested by SST (Jacobs & Jaques, 1987, 1990, 1991), both researchers concluded from their interviews that the purposes of these networks were to facilitate (a) information acquisition and (b) the implementation of the executive leader's agenda. However, unlike with planning and boundary management, no studies have established an empirical link between network development or consensus building (as executive leader performance requirements) and organizational success. Thus, the empirical question of whether the effective accomplishment of these particular requirements adds value to the organization remains.

Frame of Reference

Relatively few nonmilitary studies have examined empirically the question of whether executive leaders add value to the organization by developing a complex cognitive map of the organization and its environment. Most of the survey studies have focused on measuring behaviors or requisite work activities, not cognitive activities. Kaplan's (1986) interviews with 25 executive leaders did refer to a need to develop a broad organizational perspective. His study also included an analysis of examples of effective and ineffective general managers (GMs) provided by the interviewees. He concluded the following from his observations:

> The multifunctional scope together with the sheer bulk of the general manager's domain pose a stiff challenge. By definition, the job requires the incumbent to grasp, though not necessarily master, the full range of functions (marketing, sales, manufacturing, R&D, finance) and at the same time to transcend a functional perspective to achieve a holistic view of the business. . . . The thumbnail sketches provide a data point here: six of the GMs classified as effective were seen as understanding the business as a whole, as taking a broad view; three of the ineffective ones were downgraded for not doing so. (p. 192)

This illustrates the importance of an executive frame of reference. However, this observation was grounded in an unsystematic interview-based methodology that did not directly measure the content and structure of executive leader maps. Three other studies provided data related to the notion of requisite variety that is at the heart of SST and its propositions regarding executive leaders' frames of reference. To review, the complexity of an executive leader's operating environment requires a causal map of corresponding complexity. Following ICT, these maps need to be flexibly integrated such that they change structurally in response to changes in environmental causal dimensions. Using annual reports and public statements, Fahey and Narayanan (1989) derived the causal maps of top executive leaders within a single organization over a 20-year period. This company was one of the two dominant companies in terms of market share in its industry. Leader causal maps were defined as "interconnected assertions of causality decision makers chose to reveal to the world around them" (p. 362). Fahey and Narayanan examined the association between changes in top executive leader maps and environmental dynamics. They found that the executive leader maps were fairly complex, although they still did not fully mirror the complexity of the company's environment:

> The structure of the raw and reconstructed revealed mental maps indicates that decision-makers were cognizant of the complexity of the environment. The content of the maps changed considerably from period to period [of environmental evolution]. Yet, little interconnectedness between elements of the macroenvironment and the industry was present in the maps. This may reflect a difficulty on the part of decision-makers to construct a complex and integrated view of the environment. (p. 374)

Barr, Stimpert, and Huff (1992) compared the evolution of top managers' mental maps over time in two demographically similar railroad companies. One company thrived over the 25-year span that was studied, whereas the other ceased to exist shortly thereafter. As in Fahey and Narayanan's (1989) study managerial causal maps were established from statements in annual report data over the 25-year period. Barr et al. found that causal maps from the successful company changed fairly quickly as a function of environmental change, whereas the maps from the failed company did not. Top executives from the successful company revised their cause-and-effect associations to reflect new environmental influences, whereas top executives from the failed company attempted to explain these new influences through their existing and outmoded understandings. This suggests that although both sets of executives attended to the environmental changes, only those in the successful company changed their mental causal maps accordingly.

Both of these studies represent essentially case study approaches that allow only descriptive analyses. Calori, Johnson, and Sarnin (1994) examined executive leaders in 26 companies across four different industries (brewing, car manufacturing, retail banking, and book publishing). These industries were selected to produce variance in environmental complexity. Following Streufert and Swezey (1986) and Huff and Fletcher (1990), Calori et al. used cognitive mapping techniques to derive, from in-depth, open-ended interviews with executive leaders, the comprehensiveness (i.e., differentiation) and interconnectedness (i.e., integration) of their causal maps. They also assessed a company's geographic scope and the diversity of its business portfolio as measures of environmental complexity. They found that executive leader map complexity was not associated with business diversity. However, they reported that "in firms with an international geographic scope, the CEOs' cognitive maps of the structure of the industry were more comprehensive than those of CEOs in firms with a national scope" (p. 450). They also found that "in firms belonging to a multinational foreign group the CEOs' cognitive maps of the dynamics of the industry are more complex [in terms of both comprehensiveness and interconnectiveness] than the ones of the CEOs in independent firms" (p. 452).

These studies support the notion of requisite variety that argues that executive leaders are required to develop casual maps that reflect the complexity of the organization-environment dynamics within which they operate. Unfortunately, they do not provide data on differences in the requisite quality of leader mental maps across organizational levels. Also, the evidence that such maps facilitate organizational effectiveness is limited. Fahey and Narayanan (1989) did not link variance in map quality and environmental fit with organizational performance. However, Barr et al. (1992) provided descriptive evidence of such a link. The value of these studies lies not so much in their findings as in their description of a method for studying executive leader causal maps and their possible influences on organizational processes and outcomes (see also Huff, 1990). They serve as a guide for future research.

Evaluation

Together, the nonmilitary studies supported and extended some of the tenuous findings from the military studies. Relatively longer planning time spans, boundary management, and, to a lesser extent, network development and frame of reference formation have been documented as parts of executive leader performance requirements. Furthermore, unlike in the military studies, the accomplishment of two of these requirements, planning and boundary management, were empirically linked to organizational effectiveness. Barr et al.'s (1992) case study of two companies also provided descriptive data supporting a link between the complexity of executive leaders' causal maps and organizational adaptation. The nonmilitary studies used a greater variety of research methods. Several of them also had large enough samples to permit inferential analyses instead of merely descriptive ones.

However, like their military counterparts, these studies also had several characteristics limiting their conclusions regarding executive leader performance requirements. First, a significant proportion of the studies relied on qualitative methods such as interviews, case studies, and participant observation. Although these approaches have an important place in the study of executive leadership, they must be supplemented with more quantitative, nomothetic, and controlled approaches. The nonmilitary studies are an improvement over the military studies in this regard, but they still are lacking. Second, there are still no nonmilitary multivariate studies that examine the relative contributions of different executive leader performance requirements. Some of the studies that developed importance or time allocation ratings for several executive leader functions have provided descriptive evidence for differential contributions, suggesting long-term planning as the most important executive leader performance requirement (e.g., Kraut et al., 1989; Mahoney et al., 1965). However, a more systematic approach to this question is needed. Third, few of the studies examined the link between these performance requirements and information-processing demands. This was less serious in the nonmilitary studies than in the military ones because the former were not derived from a theoretical model that suggested such a link. The lack of a conceptual framework for most of these studies leaves open the question, though, of why certain performance functions examined in nonmilitary studies are important for executive leader and organizational success.

Therefore, although the nonmilitary studies provided more support than the military studies for most of the propositions derived from conceptual complexity theories regarding executive leader performance requirements, their conclusions still need to be considered with caution.

Requisite Executive Leader Characteristics

Although executive leaders are likely to possess stronger conceptual, interpersonal, and technical skills than lower-level leaders, their analytical capacities are predicted to be the most significant determinant of their leadership effectiveness. This section examines the empirical evidence for the proposed link between high-level conceptual skills and performance. These skills include the ability to abstract a meaningful pattern, through processes of differentiation and integration, from a complex array of information. They also include the ability to develop novel and innovative solutions to complex organizational problems. Jacobs and Jaques (1987; see also Lewis & Jacobs, 1992) referred to such skills as *conceptual capacity*. Streufert and Swezey (1986) described them as reflecting flexible integrative complexity. Mumford, Zaccaro, Harding, Fleishman, and Reiter-Palmon (1993) and Mumford and Connelly (1991) emphasized creative or divergent thinking skills as well as complex cognitive and metacognitive problem-solving skills as executive leader competencies (see also Markessini, 1991; Laskey, Leddo, & Bresnick, 1990). Each of these cognitive capacities is considered to be conceptually distinct from raw mental ability or intelligence, although the correlation between the two is expected to be significant.

The conceptual models described in chapter 2 suggest the following propositions regarding requisite leader characteristics:

9. Executive leaders will possess stronger conceptual skills than lower-level leaders.

10. Executive leaders will have more complex and integrated cognitive maps of the organization and its environment than lower-level leaders.

11. The level of conceptual capacities possessed by executive leaders and the degree of flexible integrative complexity of their cognitive maps will determine performance at the executive level.

12. Executive leaders will display a stronger proclivity for thinking, reflection, and conceptual model building than lower-level leaders.

As in the previous section, this empirical review of research on leader characteristics is divided into studies using military and nonmilitary samples, respectively.

MILITARY STUDIES: CONCEPTUAL CAPACITIES

Table 3-4 summarizes military studies that focused on the identification of executive leader cognitive skills and their association with executive leader performance. A large proportion of these studies used an interview method in which top executive leaders were asked to describe the key competencies they believed were associated with effective senior leadership (Harris & Lucas, 1991; Lucas & Markessini, 1993; Markessini, 1991; Markessini et al., 1994). These studies indicated that, for the most part, top executive leaders cited complex thinking and analytical skills and the awareness of their own cognitive problem-solving processes (i.e., metacognition) as important for their work. They also included as executive leader competencies such skills as consensus building, risk taking, and dealing with uncertainty. Markessini et al. (1994) reported that civilian executive leaders attributed less importance to some conceptual abilities, risk taking, and complex mental map formation than their military counterparts. Instead, they attached somewhat more importance to consensus-building skills.

Although informative, such studies do not sufficiently address the propositions guiding this review. Interview-based methodologies have a traditional place in the identification of job content and work performance requirements, but such self-reports of requisite skills are subject to significant positivity biases. Such approaches also are based on the questionable assumption that interviewees are aware of the relationship between necessary competencies and executive leader and organizational performance. Furthermore, in the military studies, the researchers used a content-coding analysis to derive skill recommendations from interview protocols by counting the number of officers or civilian ex-

TABLE 3-4

Summary of Empirical Studies Examining Requisite Military Executive Leader Characteristics

Study	Participants	Study type	Findings
Barber (1990)	270 Army War College students (lieutenant colonels and colonels)	Survey/ descriptive	Senior military officers exhibited higher tendencies toward sensing, thinking, and judging functions of MBTI. Proportion of those scoring high on NT functions was higher than in general military population.
Harris & Lucas (1991)	8 four-star general officers, 33 three-star general officers	Structured interviews	Three- and four-star general officers identified the following as requisite knowledge and skills for their positions: multinational knowledge, knowledge of joint/ unified relationships in military, consensus-building skills, envisioning/anticipating skills, skills related to establishing organizational culture and values, and abstracting and synthesizing skills.
Horvath et al. (1994)	81 platoon, company, and battalion leaders	Structured interviews	Battalion commanders displayed greater amount of tacit knowledge than platoon leaders and company commanders. Structures of tacit knowledge representations were more complex.
Knowlton & McGee (1994)	1,650 Industrial College of the Armed Forces students (lieutenant colonels and colonels)	Survey/ descriptive	Proportion of students who scored high on NT functions of MBTI was larger than proportion reported for general military population but smaller than proportion reported for business executives. Largest proportion of students scored high on MBTI ST functions.
Lucas & Markessini (1993)	48 one-star general officers, 26 two-star general officers	Structured interviews	One- and two-star officers identified the following as requisite knowledge and skills for their positions: knowledge of joint/unified relationships in military; understanding of total Army system; problem management skills; planning and envisioning skills; and communication, networking, and consensus-building skills. They also mentioned temperament factors, such as ability to deal with uncertainty and willingness to take risks.

Study	Method	Sample	Findings
Markessini (1991)	Structured interviews	8 four-star general officers, 33 three-star general officers	Recoded data from Harris and Lucas (1991) for mention of metacognitive skills and awareness as requisite senior executive skills. Found that general officers frequently cited such skills as well as cognitive skills related to mapping ability, problem management, long-term planning, and innovative/creative thinking.
Markessini, Lucas, Chandler, & Jacobs (1994)	Structured interviews	27 executive service and senior executive service members	Civilian executives reported requisite position skills, competencies, and temperament factors similar to those reported by military counterparts. These include multinational knowledge, understanding joint/unified relationships across military service branches, understanding total Army system, consensus-building skills, envisioning skills, ability to find creative or innovative problem solutions, cognitive abilities related to complex analysis and synthesis, and temperament factors related to risk taking.
Suedfeld, Corteen, & McCormick (19860	Archival	6 Civil War generals	Developed integrative complexity scores for each of six Civil War generals. Found that for three battles won by Robert E. Lee against greater numbers of opposing forces, his score was substantially higher than that of opponent. For two of the three battles he lost, his score was lower than that of opposing commander.
Zaccaro, Marks, O'Connor-Boes, & Costanza (1995)	Survey/correlational	101 military officers, including first and second lieutenants, majors, and lieutenant and full colonels	Colonels displayed stronger complex problem-solving skills than majors or lieutenants.
Zaccaro, Mumford, et al. (1995)	Survey/correlational	1,807 military officers from second lieutenant to full colonel	Scores on measures of divergent-thinking ability and complex problem-solving skills were correlated with hierarchical level. Higher ranking officers displayed stronger cognitive skills than junior officers.

Note. MBTI = Myers-Briggs Type Indicator; N = Intuition; T = Thinking; S = Sensing.

ecutive leaders who mentioned the importance of particular skills. The descriptions provided by the researchers do not clearly indicate that responses referring to executive leader performance requirements (e.g., the need for long-term planning; consensus building) were coded differently from responses referring to requisite executive leader skills (e.g., envisioning skills, consensus-building skills, and interpersonal skills). Thus, the data from these studies provide insufficient evidence for the efficacy of requisite executive leader skills.

Interview-based or qualitative research methods do not adequately address the question of whether conceptual skills increase both in prevalence and importance at the executive leader level. Nor do they provide information on the relative importance of these skills for enhancing executive leader performance. More quantitative studies are necessary to address these questions. Unfortunately, studies examining complex conceptual skills of officers at top military ranks and the association of these skills with executive leader performance and organizational effectiveness are not available. However, data compiled by Zaccaro, Mumford, Marks, et al. (1995) indicated a significant positive correlation between the display of divergent thinking abilities and complex problem-solving skills, respectively, and military rank in officers ranging from second lieutenant to colonel. In another study, Zaccaro, Marks, O'Connor-Boes, and Costanza (1995) reported that ratings of conceptual skill reflected in the generation of solutions to ill-defined and complex problems were significantly higher for colonels than for lower-level officers. Both studies provide support for the proposition that higher-level officers exhibit stronger conceptual abilities than lower-level officers. Extrapolation of these data implies that systems-level executive leaders would demonstrate even stronger capacities.

An interesting archival study was completed by Suedfeld, Corteen, and McCormick (1986) to investigate the integrative complexity of General Robert E. Lee and five of his opposing Civil War commanders (Burnside, Grant, Hooker, McClelland, and Meade). Suedfeld et al. adapted the Sentence Completion Test of flexible integrative complexity (Schroder, Driver, & Streufert, 1967; Schroder & Streufert, 1962) for use in textual analysis and applied this approach to official dispatches, orders, and published letters to derive an integrative complexity score for each military officer. They then associated differences in integrative complexity between Lee and his opposing commanders with battle outcomes. For three battles that Lee won against heavy odds (i.e., against approximately 50% to 75% more opposing forces: Antietam, Fredericksburg, and Chancellorsville), his complexity score was substantially larger than that of his opposing commander. For two of the three battles that he lost (Wilderness and Spotsylvania), Lee's score was lower than that of the opposing commander.

Although the nature of this study precluded parametric or inferential analyses, it does offer some unusual evidence for an association between integrative complexity and military performance. However, these results need to be interpreted cautiously because of several questionable assumptions adopted by Suedfeld et al. (McGee, personal communication, March 1996). First, Antietam was treated by Suedfeld et al. as a victory for the South although many historians consider this battle to have been a stalemate. Second, the six battles selected by Suedfeld et al. for the study occurred sequentially in time: Lee won earlier battles, whereas Union generals won later ones. Because battle order reflects the effects of prolonged combat and diminishing resources on Lee, the relationship between the differential in complexity scores between Lee and his opponents and battle outcome is confounded by battle order. These and other points (e.g., Lee's physical illness at Gettysburg) mean that these results, however interesting, need to be viewed with great caution.

Horvath et al. (1994) provided some evidence of differences between lower- and middle-level military leaders in the complexity of their work-related knowledge structures. They examined the content and structure of tacit knowledge in platoon leaders and company and battalion commanders. Although these are not executive leaders, a trend toward more complexity in knowledge representations across these three levels of organizational leadership would suggest even greater complexity at executive leader levels. *Tacit knowledge* refers to "action-oriented knowledge, acquired without direct help from others, that allows individuals to achieve goals they personally value" (Horvath et al., 1994, p. 1). For military leaders, such knowledge is important for the attainment of unit and organizational goals. Horvath et al. interviewed 81 Army officers to elicit stories of leadership experiences that resulted in tacit knowledge gain. These stories were coded to identify the content of knowledge gained and then sorted into conceptual categories. These sorts were used to form dissimilarity matrices for the purpose of cluster analyses to assess knowledge structure.

Horvath et al. (1994) reported that battalion commanders were more likely than lower-level leaders to have a systems perspective of leadership that included information on managing organizational change, protecting the organization, and dealing with poor performers. Likewise, as suggested by SST, these leaders were more likely to understand how to balance short-term production requirements and long-term personnel development needs. These are primarily differences in knowledge content. The proposed complexity of leader knowledge resides not only in the amount of knowledge incorporated into cognitive models but also the structure and organization of this knowledge. The results of the cluster analyses indicated that the knowledge structures of battalion commanders were more differentiated than lower-level leaders. Horvath et al. concluded "battalion commanders' tacit knowledge for military leadership is more complexly structured, at least for the items in question, than that of company commanders and platoon leaders" (p. 22).

This study is a valuable one because it represents one of the few attempts in the literature to assess both content and structural differences in military leader knowledge. Several points need to be considered, however. First, the knowledge that was assessed represents primarily information about how to "get things done" within the organizational setting. It is a performance map, not a causal map of the system dynamics between the organization and its environment, although the latter may incorporate elements of the former. Second, the measure of structure used in this study assessed differentiation, not integration. Streufert and Swezey (1986) argued that flexible integration, not just differentiation, is the requisite organizational leadership skill. Third, as noted, the leaders examined were not at the executive leader rank. A plausible extrapolation of the data suggests that the tacit knowledge structures of executive leaders would display even greater complexity. However, this extrapolation needs empirical confirmation. Also, it is necessary to associate the complexity of these and other leader knowledge structures with leader performance.

MILITARY STUDIES: PROCLIVITY

Jacobs and Jaques (1990, 1991) proposed that a proclivity toward mental model building would be conducive to the development of potential executive leaders. They suggested that such an orientation is measured by the intuition (N; versus sensing [S]) and thinking (T; versus feeling [F]) dimensions of the Myers-Briggs Type Indicator (MBTI). They also proposed that if this proclivity is linked to senior leader development, then there should be a disproportionate percentage of NTs at higher organizational levels. Furthermore, the proportion of STs, reflecting a more immediate, action-oriented style, should be higher at lower levels of the organization.

Although a number of studies have examined such stylistic orientations in business executive leaders (see M. H. McCaulley, 1990), few, if any, have been completed on top military executive leaders (i.e., general officers). Two studies, however, administered the MBTI to colonels and lieutenant colonels (i.e., organizational-domain leaders) at the Army War College (Barber, 1990) and at the Industrial College of the Armed Forces (Knowlton & McGee, 1994). Barber found that 25% of the officers in his sample were categorized as NTs, whereas 62.3% were categorized as STs. Knowlton and McGee found that 32% of their sample were NTs and 55% were STs. The average percentages derived from the general military population (i.e., a mix of officers and enlisted soldiers) were 15% and 43%, respectively (Briggs-Myers & McCaulley, 1985). Thus, although the largest percentage of colonels were STs, the percentage of NTs in this group was higher in both samples than in the general military population. Note that, according to SST, the leaders in this sample would be classified as organizational-domain leaders. Therefore, the percentage of STs would be expected to be higher than at the systems level, but the percentage of NTs would be expected to be higher than at the production level. The trend in these samples compared to the more general military population suggests that the relative proportion of NTs among systems-level military executive leaders may be even higher; however, this requires a more definitive empirical test.

MILITARY STUDIES AND EXECUTIVE CHARACTERISTICS: EVALUATION

There has been little or no effort to test the propositions regarding requisite leader characteristics in military executive leaders with research methods that allow some degree of control and plausible causal inference. Appropriate testing of these propositions requires the effective measurement of proposed qualities such as conceptual capacity in general officers (i.e., systems-level leaders). Statistical examination of (a) the differences between these qualities and those of lower-level officers and (b) the congruence between these measures and indices of individual and organizational effectiveness is also needed. In addition, for sufficient validation of an executive leadership theory, researchers need to demonstrate a significant association between executive leader capacities and the accomplishment of executive leader performance requirements such as long-term planning, boundary and network development (see Figure 2-1). For example, perhaps the most important premise of SST is that high-level conceptual capacities help executive leaders develop the highly complex mental maps required for effective action at the top of the organization. To examine the validity of this premise, researchers need to develop measures of such mental maps and associate them with both executive leader capacities and organizational performance.

Implementation of this research strategy, or any other that provides valid evidence for the efficacy of military executive leader conceptual skills, is crucial for another simple reason. The specification of executive leader assessment and development programs for the Army needs to be grounded in a firm and empirically supported understanding of the requisite qualities that must be assessed or developed. The components of such programs (e.g., classroom instruction, work assignments, self-development) should obviously be constructed to target empirically validated requisite skills and other executive leader qualities. Validation of these executive leader qualities means a demonstration that they are indeed important for executive leader performance. Qualitative, interview-based data provide a subjective and indirect portrayal of this relationship. Such data need to be supplemented with more objective approaches.

NONMILITARY STUDIES: CONCEPTUAL CAPACITIES

Studies of executive leadership and high-level conceptual capacities are relatively rare. Bass's (1990) comprehensive *Handbook of Leadership: Theory, Research, and Managerial Applications* lists very few references to such variables as complex problem-solving skills, creativity, integrative cognitive complexity, or conceptual capacity (although frequent mention is made of general intelligence). The relatively few studies that have examined executive leader differences in creativity, integrative complexity, and complex mental map formation are summarized in Table 3-5. No nonmilitary studies have explicitly examined the SST construct of conceptual capacity and its influence on executive leader performance.[1]

Observations of executive leader skills derived from interviews with top business executive leaders (Isenberg, 1984; Kotter, 1982a, 1982b; Levinson & Rosenthal, 1984) have yielded conclusions similar to those from interviews with military executive leaders. For example, Isenberg observed from detailed interviews with 12 very senior managers, that, unlike lower-level managers, they are characterized by integrative thinking processes. Furthermore, their problem management reflects the formation of broad and integrated problem maps:

> Managers at all levels work at understanding and solving the problems that arise in their jobs. The thinking of top managers deals not with isolated and discrete items but with portfolios of problems, issues, and opportunities. These portfolios have three characteristics: (1) many problems exist simultaneously, (2) these

---

[1]Jacobs and Jaques (1991) mentioned Stamp (1988) as "the best currently available evidence for the importance of conceptual capacity in executive development" (p. 442). This longitudinal study examined the association between predicted and attained organizational levels over a 4- to 13-year span. The prediction of future organizational level was based on an assessment of conceptual capacity at Time 1 using the CPA. Correlations of this index with attained level ranged from .79 to .92. Although these numbers are impressive, they do not reflect a relationship between conceptual capacity and executive leader performance. Instead, they should be interpreted as criterion-related validity coefficients that reflect the psychometric quality of the CPA as a predictor of ascension to executive ranks.

problems compete for some part of an executive leader's immediate concern, and (3) the issues are interrelated.

The cognitive tasks in problem management are to find and define good problems, to "map" these into a network, and to manage their dynamically shifting priorities.

These processes suggest greater use of conceptual and integrative mapping skills at executive organizational levels. Nonetheless, as noted earlier, interview-based studies have provided insufficient data for the identification and assessment of executive leader conceptual skills.

Baehr (1992) presented evidence from descriptive surveys for hierarchical differences in creative ability. He measured "potential for intuitive thinking and creative and innovative behavior" (p. 100; Thurstone & Mellinger, 1957/1985) in 1358 managers at three levels in four different types of industries. The results of these surveys indicated significant differences in creative potential across managerial levels, although the differences were smaller in professional and sales hierarchies. Rusmore (1984) also reported a steady increase in cognitive creativity across groups of first-line supervisors, middle-level managers, and top-level executive leaders. However, a survey study by Chusmir and Koberg (1986) examined creativity in male and female managers at multiple organizational levels and found that hierarchical level was positively associated with creativity for women but not for men. These studies demonstrate some evidence for differences in creative thinking skills across executive levels, but they also identify some moderating influences such as the nature of the industry and gender.

Several studies have examined the relationship between executive leader creativity and organizational performance. Norburn (1986) surveyed and interviewed executive leaders from industries experiencing growth, industries experiencing turbulence, and industries experiencing decline. He found that executive leaders from growth industries were more likely to list intelligence, followed closely by creativity, as success traits. Executive leaders from declining industries and turbulent industries cited concern of others and personal integrity, respectively, as important executive leader characteristics. Rusmore and Baker (1987) reported correlations between creativity and managerial performance of $-.12$, $.19$, $.27$, and $.33$ across four organizational levels. Creative thinking capacities were found to be increasingly related to performance at higher organizational levels.

Simonton (1988) rated U.S. presidential biographical references on personality adjectives that were factor analyzed into 14 factors. One of the factors was labeled *Intellectual Brilliance* and included, among others, such adjectives as inventive, intelligent, sophisticated, complicated, insightful, and wise. This factor presumably reflected characteristics similar to those proposed by conceptual complexity theories as important for

TABLE 3-5

Summary of Empirical Studies Examining Requisite Nonmilitary Executive Leader Characteristics

Study	Participants	Study type	Findings
Baehr (1992)	1,358 managers at three levels in companies from four industries (manufacturing, sales, professional, and technical)	Survey/correlational	Executives displayed higher creative potential scores than middle- or lower-level managers. Differences were smaller in sales and professional industries.
Church & Alie (1986)	127 middle- and upper-level managers at two manufacturing plants	Survey	Upper-level management contained significantly more MBTI NS (individuals who "exhibit the conceptual ability to perceive environments as wholes and problems or events as parts of wholes," p. 33) than middle-level management.
Chusmir & Koberg (1986)	96 male and 69 female managers from 11 companies (representing service, manufacturing, retail, nonprofit, and wholesale industries)	Survey/correlational	Upper-level female managers scored higher than lower-level managers, on a measure of creative thinking processes. Upper- and lower-level male managers did not differ significantly in creativity.
Dollinger (1984)	82 owner/operators of retail and manufacturing companies (food and apparel industries)	Survey/correlational	Integrative complexity was significantly correlated with intensity of boundary management (i.e., percentage of executive's time devoted to boundary management) but not with extensive boundary management (number of external contacts made). Integrative complexity was not correlated with three indices of organizational performance. Relationship between intensive boundary management and company performance was significantly stronger under conditions of high executive complexity.

Isenberg (1984)	12 top senior company managers	Interview/ observation	Requisite executive qualities include intuitive thinking abilities, problem management skills, and ability to tolerate ambiguity and deal with anxiety.
Kotter (1982a, 1982b)	15 corporate general managers	Interview/ observation	Common personal characteristics of general managers included analytical abilities, achievement and power needs, intelligence, intuition, ability to relate easily to broad set of business specialists, and personable style.
M. H. McCaulley (1990)	MBTI database at Center for the Application of Psychological Type	Survey/ descriptive	Scores for successful executives, relatively unsuccessful executives, middle- and lower-level managers, and from general population were abstracted from tables provided. Group of successful executives contained substantially more individuals who scored high on the MBTI N and T dimensions than any other groups.
Norburn (1986)	354 executives from industries experiencing growth, turbulence, and decline	Survey/ interview	Executives from growth industries were more likely to indicate intelligence and creativity as requisite top leader characteristics than executives from turbulent or declining industries.
Reynierse (1991)	319 senior outplaced executives	Survey	Equal proportion of executives were classified as high on MBTI—ST and NT dimensions. Individuals scored as high in S, J, and I were overrepresented in this sample of executives who had lost their jobs; individuals scored as high in N, F, and P were underrepresented.
Roach (1986)	70 first-line supervisors, 161 middle-level managers, and 67 executives from multiple organizations	Survey/ descriptive	Proportion of individuals scoring on the MBTI N and T dimensions rose from 19% of supervisors to 32% of middle-level managers to 52% of executives; pattern was reversed for individuals who scored high in S and T dimensions.

(continued)

TABLE 3-5 continued			
Study	**Participants**	**Study type**	**Findings**
Rusmore (1984)	208 executives at three organizational levels	Survey/correlational	Executives displayed higher mental ability and cognitive creativity than middle-level managers and first-line supervisors.
Rusmore & Baker (1987)	208 executives at three organizational levels	Survey/correlational	General intelligence was more strongly correlated with performance at lower organizational levels; cognitive creativity was more strongly correlated with performance as one ascended the organizational hierarchy.
Simonton (1986)	39 U.S. presidents	Archival	Ratings of presidential intellectual brilliance were significantly associated with historian ratings of presidential performance. Ratings of other personal qualities were not associated with presidential performance.
Streufert (1983)	2 executives	Case study	Successful executive displayed more integrative complexity in time–event matrix derived from management simulation game than unsuccessful executive.

Note. MBTI = Myers-Briggs Type Indicator; N = Intuition; T = Thinking; S = Sensing; J = Judgment; I = Introversion; P = Perception.

executive leadership. Simonton regressed both objective (e.g., legislative outcomes) and subjective (e.g. historians' ratings) indices of presidential performance on presidential characteristics. Although Intellectual Brilliance had mixed associations with some of the objective criteria, it was the only personal quality associated with rated presidential performance.

Three studies summarized in Table 3-5 provided evidence for an association between executive leader integrative complexity and performance. One, a case study reported by Streufert (1983), compared the time–event decision-making matrices derived from an international business simulation game completed by two executive leaders (see chapter 2 and Streufert & Swezey, 1986, for additional details on this measure). Peer ratings had identified one leader as more effective than the other. Streufert found that the more effective executive leader displayed a much more integrated and multidimensional decision-making style than the less effective executive leader. Suedfeld and Rank (1976) used textual analysis to derive integrative complexity scores for revolutionary leaders who had attained public office and were categorized as either successful or unsuccessful. Successful leaders were found to have scored higher in integrative complexity at that time of their careers than unsuccessful leaders.

Both of these studies made their arguments for leader integrative complexity and executive leader effectiveness through idiographic analyses. Dollinger (1984) adopted a more nomothetic approach. He used the Sentence Completion Test (Schroder et al., 1967) to measure the flexible integrative complexity of 82 company owners. He correlated these scores with (a) the number of external constituencies (extensive boundary management), (b) the amount of time spent with external constituencies (intensive boundary management), and (c) indices of organizational performance (sales, retained earnings, and accrued owner benefits). Integrative complexity was significantly associated with intensive boundary management but not with extensive boundary management or any of the performance measures. However, integrative complexity moderated the influence of intensive boundary management on sales and accrued benefits. Dollinger interpreted this interaction as showing that boundary management time was more strongly related to performance under conditions of high information-processing capabilities. This set of results makes two important contributions. First, it is one of the few empirical studies to associate executive leader conceptual capacity with an executive leader performance requirement (i.e., boundary management). Second, it suggests that intensive boundary management alone is not sufficient for the prediction of executive leader performance. What is also necessary is the capacity to develop an integrated map of information gained from these activities. Of course, this second point is a speculative interpretation of the data. Its confirmation would require measures of executive leader mental models.

NONMILITARY STUDIES: PROCLIVITY

Although several studies have examined the distribution of decision-making styles among executive leaders and across organizational levels (Church & Alie, 1986; Reynierse, 1991; Roach, 1986), the most comprehensive examination was provided by M. H. McCaulley (1990). She presented data from the *MBTI Atlas of Type Tables* (MacDaid, McCaulley, & Kainz), incorporated the results of many studies that administered the MBTI to various samples. For the purposes of this chapter, certain samples were selected for comparison: These were (a) several samples of successful executive leaders, (b) several samples of lower-level leaders, and (c) two samples of relatively less effective executive leaders. The percentage of STs (sensing–thinking), SFs (sensing–feeling), NFs (intuition–feeling), and NTs (intuition–feeling) computed for each sample is shown in Table 3-6, along with percentages for the general population. The pattern of results suggests support for Jaques and Jacobs's (1991) proposal that a greater proportion of NTs would be evident in the upper levels of the organization, whereas a greater proportion of STs would be evident at lower levels.

These data suggest that a proclivity for mental model building is associated with upper-level management. However, although acknowledging that some types are more highly represented among senior managers, M. H. McCaulley noted that "there is evidence that all 16 MBTI types assume leadership positions" (p. 414). She and others (e.g., Knowlton & McGee, 1994) have argued that effective top-level leadership involves the development and display of both preferred and secondary orientations.

NONMILITARY STUDIES ON EXECUTIVE CHARACTERISTICS: EVALUATION

As a group, the nonmilitary studies of requisite executive leader characteristics are less idiographic and more rigorous than the military studies. Particular studies have provided empirical examinations of (a) differences in conceptual capacities across organizational levels and (b) the association between executive leader conceptual skills and organizational performance. A substantial number of studies have examined the proclivity hypothesis offered by Jacobs and Jaques (1990, 1991).

However, this body of work is deficient in several ways. First, research on the quality of executive leader maps and organizational performance is still limited. Although the studies by Barr et al. (1992), Calori et al. (1994), and Fahey and Narayanan (1989) described earlier in this chapter provided a framework for such research, they did not

TABLE 3-6

Comparison of MBTI Dimensions Across Samples of Executives and Nonexecutives

Sample	MBTI dimensions			
	ST	SF	NF	NT
Successful Executives				
Federal Senior Executives	46.0%	5.1%	8.5%	40.4%
Top Executives (from CCL)	51.4	5.8	6.5	47.0
Highly-Rated Executives (from CCL)	38.6	7.3	12.2	41.8
Top Education Leaders	56.5	9.6	30.0	28.3
Founders of Highly Successful Companies	35.9	4.4	8.8	41.1
Executives (Roach 1986)	30.0	3.0	15.0	52.0
Japanese CEOs	36.4	16.9	9.3	37.2
Japanese Executives	37.4	19.7	12.5	30.4
"Unsuccessful" Executives/Middle Managers and Supervisors				
Low-Rated Executives (from CCL)	56.5	5.6	9.9	28.3
CEOs from Limited Growth Companies	70.7	15.3	3.3	10.7
Middle Managers (Roach 1986)	46.0	11.0	12.0	32.0
Supervisors (Roach 1986)	53.0	17.0	17.0	19.0
Japanese Middle Managers (Overall)	46.7	17.2	9.5	20.8
Japanese Middle Managers (Chemical Industry)	38.8	27.1	6.4	34.5
Japanese Supervisors	29.7	52.5	9.2	8.8
General Population	38.0	38.0	12.0	12.0

Note. CCL = Center for Creative Leadership; MBTI = Myers-Briggs Type Indicator; ST = Sensing/Thinking; SF = Sensing/Feeling; NF = Intuitive/Feeling; NT = Intuitive/Thinking.

adequately address the causal role of complex maps in executive leadership. Second, although some studies have addressed Propositions 9, 11, and 12, more nomothetic research that provides the basis for more adequate generalization across types of executive leaders is still needed. Although there are considerably fewer idiographic nonmilitary studies than military studies, the number is still too large to provide a sufficient understanding of executive leadership. Third, examination of Propositions 9 to 12 requires multivariate studies that control for the possible spurious influence of other variables. For example, until such studies are completed, it is not possible to respond to the criticism that an observed relationship between executive leader conceptual capacity and performance can be attributed to such unmeasured causes as intelligence, high-level social skills, and certain dispositional orientations (e.g., tolerance for ambiguity; openness). Each of these factors may correlate to a greater or lesser degree with conceptual capacity. Fourth, the non-military studies tend not to proceed from a theoretical framework. Although the results from these studies can be interpreted through the conceptual complexity theories described in chapter 2, the questions asked were not derived specifically from these theories. Thus, the conceptual basis for why certain relationships were observed between executive leader qualities and organizational processes and outcomes remains ambiguous.

Measurement of Conceptual Complexity

The Career Path Appreciation technique (CPA) and the Strategic Leader Development Inventory (SLDI) were developed within the context of SST to assess conceptual capacity. Several measures of integrative complexity have been developed for ICT (e.g., the Sentence Completion Test, the Impression Formation Test, time-event matrices). Streufert and Swezey (1986) provided a substantial review of their psychometric qualities. (The reader is referred to that source as well as to Streufert and Streufert, 1978, for information.) However, because the SLDI was developed only recently, there is little evidence regarding its psychometric qualities. Stewart, Kilcullen, and Hopkins (1993) presented data demonstrating high internal consistency for the individual scales of the SLDI. They also found that the correlations among the dimensions on the SLDI are lower than their internal consistency coefficients, suggesting a degree of discriminant validity among the factors. However, because no other psychometric data are currently available regarding the SLDI, it will not be discussed further. Only evidence for the psychometric qualities of the CPA is reviewed. The following proposition is evaluated:

> 13. The Career Path Appreciation technique will exhibit acceptable levels of reliability, construct validity, and criterion-related validity.

CAREER PATH APPRECIATION TECHNIQUE

The CPA involves a 2-hr interview that provides data that are used to judge or rate an interviewee's current and predicted levels of conceptual capacity. Jacobs and Jaques (1990) stated that assessment of CPA data requires substantial expertise in SST and Level IV conceptual capability as defined by this theory. For this reason, the issue of interrater reliability is an important one. Lewis (1993, 1995) administered the CPA to two classes of colonels at the U.S. Army War College. He reported the same interrater reliability coefficient of .81 for each sample. Lewis (1993) also examined the internal consistency of the phrase selection task of the CPA. This portion of the CPA requires interviewees to examine nine sets of six cards that contain phrases describing approaches to work. Each of the six cards reflects a different level of work capacity. Assessees select and discuss phrases reflecting how they most and least like to work (see chapter 2 for a more extended description of the CPA and its components). Lewis reported a Cronbach's coefficient alpha for the "most" responses across the nine sets of .78. Also, the multiple correlation of the phrase selection and symbol sort tasks of the CPA with a rater's overall judgment of conceptual capacity was .76. Lewis (1993, 1995) did not, however, report the correlations among the three components of the CPA.

The construct and predictive validity of the CPA was investigated in three studies (Lewis, 1995; McIntyre, Jordan, Mergen, Hamill, & Jacobs, 1993; Stamp, 1988). Lewis (1995) interviewed and surveyed 44 students attending either the Army War College or the Industrial College of the Armed Forces. He examined the associations between conceptual capacity scores derived from the CPA and (a) Kegan's breadth of perspective concept; (b) instructor ratings of a student's strategic thinking skill, general officer potential, and peer popularity; and (c) scores from two measures of personality style, the MBTI and the Kirton Adaptation-Innovation Inventory (KAI). Breadth of perspective reflects "the capacity of the leader to take a broad view of his or her work environment, relatively unencumbered by narrow self interest or the prevailing mind set of others in the organization" (Lewis, 1995, p. 5). Conceptual capacity was expected to be significantly associated with this ability as well as with instructor ratings of strategic thinking and general officer potential. It was not expected to be associated with ratings of peer popularity or to measures of personality style. Lewis found that CPA scores were indeed significantly correlated with breadth of perspective, strategic thinking skill, and general officer potential, although the correlations were generally modest for convergent validity coefficients (rs ranged from .23 to .57). CPA scores were not correlated with peer popularity or with the extraversion-introversion and feeling-thinking dimensions of the MBTI. However, correlations with the KAI ($r = .63$) and the intuition-sensing scale of the MBTI ($r = .58$) were high for the purposes of discriminant validity. Thus, these data provided mixed evidence for the construct validity of the CPA.

McIntyre et al. (1993) completed three studies with undergraduate students to examine the construct validity of the CPA. In the first investigation, they examined the convergent validity among the CPA and the KAI, scores on two learning and performance tasks that required logical problem solving and non-linear thinking, and assessee's age. In the second study, they examined the CPA's convergence with career decision-making skills, complexity of career choices, age, creativity, and a different measure of cognitive complexity. In the third study, they examined the association between the CPA and several personality orientations as measured by the MBTI and the NEO Personality Inventory. The CPA was expected to be correlated with lower neuroticism, more openness to experience, and the intuition and perception subscales of the MBTI. In all three studies, McIntyre et al. also examined the degree of discriminant validity between the CPA and various measures of intelligence (GRE and SAT scores; Wonderlic scores).

Results across the three studies suggested that different parts of the CPA may reflect two distinct constructs—one reflecting a willingness or proclivity "to tolerate ambiguity and deal with complex environments" (McIntyre et al., 1993, p. 12) and the other reflecting an individual's level of conceptual capacity. Proclivity is reflected in performance on the phrase selection task, whereas capability is reflected in the symbol sort task. However, some of the personality measures were linked to both proclivity and capability. Also, some of the capability measures (e.g., scores on the performance tasks, measures of achievement and intelligence) displayed modest or insignificant correlations with the capability components of the CPA. Therefore, although there may be two distinct constructs within the CPA, the results of this study did not clearly distinguish between them.

McIntyre et al. (1993) reported generally high correlations between scores on the CPA and creativity. They also found that individuals who displayed high CPA scores "tend to be self-confident, able to handle ambiguity, capable of working on different projects simultaneously, and insightful" (p. 27). In general, the modest correlations of CPA scores with various measures of intelligence and achievement were sufficient to indicate discriminant validity.

The results described suggest that the CPA is conceptually multicomponential, reflecting more than one construct. However, these studies did not provide sufficient clarity regarding the validity of each of its component constructs. This lack of conceptual clarity does not prohibit the use of the CPA for assessment purposes if it can be demonstrated to be associated with executive leader performance or attainment of executive leader rank. The use of the CPA as a research tool to determine critical executive leader competencies and personality orientations is more problematic, however, because aggregate CPA scores seem to indicate multiple competencies and orientations.

Stamp (1988) provided evidence for the predictive validity of the CPA. She administered different versions of the CPA to 182 managers in four different organizations and derived predictions of their current levels of conceptual capacity. She also used Jaques's (1986) maturation curves (see Figure 2-1) along with each manager's age and current capability to predict the probable level of organizational work the manager would attain. Her criterion was the actual level attained by each manager 4 to 13 years later. The correlations between predicted and actual attained work levels found in various samples ranged from .70 to .92. These predictive validity coefficients are higher than those found in several studies (e.g., Anstay, 1977; Bray, Campbell, & Grant, 1974; Dunnette, 1972; Herriot, 1987; Hunter & Hunter, 1984) that used different procedures to predict work potential (range of correlations across these studies reported by Stamp = 14 to .78; mean r = .34).

SUMMARY

The data from the studies described indicate that the CPA has demonstrated reasonable levels of interrater reliability and internal consistency. To date, there has been no examination of test–retest reliabilities. Given that the conceptual qualities assessed by the CPA are proposed to be highly stable, studies of such reliabilities would be useful. Research on the CPA also has provided evidence for its predictive validity. The validity coefficients from Stamp (1988) are quite impressive. They suggest that the CPA can provide useful information for assessment and selection purposes.

The data on construct validity are more problematic. Stamp (1988) demonstrated that whatever the CPA measures, it predicts eventual attained organizational level quite well. Because the prediction of attained level was based on theoretically driven cognitive capability curves, the high correlations reported in Stamp's study suggest some degree of validity for the CPA as a measure of conceptual capacity. However, more direct studies of construct validity have not provided sufficient evidence for the clarity of the constructs being assessed. Indeed, the predictions made in one study (Lewis, 1995) are contradicted by the predictions made in another (McIntyre et al., 1993). Lewis proposed that the CPA should be unrelated to measures from either the MBTI or the KAI. McIntyre et al. proposed that the CPA is related to the KAI as well as to specific dimensions of the MBTI. The latter study decomposed the CPA into different (but related) constructs, which may account for these different predictions. Nonetheless, the data from these studies are not precise regarding the particular individual characteristics being measured by the CPA.

As noted earlier, this is not a problem per se for assessment uses of the CPA. However, to construct appropriate executive leader training and development programs, it is necessary to have more precise information about what individual qualities to target. Such information can be derived from a demonstrated linkage between particular skills or competencies and the successful accomplishment of necessary executive leader performance requirements. Because the CPA appears to assess multiple individual qualities, any association between it alone and such performance requirements will not provide sufficient evidence for particular key executive leader characteristics. This evidence can be ascertained from carefully controlled studies that combine the CPA with other measures of its individual components. Such studies would allow a more precise identification of particular qualities being assessed by separate parts of the CPA and, more important, the statistical control of some characteristics to ascertain the direct effects of others.

The CPA is a difficult and time-consuming measure to administer. This led McIntyre et al. (1993) to state that

> It appears unlikely that the CPA will ever see extensive
> operational use for selection purposes in military settings. The
> cost of administration is high in the first place. And the tool is
> potentially vulnerable to compromise, in the second place. (p. 28)

This is unfortunate. However, any assessment of high-level complex cognitive capabilities will probably require an assessment procedure that is more likely equally cumbersome and time consuming. Such capabilities cannot be assessed adequately through short and simple multiple-choice inventories. Constructed response tasks, which require assessees to construct or develop (rather than choose) a response to a stimulus configuration, likely will be the more appropriate assessment strategy (Ackerman & Smith, 1988; Bennett, 1993a, 1993b; Bennett et al., 1990; Sebrechts, Bennett, & Rock, 1991). The validation of such tools are problematic and may require unconventional research strategies (Bennett, 1993a, 1993b; Bennett et al., 1990; Braun, 1988). However, if conceptual capacities are significantly associated with executive leader performance requirements, then their measurement, no matter how difficult, is an important priority.

Leader Development

A complete review and evaluation of all leadership development efforts is beyond the scope of this book. Instead, the focus is primarily on interventions designed to foster the development of cognitive skills such as creative thinking, decision making, and strategic problem solving. These include what Jaques, Clement, Rigby, and Jacobs (1986) termed *psychological equipment*—the knowledge, skills, values, and temperament necessary for managerial work.

SST suggests that such skills become relatively more important as leaders ascend the organizational hierarchy. Unlike conceptual potential, these skills theoretically can be improved through targeted training. Furthermore, when executive leaders are placed in situations in which the limits of their current frames of reference are challenged, such skills can facilitate the formation of different and novel ways of construing experience. Thus, they may be highly instrumental in promoting an individual's growth in conceptual capacity within predetermined paths. This suggests the following proposition:

14. Leader training and development interventions designed to enhance decision-making and strategic problem-solving skills, creative thinking capacities, and the ability to develop more complex causal maps will demonstrate acceptable validity.

COGNITIVE SKILL DEVELOPMENT

Three studies sponsored by the ARI described the development and evaluation of programs designed specifically to enhance complex thinking skills. Stewart and Angle (1992) examined the effectiveness of a training course developed to facilitate creative problem solving. In this study, 109 college students were asked to complete material and verbal problem-solving tasks that required creative thinking. Students completed these tasks both before and after completing the course. Students also were divided into experimental and comparison groups (i.e., students from a different course). The following results were found: (a) Students in the experimental condition displayed significantly greater improvement on the material task from pretest to posttest than the controls, and (b) training increased participants' tolerance for ambiguity and their appreciation for unstructured problem solving. Stewart (1994) described an adaptation of this course for use at the Army War College. Although he did not provide a formal evaluation of the program's effectiveness, he did report the following:

> It was our's and the students' subjective assessment that this form
> of instruction was more beneficial in improving the target
> [knowledge, skills, and abilities; KSAs] than would have been any
> of the other instructional approaches used at the AWC [Army
> War College] for achieving the same ends. Also, it improved KSAs
> other forms of instructions just couldn't. (p. 25)

Although this observation represents second-hand reaction data, when added to the experimental data, it does suggest some promise for the usefulness of this course in training creative problem solving.

Zsambok (1993a, 1993b) developed a training program to help senior military officers institute effective strategic decision making in their teams. On the basis of previous theoretical work and observations of strategic decision-making teams, Zsambok specified 10 key behaviors associated with effective team performance. The first four (defining roles and functions, engaging team members, compensating actions, and avoiding micromanagement) fostered a greater sense of team identity. Four additional behaviors fostered the team's conceptual level or the intelligence of its problem solving and decision making actions. These were envisioning goals and plans, focusing on time horizon and range of factors, detecting gaps and ambiguities, and achieving situation assessment by diverging and converging. The final two behaviors, adjusting team performance action and time management, referred to team regulatory mechanisms. These behaviors were integrated into the Advanced Team Decision Making (ATDM) model. Zsambok designed a training program to foster knowledge of the ATDM model. This program contained instructional material on the model, a strategic decision-making exercise, and materials designed to facilitate team self-appraisal and feedback during the exercise.

Zsambok (1993a) administered an early version of this program at the Air Force Institute of Technology. Although her description of this study was limited, she reported that "trained observers found that the treatment team improved by 73% in its use of key decision-making behaviors, while the control team . . . improved by just 28%" (p. 2). The experimental team exhibited a lower productivity baseline than the control group but surpassed the control group by the final two (of four) performance sessions. Zsambok (1993a, 1993b) also administered the program at the Industrial College of the Armed Forces. Thirty-eight teams completed a survey designed to assess the model. The results indicated that the ATDM model was perceived as reflecting behaviors associated with high team performance and that learning and practicing ATDM resulted in (a) greater understanding of effective team behaviors and (b) improvements in reported team performance quality. Although the data from the Industrial College of the Armed Forces reflect reaction criteria, they suggest that the ATDM model may be a useful vehicle for enhancing complex thinking and problem-solving skills in senior leadership teams.

Streufert, Nogomi, Swezey, Pogash, and Piasecki (1988) designed a training program to facilitate the development of flexible, integrative thinking in managers. This program involves the use of quasi-experimental simulation techniques in which a trainer has control over the flow and presentation of information to trainees as well as control over other task characteristics, events, and demands. Within this controlled context, trainees make decisions in response to complex problem scenarios. The simulation is designed to assess the structure (e.g., differentiation, integration) of an individual's decision making. The training program also provides instructions to participants regarding how to think in integrated and complex ways.

Streufert et al. (1988) described an experiment in which one group of managers received the training simulation exercise with its instructional unit on the structure of flexible and integrative information processing. They also received information on what functions they should accomplish to be successful in the kinds of problems represented in the exercise. Thus, they received both content-specific and information-structuring instructions. A second group received only the content-specific training, and a third group received no training at all. All groups participated in one simulation before training and in a different simulation after training. Streufert et al. reported that after training both the content and structuring and content-alone groups showed gains in performance. The control group exhibited no performance gains. The group of managers who received content and information structuring recorded greater gains in performance. These results suggest some success, then, in developing complex cognitive skills through a combination of simulation techniques and instructional materials. The ARI has sponsored the development of similar training programs for use in the military (Swezey, Streufert, Criswell, Unger, & van Rijn, 1984).

EVALUATION

The studies summarized in this section evaluated prototypic training programs designed to enhance the cognitive skills of potential executive leaders. The data from these studies demonstrate the promise of the training programs. However, the interventions are primarily instructional-based programs. Little attention has been directed to the role of unit assignments and self-development efforts in pushing leaders to adjust their current frames of reference in favor of more complex ones that incorporate a wider span of causal factors. If, as suggested by SST, the construction of new and more complex organizational causal maps is a requisite for effective senior leadership, evaluations of senior leadership development programs need to include criteria that document such cognitive changes.

Conceptual Complexity Theories: General Conclusions

The following general conclusions can be drawn from the research model presented in Figure 3-1 and the empirical review offered throughout this chapter:

- Long-term planning, engagement with the organization's external environment, consensus building, network development, and construction of organizational causal maps are more important role performance requirements for executive leaders than for lower-level leaders. This has been demonstrated in both military and nonmilitary samples.

▪ The successful accomplishment of these executive leadership requirements, particularly long-term planning and boundary management, is associated with greater organizational performance. This has been demonstrated in nonmilitary samples but not in military ones.

▪ Upper-level leaders exhibit stronger conceptual skills than lower-level leaders. This has been demonstrated in both military and nonmilitary studies.

▪ The conceptual capabilities of executive leaders are associated with higher executive leader and organizational performance. This has been demonstrated in nonmilitary samples, but not military ones.

▪ Executive leaders display stronger proclivity for mental model building than lower-level leaders. This has been demonstrated in both military and nonmilitary samples, although higher ranking executive leaders have been examined in nonmilitary studies than in military studies.

▪ Proclivity for mental model building has not been associated with successful executive leader development or with the successful accomplishment of executive leader performance requirements.

▪ The CPA has demonstrated acceptable interrater reliabilities, internal consistency, and criterion-related validity. However, its construct validity has not been amply demonstrated.

▪ Existing military senior leader development programs have not yet demonstrated sufficient validity in terms of enhancing high-level conceptual capacities in rising military executive leaders.

These conclusions suggest that a sufficiently clear picture exists regarding the nature of executive leader work. Performance requirements appear to be comparable in military and nonmilitary leadership domains. These requirements change across organizational levels such that they impose greater and more complex information-processing demands in upper-level positions. Thus, top executive leaders need to respond to the complexity created by (a) greater long-term planning requirements, (b) the creation of organizational policies that reflect the conclusions of such planning, and (c) the development of organizational networks that provide information to the executive leader and facilitate implementation of his or her agenda. Finally, an executive leader's responses to all of these requirements is grounded in the meaning or sense of understanding (i.e., the frame of reference) he or she derives from reflecting on the multiple causal influences operating on the organization. This development of a frame of reference is the means, then, by which executive leaders add value to their organizations.

The review in this chapter indicates that the empirical investigation of executive leaders' mental maps and their influence on organizational action is at a very early stage. The focus has been primarily on developing techniques to assess such maps and associating their structures with environmental dynamics. There is a significant need, particularly in military settings, to examine how an executive leader's frame of reference influences the subsequent process of executive leadership and particularly the accomplishment of executive leader position requirements. Researchers also need to associate the quality of executive leaders' mental maps with organizational action and performance. Calori et al. (1994) provided some intriguing evidence of this association in their descriptive study of eight companies. However, the sample was too small for a systematic investigation of what impact executive leader causal maps have on leadership and organizational processes.

According to SST, the usefulness of an executive leader's frame of reference is based on the requirement for long-term planning. As noted, a significant number of studies in both military and nonmilitary domains have demonstrated that such planning is an important executive leader position requirement and that (in nonmilitary samples) it does influence organizational performance. However, SST specifically postulates a long time horizon—20 years and beyond—for top organizational executive leaders. This premise has been sharply criticized on two grounds. First, such planning can produce a degree of rigidity in executive leader thinking that is organizationally dysfunctional, particularly in turbulent environments (Streufert & Swezey, 1986). Second, the performance demands of executive leaders require a more short-term operational focus in addition to a strategic perspective (Isenberg, 1984). That is, observations of top management work have indicated a substantial amount of time spent on short-term projects with little time devoted to the kind of reflective thought required for a 20- to 50-year planning cycle (Mintzberg, 1973, 1975, 1994).

The data from the various studies described in this chapter suggest that the long-term orientation of an executive leader probably extends at most 5 to 10 years into the future. Markessini et al.'s (1994) study of nonmilitary executive leaders indicated that the leaders could envision further into the future. Likewise, Lucas and Harris (1993) demonstrated similar capabilities in Army general officers. However, there is no evidence that such envisioning capability is necessary or even useful to the successful accomplishment of executive leader work in these domains. Kotter's (1982a, 1982b) data from interviews with top executive leaders indicated that they may include a 5- to 20-year perspective in their strategic agendas (see Figure 3-3). However, this perspective is reflected only in vague notions about what financial picture is desired by the executive leader, what products should be developed, and what type of organization is preferred by the executive. The precise usefulness of these vague notions for the executive and the organization remains to be demonstrated.

Other research has offered two interesting notions about work time span that may resolve the differences between SST and other approaches to executive leadership. One notion refers to the time span diversity within an executive leader's strategic portfolio (Calori et al., 1994). Executive leaders do not merely need to have a long-term perspective, they also need to balance an array of strategic projects that vary in their requisite time horizons. This is perfectly compatible with the premise of SST that executive leaders must have the capability to envision far into the future. The mix of diverse time horizons adds to the information-processing requirements confronting the executive leader, thereby enhancing the need for high conceptual capacity. The notion of diverse time horizons is also suited to those theories that argue that a significant proportion of executive leader work reflects short-term operational requirements. As suggested by Calori et al., the diversity of an executive leader's strategic portfolio appears to be more directly linked to organizational performance than the furthest horizon of executive leader planning.

The second notion, offered by Thomas and Greenberger (1995) and Ringle and Savickas (1983), argues that the 20-year-plus time span proposed by SST does not necessarily have to mean an orientation of that duration. That is, the time span incorporated into executive leader thinking may reflect a retrospective as well as a prospective focus for the organization and its environment. Thomas and Greenberger suggested, for example, that an executive leader's 20-year perspective may include the previous 10 years as well as the future 10 years. Zaccaro et al. (1995) argued for a similar notion regarding leader visions. They suggested that an effective vision includes not only information about the organization and its environment at some future point in time but also an understanding of how the organization got to its present state and how the future desired for the organization by its executive leader relates to its past. Such long time spans fit the executive leader performance requirements and conceptual skills advocated by SST. However, these time horizons are not so far in the future as to be impractical for strategic considerations.

Thomas and Greenberger (1995) argued that issues related to leadership and time orientation have been largely unexplored. They proposed a model that includes time orientation as an important component of leadership and organizational performance. Given its centrality in SST, additional research needs to be directed at how time orientation is operationalized in executive leader work. This review suggests the following key issues: (a) the influence of time diversity versus extent of horizon on executive leadership and organizational performance; (b) time span as reflecting a past, present, and future orientation; and (c) the relative contribution to the explanation of executive leader work made by different definitions of time span (e.g., task time span, planning time span; envisioning horizon; Markessini et al., 1994).

A recurring theme in this empirical review of conceptual complexity theories of executive leadership has been that there have been few or no attempts in executive leadership research, particularly in the military, to associate successful accomplishment of executive leader performance requirements with executive leader and organizational performance. SST argues that long-term planning, boundary management, network development, consensus building, and, particularly, causal map development are the means by which executive leaders add value to their organizations. These requirements are then used to propose key executive leaders competencies that facilitate their accomplishment. However, if there is no empirical evidence associating executive leader role or performance requirements with organizational effectiveness, then there is not a sufficient basis for validating the efficacy of certain prescribed competencies. The necessity for this evidence is the basic premise of the research model in Figure 3-1. Also, if executive leader competencies are not validated, or if they are misspecified, then the construction of executive leader development programs that target these competencies may be misdirected and ineffective. The key to validation, then, lies in defining and operationalizing the criteria for successful executive leadership and using those criteria to validate the models of such leadership that have driven the corresponding development of senior leadership training programs.

Behavioral Complexity Theories: Conceptual Review and Evaluation

4

The preceding two chapters focused on the information-processing demands confronting executive leaders and their requisite need for high-level conceptual skills. This chapter and the next focus on the level of social demands that must be considered by executive leaders when formulating action plans and the resulting need for them to have the capacity for behavioral complexity. *Behavioral complexity* refers to an executive leader's ability to manage multiple organizational roles that call for very different, and sometimes competing, behavior patterns. Indeed, Denison, Hooijberg, and Quinn (1995), major proponents of this approach, described effective leadership as "the ability to perform the multiple roles and behaviors that circumscribe the requisite variety implied by an organizational or environmental context" (p. 526).

Social and Behavioral Complexity

Behavioral complexity and cognitive complexity are ultimately related. Because the problem situations confronting executive leaders are complex, their solutions and their implementation should be correspondingly complex. Cognitive capacities promote the development of these complex plans, whereas social capacities facilitate their implementation within complex social environments. Along these lines, Denison et al. (1995) argued that

> cognitive complexity . . . may well be a necessary condition for the effective practice of leadership. Behavioral complexity, however, must certainly be the sufficient condition. Leadership

must inevitably be performed through action, not cognition, and
it would thus appear to be time for leadership researchers to
begin to develop theories of behavioral as well as cognitive
complexity. (p. 524)

Following this argument, there are three important points to be
made regarding behavioral complexity and executive leadership. First,
cognitive complexity and behavioral complexity are not independent.
Theories of social intelligence have grounded the ability to display diverse and situationally appropriate social responses in the development
of elaborated cognitive representations, or schemas, of critical components that comprise the social environment (Cantor & Kihlstrom, 1987;
Zaccaro, Gilbert, Thor, & Mumford, 1991). Second, one might view cognitive complexity and behavioral complexity as contributing respectively
to the direction-setting and operational aspects of strategic leadership
(Gardner & Schermerhorn, 1992). Cognitive complexity facilitates the
development of a viable and integrated vision or strategy for the organization, whereas behavioral complexity contributes to its implementation within the organization and its external environment. Both are
necessary, yet neither is sufficient for effective executive leadership.
Third, the need for behavioral complexity in executive leaders is driven
by the existence of social complexity in their organizational operating
environments. This is an application of the law of requisite variety used
by Jacobs and Jaques (1987; Jacobs & Lewis, 1992) to explain the necessity for cognitive complexity. The existence of social complexity creates the need for behavioral complexity.

What factors create social complexity for the executive leader? One
factor is related to the performance requirement that executive leaders
coordinate and supervise the activities of different departments within
the organization. Organizations contain multiple subsystems that can be
distinguished by their functions (Katz & Kahn, 1978). As suggested by
Katz and Kahn, functions can be described in terms of input processes
(the acquisition of organizational resources), throughput processes (the
transformation of raw materials and resources into organizational products), and output processes (the distribution of finished products to organizational consumers). For example, production subsystems in the organization are primarily concerned with throughput processes, whereas
sales subsystems are oriented toward output. Human resources departments focus on input processes, whereas other subsystems within the
organization can be termed boundary-spanning subsystems that focus
on managing and acquiring information about the environment. Although the latter function is inherently part of the executive leader's
role (Katz & Kahn, 1978), some organizational subsystems possess specialized boundary-spanning roles (e.g., marketing departments). The
various constituencies associated with input, throughput, and output

processes often will make different and conflicting demands on the executive leader and, accordingly, will require different behavioral responses.

The functional diversity just described represents the social complexity of a single organization. For corporate executives (i.e., Strata VI and VII leaders, according to Jacobs & Jaques, 1987), this diversity is compounded for the executive leader with more than one company under his or her purview. Just as different functional departments within an organization present an executive leader with conflicting social (and therefore behavioral) demands, different organizations present a diversity of cultures, needs, and requirements for him or her to consider.

This is a macroanalysis of organizational social complexity. A microanalysis reveals similar social diversity. Bentz (1987) argued that executive leader success requires the ability to handle the degree of "scope/scale" that exists in large organizations. Scope refers to the number of functional units under an individual's control. Scale refers to the internal complexity and diversity that exists "within and across units managed, within and across varieties of personal relations, and across decisions made" (pp. 1–2). That is, functional units, and individuals within them, are not homogeneous in terms of their needs, demands, temperaments, and social requirements. The same is true of the management team that reports to the top executive leader. This interpersonal diversity adds to the social complexity executive leaders need to consider in formulating action plans (Zaccaro, Gilbert, et al., 1991).

Another characteristic of executive leader social complexity that requires behavioral complexity is the boundary management aspect of top organizational leadership. Executive leaders engage in a number of different boundary-spanning functions (Gilmore, 1982). For example, at one level, boundary spanning means managing the interactions and representations of a leader's subordinates to higher organizational authorities. Thus, leaders act as intermediaries between their subordinates and supervisors. At another level, such as for senior executive leaders, boundary spanning entails managing such activities as the interactions between the organization as a whole and its board of directors. Quite often, the demands made by various constituencies conflict, requiring the delicate balancing of differing behavioral expectations (Tsui, 1984a, 1984b). Executive leaders also typically are required to manage the boundary between the organization and an often complex and dynamic environment. This may involve interactions with political constituencies and regulators, consumers of organizational products, sources of organizational materials and financial resources, shareholders, and community leaders. Each of these constituencies requires a range of very different actions from the executive leader.

Still another characteristic of executive social complexity is the requirement that senior leaders balance competing macro-level demands from both the organization and its environment (Hart & Quinn, 1993; Quinn, 1984). Executive leaders often are required to promote organizational adaptation and innovation in response to dynamic environmental conditions. However, the establishment of an organizational culture that favors innovation and change can at times work against the order and predictability required for successful collective action (Weick, 1979). Thus, executive leaders need to create an organization that is both flexible and predictable—that is, one that is adaptive to environmental change yet has the stability necessary for organized responses from large numbers of individual members (Jonas, Fry, & Srivastva, 1990). This paradox in turn produces several competing social role requirements for the executive leader (Hart & Quinn, 1993).

The existence of social complexity in the operating environments of executive leaders means that successful leadership entails the effective management of multiple social roles and corresponding behavior patterns. This premise is the basis for the three conceptual theories described in this chapter. The first is Mintzberg's (1973, 1975) classification of managerial roles. Although this classification does not have the framework of a formal model or theory, it is important because it delineates the different behavior patterns required of executive leaders. In addition, it serves as a basis for subsequent research on managerial behavioral complexity. The other two theories, Tsui's multiple constituency framework (Tsui, 1984a, 1984b) and Quinn's Competing values framework (Hooijberg & Quinn, 1992; Quinn, 1984, 1988), are more explicit about the need for executive leaders to balance conflicting demands and behavior patterns. As with the other conceptual perspectives described in this book, these theories are examined through the following four themes: (a) executive leader performance requirements; (b) requisite executive leader characteristics; (c) measurement of behavioral complexity; and (d) leader development.

Nature of Organizational Leadership

The social complexity confronting top executives suggests that organizational leadership entails the enactment of multiple roles. This premise is articulated by each of the models described in this section.

MINTZBERG'S MANAGERIAL ROLES: NATURE OF EXECUTIVE LEADER PLANNING

The image of the executive leader that is suggested by the conceptual complexity theories is that of the reflective, long-term planner. This is an image that Mintzberg (1973, 1975) explicitly rejected. He noted, "The traditional literature notwithstanding, the job of managing does not breed reflective planners; the manager is a real time responder to stimuli, an individual who is conditioned by his job to prefer live to delayed action" (Mintzberg, 1975, p. 51). According to Mintzberg, executive leaders make decisions relatively quickly, often without the aid of extensive cost-benefit analyses. At times, decisions are made on the basis of trust for the proposer of the project rather than on any systematic analysis of the project's strengths and weaknesses in accordance with organizational direction.

Executive leader work is characterized as action oriented and filled with many different, brief, and discontinuous tasks. Mintzberg (1973, 1975) calculated that among the chief executive officers (CEOs) he observed, one half of their activities consumed less than 9 min, with only 10% lasting longer than 1 hr. The range of tasks performed reflected a variety of very different managerial roles. Although stratified systems theory (SST) argues for some of the same top executive leader roles, two differences are apparent. First, executive leader work is directed equally inward and outward with respect to the organization. SST places a bit more emphasis on the external systemic focus of top management. Mintzberg's role set includes this focus; however, several of the roles also reflect day-to-day operational activities and direct management. Indeed, Mintzberg's analysis of the time executive leaders spent with various constituencies reported an almost even split between external (44%) and internal (48%) groups (7% of the executive leaders' time was spent with directors and trustees). A second nuance of difference between the two perspectives is the one alluded to earlier. Whereas SST places a disproportionate emphasis on planning and strategy making, Mintzberg argued that all of the different managerial roles are equally important to successful executive leadership performance. This suggests that the primary emphasis of SST on conceptual capacity as the most critical executive leadership skill may be misplaced—an argument pressed by others as well (e.g., Boal & Whitehead, 1992).

This is not to say that Mintzberg's role set rejects planning as part of executive leadership. Nor does his classification system discount the need for an integrated understanding of the organization and its environment (i.e., the frame of reference espoused by SST). In a recent contribution to his theory, Mintzberg (1994) provided an interesting perspective on executive leader planning. He defined *planning* as a "formalized procedure to produce articulated result, in the form of an integrated system of decisions" (p. 31). *Planners* are individuals "without line (operating) responsibilities and so with time on their hands to worry about the future of the organization" (p. 32). What then are managers? Mintzberg noted the following:

> Effective managers . . . have their fingers on the pulse of the organization and its external context through their privileged access to soft data. But as described in the planning dilemma, they lack the time and inclination to study the hard data. The nature of their work favors action over reflection, quick response over long term consideration, the oral over the written, getting information rapidly over getting it right. Someone has to take the time to study the hard facts—shifts in consumer buying habits, realignments of competitive positions, changes in product mixes, and so on—and ensure that their consequences are fed into the strategy making process. (1994, p. 368)

Mintzberg nominated the planner for the role of providing the data analysis and information interpretation needed for managerial decision making. These are individuals who take the long-term perspective, consider this perspective in the context of their analysis, form the "picture," and then provide their interpretation to the senior manager. It is the planner who does the long-range reflection and analysis, whereas the manager makes the necessary strategic decision. This does not absolve the executive leader from needing or using a long-term perspective, but it does suggest that such a perspective is more typically the province of the executive's (planning) staff, whereas his or her typical work focus may be more short-term.

Mintzberg's Integrated Managerial Role Set

Mintzberg (1973, 1975) used intensive structured observation methods to record and analyze the work of five CEOs. He identified 10 managerial roles subsumed under three headings. These roles are listed in Table 4-1. The first role category reflects *interpersonal* roles. These roles emerge from the formal and position authority of the executive leader. They include activities related to both ceremonial or symbolic representation of the organization to outside constituencies (*figurehead*) and interaction with myriad external constituencies that become potential sources of information critical to organizational functioning (*liaison*). Interpersonal roles also include hiring, training, and motivating subordinates and staff members (*leader*). These roles, as a set, provide the social contacts (and context) for *informational* roles. This second role set reflects activities centered on the acquisition and dissemination of information. The first role in this set involves the acquisition of information from sources within and outside the organization, as well as from contacts

TABLE 4-1

Mintzberg's Managerial Roles

Role	Activities
Interpersonal roles	
Figurehead	Perform duties of ceremonial or symbolic nature.
Leader	Perform duties related to hiring, training, and motivating subordinates.
Liaison	Make contacts and develop networks outside vertical chain of command.
Informational roles	
Monitor	Gather information regarding organizational effectiveness from both internal and external sources.
Disseminator	Communicate information to subordinates and other organizational personnel; facilitate communication among subordinate units.
Spokesperson	Communicate information about organization to constituencies outside organizational unit or constituencies outside organization.
Decisional roles	
Entrepreneur	Initiate and encourage projects and strategies that facilitate organizational adaptation to changing environmental conditions.
Disturbance handler	Provide appropriate responses to unexpected events and crises.
Resource allocator	Allocate resources to organizational units in accordance with managerial priorities.
Negotiator	Represent organizational units in negotiations; facilitate negotiations with and among organizational subunits.

developed in the liaison role (*monitor*). This information is then distributed to key organizational personnel. The manager also facilitates communication among disparate subordinate units (*disseminator*). Finally, the manager is a source of information to constituencies outside the organization or at least outside his or her organizational unit (*spokesman*). The purpose is to inform constituencies that are critical to the input and output processes of the organization (e.g., suppliers, shareholders).

In addition, Mintzberg (1973, 1975) noted in his observations of CEOs that each played a central part in organizational decision making.

Accordingly, he specified four *decisional* roles. The first such role involves the initiation and encouragement of new ideas and innovations that facilitate organizational adaptation to changing environmental conditions (*entrepreneur*). This role more often than not reflects proactive behaviors. However, a significant portion of managerial activity is taken in response to unexpected events and crises (*disturbance handler*). Also, when making decisions, managers often are distributing organizational resources (including their time) according to established strategic priorities (*resource allocator*). Finally, because senior managers oversee several subordinate units and need to interact with multiple constituencies associated with the organization, they often are required to arbitrate or mediate disputes or bargain on behalf of the organization (*negotiator*).

These 10 roles emphasize the two central aspects of executive leader work mentioned frequently in this book: boundary management and organizational maintenance. Several of Mintzberg's (1973, 1975) roles reflect the manager's need to interact with external individuals and groups (e.g., figurehead, liaison, spokesman, and negotiator). Other roles emphasize orienting the organization with respect to its environment, either by keeping critical subordinate units informed of environmental conditions (e.g., disseminator), or by altering organizational priorities in response to changes in these conditions (e.g., entrepreneur). The remaining roles reflect activities devoted to maintaining stability in organizational functioning. Thus, Mintzberg's roles reflect leadership functions prescribed by a number of early theorists of organizational leadership (e.g., Barnard, 1938; Hemphill, 1950; Katz & Kahn, 1966, 1978; Krech & Crutchfield, 1948; Selznick, 1957).

All of Mintzberg's (1973, 1975) roles are considered critical for effective senior leadership. Indeed, Mintzberg argued that these roles form an integrated whole or gestalt. The interpersonal roles are used to build the contacts and sources that allow the successful accomplishment of informational roles. The informational roles are critical in making and implementing organizational decisions. Successful leadership therefore requires the ability to accomplish all 10 roles. Because each role presumably reflects a different constellation of behaviors, this means that executive leaders are required to display many different behavior patterns according to the requirements of particular managerial tasks. Furthermore, given the rapid pace of executive management work described by Mintzberg, executive leaders need the ability to shift quickly among roles (and behavior patterns).

Mintzberg (1973, 1975) did not specify how the number and nature of managerial roles change across organizational levels. Because his classification emerged from his observations of CEOs, the assumption is that his 10 roles are reflective of executive-level leadership. It is possible to speculate that (a) the contextual complexity of accomplishing each role changes qualitatively at higher organizational levels or (b) some of the roles (e.g., entrepreneur) become less important and perhaps even non-existent at lower levels. These must remain speculations, however, because Mintzberg did not explicitly address differences in managerial functioning by level. He did, however, argue that the amount of time devoted to each role varies by managerial job function. For example, although Mintzberg argued that all three types of managers studied completed elements of all three central leadership roles, he noted from his observations that sales managers spent more time on interpersonal roles, production managers on decisional roles, and staff managers on informational roles.

Unlike other approaches to behavioral complexity that stress the incongruent quality of required executive leader characteristics and the need for executive leaders to balance conflicting demands, Mintzberg's (1973, 1975) classification of senior management roles does not assume conflict or incongruence among any of the behavioral roles. Instead, the roles are presumed to be integrated into a coherent gestalt. Mintzberg noted, "No role can be pulled out of the framework and the job left intact" (1975, p. 59).

TSUI'S MULTIPLE CONSTITUENCY FRAMEWORK

Tsui (1984a, 1984b) argued that leader success, and by extension, organizational effectiveness, was a function of the leader's reputational effectiveness. She defined *reputation* as "the effectiveness as perceived from the perspective of the individual or a specific group of individuals who are satisfied with the job behavior and activities exhibited by the manager being evaluated" (Tsui, 1984b, p. 65). Each leader is embedded within a role set that contains multiple role senders (Katz & Kahn, 1978). Role senders include subordinates, peers, and superiors within the organization as well as constituency groups outside the organization. These role senders are likely to have expectations of the leader that reflect their different functional specializations, work objectives, personal and group goals, and personal career aspirations. When these role expectations diverge significantly, a leader who is in the middle of this role set will receive different, often conflicting, role information. For example, Tsui argued that the behaviors required by a leader's superiors are likely to be different from, and indeed may be negatively related to, the behaviors prescribed by his or her peers or subordinates. However, she noted that to be perceived as effective by multiple relevant constituencies, a leader needs to meet the different role requirements of all key role senders. Thus, for a leader, success is likely to depend on maintaining a delicate balance of conflicting role behaviors.

Tsui's (1984a) multiple constituency framework of managerial effectiveness is illustrated in Figure 4-1. Managerial and organizational effectiveness is determined jointly by the reputational effectiveness established with superiors, subordinates, and peers as well as reflecting the leader's own expectations and role priorities. Reputational effectiveness is determined by the degree to which managerial role behavior is perceived as successfully reflecting the confluence of behaviors expected by separate organizational constituencies. Tsui argued that organizational, interpersonal, and personal factors influence the nature of managerial role sending. Relevant organizational factors include authority structure, organizational strategy, degree of vertical and horizontal differentiation, and reward structures. Interpersonal factors include the degree of credibility and political power possessed by both different role senders and the focal leader. Role senders with high credibility and clout will more likely command the attention of the leader, whereas leaders with high credibility and power will be able to shape the role expectations of others more effectively. Personal factors include the power motives or influence needs of the leader and role senders, as well as the level of aspirations and expectations established by both the leader and the role senders.

Tsui (1984b) incorporated Mintzberg's role classification into her framework by proposing that different constituencies will vary in their expected frequencies of each of the role behaviors. She argued, for example, that the spokesperson and liaison roles are more instrumental for reputational effectiveness perceived by peers than by subordinates or superiors because a manager's peers rely heavily on information exchange to coordinate their own work efforts. Tsui suggested that subordinates emphasize the leader, resource allocation, and environmental monitoring roles because such activities help structure and give meaning to their own work. Finally, a leader's superiors are more likely to favor entrepreneurial roles. Note that an effective leader is required to be responsive to all of these constituencies with their differing role expectations. Accordingly, Tsui proposed that a leader's perceptions of his or her own reputation depends on the successful accomplishment of all of these roles.

Tsui's framework (1984a, 1984b) supports the premise that successful leaders need to display a complex array of different behaviors. However, Tsui did not clearly specify how role expectations from multiple constituencies vary as one ascends organizational levels. That is, Tsui did not indicate how junior leaders differ from senior leaders in determinants of reputational effectiveness. She did suggest that leaders in boundary-spanning roles need to respond not only to superior, peer, and subordinate role requirements, but also to the demands of constituencies outside the organization. Because senior leaders are more likely to be

FIGURE 4-1

Multiple-Constituency Framework of Managerial Effectiveness

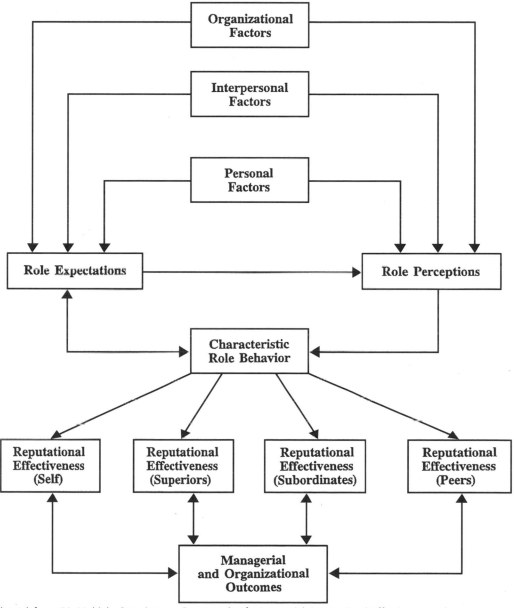

Adapted from "A Multiple-Constituency Framework of Managerial Reputational Effectiveness," by A. S. Tsui, in *Leaders and Managers: International Perspectives on Managerial Behavior and Leadership* (p. 32), by J. G. Hunt, D. Hosking, C. A. Schriesheim, and R. Stewart (Eds.), 1984, New York: Pergamon Press. Copyright 1984 by A. S. Tsui. Adapted with permission.

engaged in boundary-spanning activities than junior leaders, they need to account for the role requirements of external groups more so than their junior counterparts. Also, at higher organizational levels, leaders are increasingly likely to have multiple subordinate groups reflecting different job functions reporting to them. Each subordinate group could convey substantially different role expectations. Thus, executive leaders must balance a more complex constellation of subordinate demands than junior leaders, who may have only one subordinate group to account for. Thus, although Tsui's framework does not explicitly propose differences across organizational levels, it does support the premise that social and behavioral complexity are greater for senior leaders than junior leaders.

QUINN'S COMPETING VALUES FRAMEWORK

Although Tsui (1984a, 1984b) emphasized the need to balance different role demands from multiple constituencies, the notion of conflict is not an inevitable aspect of her framework. A politically skillful or powerful leader can reconcile competing role requirements to form a coherent and consistent whole. For such a leader, behavioral requirements become consistent across different organizational groups. Quinn's competing values framework (Hart & Quinn, 1993; Hooijberg & Quinn, 1992; Quinn, 1984, 1988), however, argues that conflicting values and therefore opposing behavioral requirements are inherent in the nature of organizational executive leadership. Furthermore, Quinn argued that opposing values are of equal value to overall leader effectiveness. Therefore, leader effectiveness entails the mastery of countervailing behavior patterns.

Quinn's leadership values are derived from a model of organizational effectiveness that incorporates three sets of competing values (Quinn & Rohrbaugh, 1981; Rohrbaugh, 1981). The first is flexibility versus stability. Organizations are expected to be flexible and adaptive in response to environmental change as well stable and predictable in their operating procedures. Second, organizational effectiveness can be described in terms of an emphasis on the well-being of individual members versus the well-being of the organization as a whole. The former reflects a more internal focus, whereas the latter reflects the organization in relation to its external environment. Finally, values differ in terms of a process or outcomes focus.

As applied to organizational leadership, these dimensions produce four sets of competing behavioral role requirements (Quinn, 1984). These roles and requisite behavioral patterns are summarized in Figure 4-2. The dimensions of flexibility–predictability and internal focus–external focus produce four quadrants. The first, reflecting flexibility and

FIGURE 4-2

Quinn's Competing Values Framework

	Flexibility/Internal Focus		**Predictability/External Focus**
Mentor	*Shows consideration.* Is aware of individual needs, actively listens, is fair and objective, supports legitimate requests, attempts to facilitate individual development.	**Director**	*Provides structure.* Engages in goal setting and role clarification, sets objectives, monitors progress, provides feedback, establishes clear expectations.
Facilitator	*Facilitates interaction.* Is interpersonally skilled, facilitates group processes, encourages expression, seeks consensus, facilitates compromise.	**Producer**	*Initiates action.* Is concerned about task, stimulates appropriate performance in group members and others necessary for task completion.
	Flexibility/External Focus		**Predictability/Internal Focus**
Innovator	*Envisions change.* Seeks new opportunities, encourages and considers new ideas, is tolerant of ambiguity and risk.	**Coordinator**	*Maintains structure.* Maintains stability and flow of work by scheduling, coordinating, solving problems, and ensuring rules, standards, and deadlines are understood and met.
Broker	*Acquires resources.* Develops interpersonal contacts, monitors environment, amasses power and influence, maintains external image of unit, secures resources.	**Monitor**	*Provides information.* Deeply comprehends task of group, constantly collects and distributes information, facilitates development of shared meanings, develops group sense of continuity and safety.

From "Applying the Competing Values Approach to Leadership: Towards an Integrative Framework," by R. E. Quinn, in *Leaders and Managers: International Perspectives on Managerial Behavior and Leadership* (p. 32), by J. G. Hunt, D. Hosking, C. A. Schriesheim, and R. Stewart (Eds.), 1984, New York: Pergamon Press. Copyright 1994 by Pergamon Press, and "Behavioral Complexity and the Development of Effective Managers," by R. Hooijberg and R. E. Quinn, in *Strategic Leadership: A Multiorganizational Perspective*, 1992, Westport, CT: Quorum Books. Copyright © 1992. Reprinted by permission of Jossey-Bass, Inc., a subsidiary of John Wiley & Sons, Inc.

internal focus, indicates that leaders are required to develop and nurture subordinates and promote open interactions among them. Thus, leaders must act in the roles of mentor and facilitator, respectively. These roles compete with roles defined in the opposing quadrant of predictability and external focus. Leaders need to provide structure and initiate action. These actions, reflecting the director and producer roles, conflict with the mentor and facilitator roles, respectively, because the need for task-oriented actions may be incompatible with the requirement to develop subordinates and promote a harmonious work environment.

The quadrant reflecting flexibility and external focus suggests that leaders need to be creative in developing new ideas and products in response to environmental changes. In addition, leaders must attend to resource acquisition and particularly to organizational growth. These leader roles are defined as innovator and broker, respectively. They compete with roles that reflect predictability and internal focus. The coordinator role (competing with the innovator role) is necessary to maintain organizational stability and control of operating procedures. Innovation means disruption of and change to these procedures. The role of monitor reflects information acquisition and distribution within the organization; this competes with the broker role because in the latter role leaders acquire information from outside the organization.

Hooijberg and Quinn (1992) argued that organizational leadership requires significant behavioral complexity. Effective leaders will enact more of the roles in the competing values framework than ineffective leaders. Also, effective leaders will balance these roles such that one role is not emphasized disproportionately. Less effective leaders will either not display any of the roles or will display one role more than the others. Because each role has a countervailing role, the enactment of multiple roles requires significant leadership skill. Thus, for example, leaders need to be innovative and adaptive regarding the organization's operating environment while at the same time maintaining stability and structure within the organization. Also, leaders must develop their subordinates by creating a nurturing environment while also being task focused and structuring to complete production goals in a timely manner. Behavioral complexity is thus defined as the skillful balancing of multiple leadership roles in accordance with organizational requirements.

Hooijberg (1996) extended these notions by specifying two dimensions of behavioral complexity: behavioral repertoire and behavioral differentiation. *Behavioral repertoire* refers to the variety of behaviors an executive leader can enact in response to situational demands. The broader the leader's repertoire, the more effective the leader can be across diverse organizational contexts. Furthermore, as social complexity within organizations increases, the more necessary a broad behavioral repertoire becomes.

Hooijberg (1996) noted that the extent of a manager's repertoire was necessary, but not sufficient, for effectiveness. Managers and executives also need the ability to apply appropriate responses to particular situations. Hooijberg described this ability as *behavioral differentiation*. He noted that "the concept of behavioral differentiation refers to the ability of managers to perform the leadership functions they have in their behavioral repertoire differently (more adaptively, more flexibly, more appropriately, more individualized, and situation specific) depending on the organizational situation" (p. 922).

Quinn, Hooijberg, and their colleagues did not explicitly specify differences in role requirements between junior and senior leaders. However, the competing values framework is based on an integration of organizational effectiveness theories, suggesting that it applies to senior leaders. Indeed, Hart and Quinn (1993) specified the roles as "executive roles" and called their approach a model of executive leadership. Nonetheless, one may speculate that junior leaders are likely to enact one or a few of the roles, perhaps those from a single quadrant. For example, lower-level leaders may be focused on providing direction and initiating action for subordinates. They may otherwise be concerned with monitoring and coordinating functions or with subordinate development. Lower-level leadership, however, does not exclude the need to enact conflicting roles. According to Jacobs and Jaques (1987), leaders at Stratum III (production domain) often need to provide direction and nurture subordinate development. Thus, a degree of behavioral complexity may be required even at lower organizational levels. A key difference may be that senior leaders have a wider array of competing roles to enact.

Quinn (1988) completed research with managers at different organizational levels that suggested that effectiveness required varying needs to accomplish all of the identified roles. He clustered effective managers at several levels and developed a profile of each. At middle organizational levels, managers could be effective by emphasizing either (a) the roles of mentor, facilitator, innovator, and broker (called *open adaptors*) or (b) the roles of director, producer, coordinator, and monitor (called *aggressive achievers*). Note that managerial effectiveness can be attained without necessarily displaying competing values. At higher organizational levels, effective managers begin to display competing values, although not all four sets are displayed. Quinn identified the *committed intensives* (high scores on the innovator, producer, monitor, and facilitator roles), *peaceful team builders* (high scores on all roles but broker and producer), and *conceptual planners* (high scores on all roles but monitor and coordinator). At the top of the organization (i.e., top executives), effective managers were those who displayed high scores on all roles (called *master managers*). Although this is an empirically driven differentiation, these patterns suggest organizational-level differences in the need to adopt and balance the full range of competing roles.

Requisite Executive Leader Characteristics

Although a number of studies have examined the multiple role and behavioral requirements of executive leadership, few have investigated the leader skills and characteristics that promote behavioral complexity. One possible explanation for this relative lack of attention is that as the behavioral requirements of senior leadership multiply, it becomes necessary to posit a correspondingly expanding list of skills that facilitate each behavior pattern. For example, if one begins with Baehr's (1992) comprehensive list of 16 leader activities, then one needs to specify the leader knowledge, skills, abilities, and other dispositional orientations that lead to the effective display of each activity pattern. The leader qualities that produce successful objective setting and planning are likely to be different from those facilitating effective team building. Likewise, each of Mintzberg's 10 managerial roles generally will emerge from very different constellations of leader qualities. Also, because leader behaviors are likely to be multiply determined, a list of influential variables producing behavioral complexity can be significantly greater that the number of role behaviors required of the leader.

Nonetheless, Mintzberg (1975, p. 61) specified several managerial skills linked to his role classification:

- Developing peer relations (networking);
- Carrying out negotiations;
- Motivating subordinates;
- Resolving conflicts;
- Establishing information networks and disseminating information;
- Making decisions under ambiguity;
- Allocating resources (including one's own time); and
- Applying introspective skills.

These behaviors and the abilities that foster them promote the accomplishment of Mintzberg's managerial role set. They fit into the categories of interpersonal and conceptual skills that are the basis of most leader skill typologies (Katz, 1955; Mann, 1965; Yukl, 1994). Many of these skills apply to managers at most, if not all, organizational levels. Thus, they are not informative in terms of the skills that differentiate effective junior managers from effective senior leaders.

Tsui (1984a) proposed that high reputational effectiveness across multiple constituencies is associated with strong power motives and influence needs in focal managers. Leaders with high power motivation are likely to be more successful in shaping the expectations of different constituencies to make them more congruent with their own. Also, a strong need to influence others has been associated with a desire to work hard on behalf of others (McClelland, 1961). Accordingly, leaders with such needs are likely to be more committed to addressing the role expectations of multiple and different organizational constituencies. Tsui did not adopt the premise that power and influence needs become more or less important at different organizational levels.

Quinn (1984) proposed trait clusters for each of the roles in his competing values framework. Table 4-2 lists these clusters by leader role. Each role is defined as emerging from qualitatively different sets of leader characteristics. Thus, this theory presumes that leaders with high behavioral complexity possess all of these characteristics. This premise is interesting in that it appears to suggest competing dispositional orientations in the same leader. For example, the innovator and broker roles are proposed as requiring "an inventive, risk-taking style" (Quinn, 1984, p. 19). However, the competing roles of coordinator and monitor suggest a more conservative and cautious style. Likewise, the producer and director roles are linked to a task-driven style, whereas the competing roles of facilitator and mentor suggest a person-oriented and relaxed work style. Thus, leader effectiveness appears to be grounded in the balancing of different dispositional orientations.

The focus on different behavioral styles forces an emphasis on multiple trait clusters and ignores the substance of leader behavioral complexity. Day and Lord (1988) suggested that rather than focusing narrowly on leader styles, theories of executive leadership should include such factors as analytical, perceptual, and conceptual leader abilities. These characteristics can facilitate the emergence of integrated and complex behavior patterns. Accordingly, Hooijberg and Quinn (1992) argued that cognitive complexity is a determining condition for behavioral complexity. They suggested that cognitive complexity helps leaders understand the four sets of leader roles with their competing underlying values and philosophies. Furthermore, high-level cognitive skills promote the integration of these competing skills.

Here, then, is a basis for behavioral complexity: Effective executive leaders need appropriate cognitive skills to understand the requisite complex behavior patterns. Streufert and Swezey (1986) noted that successful leaders displayed flexible integrative complexity in the leadership domain, meaning that they differentiated among alternate leadership activities and integrated them into a coherent and flexible theory. If one accepts the premise that the need to balance competing role and be-

TABLE 4-2

Proposed Trait Clusters for Quinn's Competing Values Framework Leader Roles

Role	Trait cluster
Mentor	*Caring, empathetic*: Is concerned about individuals, is alert to their problems and needs, sees individuals as valued resources.
Facilitator	*Process oriented, diplomatic, tactful*: Has good interpersonal skills; facilitates group interaction, cooperation, and cohesion.
Monitor	*Technically expert, well prepared*: Is well-informed, knowledgeable regarding group work, competent, highly expert in technical matters.
Coordinator	*Dependable, reliable*: Is consistent, predictable; seeks to maintain continuity and equilibrium.
Director	*Decisive, directive*: Is conclusive and determinative; can rapidly plan work and provide direction.
Production	*Task oriented, work focused*: Is action oriented, highly generative; invests great energy, derives much satisfaction from productive work.
Broker	*Politically astute, resource oriented*: Is very aware of and sensitive to external conditions, particularly those related to legitimacy, influence, and resource acquisition.
Innovator	*Innovative, clever*: Is innovative, conceptually skilled; seeks unique opportunities and improvements.

Also adapted from R. E. Quinn (1988). Figure 10. Competing Values Framework of Leadership Roles. In R. E. Quinn (Ed.), *Beyond Rational Management: Mastering the Paradoxes and Competing Demands of High Performance* (p. 86). San Francisco, CA: Jossey-Bass. Copyright 1988 by Jossey-Bass. Adapted with permission of the publisher. And adapted from R. Hooijberg and R. E. Quinn (1992). Behavioral Complexity and the Development of Effective Managers. In R. L. Phillips & J. G. Hunt (Eds.), *Strategic Leadership: A Multiorganizational-Level Perspective*. Westport, CT: Quorum Books. Copyright 1992 by Quorum Books. Adapted with permission of publisher.

havioral requirements is stronger at higher organizational levels, then, as suggested by Streufert and Swezey, flexible integrative complexity becomes more important for executive leaders than for lower-level managers.

Zaccaro, Gilbert, et al. (1991) suggested that social intelligence might also be instrumental in the display of behavioral complexity. They defined *social intelligence* as the ability to perceive critical situational contingencies and enact the leader roles most appropriate for each situation. They also tied this ability to effective leadership. Social intelligence includes skills related to social perceptiveness and behavioral flexibility. Behavioral flexibility has two determining components: a broad response repertoire and the cognitive capacity to adjust and match be-haviors to particular social demands (Paulus & Martin, 1988). Leaders who can enact different leader roles are likely to possess a broad be-havioral repertoire. However, this repertoire is not helpful unless leaders also can match different role behaviors with situational role require-ments. This is accomplished through elaborated cognitive representa-tions that effectively encode significant elements of the executive leader's social world and provide information about the most appropri-ate responses across a variety of social situations (Zaccaro, Gilbert, et al., 1991). Note that the development of these cognitive frameworks re-quires the kinds of conceptual skills proposed by the conceptual com-plexity theories of executive leadership.

In summary, the specification of executive leader roles and their social complexity has been linked to a delineation of requisite mana-gerial skills. Less attention, however, has been given to managerial ca-pabilities that specifically lead to an ability to handle competing role responsibilities. Hooijberg and Quinn (1992) linked the cognitive com-plexity approaches to executive leadership with their own approach by arguing that strong conceptual skills promote behavioral complexity. This viewpoint is supported by theories of social intelligence that argue that elaborate cognitive theories of a complex social domain facilitate appropriate social behavior. This suggests that executive leadership may best be explained by a combination of the cognitive and behavior com-plexity perspectives. This is a significant basis for the integrated execu-tive leadership model that is proposed in chapter 10 of this book.

Measurement of Behavioral Complexity

The research on behavioral complexity and the nature of executive lead-ership suggests two key measurement issues. The first is the empirical assessment of roles and activity patterns displayed by executive leaders. Several psychometrically sound inventories of managerial jobs have been developed and applied to the study of executive leadership. These include the Work Analysis Forms (Stogdill & Shartle, 1958), the Exec-utive Position Description Questionnaire (Hemphill, 1960), the Leader Behavior Description Questionnaire (Form XII; Stogdill, 1963), the Management Position Description Questionnaire (Tornow & Pinto, 1976), the Management Practices Survey (Yukl, Wall, & Lepsinger, 1990), the Leadership Observation System (Luthans & Lockwood, 1984), and the Management and Professional Job Functions Inventory (Baehr, 1992). These inventories provide a relatively common description of the range of executive leadership behavioral requirements (see also Yukl, 1989, p. 95). Behavioral complexity can be assessed by observing the degree to which respondents display high scores on multiple behavioral categories (e.g., McCall & Segrist, 1980; Morse & Wagner, 1976; Pavett & Lau, 1982).

This approach, however, does not directly assess an individual's ability to effectively enact competing or conflicting roles. As noted previously, Tsui (1984b) and Hooijberg and Quinn (1992) specified behavioral complexity as the balancing and display of conflicting behavioral patterns. The inventories listed do not specifically identify the variety of leadership behaviors in terms of competing role requirements. A measurement technique that defines such competing role patterns would be closer to the conceptual meaning of behavioral complexity. Denison et al. (1995) described an inventory that directly assesses the eight countervailing leadership roles of Quinn's competing values framework. This inventory is shown in Figure 4-3. High scores across the competing roles indicate effective displays of behavioral complexity. Hooijberg and Quinn (1992, p. 165) applied the following formula (Bobko & Schwartz, 1984) to a similar instrument to assess behavioral complexity:

$$\text{Integration} = [(k - 1) - (|X - Y|)] * [(X + Y)/2],$$

where

k = range of integral response on scale (1 = *manager never performs role*; 7 = *manager almost always performs role*);
X = scores on one role (e.g., mentor role); and
Y = scores on competing role (e.g., director role).

This formula creates an index of integrative balance among contrasting leader roles. High scores on this index indicate that leaders are displaying high but relatively equal levels of competing roles. Likewise, leaders who display equally moderate levels on competing roles will score higher on this index of behavioral complexity than leaders who may score higher on one role but lower in a competing role. To fully assess behavioral complexity, integration scores are computed for the four dimensions of contrasting roles in the competing values framework (i.e., mentor vs. director, facilitator vs. producer, monitor vs. broker, and coordinator vs. innovator). This index, combined with the job inventories described earlier, appears to provide an effective assessment approach to examining executive leader behavioral complexity. Research using this approach is described in chapter 5.

FIGURE 4-3

Leader Roles Measure

Questionnaire Items By Role

1	2	3	4	5	6	7
almost never	very seldom	seldom	occasionally	frequently	very frequently	almost always

The Innovator Role (0.66)
    1. Comes up with inventive ideas.
    2. Experiments with new concepts and ideas.
The Broker Role (0.72)
    3. Exerts upward influence in the organization.
    4. Influences decisions made at higher levels.
The Producer Role (0.79)
    5. Sees that the unit delivers on stated goals.
    6. Gets the unit to meet expected goals.
The Director Role (0.80)
    7. Makes the unit's role very clear.
    8. Clarifies the unit's priorities and directions.
The Coordinator Role (0.70)
    9. Anticipates workflow problems, avoids crisis.
    10. Brings a sense of order into the unit.
The Monitor Role
    11. Maintains tight logistical control.
    12. Compares records, reports, and so on, the detect discrepancies.
The Facilitator Role (0.62)
    13. Surfaces key differences among group members, then works participatively to resolve them.
    14. Encourages participative decision making in the group.
The Mentor Role (0.87)
    15. Shows empathy and concern in dealing with subordinates.
    16. Treats each individual in a sensitive, caring way.

Effectiveness Items

In this section we would like to know your general overall assessment of the person as a managerial leader. In answering the following questions, please circle the appropriate number.

1. Meeting of managerial performance standards:
    Below most standards   1 2 3 4 5   Above most standards
2. Comparison to person's managerial peers:
    Worse manager than peers   1 2 3 4 5   Better managers than peers
3. Performance as a role model:
    Poor role model   1 2 3 4 5   Excellent role model
4. Overall managerial success:
    A managerial failure   1 2 3 4 5   A managerial success
5. Overall effectiveness as a manager:
    Ineffective manager   1 2 3 4 5   Effective manager

Leader Development

To the extent that behavioral complexity is necessary for successful executive leadership, leader development, then, involves expanding a rising leader's capacity to enact and integrate a wider range of competing leadership roles. Hooijberg and Quinn (1992) provided a conceptual framework for leader development based on this premise. They also offered an example of such an intervention.

The basic premise of their approach to leader development (Hooijberg & Quinn, 1992) is that greater behavioral complexity emerges when leaders break from habitual behavioral patterns at work and begin to learn and enact new role behaviors. As leaders become more skilled in new roles, they expand their behavioral repertoires and, correspondingly, their capacity to integrate the new roles with prior learned responses. The critical dynamic for successful executive leader development in this framework becomes environmental influences and events that will trigger the leader's initiative to break from comfortable routines and learn new role behaviors. Hall (1987) suggested that triggering events can result from (a) changes in the organizational or societal environment; (b) a leader's mentors and role models who themselves either demonstrate behavioral complexity or provide the opportunity for leaders to explore new role requirements; and (c) personal changes that motivate the leader to make changes in his or her work routines. Hooijberg and Quinn (1992) also argued that leader development interventions designed to enhance behavioral complexity are more effective when participants voluntarily seek to change their habitual routines. When such changes are forced on leaders, they may react by resisting; they also are not likely to be motivated to explore new role options.

To develop behavioral complexity, then, junior leaders need to be encouraged to break from routine role behaviors and provided the opportunity to learn and practice new leader role patterns. Hooijberg and Quinn (1992) described an example of a leader development intervention that uses this approach to enhance behavioral complexity (i.e., Project LEAD). This program provides a discourse on different managerial roles required for effective organizational leadership. It then challenges leaders to examine and change their habitual work roles. It promotes leaders' reflection on their work practices with the goal of understanding the need for role expansion. Participants then develop follow-up action plans to be implemented at their worksite and reviewed in subsequent (i.e., 6 to 8 months later) training sessions.

This program avoids the training of specific behavior patterns in favor of a cognitive reframing approach that encourages the emergence of skills and abilities supporting different roles. Several theorists have questioned the effectiveness of specific behavior training when the performance domain is likely to be substantially different from the training domain (P. L. Ackerman, 1986, 1987; Fleishman & Mumford, 1989a, 1989b). Such is the case for leadership (Mumford, Zaccaro, Harding, Fleishman, & Reiter-Palmon, 1993). The approach described by Hooijberg and Quinn (1992) appears promising in that it focuses on expanding the array of managerial roles that the leader can effectively enact. That is, the program is grounded in developing through experience and reflection the more elaborate social knowledge representations associated with the display of more complex social behavior in organizations.

Summary

How well do theories of executive behavioral complexity reflect Day and Lord's (1988) suggestions for a systematic theory of executive leadership? Regarding the nature of executive leader performance requirements, the answer is that they provide some but not all of the components suggested for such a theory. The central mechanism through which executive leaders influence organizational performance is their display and balancing of different requisite organizational roles. This behavioral complexity provides an effective response to the social complexity that is inherent in executive leader work. Accordingly, leader effectiveness becomes operationalized by how well leaders can accommodate different organizational constituencies that demand different role constellations from them (see Tsui, 1984b). Furthermore, these theories are grounded in either (or both) role theory or organization theory. For example, Quinn (1984, 1988) developed his theory from an integration of four organizational effectiveness theories—human relations, open systems, internal process, and rational goal. Each of these theories corresponds to one of the four quadrants of Quinn's Competing Values Model. Tsui (1984a, 1984b) developed her framework from the central premises of role theory and the notion of role conflict (e.g., Katz & Kahn, 1978; Merton, 1957). Thus, these approaches reflect the theoretical base suggested by Day and Lord.

Where these theories fall a bit short, at least in comparison with SST (described in chapters 2 and 3), is that they do not articulate clearly and precisely the differences in performance requirements between upper- and lower-level organizational leaders and where in the organizational hierarchy the shifts in these requirements occur. Some inferences can perhaps be derived from each theory. Some empirical studies based on these theories and hypothesized hierarchical differences in role behavior have been completed (e.g., Pavett & Lau, 1982; Quinn, 1988). However, these theories do not offer systematic differences. This becomes problematic in terms of deriving leader competencies that change as one ascends organizational levels. It also inhibits the development of multilevel leader development programs.

Also, unlike SST, the behavioral complexity theories do not clearly delineate the capacities and skills that contribute to the effective display of diverse executive leader roles. Mintzberg (1975) and Quinn (1984) described characteristics that contribute to individual roles, but they did not indicate qualities that facilitate the integration of these roles, particularly those that are proposed as competing. Hooijberg and Quinn (1992) argued that cognitive complexity is one element of behavioral complexity. However, they did not fully articulate the rationale for this connection, except that this conceptual skill helps leaders understand (and presumably integrate) all of their roles. Zaccaro, Gilbert, et al. (1991) provided a rationale by arguing that behavioral flexibility, a integral element of behavioral complexity, is grounded in elaborate social knowledge structures such as event schemas and behavioral scripts. Cognitive complexity would presumably contribute to the effective development of these knowledge structures. Thus, there is a conceptual basis for delineating individual characteristics associated with executive leader behavioral complexity. However, this basis needs to be articulated more systematically in terms of characteristics that distinguish upper- and lower-level managers and successful from unsuccessful executive leaders.

Although both SST and Integrative Complexity Theory provide measurement tools for the assessment of complex cognitive skills, the behavioral complexity theories do not offer tools with which to assess complex social skills. This inhibits direct empirical testing of their major postulates. However, Hooijberg and Quinn (1992) provided a method of scoring data from ratings of managerial behavior to produce an index of role balance. This index, and other similar approaches, can provide a basis for assessing the antecedents and consequences of behavioral complexity.

A final element of a well-rounded executive leadership theory is the specification of principles to guide the development of potential senior executive leaders. Hooijberg and Quinn (1992) and Quinn, Faerman, Thompson, and McGrath (1990) provided such a framework for the development of behavioral complexity. This approach shares with SST the notion that increased job challenges will induce a break from habitual ways of thinking and behaving to produce more complex patterns that are more suited for executive leader work. Unlike the fundamental executive leader characteristic proposed by conceptual complexity theories (i.e., conceptual capacity), the skills proposed as the basis for executive leader behavioral complexity may be altered by specific targeted developmental interventions.

In summary, the behavioral complexity theories provide a conceptual framework that complements quite well the theories described in chapter 2. Several researchers have argued that the competencies, skills, and behaviors described in both frameworks are necessary for effective executive leadership (Boal & Whitehead, 1992; Hooijberg & Quinn, 1992; House, 1992; Sashkin, 1992). Cognitive capacities provide the rationale for organized executive leader action, whereas behavioral or social capacities provide the means of implementing planned actions in complex social domains. Thus, understanding executive leadership and facilitating its development most likely requires an integration of the conceptual complexity and behavioral complexity approaches.

Behavioral Complexity Theories of Executive Leadership: Empirical Review and Evaluation

5

C hapter 4 reviewed and evaluated several behavioral complexity theories of executive leadership. This chapter examines empirical research that offers data supporting these theories. However, the research base regarding behavioral complexity theories is much more limited than that reviewed in chapter 3 for the conceptual complexity theories of executive leadership. Part of this relative paucity of research is attributable to the fact that the theoretical development of behavioral complexity theories has lagged significantly behind the development of stratified systems theory (SST). For example, the specification of executive leader characteristics in behavioral complexity theories is not as elaborate as it is in other approaches, nor has the measurement of behavioral complexity or its development progressed much beyond the work of Quinn and his colleagues (Quinn, 1984, 1988; Hooijberg & Quinn, 1992). Thus, the empirical research base for this conceptual framework is smaller than for other executive leadership perspectives.

However, a number of studies have provided data regarding the socially complex nature of executive leader work and the corresponding requirement for managerial behavioral complexity. Furthermore, several studies of lower- and middle-level managers regarding some individual characteristics that may be associated with greater displays of behavioral complexity have been completed. These studies provide some insight into the validity of this conceptual framework and may serve as a basis for future research with executive-level leaders.

Research Model

Figure 5-1 presents a research model for behavioral complexity theories that is similar to the one used to illustrate the conceptual complexity

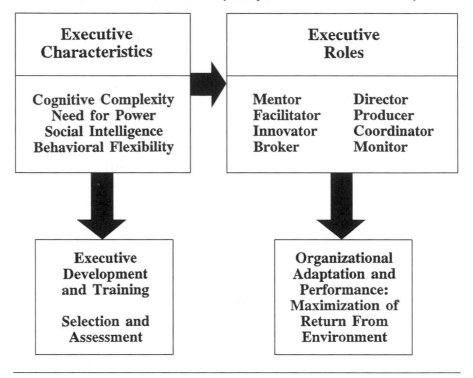

FIGURE 5-1

Research Model of Behavioral Complexity and Executive Leadership

theories (see Figure 3-1). This model includes the executive leader characteristics and roles that, according to behavioral complexity, should contribute to organizational effectiveness. The research reviewed in this chapter is considered in terms of (a) the proposed contents represented in each box (e.g., Do the executive leader roles described by behavioral complexity theories accurately reflect executive-level functioning?) and (b) the relationships suggested among the elements of the model (e.g., Is the accomplishment of multiple executive leader roles significantly associated with organizational gain?).

According to behavioral complexity theories, because of greater social demands and complexity at upper organizational levels, executive leaders are required to enact multiple roles to facilitate organizational adaptation and performance. The roles indicated in Figure 5-1 (i.e., mentor, facilitator, innovator, broker, director, producer, coordinator, and monitor) are those proposed by Quinn (1984, 1988; Hooijberg & Quinn, 1992); they are fairly compatible with the managerial roles identified by Mintzberg (1973, 1975; see Hart & Quinn, 1993, for a comparison). Likewise, in line with Tsui's (1984a, 1984b) multiple constituency framework, these roles reflect the needs and demands of the multiple constituencies that executive leaders must balance in accomplishing their work. Executive leaders add value to the organization when they are able to enact each and all of these roles successfully; that is, organizational effectiveness is determined by the ability of top executive leaders to display behavioral complexity.

As described in chapter 4, the display of behavioral complexity is facilitated in part by four executive characteristics: (a) cognitive complexity (Hooijberg & Quinn, 1992); (b) need for power (Tsui, 1984a); (c) social intelligence (Zaccaro, Gilbert, Thor, & Mumford, 1991); and, in particular, (d) behavioral flexibility (a subcomponent of social intelligence; Zaccaro et al., 1991). Behavioral complexity research needs to link these characteristics to the display of multiple executive leader roles and organizational performance and adaptation. Furthermore, measurement tools need to be validated regarding the extent to which they assess behavioral complexity or corresponding executive leader characteristics. Likewise, leader development efforts should be evaluated according to their efficacy in fostering behavioral complexity.

The research questions that are the focus of this chapter are derived from the model in Figure 5-1. These questions center on the following recurrent themes: (a) nature of executive leader roles, (b) requisite executive leader characteristics, (c) measurement of behavioral complexity, and (d) leader development and assessment.

Nature of Executive Leader Roles

Behavioral complexity theories propose that executive leaders face greater and more complex social demands than lower-level managers. These demands result from (a) requirements that executive leaders manage, integrate, and coordinate the activities of multiple rather than single organizational units; (b) the necessity of executive leaders to rely on more indirect forms of social influence and persuasion to foster organizational change; and (c) the responsibility of top executive leaders to represent the organization to a variety of outside stakeholders, each with different expectations of the organization (i.e., engage in boundary management with diverse environmental constituencies). These different demands create diversity in executive leader role requirements and a greater need for behavioral complexity.

These notions lead to the following propositions:

1. Executive leaders enact a greater variety of behavioral roles than lower-level leaders. These roles reflect differing work orientations (e.g., innovation vs. stability; production vs. personnel development; external broker vs. internal manager).
2. The successful accomplishment of multiple executive leader roles will be positively associated with organizational effectiveness.

EXECUTIVE LEADER ROLES

Two aspects of executive leader role accomplishment are the number of different roles the executive enacts and the frequency of role shifting that occurs during executive work. Each aspect is considered.

Breadth of Executive Leader Roles

The question of what behavioral roles are required for the successful completion of executive leader work has been considered by several researchers using a variety of methods: (a) analyses of subject matter experts (e.g., Luthans & Lockwood, 1984), (b) factor analyses of job description surveys (e.g., Baehr, 1992; Morse & Wagner, 1978; Tornow & Pinto, 1976; Tsui, 1984), and (c) analyses of managerial importance and time-spent ratings of job activities (Kraut, Pedigo, McKenna, & Dunnette, 1989; Mahoney, Jerdee, & Carroll, 1965; Page & Tornow, 1987). A sample of these studies and their findings are described in Table 5-1.[1]

The results of these studies indicate that there are a wide variety of executive roles, as suggested by the behavioral complexity theories. Most of the classifications contain role activities that are congruent with several, if not all, of Mintzberg's (1973, 1975) managerial roles. Furthermore, most of these classifications contain roles and activities that can be placed in each of the four competing sets of values identified by Quinn and his colleagues (1988; Hart & Quinn, 1993). A consistent theme, for example, is the requirement that executive leaders act as external representatives of the organization as well as internal organi-

---

[1] Note that several of these studies were discussed in chapter 3 regarding propositions derived from conceptual complexity theories of executive leadership. Specifically, the premise that executive leaders engage in more long-term planning and boundary management than lower-level leaders was examined. The focus of this chapter is not only on these behavioral roles, but also on others specified by behavioral complexity theories. That is, in addition to planner and boundary manager, executive leaders are expected to enact a greater number of roles than lower-level leaders. The data from these studies therefore are useful in addressing the broader issue of expected executive leader role enactment.

TABLE 5-1

Sample of Empirically Derived Leader Role and Activity Clusters

Study	Role/activity cluster
Baehr (1992)	Setting organizational objectives
	Planning and reviewing finances
	Improving work procedures and practices
	Coordinating interdepartmental activities
	Developing and implementing technical ideas
	Providing judgment and decision making
	Developing group cooperation and teamwork
	Coping with difficulties and emergencies
	Promoting safety attitudes and practices
	Communicating
	Developing employee potential
	Supervising
	Pursuing self-development and improvement
	Implementing personnel practices
	Promoting community–organization relations
	Handling outside contacts
Hales (1986)	Acting as figurehead and unit leader
	Acting as liaison
	Monitoring, filtering, and disseminating information
	Allocating resources
	Handling disturbances
	Negotiating
	Innovating
	Planning
	Controlling and directing subordinates
Hemphill (1959)	Staff service provision
	Work supervision
	Internal business control
	Technical products and markets
	Human, community, and social affairs
	Long-range planning
	Exercise of broad power and authority
	Business reputation management
	Personal demands
	Asset preservation
Javidan & Dastmalchian (1993)	Mobilizer
	Ambassador
	Driver
	Auditor
	Servant
Kraut, Pedigo, McKenna, & Dunnette (1989)	Managing individual performance
	Instructing subordinates
	Planning and allocating resources
	Coordinating interdependent groups
	Managing group performance
	Monitoring business environment
	Representing staff

(continued)

TABLE 5-1 continued

Sample of Empirically Derived Leader Role and Activity Clusters

Study	Role/activity cluster
Lau, Newman, & Broedling (1980)	Leadership and supervision
	Information gathering and dissemination
	Technical problem solving and executive decision making
	Resource allocation
Luthans & Lockwood (1984)	Planning and coordination
	Staffing
	Training and development
	Decision making and problem solving
	Paperwork processing
	Exchange of routine information
	Monitoring and control of performance
	Motivation and reinforcement
	Discipline and punishment
	Interaction with outsiders
	Conflict management
	Socialization and politicking
Mahoney, Jerdee, & Carroll (1965)	Supervisor
	Planner
	Generalist
	Investigator
	Coordinator
	Negotiator
	Evaluator
	Multispecialist
McCall & Segrist (1980)	Leader
	Liaison
	Entrepreneur
	Environmental monitor
	Resource allocator
	Spokesperson
Morse & Wagner (1978)	Motivation and conflict management
	Development
	Organization and coordination
	Strategic problem solving
	Information management
	Environment and resource management
Page & Tornow (1987)	Planning and controlling
	Strategic decision making
	Business indicator monitoring
	Supervising
	Coordinating
	Sales and marketing
	Public relations
	Consulting
	Administration
	Labor relations

(continued)

TABLE 5-1 continued

Sample of Empirically Derived Leader Role and Activity Clusters

Study	Role/activity cluster
Stogdill, Shartle, Wherry, & Jaynes (1955)	High-level policy making
	Administrative coordination
	Methods planning
	Interest representation
	Personnel services
	Professional consultation
	Maintenance services
	Inspection
Tornow & Pinto (1976)	Long-range planning
	Organizational unit coordination
	Internal control
	Product responsibility and service
	Public relations
	Technical consulting
	Strategic decision making
	Financial decision making
	Fact gathering
	Supervising
	Complexity and stress management
	Financial monitoring
	Personnel management
Tsui (1984b)	Leader
	Spokesperson
	Resource allocator
	Entrepreneur
	Environmental monitor
	Liaison
Yukl (1989)	Networking
	Supporting
	Managing conflict and building team
	Motivating
	Recognizing and rewarding
	Planning and organizing
	Solving problems
	Consulting and delegating
	Monitoring environment and operations
	Disseminating information
	Clarifying roles and objectives

zational coordinators. Likewise, more recent classifications include roles related to personnel development and mentoring as well as structuring work to meet production schedules (e.g., Baehr, 1992; Luthans & Lockwood, 1984; Tsui, 1984b; Yukl, 1989). This suggests empirical support for the premise that the nature of executive leadership includes a range of competing work requirements.

A 1994 study by Gibb provided data indicating that the frequency of Mintzberg's (1973, 1975) roles displayed by managers varied according to environmental conditions. Gibb examined Mintzberg's interpersonal, informational, and decisional roles in the context of high or low environmental complexity (i.e., number of units requiring executive leader interaction and degree of sophisticated knowledge required regarding environmental elements) and high or low environmental dynamism (i.e., rate of change in the environment). He found that managers across multiple organizational levels displayed a higher frequency of all three sets of roles under conditions of high environmental complexity as well as a higher frequency of decisional roles under conditions of environmental dynamism. These data suggest that environmental characteristics determine the necessity for executive leaders to display all of Mintzberg's managerial roles to facilitate organizational adaptation and success. Merz and Sauber (1995) also provided data illustrating the importance of environmental conditions in delimiting or enhancing the necessity of particular managerial roles.

Executive Leader Role Shifting

Behavioral complexity theories indicate that executive leader work is characterized by frequent role shifting and a constant pace of activity that requires balancing multiple work requirements. Interviews with top executive leaders and time-allocation analyses of their workdays have supported this premise. Kotter (1982a, 1982b) reported from his interviews with and observations of 15 general managers that they spent a significant proportion of their time interacting with others, addressed a wide range of topics, and often behaved in reactive rather than proactive ways. Mintzberg's (1975) observations of five executives led to his conclusion that "half of the activities engaged in by the five chief executives . . . lasted less than nine minutes and only 10% exceeded one hour" (p. 50). A similar study by Kurke and Aldrich (1983) found that almost two thirds of the activities completed by four top executive leaders lasted fewer than 9 min. Regarding balancing different organizational orientations, Jonas, Fry, and Srivastva (1990) noted from interviews with 24 chief executive leaders their efforts to maintain both stability and innovation within their organizations:

> Part of the role of the CEO [chief executive officer] is to simultaneously embody the status quo and to question it. As custodian of the firm's history he or she strives to define the strengths of the enterprise by acting as a force for stability and an expression of its culture. Equally concerned with the future, he or

she regularly asks the frame-breaking question, challenges organizational norms, and plays the maverick to stimulate creativity and innovation. (p. 40)

Time-allocation analyses of executive leader managerial activities have revealed similar patterns of multiple-role accomplishment and role shifting under time-intensive circumstances. Haas, Porat, and Vaughan (1969) found that the time allocated to seven activities performed by executive leaders (planning, negotiating, investigating, coordinating, supervising, evaluating, and other) was fairly comparable, ranging from about 10.5% (investigating) to about 24% (negotiating). Time allocated to activities in the "other" category was 3.28%. Carroll and Gillen (1987), summarizing the earlier work of Mahoney, Jerdee, and Carroll (1965), reported a wider range of time allocations, 2% to 26%, across eight activities (planning, representing, investigating, negotiating, coordinating, evaluating, supervising, and staffing). However, these data were aggregated across multiple organizational levels. In an early time-allocation study of Swedish executive leaders, Carlson (1951) found that they divided their time about equally between activities outside and within the organization. Other time-allocation studies by Stogdill and Shartle, Wherry, and Jaynes (1955) and R. Stewart (1967) illustrated similar patterns of diverse activities and contacts. After reviewing these and other studies, Hales (1986) reached the following conclusion:

A picture of managerial work as technical, tactical, reactive, and frenetic recurs across studies of time budgeting. Carlson (1951), Copeman, Luijk, and Hanika (1963), Horne and Lupton (1965), and Mintzberg (1973) all indicate that even senior managers spend little time on planning or abstract formulation, are subject to constant interruptions, hold short face-to-face meetings that flit from topic to topic and respond to the initiatives of others far more than they initiate themselves.

Differences Between Executive- and Lower-Level Leaders

An important question remains regarding whether the range and frequency of role requirements and managerial activities change as a function of organizational level. This question directly addresses the differences in work requirements between junior and senior leaders that Day and Lord (1988) suggested should be articulated by effective theories of executive leadership. Several studies have examined the differential frequency of the work roles identified by Mintzberg (1973, 1975; or those shown in Table 5-1) across organizational levels. Mahoney et al. (1965) found that leaders at all levels spent some time doing all of the activities in their classification; however, planning and generalist activities were more prevalent at higher organizational levels, whereas direct subordinate supervision was more characteristic of junior leaders. Page and Tornow (1987) found more activity associated with planning, strategic decision making, public relations, and environmental monitoring among executive leaders than lower level managers and supervisors. Supervisors were higher than executive leaders on supervising subordinates and administration. Similar findings were reported by Kraut et al. (1989), who reported that monitoring of the business environment and coordination of multiple groups increased at higher organizational levels but the frequency of activities related to subordinate instruction and management of individual performance declined.

Studies by Alexander (1979), Paolillo (1981), and Pavett and Lau (1982) focused particularly on the roles specified by Mintzberg (1973, 1975) and determined their frequency across different organizational levels. Alexander (1979) reported that two interpersonal roles (figurehead and liaison), three informational roles (monitor, disseminator, and spokesperson), and one decisional role (entrepreneur) were more frequently required at higher organizational levels. Paolillo (1981) found that 7 of the 10 roles (figurehead, monitor, disseminator, spokesperson, entrepreneur, resource allocator, and negotiator) were more important for top organizational leaders than for their lower-level counterparts. Pavett and Lau (1982) also found that most of Mintzberg's roles (figurehead, liaison, monitor, disseminator, spokesperson, resource allocator, and negotiator) increased in importance as managers ascended the organizational hierarchy. Although some differences are apparent among the three studies in the strengths of particular differences across levels, all three agree that the roles of leader, disturbance handler, and technical expert did not become more important at higher levels. In fact, Pavett and Lau demonstrated that the interpersonal role of leader was significantly more important at lower organizational levels.

Baehr (1992) provided further evidence for the hierarchical differentiation of leader role requirements. He completed a cluster analysis of 16 job functions on 1358 leaders at different levels in industry, banking, and health care organizations. The cluster analysis identified 11 clusters, with the first 3 reflecting the job functions of executive leaders, middle managers, and line supervisors. The top five activities in the executive leader cluster were (a) setting organizational objectives, (b) communicating, (c) promoting community-organization relations, (d) coordinating interdepartmental activities, and (e) handling outside contacts. Middle manager activities were characterized by (a) communicating, (b) coordinating interdepartmental activities, (c) improving work practices, (d) developing teamwork, and (e) providing judgment and decision making. The major job functions of line supervisors were (a) developing teamwork, (b) supervising, (c) coping with emergencies, (d) developing employee potential, and (e) managing personnel. Thus, executive leaders were more oriented toward planning and boundary-spanning activities than lower level managers, whereas the latter were more concerned with intraorganizational coordination and personnel supervision functions.

Summary

The data from these studies suggest three conclusions about the role requirements of organizational leaders. First, a range of behaviors reflecting boundary management, planning, coordinating, monitoring, supervising, and personnel development characterize organizational leadership work. Second, senior leaders are more likely to engage in a greater variety of these behaviors than junior leaders. They are especially more likely to engage in planning and boundary-spanning activities than junior leaders. Third, the pattern of roles required at higher organizational levels includes incongruent or conflicting behaviors. For example, the personnel development requirements reported by several of the classifications in Table 5-1 can conflict with the need for immediate action and direction. Likewise, interactions with external constituencies from a dynamic organizational environment can prompt leader behaviors that are incompatible with the internal coordination and maintenance behaviors required when working with subordinate organizational units. Thus, as suggested by Quinn (1984, 1988), balancing competing leader roles, or behavioral complexity, becomes more important at higher organizational levels.

BEHAVIORAL COMPLEXITY AND EXECUTIVE LEADER PERFORMANCE

The diversity of required executive leader roles leads to the question of whether leaders who display behavioral complexity, either by enacting a range of integrated leadership roles (as suggested by Mintzberg, 1973, 1975) or by balancing competing roles (as suggested by Tsui, 1984a, 1984b; and Quinn, 1984, 1988; Hart & Quinn, 1993), are more effective than those leaders who do not display high behavioral complexity. Morse and Wagner (1978) examined this question by comparing managers of high-performing organizational units (defined through objective product data such as profit margins) with managers of low-performing organizational units on the following job functions: (a) motivation and conflict management; (b) development; (c) organization and coordination; (d) strategic problem solving; (e) information handling; and (f) environment and resource management. High-performing units had managers who displayed significantly higher response frequencies on each of these functions than managers of low-performing units. Studies by McCall and Segrist (1980) and Pavett and Lau (1982) demonstrated significant associations between the enactment of Mintzberg's (1973, 1975) managerial roles and promotion rate and rated performance, respectively. In line with studies demonstrating the relative unimportance assigned to the interpersonal leader role for executive leaders, both studies showed that high-performing managers indicated lower responses on this role than low-performing managers.

Tsui (1984b) classified 153 managers according to their reputational effectiveness as perceived by different organizational constituencies (i.e., superiors, peers, and subordinates). Managers having high reputational effectiveness met the expectations of all three sets of constituents. Managers with low reputational effectiveness failed to satisfy any of their constituent groups, whereas partially reputationally effective managers met the expectations of a subset of constituents. High reputationally effective managers can be considered as being higher in behavioral complexity because they successfully balance potentially conflicting expectations from different organizational groups. Likewise, those with partial or no reputational effectiveness can be considered as lower in behavioral complexity because they are responsive to no organizational constituencies or to only one. Analyses of variance (ANOVAs) on four criteria of managerial performance indicated significant differences between high reputationally effective managers and both groups of less effective managers on performance appraisal ratings, intracompany promotion rates, and career advancement rates. Also, highly effective managers differed from those with no reputational effectiveness on merit increases. Thus, these findings suggest that behavioral complexity, operationalized as rated effectiveness by multiple groups with differing perspectives, was significantly associated with individual managerial performance.

Quinn and his associates have completed several studies examining behavioral complexity and both individual performance and organizational effectiveness. For example, Hooijberg and Quinn (1992) described an unpublished study by Denison, Hooijberg, and Quinn (1995) in which subordinates rated their supervisors on the eight leader roles of the competing values framework. Superiors provided ratings of each leader's effectiveness. Behavioral complexity was defined by the degree to which the profiles of each leader resembled the eight competing leader roles. Denison et al. reported from their results that effective leaders were rated as more behaviorally complex than less effective leaders.

Hooijberg and Quinn (1992) operationalized behavioral complexity using the following formula (Bobko & Schwartz, 1984) to create an index of integrative balance among contrasting leader roles:

$$\text{Integration} = [(k - 1) - (|X - Y|)] * [(X + Y)/2],$$

where

k = range of integral response scale (1 = *manager never performs role;* 7
    = *manager almost always performs role*);
X = scores on one role (e.g., mentor role); and
Y = scores on competing role (e.g., director role).

High scores on this index indicate leaders who display high but relatively equal levels of competing roles, whereas lower scores indicate
leaders who frequently enact one of the roles but not others. Integration
scores are computed for the four dimensions of contrasting roles in the
competing values framework (i.e., mentor vs. director, facilitator vs. producer, monitor vs. broker, and coordinator vs. innovator). Quinn,
Spritzer, and Hart (1991) applied this operationalization and reported
that behaviorally complex managers were rated as more effective by
their subordinates, peers, and superiors than those who scored lower in
behavioral complexity. Note that these results parallel those on reputational effectiveness across different constituencies reported by Tsui
(1984b) using a different operationalization of behavioral complexity.

Hart and Quinn (1993) examined the association between behavioral complexity and organizational outcomes such as financial performance (cash flow, profitability); business performance (sales growth,
product development, market share); and stakeholder performance
(product quality, employee satisfaction, overall performance). They con-
densed the eight competing leader roles into four categories reflecting
each of the four quadrants of their model (see Figure 4-2). *Motivators*
were characterized by flexibility and an internal focus; *analyzers* by predictability and an internal focus; *vision setters* by flexibility and an external focus; and *task masters* by predictability and an external focus. Hart
and Quinn hypothesized that the simultaneous use of all four roles by
CEOs would be associated with all three organizational performance
indices. They tested this hypothesis by using a cluster analysis to create
three groups: *high complexity* (high scores on all leader roles), *unbalanced*
(high scores on analyzer and task master roles, but low scores on competing roles), and *low complexity* (low scores on all four roles). ANOVAs
showed that organizations with leaders high on behavioral complexity
were indeed significantly stronger on all three performance criteria than
organizations with leaders who were either low in behavioral complexity or displayed an unbalanced or mixed role profile.

Hooijberg (1996) investigated the association between two dimensions of behavioral complexity—behavioral repertoire and behavioral
differentiation—and leader effectiveness, assessed through ratings from
a leader's subordinates, peers, and supervisors. Behavioral repertoire
was measured by ratings from the leader's subordinates, peers, and supervisors of how often he or she displayed a number of leadership func-

tions. Behavioral differentiation was assessed through the variance in behavioral ratings across subordinates, peers, and supervisors. Data were collected for 282 middle managers from an automotive company and 252 managers from a public utility company. Hooijberg found in both samples that the extent of a leader's behavioral repertoire was positively associated with effectiveness ratings from the leader's role set. However, the results for behavioral differentiation ratings were mixed. They were positively associated only with the effectiveness ratings by supervisors and only in the automotive sample. In fact, behavioral differentiation was negatively associated with subordinate ratings of effectiveness. Hooijberg suggested that whereas supervisors may interpret response variation by their subordinate managers as consistent with the demands of the situation, a behaviorally differentiated manager's subordinates may interpret the same variation as inconsistency in behavior and therefore perceive the manager negatively.

The results of these studies demonstrate significant support for the premise that senior leaders who display behavioral complexity are more successful than those who do not. The studies by McCall and Segrist (1980), Pavett and Lau (1982), and Hooijberg (1996) demonstrated a relationship between a leader's display of multiple leadership roles and his or her individual performance. Tsui (1984b), Denison et al. (1995), and Quinn et al. (1991) assessed behavioral complexity more directly by operationalizing it as a balancing of competing expectations and leader roles. They also found significant associations with leader effectiveness. The results of Morse and Wagner (1976) and Hart and Quinn (1993) are particularly important because they associated leader display of multiple roles and the integration of competing roles, respectively, with organizational outcomes. Senior leaders are more responsible for organizationwide effectiveness than lower-level leaders (Day & Lord, 1988). Accordingly, a critical criterion for senior leadership is the success of the organization as a whole. These two studies provide a particularly appropriate demonstration of the importance of individual senior leader behavioral skills.

EVALUATION

Studies using diverse methods have demonstrated that executive leaders are required to enact a greater variety of roles than their lower-level counterparts. These roles reflect the classifications offered by both Mintzberg (1973, 1975) and Quinn (1984, 1988; Hooijberg & Quinn, 1992). That is, executive leaders are required to be external representatives of the organization as well as internal operational managers. They also need to maintain organizational stability while creating conditions for organization innovation and change. To the degree that these arc to be viewed as contrasting roles, as suggested by Quinn (1984) and Hooijberg and Quinn (1992), then the results from these studies indicate that executive leaders are required to display more behavioral complexity than lower-level leaders.

The studies reviewed suggest that the display of behavioral complexity is associated with personal and organizational effectiveness. These studies demonstrate that the enactment of multiple managerial roles specified by Mintzberg (1973, 1975) and other theorists as well as the balancing of seemingly conflicting executive roles leads to executive success. Thus, a significant link between executive leader behavioral complexity and organizational performance, as illustrated in Figure 5-1, has been established. However, an important question remains: What individual characteristics are linked to behavioral complexity and multiple executive leader role enactment?

Requisite Executive Characteristics

There are two approaches that can be taken to examine executive leader characteristics associated with the display of behavioral complexity. The first is to examine those qualities that facilitate the accomplishment of each executive leader role. Along these lines, Mintzberg (1975) and Quinn (1984, 1988; Hooijberg & Quinn, 1992) each offered a set of managerial traits and skills corresponding to their role clusters. However, as noted in chapter 4, this approach ignores the central dynamic of behavioral complexity theories—that is, that important executive leader qualities are those that facilitate the executive leader's ability to enact multiple roles and balance competing behavioral orientations. As shown in Figure 5-1, the behavioral complexity theories of executive leadership and related approaches suggest four such characteristics: (a) cognitive complexity, (b) need for power, (c) social intelligence, and (d) behavioral flexibility: Accordingly, the following propositions are offered regarding behavioral complexity and requisite executive leader qualities:

3. Executive leaders will possess stronger cognitive complexity, need for power, social intelligence, and behavioral flexibility than lower-level leaders. These qualities also will distinguish successful from unsuccessful executive leaders.
4. Cognitive complexity, need for power, social intelligence, and behavioral flexibility will be associated with greater behavioral complexity exhibited by organizational leaders.

Studies examining cognitive complexity and executive leader action were reviewed in chapter 3. However, there has been no research regarding whether cognitive complexity facilitates the display of executive leader flexibility. Streufert, Streufert, and Castore (1968) examined the relationship between cognitive complexity and the degree to which individuals displayed 12 of Stogdill's (1963) leader behavior characteristics in a negotiation simulation game. Although some individuals with low cognitive complexity displayed higher levels of some leader behaviors, "cognitively complex leaders (with the exception of 'tolerating freedom' and 'demanding reconciliation' scores) spread their leadership styles more evenly among the various leadership characteristics" (Streufert & Swezey, 1986, p. 175). This suggests that such individuals are more likely to enact different leadership approaches (i.e., demonstrate more behavioral variability). These data, however, were collected from an undergraduate student sample; additional research with executive leaders is necessary before the determining role of cognitive complexity in behavioral complexity can be ascertained.

The same conclusion can be made for power and dominance motives as characteristics enhancing executive leader behavioral complexity. Tsui (1984a) argued that high reputational effectiveness, which reflected an ability to respond effectively to multiple constituencies, was associated with high need for power and influence. Although several studies have demonstrated a link between power needs and leadership (Harrell & Stahl, 1981; House, Spangler, & Woycke, 1991; Ross & Offerman, 1991; Stahl, 1983), such needs have not been empirically linked to behavioral complexity. Thus, the determining role of power needs in the display of multiple executive leader roles remains speculative.

Zaccaro, Gilbert, et al. (1991) argued that the degree to which executive leaders were able to select appropriate situational responses depended in large part on their ability to perceive interpersonal and system contingencies and requirements within the organization. Findings from several early studies on social perceptiveness and leadership were decidedly mixed (Bell & Hall, 1954; Campbell, 1955; Chowdhry & Newcomb (1952), Gage & Exline, 1953; Hites & Campbell, 1950; Nagle, 1954; Trapp, 1955; Van Zelst, 1952). However, many of these studies did not examine organizational managers, much less executive leaders. Furthermore, significant measurement problems have plagued the assessment of social perceptiveness and social intelligence.

Zaccaro, Zazanis, Diana, and Gilbert (1994) found a significant association between social intelligence and leadership rankings in military training groups. Gilbert and Zaccaro (1995) examined social intelligence and career achievement in military officers ranging in rank from second lieutenant to colonel. They reported that both interpersonal and system perceptiveness were significantly associated with indices of military career success. System perceptiveness, but not interpersonal perception skills, contributed significantly to the prediction of rank and career achievement, even after accounting for officer intelligence and creative thinking skills. Similar data were reported by Howard and Bray (1988). They found that skills in the perception of social cues were significantly associated with attained managerial level 8 and 20 years into a manager's career. Although these data are suggestive, they do not establish a link between social intelligence and the display of behavioral complexity. Furthermore, the samples studied did not consist of organizational executive leaders.

Behavioral flexibility is perhaps the executive leader characteristic that is intuitively linked most closely with behavioral complexity. This attribute refers to "the ability and willingness to respond in significantly different ways to correspondingly different situational requirements" (Zaccaro, Gilbert, et al., 1991, p. 322). The focus is on responding equally well to very different situational demands. Evidence for a significant association between leadership and behavioral flexibility appears in three sets of studies. The first used a rotation design in laboratory studies to investigate cross-situational stability in leader emergence (Ferentinos, 1996; Kenny & Hallmark, 1991; Kenny & Zaccaro, 1983; Rueb & Foti, 1990; Zaccaro, Foti, & Kenny, 1991). In such studies, leadership requirements and group characteristics are varied; leader emergence in one situation is then correlated with leader emergence in other situations. The general result from the studies cited previously was that although cross-situational stability was exhibited in leader emergence, emergent leaders appeared to change their responses according to situational requirements.

A second set of studies supporting a link between behavioral flexibility and leadership focused on self-monitoring as a characteristic of emergent leaders. Snyder (1974, 1979) described self-monitoring as an individual difference variable including the ability to control one's behavior in response to social cues. Paulus and Martin (1988) identified self-monitoring as reflecting primarily behavioral flexibility. Research has shown that high self-monitors differ from low self-monitors on a number of behaviors linked to leadership, including adaptiveness to new situations (Snyder, 1979), initiation of social interactions (Ickes & Barnes, 1977), boundary management (Caldwell & O'Reilly, 1982), communication effectiveness, and persuasive ability (Sypher & Sypher, 1983). Several studies in both laboratory and field settings have reported significant associations between self-monitoring scores and leadership status (Dobbins, Long, Dedrick, & Clemons, 1990; Ellis, 1988; Ellis, Adamson, Deszca, & Cawsay, 1988; Foti & Cohen, 1986; Garland & Beard, 1979; Rueb & Foti, 1990). Furthermore, Zaccaro, Foti, et al. (1991) found a significant correlation between self-monitoring and leader emergence scores averaged across four different group situations. Together, these results support a link between behavioral flexibility as operationalized by self-monitoring and leadership.

Many of the earlier studies did not examine organizational executive leaders or even lower-level managers. However, a third set of studies investigated the link between behavioral flexibility and leader career achievement and advancement. Gilbert and Zaccaro (1995) found that behavioral flexibility was significantly correlated with military career success, even when controlling for officer intelligence and creative thinking skills. Howard and Bray (1988) reported that behavioral flexibility was significantly correlated with attained managerial level both 8 and 20 years into an individual's career. Ritchie (1994) examined 24 individual characteristics, including behavioral flexibility, as part of an assessment of senior management potential. In his sample of 115 managers, approximately one half had reached middle- to upper-level management 7 years after initial assessment. Ritchie found that behavioral flexibility was one of the top three correlates of attained level. Ritchie also completed a cluster analysis of managers and derived three clusters: (a) stars, (b) overachievers, and (b) plateaued. Thirty-eight percent of the stars, 16% of the overachievers, and none of the plateaued managers were promoted to upper-level management positions. Stars achieved higher ratings of behavioral flexibility than overachievers, who scored higher than those in the plateaued group. These studies provide support for an association between behavioral flexibility as a leader characteristic and managerial career advancement.

EVALUATION

Few studies have empirically examined executive leader characteristics that specifically promote behavioral complexity. Behavioral flexibility has been the focus of the bulk of this research and appears to be associated with executive leadership potential. This construct reflects a leader's ability to switch roles or vary his or her behavior according to situational requirements (Zaccaro, Gilbert, et al., 1991). Thus, its link with executive leadership is congruent with behavioral complexity theories. The research described suggests that upper-level leaders differ from lower-level leaders in terms of this skill. However, few, if any, studies have examined behavioral flexibility solely in executive-level leaders to determine if variance in this skill is associated with variance in executive leader performance. Such research is necessary before behavioral flexibility can be considered an important executive leader competency.

It also is necessary to associate proposed executive leader characteristics, including behavioral flexibility, with specific measures of displayed role diversity and behavioral complexity. Several of the studies described have demonstrated that such executive leader diversity is associated with personal and organizational effectiveness (Denison et al., 1995; Hart & Quinn, 1993; McCall & Segrist, 1980; Pavett & Lau, 1982; Tsui, 1984b). What is missing, however, is an empirical test of the premise that such individual characteristics as cognitive complexity, behavioral flexibility, need for power, and social perception skills influence organizational performance indirectly by facilitating an executive leader's ability to be behaviorally complex. This is important because other theories of executive leadership offer these same characteristics as important executive leader competencies but suggest that different processes mediate their influence on performance. For example, conceptual capacity theories argue that cognitive complexity is important because it allows executive leaders to construct more complex frames of reference and organizational causal maps (Jacobs & Jaques, 1987; Jacobs & Lewis, 1992). Likewise, theories of charismatic leadership argue that need for power is associated with effective inspirational leadership (House & Howell, 1992). It certainly is possible that multiple mediated linkages exist between these characteristics and executive leader and organizational effectiveness. Nonetheless, these linkages need to be identified and sorted through empirical investigation.

Leader Assessment and Development

ASSESSMENT OF BEHAVIORAL COMPLEXITY

There is a significant lack of empirical research investigating the measurement of executive leader behavioral complexity and its development in potential executive leaders. As noted in chapter 4, behavioral complexity has been assessed in two ways. The first and most common way is to have managers complete work behavior inventories that specify a number of leadership activities. Behavioral complexity is operationalized by high scores across all leadership dimensions. Quinn (1988) used this approach with an instrument that assessed each of the roles in the competing values framework. The second approach is the formula applied by Hooijberg and Quinn (1992) to assess the balance executive leaders achieve across different roles. Using this formula produces assessments of higher behavioral complexity for leaders who display moderate scores across all of the roles than for leaders who score high on some roles but low on others.

Both approaches are conceptually sound in terms of assessing behavioral complexity. However, there is little if any psychometric evidence regarding these approaches. Quinn (1988) referenced an unpublished study (Quinn, Faerman, & Dixit, 1987) that found evidence for the convergent and divergent validity of the competing values framework; however, no other details such as a description of the alternative measures used (i.e., a multimethod-multitrait approach) and the specific pattern of correlations across scales were provided. Quinn also summarized the results of a factor analysis of the competing values framework. As expected, eight factors, corresponding to each of the leadership roles, were identified by this analysis. Furthermore, Quinn reported strong interitem consistencies for each subscale. These findings suggest preliminary evidence for the psychometric soundness of Quinn's competing values framework.

In a related study, Denison et al. (1995) used confirmatory multidimensional scaling analyses to examine the validity of the competing values framework as operationalized in terms of the measure shown in Figure 4-3. They asked subordinates of middle-level executive leaders to rate their supervisors on how frequently they displayed the eight competing roles. Denison et al. found that the scales on their measure demonstrated sufficient levels of convergent and discriminant validity. They also reported support for the dimensions proposed by the competing values framework. However, their analysis did not support the proposed structure of the competing roles. Likewise, no evidence has been gathered to assess Hooijberg & Quinn's (1992) operationalization of behavioral complexity in terms of their integration formula.

LEADER DEVELOPMENT

Hooijberg and Quinn (1992) also described a leader development program based on their behavioral complexity theory. The purpose of this program, called Project LEAD, is to facilitate middle-level managers to examine and reflect on their habitual work roles, with the goal of expanding their role repertoires (see chapter 4). Quinn, Faerman, Thompson, & McGrath (1990) developed a textbook on becoming a master manager to be used in conjunction with this program. Hooijberg and Quinn described the implementation of this program at Ford Motor Company. Although they did not provide any specific data to assess the effectiveness of the program in terms of reaction, learning, behavior, or organizational results, they did collect some evaluation data. They summarized these data as follows:

> The data suggest that the core program deeply impacts the existing mind-sets or paradigms of the middle managers and that the middle managers redefine self and role in the organization.

The [program's] activities lead to new patterns of behavior. . . . The outcomes of the initiatives [required by the training program] are valued in about 95 percent of the cases, but in 5 percent of the cases people are punished for their efforts. These people become disillusioned with the process and with the program itself. Those who are reinforced continue to grow and increase in self-confidence. These people continue to empower self and others. Such empowerment leads to new experiences and perspectives and to further redefinition of self and role. (pp. 172–173)

SUMMARY

Preliminary research on both the assessment and development of behavioral complexity by Quinn and his colleagues has suggested some promising directions. However, additional studies are needed to determine the validity of the proposed assessment tools as well as Project LEAD. Furthermore, the developmental approach described by Quinn is an instruction-based program. Hooijberg and Quinn (1992) argued that growth in behavioral complexity comes not only from such training but also from a supportive work environment that induces and sustains new work role behaviors. Thus, from this perspective, work challenges and a supportive superior and environment appear to be necessary elements of leader development. These factors also need to be considered in evaluating Project LEAD or other development efforts derived from behavioral complexity theories of executive leadership.

Behavioral Complexity Theories: General Conclusions

This empirical review of research related to executive leader behavioral complexity has yielded the following conclusions:

- Executive-level leadership is characterized by a greater diversity of managerial roles than lower-level leadership. These roles reflect competing work orientations such as stability versus innovation, production versus personnel development, and internal versus external focus.
- The successful accomplishment of multiple and diverse roles by executive leaders is associated with indices of personal and organizational effectiveness.
- There is limited, if any, empirical evidence linking cognitive complexity, need for power, and social intelligence to an executive

leader's successful accomplishment of multiple and diverse organizational roles.

▪ Behavioral flexibility is associated with indices of managerial career advancement and attained organizational level.

▪ There is insufficient empirical evidence regarding the validity of (a) proposed measures of behavioral complexity and (b) development of corresponding skills in rising executive leaders.

These conclusions indicate that although the specification of executive leadership as involving the balancing and accomplishment of multiple roles is fairly well-substantiated, the empirical validation of executive leader characteristics, their measurement, and their development has lagged behind significantly. Thus, the full contributions of the behavioral complexity theories to understanding key dimensions of executive leadership remain speculative until additional empirical data regarding these questions can be gathered.

Although the propositions about multiple role accomplishment by effective executive leaders have been substantiated, a question remains regarding the executive leader as a reflective planner versus the executive leader as an active operator. A similar contrast exists between the proactive versus reactive executive leader. The research reviewed in chapter 3 supported the perspective that upper-level leaders engaged in more long-term planning than lower-level managers. However, the time-allocation studies reviewed in this chapter indicated little time devoted to such planning by most executive leaders. Instead, the pace of executive leader work is reported to be frenetic and relentless, fleeting from topic to topic and often reactive rather than proactive (Hales, 1986). A reconciliation between these two observations has yet to be offered by executive leadership theorists. One possibility is that the idea of executive leader as long-term planner is based on an erroneous assumption that such planning requires significant time expenditure during an executive leader's work-day. Instead, strategic images may develop over time in pieces that are then put together in flashes of insight. Also, this creative process may occur during an executive leader's down time after work hours (e.g., while exercising, relaxing). Alternatively, the idea of the executive leader as reactive operator also may be based on an erroneous assumption that executive leaders do not operate from a systematic and coherent cognitive framework that ties together and gives meaning to their multiple daily activities. Instead, it is possible that if these activities were viewed over a long time span, a strategic focus might clearly be evident. Given that there is empirical data supporting both perspectives of executive leaders as long-term strategic planners and as short-term reactive managers, theories of executive leadership need to integrate them into a single conceptual framework.

The behavioral complexity theories of leadership provide a useful complement to the conceptual complexity theories described in previous chapters. Indeed, several researchers have argued that both cognitive and social or behavioral skills are necessary precursors to successful executive leadership (Boal & Whitehead, 1992; Boyatzis, 1982; Mumford, Zaccaro, Harding, Fleishman, & Reiter-Palmon, 1993; Ritchie, 1994). Cognitive skills are used in the processes of making sense of organizational environments and establishing organizational directions. Behavioral skills are used in the implementation, within complex social domains, of strategies, goals, and tasks that are derived from leader sense making and direction setting. Accordingly, to fully understand executive leadership, both cognitive complexity and social and behavioral complexity need to be the bases for an integrated conceptual model.

The approaches to executive leadership described in this chapter and previous chapters emphasize the operating environments of top executive leaders and the individual characteristics needed for success in these settings. The conceptual approaches examined in the next four chapters (i.e., strategic decision making and visionary and inspirational leadership theories) describe the processes of executive leadership. That is, instead of focusing on what executive leadership is, and what personal qualities characterize successful executive leaders, these theories specify how such leaders accomplish their work. Key questions from these approaches include the following: (a) How do executive leaders derive a strategy from boundary-spanning activities? (b) How is strategy made operational? and (c) How do executive leaders empower subordinates so that they adopt the leader's vision as their own and work to achieve it? These and other questions are the focus of the next four chapters.

Strategic Decision-Making Models of Executive Leadership: Conceptual Review and Evaluation

6

Models of strategic decision making and management indicate that organizational effectiveness develops from an appropriate fit between the organization and its environment. Executive leaders create and manage this fit (Bourgeois, 1985; Lawrence & Lorsch, 1967; Thompson, 1967; Wortman, 1982), which Thompson (1967) labeled *co-alignment* and described it as a match between particular organizational elements and environmental factors. Organizations operate in environments that can be either turbulent or calm regarding rate and pace of change, either rich or scarce in human and material resources, and either highly structured or random in its demands and requirements of the organization (Emery & Trist, 1965; Katz & Kahn, 1978). Each environmental condition has significant implications for the organization in terms of the structure, climate, or policy that is likely to produce the best fit and therefore result in high performance. Bourgeois (1985) stated, for example, that "in essence, flexible, organic styles and structures befit turbulent, uncertain environments, and bureaucratic, mechanistic styles are appropriate for stable, predictable environments" (pp. 548–549).

Thompson (1967) noted, however, that different environmental elements might change at different rates, contributing significantly to the complexity and difficulty of creating co-alignment. For some environmental elements that are relatively static, for example, their corresponding organizational components may operate with a fairly stable structure, following a constant set of policies. However, other environmental forces that are highly turbulent will require organizational components (i.e., structures and policies) that can adapt constantly to maintain co-alignment. For example, the organization's personnel resource pool may be very rich and predictably stable over a relatively long time span. Organizational practices regarding personnel recruitment, acquisition, and training could therefore remain fairly constant yet keep the organization adaptive and effective. However, if the organization were operating within an environment with a high rate of technological change, then its personnel as well as production systems would need to adapt at correspondingly dynamic rates. Note that differential rates of environmental dynamics require differential adaptation and alignment across organizational components.

Organizational and Environmental Co-Alignment

Executive leaders are required to find, create, and maintain organization-environment co-alignment (Bourgeois, 1985). Thompson (1967) argued that, in accomplishing co-alignment, executive leaders are responsible for developing and maintaining operational conditions that promote stability and certainty in the short term and flexibility and adaptation in the longer term. He noted that managers at lower organizational levels require defined cause-and-effect relationships that allow predictability regarding their own managerial decisions (called *technical rationality*). The task of upper-level leaders is to provide the basis for this rationality. They do so by elucidating a vision or long-term strategy for organizational action. They also explain to lower-level managers the dynamics of the organization's operating environment that make certain broad strategic decisions necessary. Both communications provide causal frames of reference that enhance predictability. Alternatively, lower-level managers need to "provide the capacities and the slack (March & Simon, 1958) which allow the organization to make demands on its environment and to take advantage of opportunities afforded by that environment" (Thompson, 1967, p. 150). That is, organizational practices need to be structured by managers at multiple levels to provide resources that allow flexibility and adaptation to dynamic organizational and environmental conditions.

This model of executive leadership corresponds to theories discussed in earlier chapters. For example, the executive leader's provision of technical rationality to lower-level organizational subsystems corresponds to the notion from stratified systems theory (SST) of the development of a frame of reference that is used to organize and give meaning to collective action at each organizational level. Likewise, the responsibility of executive leaders to find, create, and maintain organization–environment co-alignment reflects the boundary management aspects of executive leader responsibilities specified by Katz and Kahn (1978) and included by Mintzberg (1973, 1975) and Quinn (1984, 1988) in their delineations of executive leader roles. A key difference between these theories and the strategic decision-making perspectives, however, is the emphasis by the latter on executive leadership processes. That is, strategic decision-making models describe how executive leaders make the strategic decisions that are intended to facilitate organization–environment co-alignment.

Accordingly, executive leader strategic decision making can be characterized as a three-step process involving (a) environmental scanning, (b) interpretation and sense making, and (c) strategic choice and organizational responding (Daft & Weick, 1984; Milliken, 1990; J. B. Thomas, Clark, & Gioia, 1993). *Scanning* is defined as "the managerial activity of learning about events and trends in the organization's environment" (Bluedorn, Johnson, Cartwright, & Barringer, 1994, pp. 213–214; Hambrick, 1981b). Scanning attention (i.e., what environmental sectors the executive leader chooses to scan) is dictated by organizational requirements. An important characteristic of both environmental scanning and the broader process of strategic decision making is comprehensiveness. Frederickson and Mitchell (1984) defined *comprehensiveness* as "the extent to which an organization attempts to be exhaustive or inclusive in making and integrating strategic decisions" (p. 402).

Interpretation is the process of making sense or imparting meaning to information received from environmental and organizational scanning (J. B. Thomas et al., 1993). The sense-making process is essentially one of assigning information to meaningful categories. Bluedorn et al. (1994) defined these categories as *strengths*, *weaknesses*, *opportunities*, and *threats*. Strengths and weaknesses emerge from scanning and analyzing organizational characteristics. Opportunities and threats are labels assigned to issues that are perceived as either positive and having high gain potential or negative and having high loss potential. Environmental events may also be perceived as either controllable or uncontrollable (Jackson & Dutton, 1988; J. B. Thomas et al., 1993, J. B. Thomas & McDaniel, 1990). These labels influence the third step of the strategic decision-making process, strategic choice and organizational responding (Dutton & Jackson, 1987; Meyer, 1982). Thus, for example, events labeled as threats may prompt defensive organizational reactions, whereas opportunities may lead to the adoption of more risky choices.

Also, research regarding the strategic decision-making approach has emphasized top management teams (TMTs). The perspective offered by SST generally suggests the chief executive officer (CEO) as the primary, and sometimes lone, agent in developing a strategic frame of reference. The reality, however, often is that strategic thinking and decision making are collective processes occurring within teams of executive leaders. This chapter and chapter 7 review the research on TMTs. However, the next section of this chapter describes some basic strategic decision-making processes and functions that are the province of top executive leaders.

STRATEGIC MANAGEMENT FUNCTIONS

Wortman (1982) identified five major strategic management functions of the executive leader. These functions, shown in Figure 6-1, include the following: (a) analyze problems and opportunities in the organization's operating environment; (b) formulate appropriate solutions and responses from this analysis; (c) implement those solutions and responses within the organization; (d) interpret policies and operations; and (e) evaluate the effectiveness of policies and operations given organizational conditions. This model contains a significant dynamic component in that organizational feedback informs and shapes subsequent executive leader decisions and actions (Lord & Maher, 1993). Pearce and Robinson (1995) articulated a similar set of management functions incorporating the dual components of strategy formulation and strategy implementation. They described the following processes as the crux of strategic management (pp. 3–4):

1. Formulate the organization's mission, including broad statements about its purpose, philosophy, and goals.
2. Develop an organizational profile that reflects its internal conditions and capabilities.
3. Assess the organization's external environment, including both competitive and general contextual factors.
4. Analyze the organization's options by matching its resources with the external environment.
5. Identify the most desirable options by evaluating each option in light of the organization's mission.
6. Select a set of long-term objectives and grand strategies that will achieve the most desirable options.
7. Develop annual objectives and short-term strategies that are compatible with the selected set of long-term objectives and grand strategies.
8. Implement the strategic choices by means of budgeted resource allocations in which the matching of tasks, people, structures, technologies, and reward systems is emphasized.
9. Evaluate the success of the strategic processes as input for future decision making.

Although the sets of strategic management functions described by Wortman (1982) and Pearce and Robinson (1995; as well as others see Byars, 1984) differ in terms of some particulars, they both emphasize cognitive and behavioral processes that are the basis of strategic decision making by executive leaders. Accordingly, the nature of executive leadership is described not in terms of requisite role or performance requirements (as in the conceptual complexity and behavioral complexity theories), but instead in terms of how such leadership is accomplished in

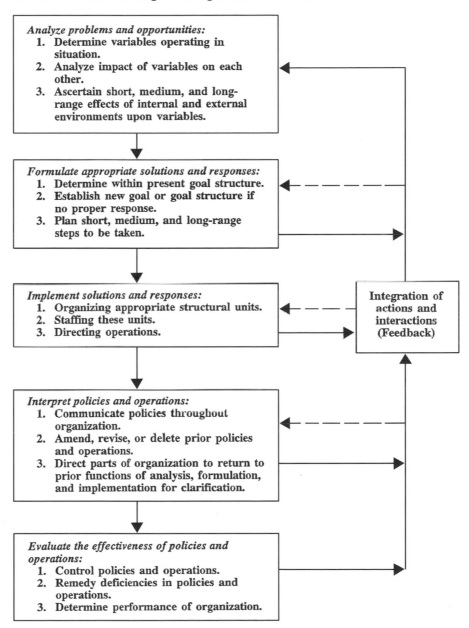

FIGURE 6-1

Executive Leader Strategic Management Functions

Analyze problems and opportunities:
1. Determine variables operating in situation.
2. Analyze impact of variables on each other.
3. Ascertain short, medium, and long-range effects of internal and external environments upon variables.

Formulate appropriate solutions and responses:
1. Determine within present goal structure.
2. Establish new goal or goal structure if no proper response.
3. Plan short, medium, and long-range steps to be taken.

Implement solutions and responses:
1. Organizing appropriate structural units.
2. Staffing these units.
3. Directing operations.

Integration of actions and interactions (Feedback)

Interpret policies and operations:
1. Communicate policies throughout organization.
2. Amend, revise, or delete prior policies and operations.
3. Direct parts of organization to return to prior functions of analysis, formulation, and implementation for clarification.

Evaluate the effectiveness of policies and operations:
1. Control policies and operations.
2. Remedy deficiencies in policies and operations.
3. Determine performance of organization.

From "Strategic Management and Changing Leader–Follower Roles," by M. S. Wortman, Jr., 1982, *Journal of Applied Behavioral Science, 18*, p. 374. Copyright 1982. Reprinted with permission of Sage Publications.

the context of aligning the organization with its environment. Furthermore, the specification of requisite executive leader characteristics is based on whether they facilitate the conduct of these processes. Thus, these models add important dimensions to the theories described in previous chapters.

These and other models of strategic decision making and management incorporate two key dimensions of leadership noted by Gardner and Schermerhorn (1992). The first is directional leadership, in which the strategic leader is responsible for establishing a vision, mission, or purpose for organizational action. The second is operational leadership, in which the strategic leader "creates the internal capacity in an organization or group actually to pursue desired direction through sustained, day-to-day performance" (p. 103). Ultimately, directional leadership provides the context for operational leadership. Thus, executive leaders formulate strategies that reflect a vision or mission for the organization and then create organizational systems to implement those strategies.

Accordingly, the executive leader is described as a reflective thinker as well as a person of action and operation. In particular, the leader as planner is crucial in several models of strategic leadership. However, several researchers have questioned the extent to which executive leaders engage in significant long-term planning in conducting their organizational roles. For example, Mintzberg (1975) noted from his observations of executive leaders that managers "are strongly oriented to action and dislike reflective activities" (p. 50). Furthermore, Isenberg (1984) stated that, "even very senior managers devote most of their attention to the tactics of implementation rather than to the formulation of strategy" (p. 84). Some models of executive succession emphasize minimal importance of strategic planning skills, matching newly hired executive leaders with established organizational strategies (see reviews by Kestner & Sebora, 1994; Szilagyi & Schweiger, 1984). This suggests that the primary focus of the executive leader may be on implementation and maintenance, not strategic activities. However, Gupta (1988) noted that even when a succession process reflects pre-existing strategies, patterns of organizational evolution and changes in environmental conditions produce a strong need for strategy change and reformulation. These contrasting perspectives are grounded in arguments about the centrality of executive leader action in strategy formulation and ultimately as a key determinant of organizational performance.

EXECUTIVE LEADER AS PRIMARY DETERMINANT OF ORGANIZATIONAL EFFECTIVENESS

Arguments about the executive leader as either strategy formulator or strategy implementer (or both) have had deep reverberations in the strategic decision-making literature. Some theorists have adopted an environmental deterministic position, arguing that organizational action and performance are strictly functions of environmental characteristics and contingencies (Aldrich, 1979; Bourgeois, 1984; Hannan & Freeman, 1977; Lawrence & Lorsch, 1967; Romanelli & Tushman, 1986). Others have presented an organizational deterministic viewpoint, suggesting that strategy emerges from previous organizational actions and existing organizational culture (Miles & Snow, 1978; Starbuck, 1983). According to this viewpoint, the organization as a whole gives rise to strategy. A related perspective, the strategic contingency approach, also stresses that the organization's pre-existing strategic orientation is instrumental in executive leader decision making (Gupta, 1984, 1988). Organizational effectiveness emerges from alignment between executive leader characteristics and this pre-existing organizational orientation. Executive leaders significantly influence organizational performance in situations in which they match the strategic characteristics of the organization. Note that the executive leader role is relatively minimized in terms of developing or formulating overall strategic orientation, although Gupta (1988) argued that, according to the strategic contingency perspective, strategy formulation and reformulation need to be considered part of executive leader activity within the contingency perspective.

An alternate approach, the strategic choice perspective, places primary emphasis on the executive leader as a strategy formulator as well as implementer without delimiting the importance of the organizational environment in constraining the choices available to the leader (Child, 1972; Hambrick, 1989; Hambrick & Mason, 1984). Executive leaders are responsible for environmental analysis and organizational planning. According to this perspective, the analysis and interpretation of environmental information is significantly influenced by an array of executive leader characteristics. The single executive leader (or the TMT) becomes a crucial arbiter of organizational strategies. That is, contrary to the view of the more deterministic approaches, "top executives matter" (Hambrick & Mason, 1984, p. 194). Differences among the strategic contingency, strategic choice, and more deterministic approaches regarding the importance assigned to senior executive leaders are examined in more detail in the next section.

The focus of these various situational decision-making and management approaches typically is centered solely on managers and executive leaders at top organizational levels rather than differences across levels. For example, Hambrick (1989) wrote,

> The study of strategic leadership focuses on the people who have overall responsibility for the organization. . . . I prefer "strategic leadership" because it connotes management of an overall enterprise, not just a small part; and it implies substantive decision-making responsibilities, not only the interpersonal and social dimensions typically associated with the word "leadership" alone. (p. 6)

Similar to general distinctions made between lower- and upper-level leaders, Drenth and Koopman (1992) distinguished junior and senior leaders in terms of strategic decision making. Specifically, senior leaders were found to be responsible for strategic and policy decisions having medium- and long-term implications. Such decisions often are ill-defined, unstructured, and ambiguous. Drenth and Koopman differentiated such decisions further into strategic decisions relevant for the future of the organization and tactical decisions related to organizational control systems or to the implementation of policy. Junior leaders were found to make operational decisions reflecting a short-term perspective and that are relatively structured and concerned with day-to-day organizational operations. Because executive leaders have primary responsibility for directional or policy-making decisions, models of strategic choice and planning limit their focus to these individuals.

In summary, strategic management models of executive leadership emphasize organizational decision making and the role of executive leaders in making, guiding, and implementing strategic decisions. Such models, however, differ significantly regarding the contribution to organizational effectiveness to be attributed to executive leaders. These different approaches are considered in more detail in the following sections. The emerging literature regarding the nature and influence of TMTs is also described in terms of understanding the process of executive leader decision making.

Nature of Organizational Leadership

The discussion of what leadership entails from the strategic decision-making perspective necessitates first a specification of how much weight executive leadership is given in determining organizational performance. Different strategic decision-making models of leadership vary on this question. Some models, called deterministic models, place great weight on environmental or organizational factors, and others, such as normative and strategic choice models, cite the decisions and actions of top leaders as strongly influential.

DETERMINISTIC MODELS OF EXECUTIVE LEADERSHIP

Deterministic models minimize the contribution of executive leadership to organizational performance. Instead, such models cite environmental factors or organizational culture and tradition as the prime progenitors of organizational strategy.

Environmental Deterministic Models

Environmental deterministic models of organizational strategy postulate that strategic choices are determined by the organization's environmental conditions. One such approach, resource dependence theory (Pfeffer & Salancik, 1978), proposes that organizational actions are constrained by the availability of necessary resources in the environment and the organization's degree of dependence on those resources. Organizational dependence is determined by how critical the resources are for organizational functioning, the discretionary power accrued to suppliers regarding access to and regulation of resources, and the number of competitive suppliers. When faced with high resource dependence, organizations attempt to adapt by acquiring greater control over resource suppliers (i.e., through mergers or acquisitions) or by diversifying organizational outputs to avoid relying on a single source for organizational survival. The role of executive leaders, then, is primarily a reactive one in which organizational actions are determined by resource munificence or scarcity. Executive leaders attempt to broker conditions favoring resource control; however, they remain subject to an environment that, if highly turbulent, can render those conditions obsolete very quickly.

Population ecology models (Hannan & Freeman, 1977) go further by ignoring organizational attempts to adapt and gain control over resource supplies. Instead, they emphasize populations of organizations that occupy an environmental niche. Characteristics of the environment determine which organizational form (defined as organizational structure and institutionalized response patterns) is likely to survive and likely to fail. Hannan and Freeman argued that because of inertial forces related to political constituencies with a stake in the status quo, sunk costs in existing operations, and the high ambiguity and risk associated with the unknown dimensions of fundamental organizational change, organizational forms are not likely to change. Thus, according to these models, executive leaders have little or no role in organizational effectiveness except to ride the forces of environmental dynamics.

Organizational Deterministic Models

Organizational deterministic models shift the impetus for strategic choices from executive leaders and place it in the organization's environment. Other approaches that reflect determinism retain responsibility for strategic decision making within the organization but place it on the organization as a whole, not necessarily on executive leaders. Thus, strategy emerges from collective organizational actions that in turn reflect the organization's cultural predisposition (Starbuck, 1983). The role of executive leaders is to (a) provide post hoc meaning and understanding to organizational actions (Cowan, Foil, & Walsh, 1992) and (b) facilitate the implementation of strategic choices. Miles and Snow (1978) offered a classification of four organizational types that yield different generic strategies for organization-environment interactions. Defenders are organizations that stress efficiency and product stability. Prospector organizations emphasize product innovation and development. Analyzers produce and market products developed by others, and reactor organizations trail their industries in adopting new products. Although Lord and Maher (1993) used this classification to describe types of strategic leaders, these categories were intended to describe stable organizational patterns of action, not individual leader actions. Thus, strategic choices reflect these organizational orientations rather than the predilections of executive leaders.

Gupta's (1984, 1988) strategic contingency approach is an organizational deterministic model that emphasizes the primary role of executive leaders as strategic implementers. This approach defines organizational strategy as a determinant, rather than consequence, of executive leader selection. Gupta (1988) noted the following:

> By definition, the notion that matching executives to organizational strategies enhances organizational performance assumes that strategies get specified prior to executive selection. In other words, for most CEOs, strategies are assumed to be a given and the CEO's primary task is assumed to consist of the implementation rather than formulation of strategies. (p. 160)

Accordingly, organizational effectiveness derives from a match between the strategic orientation of the organization and the individual characteristics of its executive leaders. Thus, to extend Miles and Snow's (1978) classification, organizations with a prospecting strategy are more likely to be successful with executive leaders who are risk takers than those who are risk aversive. Alternatively, organizations with a defensive posture may thrive under risk-aversive executive leaders. Gupta and Govindarajan (1984) offered a similar argument regarding build versus harvest strategies. A build strategy focuses on increasing and maximizing an organization's market share, whereas a harvest strategy emphasizes maximizing short-term profits and cash flow. Gupta and Govindarajan argued that executive leaders who have high risk-taking propensities and tolerance for ambiguity would facilitate performance in companies with a build strategy but hinder it in those with a harvest strategy.

This analysis emphasizes organizational strategic contingencies rather than environmental contingencies. Organizational effectiveness is based on alignment between leader characteristics and organizational strategic orientation. However, as suggested by the deterministic models, organizations are likely to suffer if their strategies are not consistent with organizational conditions. This is not to say that only one strategy is appropriate for success; multiple strategic choices may be appropriate or suitable within a common environmental framework. Thus, strategic contingencies may not necessarily be fully congruent with environmental contingencies. However, the categories of acceptable choices are likely to be constrained by such contingencies. This led Gupta (1988) to suggest that, "accordingly, an organization's environmental context has the potential to exert a direct contingency impact on the composition and characteristics of executive leadership in addition to an indirect impact via the imposition of constraints on strategic choice" (p. 164).

Gupta also observed that periods of organizational change often coincide with CEO change (Virany, Tushman, & Romanelli, 1985). Furthermore, periods of strategic stability in organizations can be altered by sudden and significant strategic change. This suggests that CEOs may have a role in strategy formulation during these periods. However, it is not clear that it is the executive leader who prompts the organizational change; instead, he or she may be in the advantageous position of capitalizing on forces impelling change and influencing the direction of that change. Gupta presented three types of scenarios involving CEO tenure and organizational strategy. Type I scenarios involve CEOs as strategic formulators and reflect the approach of Hambrick and Mason (1984), described later as a strategic choice model, in which organizational strategies are defined as consequences of executive leader characteristics. Type II scenarios reflect the more traditional strategic contingency approach and define executive leaders as primarily involved in strategic implementation. The influence of executive leader characteristics on organizational performance is moderated by the organization's strategic orientation. Type III scenarios view executive leaders as both strategy formulators and implementers. Thus, in these latter scenarios, executive leader characteristics can have both direct and moderated influences on organizational performance. Gupta argued for the need to disentangle these different scenarios in research on executive leadership and organizational strategic management.

RATIONAL/NORMATIVE MODELS OF EXECUTIVE LEADERSHIP

Whereas deterministic models of executive leadership minimize the proactive role of executive leaders, rational/normative models suggest that such leaders are the central focus of strategic decision making. Their responsibility is to decide on organizational directions based on (a) careful analysis of environmental contingencies and organizational strengths and weaknesses and (b) application of objective criteria to strategic choices to determine the most appropriate organizational strategy (Bourgeois, 1984, 1985; Hitt & Tyler, 1991; Pearce, 1981). This process is grounded in a rational and comprehensive analysis of strategic alternatives to determine optimal organizational choices.

Executive leaders are expected to analyze an array of critical information that points to the best-fitting strategy for the organization. This suggests a slow, deliberative process that can be quite time consuming. Whether such a decision-making style is appropriate in a rapidly changing or high-velocity environment in which time is short and critical information may be lacking has been questioned (Bourgeois & Eisenhardt, 1988). Some theorists have argued that such conditions produce an orientation toward satisfying strategies instead of toward maximizing organizational outcomes (Cyert & March, 1963; Simon, 1957). Executive leaders use a number of cognitive heuristics to reduce information-processing times in situations of high information load and complexity. Strategic decision making using rational and comprehensive information processing is reserved for structured and bureaucratic organizations operating in relatively stable environments (Frederickson & Mitchell, 1984).

Bourgeois and Eisenhardt (1988) argued alternatively that comprehensive and rational decision processes are linked to organizational effectiveness even in high-velocity environments. They examined the strategies, performance, and top executive leaders of four microcomputer companies. They also examined the decision-making processes that produced a "strategic repositioning or redirection" of each organization (p. 819). Their analyses suggested that in rapidly changing environments, executive leaders of the more effective organizations still engaged in thorough and formal strategic planning. For example, in contrast to the organizations with declining or mediocre performance, executive leaders in the organization with increasing performance were described as having "(1) analyzed their industry, (2) conducted a competitor analysis, (3) identified the firm's strengths and weaknesses, (4) identified the target market, and (5) developed the strategy" (p. 827). According to Bourgeois and Eisenhardt, these actions are necessary, particularly in high-velocity environments for executive leaders to a gain a sense of control and order.

Rational/normative models place greater emphasis on the executive leader as the focal point of organizational strategy development than the deterministic models. However, strategic decisions are still determined largely by organizational characteristics and environmental contingencies. Executive leaders only add their information-processing capacities and ability to conduct the comprehensive strategic decision-making processes and planning prescribed by rational/normative models of strategy development.

STRATEGIC CHOICE MODELS OF STRATEGIC LEADERSHIP

Strategic choice models of strategic leadership accept the premises of the previously described models, that is, (a) the influential role of organizational environments in strategic decision making and (b) the central role of executive leaders as information processors. However, strategic choice models also argue that psychological and other individual characteristics of executive leaders influence the interpretations and conclusions they make from environmental information; the strategies they derive from this information processing; and, hence, subsequent organizational action and effectiveness (Child, 1972; Hambrick, 1989; Hambrick & Mason, 1984).

In describing one such model, the upper echelons model, Hambrick (1989) noted the following:

> In the face of the complex, multitudinous, and ambiguous information that typifies the top management task, no two strategists will identify the same array of options for the firm; they will rarely prefer the same options; if, by remote chance, they were to pick the same options, they almost certainly would not implement them identically. Biases, blinders, egos, aptitudes, experiences, fatigue, and other human factors in the executive ranks greatly affect what happens to companies. (p. 5)

Strategic choice theories view executive leaders as both strategy formulators and strategy implementers. They are expected to establish internal organizational structures and mechanisms that reflect their strategic direction and facilitate the organization's adaptation to the environment. Furthermore, executive leaders are expected to attend to the environment, both in its current form and its likely or expected direction. The executive leader's interpretation of the environment produces the framework for actions that (it is hoped) align the organization with current and emerging environmental forces.

In general, these prescriptions for action and the nature of executive leader work are consistent with those of rational/normative models of strategic management. The difference lies, however, in the nature of environmental processing and interpretation by executive leaders. Whereas rational/normative models suggest careful and comprehensive environmental analysis by executive leaders, strategic choice models accept the "bounded rationality" perspective of information processing under less than optimal conditions (Cyert & March, 1963; Simon, 1957). They argue that the environment is too complex and too information-rich for the executive leader to fully comprehend all possible outcomes (Hambrick & Mason, 1984). Instead, the executive leader must be selective about what he or she perceives and thinks about the organization's environment.

Hambrick and Mason (1984) argued that the situation confronting the executive leader, defined as "all potential environmental and organizational stimuli" (p. 195), is screened by his or her cognitive base and values. *Cognitive base* refers to the leader's cognitive models and beliefs, which are used to apply order and structure to a chaotic array or information. Following March and Simon (1958), Hambrick and Mason defined the executive leader's cognitive base as including the following elements:

- Knowledge or assumptions about future events,
- Knowledge of alternatives, and
- Knowledge of consequences attached to alternatives. (p. 195)

Donaldson and Lorsch (1983) outlined a similar set of cognitive constraints on executive leader decision making. They argued that executive leaders analyze environmental complexity by drawing on beliefs developed from their own experiences and shared beliefs acquired from predecessors. These beliefs transform environmental uncertainty into more understandable and familiar terms. Donaldson and Lorsch defined three sets of executive beliefs. The first set includes beliefs about the organization's competence—that is, "what the organization's economic, human, and technical resources can—and cannot—accomplish: the kinds of economic activity the firm should undertake and how this activity is to be conducted" (p. 80). The second set of beliefs are understandings and perceptions of the organization's financial self-sufficiency, or its relative independence from resource suppliers. The third set includes the executive leader's understanding and judgment about an organization's ability and propensity to undertake risks. For Donaldson and Lorsch, these beliefs "act as a filter through which management perceives the realities facing its firm" (p. 79).

Hambrick and Mason (1984) proposed that executive leader values also act as an important influence on strategic choices. After a review of the literature on values, Hambrick and Brandon (1988) identified six categories of values that can influence executive leader behavior. These categories, shown in Table 6-1 along with their corresponding value definitions, influence executive leader action in two ways. First, they predispose the executive leader to specific actions. This predisposition or "behavioral channeling" occurs despite facts and information regarding more appropriate actions and is more likely to result from strongly held

TABLE 6-1

Executive Leader Values

Dimension	Values
Collectivism	Wholeness of humankind and social systems; regard and respect for all people
Duty	Integrity of reciprocal relationships; obligation and loyalty
Rationality	Fact-based, emotion-free decisions and actions
Novelty	Change; the new and the different
Materialism	Wealth and pleasing possessions
Power	Control of situations and people

Note. From "Executive Values," by D. C. Hambrick and G. Brandon, in *Strategic Management Policy and Planning, Vol. 2. The Executive Effect: Concepts and Methods for Studying Top Managers* (p. 14), by D. C. Hambrick (Ed.), 1988, Greenwich, CT: JAI Press. Copyright 1988 by JAI Press. Adapted with permission from Elsevier Science.

values. Second, values screen environmental stimuli, selecting information that is likely to be supportive of valued orientations.

An executive leader's beliefs and values narrow and limit his or her field of vision regarding incoming environmental stimuli. That is, the executive leader's attention is likely to be drawn only to the parts of the environmental information that are congruent with the predisposing orientation produced by existing cognitive biases and values. Furthermore, of this information, only a subset is selectively perceived, and an even smaller subset is interpreted. This narrowing field of attention and assignment of meaning affects subsequent executive leader judgments and eventual strategic choices. In this way, strategic choice becomes a process of bounded rationality that reflects the idiosyncrasies and personal orientations of top organizational decision makers rather than a comprehensive and rational process (Hambrick & Mason, 1984).

These arguments place significant weight on the perceptual filters used by executive leaders. In some ways, such filters can improve the understanding executive leaders have of a complex and ambiguous environment (Starbuck & Milliken, 1988). However, they also can reduce the accuracy of information acquired by the executive leader or focus his or her attention on less relevant or meaningless parts of the environment. Starbuck and Milliken described two general types of perceptual filtering that can produce distorted strategic processes. One type reflects distortions in environmental scanning or "noticing," that is, "where to look and what to see" (p. 43). The other type is distortions in sense making and the assignment of meaning. The latter type of perceptual filtering includes distortions in framing an issue, predicting the consequences of an issue, and attributing the causes of issues and outcomes. Starbuck and Milliken noted that such distortions and errors are not necessarily fatal in executive leader decision making. In fact, they can be helpful when they (a) help executive leaders acquire understanding and therefore control over a chaotic environment and (b) lead executive leaders to pursue objectives that by more rational/normative criteria might be considered unattainable but are achieved because of executive leader energy and self-confidence.

Starbuck and Milliken's (1988) types suggest that a critical aspect of strategic decision making by executive leaders is the meaning they attribute to information gained from environmental scanning activities (see also Bluedorn et al., 1994). Dutton and Jackson (1987; Jackson & Dutton, 1988) proposed two fundamental categories of meaning that can be assigned by executive leaders to perceived environmental events: opportunity or threat. Events that are interpreted as opportunities are perceived as positive ones in which organizational gain is possible and a significant amount of control can be exerted by the organization over the event. Threatening events are those that are perceived as negative and entailing significant potential loss and being relatively uncontrollable.

According to Dutton and Jackson (1987), the labeling of an event as an opportunity or a threat has specific implications for organizational actions. They proposed, for example, that when an issue is labeled an opportunity there will be greater involvement by organizational members in its resolution and that involvement will extend to lower organizational levels than when an issue is labeled as a threat. Furthermore, when an event is labeled a threat, executive leader responses are more likely to be directed toward the internal operating environment of the organization in an effort to increase perceived control over the event and reduce its potential for loss. Alternatively, when an event is perceived as an opportunity, executive leaders are more likely to respond proactively to change the external environment in a manner that reflects increased perceptions of control and gain. Finally, because decision makers react more strongly to potential loss than to potential gain, perceived threats will engender more large-scale actions than perceived opportunities. Taken together, these proposals indicate the critical nature of the meaning executive leaders assign to environmental events. For this reason, how the personal characteristics of executive leaders influence the assignment of such meaning is an integral part of strategic choice theories.

TOP MANAGEMENT TEAMS

Over the past 15 years a substantial body of research has developed regarding TMTs. The central premise of this research is that the activities of executive leadership are not the domain of a single individual, but rather are dispersed or shared by executive leaders aggregated at the top of the organization. Hambrick (1994) described this as follows:

> The top group operates at the boundary of the organization and its environment (Mintzberg, 1973). It must monitor and interpret external events and trends, deal with external constituencies (ranging from security analysts to key distributors), and also formulate, communicate, and monitor the organization's responses to the environment. (p. 175)

TMTs then have the boundary-spanning, direction-setting, and strategic implementation responsibilities that have been described as typically the province of a single top executive leader. An often-cited advantage to a team-based approach to executive leadership is that the organizational environment and the corresponding sense-making demands are too complex for any single individual to manage. Instead, a collection of executive leaders may be able to apply a greater reservoir of cognitive resources to the scanning, interpretation, and construction of meaning from complex environmental stimuli (Jacobs & Jaques, 1987). These information-processing activities are facilitated when the team authority structure is fairly informal and characterized by high levels of participation and interaction (J. B. Thomas & McDaniel, 1990). Along these lines, Jacobs and Jaques (1987) noted that

> the CEO and the executive vice presidents [EVPs] of a corporation should have a working relationship that is different from that of the relationship between the stratum V manager and his or her subordinate managers. In the latter case, a clear line organization exists, and the relationship is usually directive in nature. In the corporate case, the CEO and the EVPs form a more collegial working group in which relationships are less directive and in which clear line relationships are deliberately de-emphasized. The utility of this collegium as an uncertainty reducing mechanism would seem to be quite high.

Jacobs and Jaques (1987) described two central uncertainty-reducing mechanisms provided by TMTs. First, when authority relationships are weakened, or at least suppressed, lower-level individuals are more likely to contribute to the identification of meaningful patterns in the organization's environment. In a strong authority arrangement, conformity pressures would likely result in such individuals adopting with little question the patterns discerned by their superiors, even if such patterns were inaccurate. Second, if the TMT is composed of individuals of varying functional expertise, the team as a whole has considerably more resources (what might be called "collective conceptual capacity") to develop more complex representations of the organization's operating environment. These factors led Jacobs and Jaques to suggest that "it would in theory be possible for a corporate collegium to deal with a more structured environment than could individuals" (p. 44).

Top Management Team Demographics

The idea of a TMT as a more adaptive and comprehensive information-processing mechanism leads to the prediction that heterogeneous teams are likely to be more successful than homogeneous teams. In the TMT literature, team composition and demography has been examined in terms of four key variables: (a) organizational and team tenure, (b) age, (c) functional and occupational specialties, and (d) educational backgrounds (Bantel, 1993; Hambrick, 1994; A. I. Murray, 1989). The information-processing capacity of a TMT is defined in terms of the level of resources available to the team and the diversity of those resources. High educational levels and broad functional experiences bring more information-processing capacity to the team (Bantel, 1993; Bantel & Jackson, 1989; Wiersema & Bantel, 1992). Some researchers have proposed that the average age of TMT members is related to the level of cognitive resources available to the team (Taylor, 1975). This effect, however, may be attributable to a likely association between age and amount of functional experience. That is, the effects of age on the team's resource capacity may be spurious as a result of its correlation with other predictors of team cognitive capacities. Other researchers have argued that younger executive leaders bring stronger cognitive skills to strategic decision making (Bantel & Jackson, 1989).

Another effect of average age of TMT members that has been cited by several researchers has been on the team's propensity for risk taking and proposing strategic changes (Bantel & Jackson, 1989; Hambrick & Mason, 1984; Wiersema & Bantel, 1992). Teams with, on average, younger executive leaders are more likely to pursue innovative and risky strategies than teams with older members. The following are some of the reasons suggested for this difference: (a) some cognitive abilities may decay over time; (b) younger executive leaders are more recently educated and may therefore have superior technical knowledge than older executive leaders; (c) older executive leaders may be more invested in and therefore committed to the organizational status quo; (d) younger executive leaders may have more favorable attitudes regarding risk taking; and (e) older executive leaders are more likely to be concerned with career and financial security than their younger counterparts and therefore be less willing to threaten their personal status (Bantel & Jackson, 1989; Hambrick & Mason, 1984; Wiersema & Bantel, 1992).

Several researchers have argued that team heterogeneity in functional and educational backgrounds would influence team information processing by increasing the likelihood that multiple and diverse strategic perspectives would emerge during team interactions (Bantel, 1993; Wiersema & Bantel, 1992). This effect becomes more important as the problems confronting the team become more novel and ill defined. Because turbulent environments are likely to give rise to such problems, Hambrick and Mason (1984) argued that team heterogeneity in functional expertise, experience, and education is positively associated with organizational profitability in such circumstances. However, team homogeneity would likely be positively related to organizational growth in more stable conditions. Researchers have also argued that homogeneity in age and organizational tenure within the team will result in greater ability to reach consensus more quickly about strategic issues and therefore greater strategic clarity for the team (Bantel, 1993; Hambrick & Mason, 1984; A. I. Murray, 1989). The proposed effects of age heterogeneity on team innovation and effectiveness, however, are more complex (Bantel & Jackson, 1989; Wiersema & Bantel, 1992). Diversity in the age of team members is likely to contribute to corresponding diversity in information, ideas, and perspectives available to the team. Conversely, age heterogeneity may adversely influence team cohesion, impairing team processes and therefore team effectiveness.

These contributions suggest that heterogeneity and homogeneity exert contradictory influences on TMTs. O'Bannon and Gupta (1992) developed a conceptual reorganization of this literature in which they described two dimensions of heterogeneity and homogeneity. The first, defined as *cognitive diversity*, results from diversity of education, functional background, and experiences. This diversity provides the team with more perspectives, information, and decision-making resources; it also fosters more creative thinking and problem solving within the team. The second dimension, *social cohesion*, is derived from homogeneity in age, values, and cultural backgrounds. Social cohesion leads to better communication and greater acceptance and faster implementation of decisions (Zenger & Lawrence, 1989). Thus, these two dimensions have different consequences for team processes and team outcomes. The central point is that the demographic characteristic on which the team is homogenous or heterogeneous has a significant effect on whether diversity (or uniformity) will be deleterious for TMT functioning. Empirical studies have begun to distinguish the effects of team heterogeneity and homogeneity (e.g., Bantel, 1993; Daboub, Rasheed, Priem, & Gray, 1995; Elron, 1997; Priem, 1990; Wiersema & Bantel, 1992).

Top Management Team Behavioral Integration

Other important dimensions of TMTs are their social dynamics and processes. Hambrick (1994) suggested that such elements represent a fundamental way of distinguishing the nature of top leadership groups. Specifically, executive leader groups can be differentiated by their degree of behavioral integration. According to Hambrick (1994),

> behavioral integration is the degree to which the group engages in mutual and collective interaction. In the context of top management groups, behavioral integration has three major elements: (1) quantity and quality (richness, timeliness, accuracy) of information exchange, (2) collaborative behavior, and (3) joint decision making. Thus, behavioral integration is a "meta-construct" for describing various elements of group process— more encompassing than only amount of internal communication (Katz, 1982), communication quality (O'Reilly, Snyder, & Boothe, 1993), or collaboration. (pp. 188–189)

Hambrick's (1994) notion of behavioral integration is an important lens through which management team or group processes should be examined.[1] High behavioral integration carries with it both the advantages (e.g., more information diversity, greater commitment to action) and disadvantages (slower action and reaction; process loss, Steiner, 1972; greater potential for conflict) of collective processes. Thus, most models of TMT or group variables, processes, and outcomes (e.g., Bantel, 1993; Hambrick & Mason, 1984; K. G. Smith, Smith, Olian, & Sims, 1994; Wiersema & Bantel, 1992) are likely to be significantly moderated by the level of behavioral integration within the team.

Hambrick (1994) proposed that behavioral integration is influenced by the organization's size, the breadth of its domain, its characteristic business strategy (e.g., defender versus prospector; Miles & Snow, 1978), its level of organizational flexibility, and the dynamism of its operating environment. In turn, the level of behavioral integration within the TMT determines its shared awareness and interpretation of the organization's environment, its pursuit of organization-wide change in response to environmental change, the speed of strategic implementation, and the deterioration of organizational performance in response to change. When behavioral integration is low, organizational coordination begins to decay as department leaders take more independent actions. Hambrick (1994) argued that "organizations led by TMGs [top management groups] lacking in behavioral integration are at a disadvantage in responding to major environmental shifts" (p. 200). Hambrick highlighted the importance of the dynamics of TMTs, a theme that has been

---

[1]Several researchers have distinguished *teams* and *groups* by arguing that teams are more interdependent and have a stronger collective identity than groups (Hambrick, 1994; Morgan, Glickman, Woodard, Blaiwes, & Salas, 1986; Salas, Dickinson, Converse, & Tannenbaum, 1992). Hambrick argued that researchers who examine top management collectives refer not only to tightly integrated teams, but also to more loose conglomerations of managers. Accordingly, he suggested that the term *top management group* is "a less presumptuous label" than *top management team* (p. 173).

the focus of several studies (e.g., Amason, 1996; K. G. Smith et al., 1994).

Executive Leaders and Top Management Teams

Although there is a large and growing literature on TMTs, few studies have focused specifically on the relationship between the executive leader and his or her team, and specifically how executive leaders manage or lead their teams. Several theories discussed in this book have described executive leaders as providing vision and strategies to their teams. Such leaders also specify organizational values and direction. However, despite vast theoretical and empirical literatures on both leadership (Bass, 1990; Yukl, 1994) and team and group dynamics (Forsyth, 1990; McGrath, 1984), there has been surprisingly little conceptual research on precisely how leaders create and direct team processes to achieve collective success (Marks & Zaccaro, 1997). Leadership theories have tended to regard team properties primarily as moderator or situational variables that cue appropriate leader behaviors (e.g., Fiedler, 1964; House & Dessler, 1974; Kerr & Jermier, 1978; Kerr, Schriesheim, Murphy, & Stogdill, 1974) not as critical mediators of leader influences on collective task performance (see exceptions by Kolodny & Kiggundo, 1980, and Yukl, 1989, 1994). Alternatively, team performance models have either ignored leadership processes altogether (Hirokawa, 1985; McGrath, 1991) or treated them as just one of many important team performance functions (Gladstein, 1984; Salas, Dickinson, Converse, & Tannenbaum, 1992) instead of perhaps the team component that drives and orchestrates all other such functions. Thus, in summarizing future research needs regarding team performance, McIntyre and Salas (1995) raised some critical questions related to the behaviors that define effective team leadership and the corresponding knowledge, skills, and abilities and other characteristics that enable such behaviors.

Although these observations have been made about research on leadership and teams in general (Marks & Zaccaro, 1997), they apply particularly to TMTs. Furthermore, TMTs have qualities and attributes that make them unique from other types of teams. Thus, models of TMT leadership are qualitatively different from other team leadership models. Nonetheless, Marks and Zaccaro identified some general mechanisms through which executive leaders influence team effectiveness. Their model can apply to executive leader–TMT relationships. According to Marks and Zaccaro's model, team performance emerges from four effective processes within teams: cognitive, motivational, affective, and coordination. *Cognitive processes* refers to the development and emergence of a shared mental model, or common understanding, among team members regarding expected collective behavior during team action (Cannon-Bowers, Salas, & Converse, 1990, 1993; Klimoski & Mohammed, 1994; Minionis, Zaccaro, & Perez, 1995). Team cognitive processes also include the collective information processing that occurs when a team confronts task and problem situations. A complete review of group information-processing models is beyond the scope of this book; however, basic cognitive team processes include (a) developing a shared understanding of team problem parameters and processing objectives; (b) using individual and shared knowledge structures to define solution alternatives; (c) evaluating and reaching consensus on an acceptable solution; (d) planning and implementing actions regarding the selected solution; and (e) monitoring the implementation, outcomes, and consequences of the selected solution (Hinsz, Tindale, & Vollrath, 1997).

By virtue of the attributes of individual team members and of the team as a whole, TMTs typically have a significant amount of cognitive resources to apply to team interaction and decision making. One responsibility of the executive leader is to harness these resources and organize their use effectively in team action. For example, shared mental models of expected team and member actions serve as key mechanisms by which leaders structure and regulate team performance. Leaders inculcate in team members an understanding of the team's purpose and direction, the action steps necessary to fulfill this purpose and direction, and the role requirements for each team member. In essence, team leaders convey their own understandings and mental models of the problem situation as derived from their boundary spanning activities. Thus, leadership processes and the quality of a team leader's mental models become key determinants of subsequent team mental models. Furthermore, team mental models mediate the influence of leadership on team coordination and team performance.

Another influence of executive leadership on TMT cognitive processes is facilitating team information-processing activities. The executive leader often will assume several of these processes, including problem construction, definition of solution alternatives, and implementation planning, especially early in team development. However, this does not excuse other team members from these responsibilities. In constructing team problems, deriving solutions, and planning their implementation, executive leaders draw heavily on the functional expertise and diversity within the TMT. They coordinate the contribution and combination of team knowledge and information resources; where gaps exist, they make necessary interpretations and decisions (Hinsz et al., 1997; Kozlowski, Gully, Salas, & Cannon-Bowers, 1996).

One of the most critical leadership influences on the cognitive processes underlying team effectiveness is fostering collective metacognitive processing in the team, especially after major strategic decision-making episodes (Kozlowski et al., 1996). *Metacognition* refers to reflection on the cognitive processes used in problem solving; it represents "knowledge and cognition about cognitive phenomena" (Flavell, 1979, p. 906). Sternberg and his colleagues described metacognitive processes as executive leader functions that control the application and operation of cognitive abilities and skills (Davidson, Deuser, & Sternberg, 1994; Sternberg, 1985).

To achieve a high level of expertise that promotes adaptation in a dynamic operating environment, team members need to set aside time to consider, both individually and collectively, the consequences of their strategies, how they considered and arrived at a team solution, and how they worked together to implement the selected solution. This is a difficult process to initiate and complete successfully. When a team has succeeded at a task, members may not see the need for reflecting on collective information-processing and interaction patterns. When a team fails, members are more likely to engage in such reflection, but it may be focused on fixing blame, resulting in negative consequences for subsequent team cohesion and efficacy. The team leader needs to manage this process so that it occurs when necessary but is a constructive exercise that strengthens the team.

Motivational processes reflect team members' willingness and motivation to work hard on behalf of the team. The development and facilitation of such processes can be particularly difficult in TMTs because it is highly likely that most, if not all, team members will be leaders of other organizational teams. Their motivation may be directed toward the needs and success of other constituent teams. Thus, the executive leader needs to direct these motivational forces toward the goals of the TMT and the organization as a whole.

Affective processes include the development and maintenance of a team's emotional climate. Because TMTs are likely to be functionally diverse, there is likely to be a similar diversity of perspectives within the team (i.e., cognitive diversity; Miller, Burke, & Glick, 1998), with a greater chance for disagreements and even acrimony in team interactions. Amason and Sapienza (1997) studied 48 TMTs and reported a significant correlation between the amount of cognitive diversity and affective conflict:

> Recent research seems to suggest that the ability to arouse cognitive conflict without allowing affective conflict is a key to gaining the "benefits of conflict without the costs" (Eisenhardt & Zbaracki, 1992, p. 34). Thus, a better understanding of the conditions that can lead to cognitive and affective conflict is important. . . . Our ability to induce conflict outstrips our ability to manage its effects. Thus conflict can be like Pandora's box; once opened, its forces become difficult to control. That cognitive

and affective conflict often occurs together suggests the need for caution. (p. 511)

The executive leader's task is to foster the effective display of cognitive diversity within the TMT without engendering affective conflict or motivational decrements. Amason and Sapienza (1997) suggested that increasing mutuality can counteract affective conflict without necessarily reducing cognitive diversity. They defined *mutuality* as "the extent to which TMT members believe they are mutually accountable and responsible and will share in the consequences of their strategic decisions" (p. 499). The development of such mutuality in TMTs is thus a major executive leader responsibility.

Coordination processes refers to the dynamics among TMT members that help them act and react to organizational and environmental contingencies as a highly interdependent unit. Fleishman and Zaccaro (1992) described a taxonomy of team performance functions that classified activities required for effective team coordination and integrated performance. This taxonomy has undergone several iterations (see Fleishman and Zaccaro, 1992, for a review) until reaching its current form, which contains the following seven superordinate functions:

1. Orientation functions,
2. Resource distribution functions,
3. Timing functions,
4. Response coordination functions,
5. Motivational functions,
6. Systems monitoring functions, and
7. Procedure maintenance functions.

Although these functional labels were developed to explain generic team coordination processes, they can be applied, with minor modification, to TMT processes directed at strategic task accomplishment. Indeed, several are incorporated in Hambrick's (1994) notion of behavioral integration.

Orientation functions are communication processes used by team members to acquire and exchange specific information required for strategic decision making. Resource distribution functions are activities such as the assignment of members to specific tasks during collective action, the distribution of requisite material resources across subtasks, and the balancing of task load across members. Timing functions include activities by team members to coordinate the pace and speed of task accomplishment. Team pacing incorporates activities regulating the speed of task completion for the team as a whole as well as for individual team members. Response coordination functions include the specific sequencing of member activities and their timing in relation to the occurrence of other team actions. Motivational functions are team interactions geared toward procuring the commitment of members to team task accomplishment and their willingness to work hard on behalf of the group.

Systems monitoring functions include actions directed at the detection of errors in the nature and timing of member activities. Procedure maintenance functions are team monitoring activities designed to ensure compliance with established performance standards.

The coordination tasks of executive leaders who are managing TMTs are significant because each manager within the team in turn typically manages an organizational subunit. Thus, Fleishman and Zaccaro's (1992) coordination functions may extend to organization-wide coordination efforts.

The body of conceptual and empirical research on the nature of TMTs that has emerged over the past 10 to 15 years represents an important extension of the primarily person-centered focus that dominated previous research on executive leadership. Many researchers have argued that there are limits on single individuals in terms of their information-processing abilities and other cognitive capacities required for organizational sense making, particularly within complex and turbulent environments (Cyert & March, 1963; Jacobs & Jaques, 1987; March & Simon, 1958). TMTs, particularly those with high behavioral integration, can presumably bring a larger pool of cognitive resources to the complex tasks required for executive leadership. Alternatively, dysfunctional team processes may interfere with other executive leader performance requirements (cf., Steiner, 1972). Thus, the notion of TMTs represents a rich and complex extension of executive leadership models. This extension should prove to be productive if knowledge from group dynamics research is combined with current knowledge of executive leadership processes and performance requirements.

Requisite Executive Leader Characteristics

Strategic choice models of executive leadership define the work of executive leaders as strategy formulation and strategy implementation. Executive leaders often are required to interact within complex and turbulent environments, develop innovative strategies in alignment with such environments, and interact with and coordinate multiple organizational subsystems and constituencies. Also, strategies that are innovative may need to be "sold" to lower-level leaders who are accustomed to and comfortable with the status quo. Consequently, executive leader characteristics need to enhance environmental analysis and planning,

TABLE 6-2

Executive Leader Characteristics Associated With Effective Strategic Decision Making

Domain	Characteristic
Demographics	Age
	Functional track
	Career experiences
	Education
	Socioeconomic background
	Financial position
	Team characteristics
Cognitive abilities	Inductive reasoning
	Deductive reasoning
	Creativity
	Cognitive complexity
Expertise and knowledge	General management
	Output expertise
	Throughput expertise
Motivation	Need for achievement
	Self-efficacy
Personality	Locus of control
	Risk propensity
	Flexibility

innovative decision making, the selling of selected strategies to subordinates, the coordination of organizational systems when implementing strategy, and other executive leader strategic management functions (see Figure 6-1). As summarized in Table 6-2, several executive leader characteristics have been proposed by strategic management theorists as facilitating these functions.

DEMOGRAPHIC CHARACTERISTICS

Hambrick and Mason (1984) suggested that observable characteristics and background factors of executive leaders are critical influences on strategic decision making. They specified seven key demographic characteristics: age, functional track, career experiences, education, socioeconomic background, financial position, and team characteristics. *Functional track* refers to functions associated with the output processes of the organization (e.g., marketing, sales, and research and development); the throughput processes (e.g., production and accounting); and the regulatory and boundary-spanning processes (called "peripheral functions" by Hambrick & Mason; e.g., law and finance). *Financial position* refers to percentage of stock ownership of top executive leaders and the amount of income derived from salaries, bonuses, and so forth. *Team characteristics* reflect heterogeneity and diversity among the TMT.

Several of these observable characteristics are actually markers of psychological influences. For example, Hambrick and Mason (1984) proposed that organizations led by younger executive leaders are more likely to pursue unconventional and novel strategies than organizations led by older executive leaders. In such instances, age reflects differences in propensity for risk taking. Likewise, functional track, career experiences, and education are indicators of the executive leader's level of knowledge and expertise. Hambrick and Mason also suggested that socioeconomic background and financial position reflect motivational orientation regarding achievement, recognition, and aspirations. Finally, team homogeneity and diversity were linked with conformity dynamics among executive leaders and their responsiveness to a turbulent environment. Therefore, although demographic characteristics are prominently cited in the literature as critical influences on executive leader decision making, their effects likely reflect the influence of other psychological and less observable characteristics as well.

COGNITIVE ABILITIES

The requirements of executive leader strategy formulation and implementation demand a significant amount of cognitive ability. Rational/deterministic models of strategic leadership argue that executive leaders comprehensively scan organizational environments and, through extensive analyses of acquired information, determine appropriate strategies. This suggests that executive leaders need significant inductive and deductive reasoning skills. Hitt and Tyler (1991) argued that executive leaders also require greater cognitive complexity, defined as the structural complexity and degree of differentiation in an individual's cognitive system (Schneir, 1979). Cognitive complexity helps executive leaders perceive multiple strategic options, understand the various characteristics of each option, and discern the range of outcomes that each option can create under changing environmental circumstances.

Because of the complexity of organizational environments, executive leaders often confront novel, ill-defined problems and scenarios (Mumford et al., 1993). Effective organizational responses may require that executive leaders develop innovative and unique solutions. Thus, another critical cognitive ability that influences executive leader strategy making is creativity and divergent thinking skills. Leidecker, Bruno, and Yanow (1988) noted, for example, that in the founding, entrepreneurial stages of organizations, executive leaders need to have among others, creative problem-solving skills.

EXPERTISE AND KNOWLEDGE

Hambrick and Mason (1984) noted that knowledge of different output and throughput functional areas was related to the focus and quality of executive leader decision making (see also Hambrick, 1981b). According to Hambrick and Mason,

> "output functions"—marketing, sales, and product R&D [research and development]—emphasize growth and the search for new domain opportunities and are responsible for monitoring and adjusting products and markets. "Throughput functions"— production, process engineering, and accounting—work at improving the efficiency of the transformation process. (p. 199)

Hambrick and Mason proposed that experience with output organizational functions was positively associated with organizational growth. Furthermore, they suggested that in stable environments, experience in throughput processes was associated with profitability, whereas in turbulent environments, output functional experience was more critical. Some researchers have argued that executive leaders tend to bring their own functional perspective to strategic decision making (Dearborn & Simon, 1958). However, Hitt and Tyler (1991) noted that executive leaders typically have a range of functional experiences. Thus, their beliefs and knowledge structures represent an integration of these experiences. Similarly, Hoffman and Hegarty (1993) proposed that different areas of expertise are associated with innovative decision making, including general management; marketing and product research and development; and finance, personnel management, and production.

MOTIVATIONAL CHARACTERISTICS

Strategic decision making requires energy and high motivation. Several researchers have proposed that successful strategic leadership is associated with high levels of need for achievement. High achievement needs are associated with personal striving to accomplish difficult but attainable goals (McClelland, 1961). Miller and Toulouse (1986) argued that executive leaders with high achievement needs will pursue broad strategies and be very analytical and proactive and adopt a long-term perspective in the development of those strategies. However, they also proposed that such executive leaders also will be risk aversive because as risk increases the chance for successful achievement declines.

Cowan et al. (1992) related executive leader self-efficacy to the quality of organizational strategy formulation and implementation. *Self-efficacy* refers to an executive leader's perceptions of his or her competence and capabilities to bring about desired outcomes (Bandura, 1986; Wood & Bandura, 1989). High self-efficacy leads to persistence in the face of challenge and the willingness to confront difficult tasks (Bandura, 1986; Locke & Latham, 1990). High self-efficacy is also associated with strong perceived control. Because opportunistic events are interpreted as more controllable (Dutton & Jackson, 1987), executive leaders with high self-efficacy are more likely to perceive environmental events as opportunities. However, their strong sense of competence also means that they may handle threatening events better than executive leaders with low self-efficacy.

PERSONALITY CHARACTERISTICS

A prominent dispositional quality of executive leaders that has been associated with strategic decision making is locus of control (Miller, Kets De Vries, & Toulouse, 1982). *Locus of control* refers to the amount of mastery an executive leader believes he or she has over situations and events (Rotter, 1966). Individuals with an internal locus of control believe they have substantial influence over events and that their efforts can determine their outcomes. An external locus of control is associated with beliefs of uncontrollability and that outcomes are a function of luck or fate. These differences in control orientation have significant implications for an executive leader's desire to pursue innovative and risky strategies. For example, Miller et al. noted that

> because internal executives are more convinced of their abilities to influence their environments, they proceed to do so.
> Confidence in one's potential impact breeds actions. In contrast, external executives are likely to be more passive because they believe events to be beyond their control. (p. 239)

Miller et al. (1982) argued that because executive leaders with an internal locus of control are more action oriented and better able to handle stress they will more likely develop organizational strategies that are more innovative and risky. Furthermore, such executive leaders are likely to be more proactive and use a longer time horizon in their planning.

Risk propensity is significantly associated with strategic and innovative decision making (Baird & Thomas, 1985; Hitt & Tyler, 1991). Executive leaders with a strong risk orientation are more likely to attend to ambiguous and threatening decision options in the organization's environment, use a narrower range of criteria to evaluate those options, and incorporate them into organizational strategies than executive leaders with a low risk orientation (Kogan & Wallach, 1964; Williams, 1965). Howell and Higgins (1990) proposed that risk-taking propensity was significantly associated with entrepreneurs and champions of innovation.

A critical quality in organizational strategy development is adaptability to a dynamic and volatile environment. Miller and Toulouse (1986) argued that flexibility is an important executive leader characteristic. Executive leaders high in flexibility are likely to react more favorably to changing environmental conditions and have more adaptive strategies. Such flexibility can assist executive leaders in working with different kinds of environmental information. In addition, it can facilitate leaders' efforts to persuade multiple organizational constituencies of their proposed direction and mission (Zaccaro et al., 1991).

Measurement

Strategic choice theorists have not yet attended systematically to executive leadership measurement issues. Instead, most empirical studies have used established measures of executive leader characteristics (e.g., Howell & Higgins, 1990; Miller & Toulouse, 1986; Miller et al., 1982). Outcome measures typically are organization-level outcomes, whereas measures of environmental characteristics and organizational structure serve as moderator or predictor variables (e.g., Khan & Manopichetwattana, 1989).

However, a critical focus of measurement in this domain is the assessment of environmental scanning activities. All models of executive leadership and strategic management highlight the importance of executive leader activities in scanning and assessing the organizational environment. Such activities are the basis for subsequent effective executive leader strategy development and long-term planning. Accordingly, the assessment of environmental scanning is a central issue in research on executive leadership.

Hambrick (1981b, 1982) assessed executive leader scanning of four types of environments (1981b, p. 257): output environments (i.e., "external product/market trends or events"); throughput environments (i.e., "external developments bearing on the processing or delivery of products/services"); administrative environments (i.e., "external developments bearing on the determination of roles and relationships in the organization"); and regulatory environments (i.e., "government regulations, taxes, sanctions, accreditations, litigation, etc."). He asked executive leaders to rate (a) how frequently they learned of events in each environmental sector; (b) how interested they were in each environmental sector; and (c) how much time they spent scanning each sector. ratings were combined to create a scanning index for each type of environment. Hambrick (1981b) reported sufficient validity and reliability. Farh, Hoffman, and Hegarty (1984) examined the convergent and discriminant validity of this scale, and although they reported significant problems with the timespent measure, they found strong evidence for the validity of the frequency and interest measures.

Another central issue in evaluating strategic decision-making models of executive leadership is the selection of criteria. Almost universally, the criteria of choice have been organizational outcomes and performance. This is appropriate given that strategic decision-making models of executive leadership define leader effectiveness almost entirely through organizational success and growth. However, most of the studies in this area have used private industries and financial or business performance indices. For example, Hambrick and Mason (1984) presented a widely cited model of strategic choice and executive leadership that defined performance in terms of profitability, variations in profitability, growth, and survival. Strategic choices were defined in terms of such variables as product innovation, diversification, acquisition, financial leverage, administrative complexity, and response time. Although these criteria have particular relevance for business industries, few, if any, of them can be applied to strategic leadership in nonprofit, military, or government organizations. To examine strategic decision making and leadership in such organizations, researchers need to attend carefully to this criterion problem, with the goal of developing more applicable outcomes measures for use with these organizations.

Leader Development

Researchers and theorists have devoted relatively little attention to leader development regarding strategic decision making. The research on leader characteristics suggests that executive leader expertise and functional experience are perhaps the strongest influences on strategy-making effectiveness (Hitt & Tyler, 1991; Hoffman & Haggerty, 1993). Executive leaders with experience and expertise across multiple functional domains are more likely to be successful than executive leaders with more limited experiences. Thus, developmental interventions that emphasize diverse functional experiences and assignments for junior leaders may be effective in facilitating the development of the expertise needed for successful executive leader strategy formulation.

The rational/normative models of executive leadership emphasize environmental analysis and problem solving. Hitt and Tyler (1991) found that, compared with industry characteristics and personal qualities of organizational executive leaders, objective environmental criteria explained the most variance in acquisition decisions. This suggests that the development of the analytical and problem-solving skills of potential executive leaders should also contribute to subsequent effectiveness in strategy-making roles. Empirical research is needed, however, to assess such interventions and their effects on strategic decision making.

Summary

Strategic decision-making models have focused almost exclusively on upper-level executive leaders. Such leaders typically are those most responsible for the strategic formulation and implementation processes these models are intended to describe. Thus, the question of cross-level differences in performance requirements is less relevant to these models than to those discussed in earlier chapters. Accordingly, they do not provide conceptual answers to the question of qualitative differences in leadership across organizational levels. Also, they offer little regarding measurement and development issues.

Strategic decision-making models are quite important, however, because they provide a conceptual description, beyond those of other models discussed in this book, of how executive leaders function and work as strategic planners. Organizational effectiveness is defined in part as a function of how well the executive leader (a) scans and interprets the environment; (b) uses this information to develop a viable strategic plan; and (c) implements this plan. The specification of requisite executive leader characteristics follows from these strategic decision-making processes. Key executive leadership qualities include cognitive abilities, expertise and knowledge, and specific motivational and personality characteristics. At least one model proposes each of these qualities as facilitating strategic decision-making processes.

The strategic decision-making models of executive leadership add conceptual depth to the leadership perspectives described in chapters 2 to 5. For example, because strategic analysis and implementation require more than one executive leader role, the strategic decision-making models augment the behavioral complexity perspective quite well. Also, SST proposes that the executive leader adds value to the organization by constructing a causal frame of reference of the organization within its operating environment. This frame of reference then becomes a guide for collective action. This theory does not specify, however, how such a frame of reference is constructed. Strategic decision-making models (including the empirical research stimulated by these models that is discussed in chapter 7) describe the scanning and interpretive processes that may contribute to the formation of such frames of reference. Furthermore, they provide valuable insight into the processes of strategic implementation that follow from an established organizational causal map. Unlike the perspective offered by SST, strategic management research highlights the role of TMTs in fostering these processes. Indeed, the functional heterogeneity that is typically characteristic of such teams may promote frame building and strategic implementation across different organizational units. This perspective, then, moves organizational leadership from an individual process to a social one.

In summary, the strategic decision-making models provide suggestions regarding how executive leaders make strategic decisions that facilitate organization–environment co-alignment. However, they do not specify how leadership changes across organizational levels. Nor do they offer formal measurement and development prescriptions for executive leadership. Nonetheless, when combined with the models described earlier, they provide a richer perspective of executive leader cognitive and behavioral contributions that can help organizations thrive within complex and dynamic environments.

Strategic Decision-Making Models of Executive Leadership: Empirical Review and Evaluation

7

The strategic decision-making models of executive leadership examined in chapter 6 focused primarily on decision-making processes and the executive leader characteristics that facilitate those processes. Empirical research exists regarding (a) the role of executive leaders in organizational strategy formation and implementation and (b) how executive leader cognitive or decision-making processes affect organizational performance. The conceptual and empirical reviews of the executive leadership models described in this book have been grounded in variations of the following themes: (a) nature of executive leadership; (b) requisite executive leader characteristics; (c) measurement; and (d) leader development. Little, if any, systematic empirical research has been completed on measurement of executive leader processes and on executive leader development from the perspective of the strategic decision-making models. Therefore, these themes are not examined in this chapter.

As noted by Hambrick (1989), strategic decision-making models of executive leadership have focused on top organizational executive leaders, not on qualitative differences in leadership across organizational levels. Organizational executive leaders are responsible for strategic planning and organization-wide strategic implementation. Lower-level leaders generally operate within the implementation plans established at higher levels; they are responsible for carrying out these plans in terms of day-to-day operations. Their own managerial decision making reflects the short- or near-term operationalization of organizational strategies (Drenth & Koopman, 1992). This distinction is congruent with the conceptual complexity theories reviewed in chapters 2 and 3, particularly stratified systems theory (SST). As indicated in chapter 3, there is considerable empirical support for these proposed cross-level differences. The remainder of this chapter will examine only executive-level strategic decision-making processes.

Research Model

The research model presented in Figure 7-1, which is similar to the models presented in chapters 3 and 5, indicates proposed key executive leader characteristics and executive leader strategic decision-making processes. It also specifies that (a) executive leader characteristics are linked to the successful accomplishment of executive leader decision-making processes, and (b) effective executive leader strategic decision making is associated with organizational adaptation and maximization of return from the environment.

Three generic executive leader strategic decision-making processes have been identified in the strategic management literature. The first is environmental scanning and interpretation, or strategic sense making (J. B. Thomas, Clark, & Gioia, 1993). If organizational performance is maximized by strategic co-alignment between the organization and its environment, then knowing and understanding the environment becomes an important precursor to adapting organizational action to environmental changes. Organizational adaptation is grounded in the sec-

FIGURE 7-1

Research Model of Strategic Decision Making and Executive Leadership

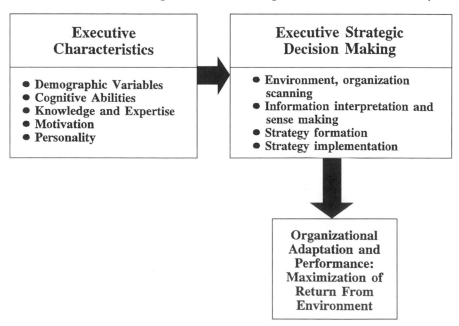

ond generic executive leader strategic decision-making process—strategic planning and formation. Such planning is likely to proceed from the longest time horizon that affords maximum environmental adaptation. That is, under conditions of environmental turbulence, strategic plans are likely to reflect specific actions within relatively short time spans, emphasizing flexibility if conditions warrant change. When environmental conditions are relatively stable, however, strategic plans can be specified in more detail over longer time spans. As described in earlier chapters, some researchers have argued that little executive leader time is actually devoted to strategic planning and strategy formation (Isenberg, 1984; Mintzberg, 1973, 1975); however, the preponderance of empirical evidence favors the specification of strategic planning as an essential element of executive leader work (see chapter 3).

The third generic executive leader strategic decision-making process is strategy implementation within the organization. Whereas the first two processes emphasize executive leader cognitive functions, strategic implementation reflects executive leader action or behavior. Strategic implementation involves translating long-term or grand strategies into shorter-term (i.e., annual) objectives and functional strategies (Hrebiniak & Joyce, 1984; Pearce & Robinson, 1995). *Functional strategies* were defined by Pearce and Robinson as "the short-term activities that each functional area within a firm must undertake in order to implement the grand strategy" (p. 310). The effectiveness of implementation is likely to depend, then, on how well these objectives are operationalized and measured (Hrebiniak & Joyce, 1984).

The models described in chapter 6 proposed several executive leader characteristics that facilitate strategic decision making. These include (a) demographic characteristics; (b) cognitive abilities; (c) expertise and knowledge; (d) motivational qualities such as those need for achievement and self-efficacy; and (e) personality characteristics such as locus of control and risk propensity. Empirical research should link these executive leader characteristics not only to organizational performance but also to the quality of executive leader strategic decision-making processes.

Nature and Influence of Executive Leader Strategic Decision Making

The conceptual models described in chapter 6 suggest the following propositions regarding the nature and influence of executive leader strategic decision making:

1. Executive leader decision making and actions will have an incremental influence on organizational adaptiveness beyond the influences of environmental contingencies and organizational characteristics.
2. Executive leader environmental scanning and interpretation will be associated with more effective organizational strategies.
3. The quality of strategic plans formed by executive leaders will be positively associated with organizational performance.
4. The quality of executive leader actions related to strategic implementation will be positively associated with organizational performance.

LEADERSHIP VERSUS ENVIRONMENT

Some strategic management theories have indicated that organizational effectiveness is grounded not in the actions of executive leaders but in either environmental conditions or the prevailing organizational culture, or both (Aldrich, 1979; Bourgeois, 1984; Hannan & Freeman, 1977; Lawrence & Lorsch, 1967; Miles & Snow, 1978; Romanelli & Tushman, 1986; Starbuck, 1983). The studies reviewed in chapter 1 regarding the significant effect of executive leaders provide support for strategic decision-making models favoring a strong role for top organizational leaders. However, they did not compare rational/normative models of strategic leadership with strategic choice models. The former models emphasize the rational and comprehensive consideration of objective environmental criteria, whereas the latter suggest that a variety of executive leader motivational and personality characteristics also explain variance in strategic decision-making processes.

Hitt and Tyler (1991) examined the relative contributions of these influences and industry characteristics to simulated acquisition decisions made by top organizational executive leaders. Industry characteristics reflected deterministic influences (i.e., independent of leadership) on organizational decisions. Objective criteria presumably captured the influence of rational/normative processes by organizational executive leaders. Hitt and Tyler also measured several executive leader characteristics, including age, amount and type of work experience, cognitive complexity, and risk orientation. They found that all characteristics explained significant variances in simulated acquisition decisions by executive leaders, suggesting that strategic decision making is influenced independently by (a) uncontrollable environmental effects, (b) rational analysis of objective criteria to determine appropriate strategy, and (c) executive leader personal characteristics. Hitt and Tyler also found that several executive leader characteristics moderated the influence of objective characteristics on leader decisions, suggesting significant support for strategic choice models.

These studies support a prominent role for executive leaders in organizational performance and suggest that characteristics in addition to information-processing skills and cognitive abilities are likely to mediate this influence. Hitt and Tyler's (1991) study is particularly useful because it partitioned variance in organizational decision making and environmental characteristics, rational analysis of environmental and organizational characteristics, and executive leader characteristics. Their results support Proposition 1.

The significant influences of both executive leader characteristics and rational/normative analysis of objective criteria reported by Hitt and Tyler (1991) imply that executive leader sense making is important for organizational performance. The next section reviews the direct evidence regarding this link.

SENSE MAKING, STRATEGIC PLANNING, AND ORGANIZATIONAL PERFORMANCE

Organizational performance is determined by the quality of linkages among executive leader scanning, interpretation, and choices (Daft & Weick, 1984; Milliken, 1990; J. B. Thomas et al., 1993). J. B. Thomas et al. examined these linkages and their association in a survey of 156 hospital chief executive officers (CEOs). Each participant responded to two scenarios that were used to assess respondents' typical scanning and interpretation activities. Both the comprehensiveness and source (i.e., internal vs. external) of scanning were measured. Furthermore, interpretation and sense making were measured according to whether events were labeled as positive or negative and controllable or uncontrollable. J. B. Thomas et al. then assessed executive leader strategic choices in terms of the introduction of new products, services, and technologies into their hospitals during the 3-year period following the assessment of executive leaders' scanning and interpretation patterns. Organizational performance after strategic change was also assessed using three measures of performance: (a) hospital occupancy rates, (b) profits per discharge, and (c) admissions.

J. B. Thomas et al. (1993) used path analytical techniques to assess the associations between strategic decision-making processes and organizational performance. They found that the comprehensiveness of scanning was significantly associated with the labeling of a strategic issue as both positive (or representing potential gain) and controllable. Whether scanned information came from internal or external sources did not influence sense-making processes. However, both information source and the labeling of an issue as controllable influenced product and service changes. According to J. B. Thomas et al., "When top managers interpreted strategic issues as controllable, they tended to act upon that perception by adding products and services to their hospital offerings" (p. 255). These product changes were significantly associated with higher subsequent organizational performance. Furthermore, they found fully mediated linkages between scanning comprehensiveness and product changes through influences on issue interpretation. That is, scanning comprehensiveness affected product and service changes selected by hospital executive leaders, and therefore organizational performance, by influencing whether a strategic issue was labeled controllable or uncontrollable.

J. B. Thomas et al.'s (1993) study provided support for both Propositions 2 and 3—that is, that (a) executive leader environmental scanning and interpretation will be associated with more effective organizational strategies, and (b) the quality of strategic choices will be associated with more effective organizational strategies. Their study also highlighted the importance of organizational and environmental scanning comprehensiveness for effective strategic decision making. Bourgeois and Eisenhardt (1988) report similar findings in their examination of four companies in a high-velocity environment. They found that executive leaders of companies with performance described as "taking off" or "stellar" made strategic decisions after (a) a wide search for decision options and alternatives and (b) a comprehensive, "rational" analysis of those options. Executive leaders of poorer performing firms used a more constrained search for options and a satisficing analysis to make strategic decisions. Other studies have reported that scanning frequency increases when the organizational environment becomes more uncertain (Daft, Sormunen, & Parks, 1988; Sawyerr, 1993). Furthermore, Daft et al. reported that the correlation between environmental uncertainty and scanning frequency was stronger for high-performing organizations than for low-performing organizations. Dean and Sharfman (1996) examined similar themes in a study of 24 organizations representing 16 industries. They found that how extensively top executive leaders sought and analyzed strategic information was positively associated with perceived strategic decision-making effectiveness. However, unlike other researchers, they did not find that the association between the extensiveness of information processing was more strongly related to effectiveness in unstable environments compared with stable environments.

Although these studies have provided support for the usefulness of scanning comprehensiveness, they also have raised questions about the role of environmental conditions. Other researchers have also emphasized the limits and limitations of this process. For example, bounded rationality produced by human cognitive limits leads to satisficing strategies that preclude strategic comprehensiveness (Cyert & March, 1963;

March & Simon, 1958). The more unpredictable and uncertain the organizational environment, the more likely attempts to be comprehensive will prove to be dysfunctional. Frederickson and Mitchell (1984) found support for this notion in a study of 109 executive leaders from 27 organizations in an unstable business environment. Each executive leader responded to decision scenarios designed to elicit his or her organization's patterns of scanning and strategic comprehensiveness. Correlations between these measures and organizational performance, with size partialled out, indicated that the comprehensiveness of situation diagnosis, alternative generation, alternative evaluation, and decision integration were negatively associated with organizational return on assets and sales growth. Frederickson (1984) examined responses to similar measures by 152 executive leaders from 38 organizations operating within a stable environment. In this study, comprehensiveness was positively associated with return on assets but not sales growth. Frederickson and Iaquinto (1989) replicated these findings with a sample of 159 executive leaders from 45 organizations in either stable or unstable environments. These studies by Frederickson and Frederickson and Iaquinto suggest that the effects of strategic comprehensiveness are significantly moderated by environmental conditions.

Another important influence on the efficacy of scanning comprehensiveness is the accuracy of executive leaders' perceptions of the dynamics within important environmental sectors. Bourgeois (1985) examined executive leaders' environmental perceptual accuracy and the influence of accuracy on economic performance. Accurate perceptions should facilitate higher quality planning and therefore more appropriate strategic decisions. Executive leaders were asked to report their perceptions of uncertainty regarding customer, supplier, competitor, sociopolitical, and technological components of their respective organizational environments. Using industry statistics, Bourgeois also computed objective indices of environmental volatility. He found that divergence between executive leader perceptions of environmental uncertainty and actual environmental conditions was negatively associated with organizational economic performance. That is, as executive leaders' perceptions of their environments became more inaccurate, organizational performance suffered.

These studies indicate that environmental scanning and interpretation should produce more effective organizational strategies. However, this relationship may vary according to environmental conditions. These findings support the importance of strategic planning for organizational performance. As noted in earlier chapters, this premise does have its detractors. Chapter 3 presented an empirical review of this relationship, with an emphasis on the meta-analysis performed by C. C. Miller and Cardinal (1994). Reviews by several other researchers emphasized that the tenuous associations generally observed between strategic planning and organizational performance may be attributed to (a) measurement issues and (b) contingency variables (Boyd, 1991; Pearce, Freeman, & Robinson, 1987; Shrader, Taylor, & Dalton, 1984). Miller and Cardinal's meta-analysis controlled for several organizational, environmental, and measurement contingency variables; measurement deficiencies; and environmental turbulence. Their analysis included 35 studies of the planning–performance relationship. Miller and Cardinal reported small but significant corrected overall correlations between planning and growth (corrected $r = .17$) and between planning and profitability (corrected $r = .12$). These correlations were stronger when (a) data were derived from organizational informants rather than archival sources; (b) planning was operationalized in terms of both formal and informal activities rather than standardized procedures alone; and (c) planning measures occurred before the assessment of performance and researchers ensured that strategic planning did not change appreciably before performance was assessed. Furthermore, planning–growth correlations were enhanced when industry effects were controlled, whereas planning was more strongly associated with organizational profitability in high-turbulence environments than in low-turbulence environments.

C. C. Miller and Cardinal's (1994) meta-analytical review of the strategic planning and performance literature provided substantial support for Proposition 3—that is, that strategy formation is linked to effective organizational performance. Miller and Cardinal's research is noteworthy because it examined and controlled for several previously mentioned moderators of this relationship. In particular, executive leader planning appears to become more important as environmental complexity and ambiguity increase. This finding is consistent with the premise of the conceptual complexity theories that argue greater organizational and environmental complexity require more complex cognitive processes and skills (i.e., the law of requisite variety; Jacobs & Jaques, 1987).

STRATEGIC IMPLEMENTATION AND ORGANIZATIONAL PERFORMANCE

The studies reviewed thus far have emphasized strategy formation and performance. The question remains whether strategy formation is necessary and sufficient for effective organizational performance or the effectiveness of strategy implementation provides joint or additive influences on important organizational outcomes.

Unfortunately, few, if any, studies have assessed the unique contributions of strategic implementation tactics to organizational effectiveness beyond the contributions of strategy formation. Many studies of strategic analysis and formation appear to have subsumed implementation processes in their measures of strategic change. For example, J. B. Thomas et al. (1993) found a significant link between the introduction of new products and services in hospitals and subsequent hospital performance. Because product or service changes occur at multiple organizational levels, it can be assumed that this finding indirectly reflects successful implementation. However, it is necessary to examine this link more directly.

Strategic implementation can be examined in terms of four subprocesses: (a) the operationalization of grand strategies into more specific and time-bounded tasks and activities; (b) the communication of organizational strategy, including its operationalization into tasks and activities, to subordinates; (c) the garnering of subordinate commitment to strategic changes, and of their motivation to follow through with these changes; and (d) the monitoring of strategic implementation activities to ascertain effective strategic change. Few studies have explicitly associated the first two of these subprocesses with successful organizational performance and adaptation. However, it is unlikely that organizational strategic change can be at all successful without effective operationalization and communication of executive leader strategic intent throughout the organization. Furthermore, the level of communication should be congruent with the degree of uncertainty present in the operating environment; that is, greater communication should occur in more unstable environments. Along these lines, Morrow (1981) found that higher unit communication increased organizational effectiveness under conditions of environmental turbulence, but reduced it when the environment was stable.

Chapter 9 examines the efficacy of executive leader behavior designed to empower subordinates and facilitate their commitment to strategic change. Related research by Wooldridge and Floyd (1990) found that when middle-level managers from 11 banks and 9 manufacturing organizations participated in strategy formation, their commitment to and understanding of the strategic change was greater than when their participation was more limited. In addition, the strategic involvement of these managers resulted in higher economic performance. Research on the monitoring and evaluation of subordinate activities has also linked these strategic control mechanisms to organizational effectiveness. *Strategic control* refers to the use of feedback and feedforward processes designed to inform leaders and subordinates of strategic implementation effectiveness (Schreyogg & Steinmann, 1987). A few studies have associated the use of strategic controls with strategic innovation (Hitt, Hoskisson, Johnson, & Moesel, 1993) and organizational effectiveness (Govindarajan, 1988; Gupta, 1987). However, further empirical research is necessary to broaden understanding of how executive leader monitoring and other strategic implementation processes are associated with organizational performance, particularly under different environmental contingencies.

TOP MANAGEMENT TEAM PROCESSES AND ORGANIZATIONAL PERFORMANCE

The research examined thus far has not addressed how top management team (TMT) processes influence environmental scanning, interpretation, strategy formation, and strategy implementation. Two categories of variables can be used to examine these relationships. The first is the demography of the TMT. These variables are discussed in the next section on executive leader characteristics and strategic decision making. The second category includes variables related to the informational and social processes within the TMT that influence team members' perceptions and interpretations of strategic issues, their selection of strategic choices, and their implementation of strategic plans. These processes are examined in this section.

Sutcliffe (1994) examined how TMT structure and information-acquisition processes influenced team perceptual accuracy, or the congruence between team members' perceptions of environmental conditions and actual conditions. *Structure* referred to the centralization of decision-making authority within the team. High centralization was found to increase the likelihood that subordinate members would conform to prevailing perspectives in their scanning and interpretation of environmental events (Jacobs & Jaques, 1987; Schwenck, 1984). Such conformity, however, may decrease perceptual accuracy. Sutcliffe also examined the level of environmental scanning and organizational performance monitoring completed by the TMT. Higher levels of both were expected to increase team perceptual accuracy. Executive leader teams from 65 organizations completed survey measures of environmental perceptions, decision-making centralization, environmental scanning, and performance monitoring. Objective measures of environmental instability and munificence were gathered from archival data. Sutcliffe found that perceptual accuracy regarding environmental stability was predicted by greater scanning among team members and less centralization. Accurate perceptions of environmental munificence were predicted marginally by team environmental scanning activities.

Sutcliffe's study (1994) focused on the congruence between TMT members' perceptions of the environment and actual environmental conditions. Implicit in this study was the premise that agreement among team members about the environment has some importance for team and organizational performance. Iaquinto and Frederickson (1997) examined a variation of this premise by exploring the relationship between agreement among team members about the comprehensiveness of the team's strategic decision-making processes and organizational performance, measured as return on assets. Thus, their focus was on the congruence across team member perceptions of their own decision-making processes. They collected survey data from 95 TMTs, assessing agreement about decision-making processes, team tenure, team size, and past performance. They found that the level of agreement was positively associated with organizational return on assets, even when past performance was controlled for. Although size and tenure of the TMT did not affect level of agreement, organization size had a negative influence on agreement about the team's decision-making processes. This can be attributed to the possibility that larger organizations are likely to be more differentiated, with more functionally diverse TMTs. This may in turn foster more internal team conflict, or at least more difficulty in reaching agreement about strategic decision-making processes.

J. B. Thomas and McDaniel (1990) examined how the information-processing structure of TMTs influences information interpretation. *Information-processing structure* was defined in terms of the degree of participation, interaction, and formalization within the team. High levels of participation and interaction along with low use of formalized procedures were determined to increase the information-processing capacities of the TMT as a whole. Accordingly, these characteristics were expected to result in high information use during strategic interpretation. High team information capacity was proposed to reduce the likelihood that the TMT would experience information overload and stress. Therefore, the TMT and its members would be less likely to label environmental events as threatening and uncontrollable. Thomas and McDaniel found support for these hypotheses in a survey of 151 hospital executive leader teams.

J. B. Thomas, Shankster, and Mathieu (1994) examined the relationship between team information-processing structure and the interpretation of strategic and political issues. *Strategic issues* were defined as those concerned with the organization's overall mission and its market position. *Political issues* were characterized as those involving conflict and negotiation among organizational executive leaders regarding their meaning and control. Thomas et al. also examined the degree of political activity (e.g., power acquisition, coalition building) within the TMT and the strength of its organizational identity. Results of surveys gathered from TMTs in 178 educational institutions indicated that team identity and political activity were associated with both strategic and political interpretation. High team identity was linked with greater levels of strategic interpretation and less political interpretation; team political activity was linked to high levels of both types of interpretation. Information-processing capacity was not associated with strategic interpretation, but it was linked to a lower likelihood that an issue would be interpreted as political.

These two studies by Thomas and his colleagues (J. B. Thomas & McDaniel, 1990, and J. B. Thomas et al., 1994) suggest that high levels of participation and interaction in TMTs facilitate strategic interpretations. Arguably, these processes increase the cognitive resources that the TMT as a whole can devote to strategic decision making. However, Korsgaard, Schweiger, and Sapienza (1995) used an experimental design with strategic decision-making teams composed of middle- and upper-level managers to examine how member involvement in decision making contributed to commitment to team decisions, trust in the team leader, and perceptions of procedural justice. Korsgaard et al. manipulated leader consideration of member inputs and influence of these inputs on team decisions. They found that both leader consideration and member influence increased perceptions of fairness, strength of post-decision attachments to the group, and post-decision trust in the leader. Furthermore, leader consideration significantly affected decision commitment when member influence was low. Consideration had no effect when influence was high. This suggests that leader attention to member contributions can result in positive team outcomes even when these inputs do not influence final decisions.

A theme across the studies described is that high participation and involvement by TMT members in strategic decision making should facilitate the team's information-processing capacities and social dynamics. However, greater team interactions could also increase the likelihood of team conflict, which may constrain effective strategic decision making. Indeed, Jacobs and Jaques (1987) noted that the importance of top executive leader teams that establish collegial relationships is that members feel more able to disagree with prevailing perspectives and thus are more likely to detect environmental signals. However, the possibility of conflict in such teams is greater than when members operate within a single perspective.

Along these lines, Amason (1996) examined two forms of conflict in TMTs: cognitive conflict and affective conflict. *Cognitive conflict* refers to conflict among team members that "is generally task-oriented and focused on judgmental differences about how best to achieve common objectives" (p. 127). Cognitive conflict is considered helpful to team decision quality because it results in diversity and integration of multiple perspectives. *Affective conflict* "tends to be emotional and focused on personal incompatibilities or disputes" (p. 129). Affective conflict inhibits decision consensus and impairs decision quality. Amason provided support for these proposed differences from surveys of 48 TMTs in food-processing companies. He also examined these relationships in a second sample from five furniture manufacturing companies. He found that cognitive conflict was positively related to the quality, understanding, and acceptance of TMT decisions; affective conflict adversely influenced these outcomes.

Amason's (1996) findings, combined with those described earlier, indicate that TMT processes regarding the exchange of different strategic perspectives within a positive and tolerant environment improve several aspects of strategic decision making. The research by Sutcliffe (1994) and by Thomas and his colleagues (J. B. Thomas & McDaniel, 1990, and J. B. Thomas et al., 1994) suggests that TMT information-processing capacities facilitate environmental scanning and interpretation. The findings reported by Korsgaard et al. (1995) and Amason indicate that TMT interaction processes also influence outcomes important for strategic implementation, including acceptance of team decisions and commitment to their success. Thus, research on TMTs has provided support for Propositions 2 and 3. Given the results of the studies reviewed earlier supporting the link between executive leader strategic decision making and organizational performance, team management processes that improve such decision making should also facilitate organizational effectiveness.

SUMMARY

Research has provided support for three of the four propositions offered at the beginning of this section. Day and Lord's (1988) analysis of previous executive succession studies as well as Barrick, Day, Lord, and Alexander's (1991) follow-up study demonstrated the usefulness of executive leadership for organizational performance. Weiner and Mahoney (1981); J. E. Smith, Carson, and Alexander (1984); and Hitt and Tyler (1991) provided additional evidence of this usefulness. Other studies reviewed also suggested that the value of executive leaders resides in part in the quality of their strategic decision making. Specifically, environmental analysis and strategy formation contribute to organizational effectiveness, which has been defined as adaptiveness within its environment. However, there are few studies that specifically and uniquely (i.e., controlling for the quality of strategy and strategy-formation processes) linked strategic implementation processes to organizational performance. Thus, Proposition 4 remains unsupported.

This empirical review has suggested that team management processes are important in strategic decision making. The conceptual complexity theories discussed in chapters 2 and 3 highlight the complex operating environment in which executive decision makers must function. However, the emphasis of those models is on the frame-of-reference-making conceptual capacities of the top decision maker. The research on TMTs has proposed that the construction of a strategic frame of reference is as much a social process as a cognitive one. Conceptual capacities are, of course, quite critical for mapping the strategic environment. Indeed, TMTs composed of executive leaders with high levels of such capacities and varying functional expertise are likely to be far more adept at such mapping than any single executive leader. Nonetheless, as Amason's (1996) results indicated, the social dynamics of such teams must be carefully established and maintained to encourage success.

Requisite Executive Leader Characteristics

If executive leader and TMT scanning, interpretation, and strategic choices are linked to organizational performance, then personal and team characteristics that facilitate these strategic processes should contribute to overall executive leader effectiveness. The various strategic decision-making models described suggested several important executive leader characteristics: (a) demographic characteristics; (b) cognitive abilities; (c) expertise and knowledge; and (d) motivational and personality characteristics. These personal characteristics influence executive leader performance by improving the quality of scanning, interpretation, strategy formation, and strategy implementation. Accordingly, the following propositions are offered:

5. Characteristics such as age, education, socioeconomic background, financial position, and team demographics will be associated with environmental scanning, information interpretation, strategy formation, and strategy implementation by executive leaders, as well as with overall organizational performance (the direction of association will differ with each characteristic).

6. Executive leader cognitive abilities will be positively associated with environmental scanning, information interpretation, strategy formation, and strategy implementation by executive leaders, as well as with overall organizational performance.

7. Functional expertise and executive leader knowledge will be positively associated with environmental scanning, information interpretation, strategy formation, and strategy implementation by executive leaders, as well as with overall organizational performance.

8. Need for achievement and executive leader self-efficacy will be positively associated with environmental scanning, information interpretation, strategy formation, and strategy implementation

by executive leaders, as well as with overall organizational performance.

9. Locus of control, risk propensity, and flexibility will be associated with certain patterns of environmental scanning, information interpretation, strategy formation, and strategy implementation by executive leaders, as well as with innovative decision making and overall organizational performance (the direction of association will differ with each dispositional characteristic).

DEMOGRAPHIC CHARACTERISTICS

Several studies have provided support for Proposition 5. Hitt and Tyler (1991) reported that executive leader age and education moderated how objective environmental characteristics influenced acquisition decisions. Taylor (1975) found that executive leader age was positively related to amount of information sought and the accurate diagnosis of such information. Age was negatively related to decision speed. Grimm and Smith (1991) reported that executive leader age was linked to the probability of making strategic changes: Younger executive leaders made such changes more readily than older executive leaders. Other studies have shown that longer executive leader tenure in an organization or industry was associated with more information-processing limitations; less likelihood that strategic issues would be interpreted as having political connotations; and persistence in using previously attempted strategies, even when their effectiveness is suspect (Boeker, 1997; Hambrick, Geletkanycz, & Frederickson, 1993; D. Miller, 1991; J. B. Thomas et al., 1994).

Several researchers have examined the average level and range of demographic characteristics of TMTs. Bantel and Jackson (1989) found that a TMT's average educational level, but not average age or tenure, was positively associated with team innovativeness in strategic decision making. Wiersema and Bantel (1992) also reported similar findings regarding strategic changes, except that average team tenure was negatively related to the likelihood of making strategic changes. Also, the heterogeneity of educational specialization within the TMT predicted strategic change decisions. Greening and Johnson (1997) found that TMT heterogeneity exhibited a curvilinear relationship with an organization's ability to manage organizational or environmental crises. Moderate levels of diversity resulted in less severe crises than did high or low diversity. This relationship was found for age and tenure heterogeneity, but not for educational diversity. Also, although moderate functional diversity was better than low diversity for crisis management, high functional diversity did not result in negative effects. Elron (1997) reported that cultural heterogeneity within TMTs in multinational organizations was positively associated with issue-based conflict and also with rated TMT performance. Cultural heterogeneity contributes to cognitive diversity within the TMT and therefore increases the cognitive resources and perspectives available for team decision making. Together, these studies point to the importance of some demographic characteristics for strategic outcomes.

Other studies have linked TMT demographics to strategic processes. For example, Sutcliffe (1994) examined the effects of TMT tenure, or the length of time the team had been together, on the accuracy of members' environmental perceptions. She found that tenure significantly improved perceptions of environmental munificence. Finkelstein and Hambrick (1990) reported that TMT tenure was significantly linked to strategic persistence and conformity. Teams that were together longer tended to persist with a strategy and therefore exhibit more stability over time. They also were likely to exhibit greater conformity to the predominant strategic tendencies within an industry, demonstrating less innovativeness and creativity. Finkelstein and Hambrick indicated that these effects were stronger in industries in which leaders had greater discretion in strategic decision making. Boeker (1997) found that TMT tenure was negatively associated with measures of strategic change: TMTs that were together longer were less likely to make such changes. However, he also found that diversity in TMT tenure was positively associated with the degree of strategic changes made by the team. Tenure diversity is likely to increase the number of perspectives and fresh ideas available to the team, creating a more favorable climate for change. Amason and Sapienza (1997) examined TMT size and its effects on team processes. Because larger teams have access to more resources, size can have the same influences as tenure diversity. Accordingly, Amason and Sapienza reported that TMT size was positively associated with both cognitive conflict and affective conflict. As expected, larger teams had more perspectives and cognitive resources at their disposal than smaller teams. However, they also had more difficulty resolving member differences without evoking negative affective responses within the team. Finally, A. I. Murray (1989) examined a single index of team homogeneity–heterogeneity that combined age, organizational tenure, team tenure, and occupational and educational background. He found that team homogeneity facilitated team interactions under conditions of intense competition. However, team heterogeneity fostered adaptability under conditions of environmental change.

The effect of heterogeneity on TMTs has been theorized as operating through the increase in cognitive perspectives and resources that diversity in age, tenure, and functional backgrounds provides to the team (e.g., Bantel & Jackson, 1989; Lant, Milliken, & Batra, 1992; C. C. Miller, Burke, & Glick, 1998; Wiersema & Bantel, 1992). That is, team demographic diversity leads to team cognitive diversity. Most studies addressing this issue have not tested this link directly; instead, demographic diversity has been related directly to organizational and team outcomes, producing mixed findings. Although cognitive diversity can produce more and different perspectives, it may also confound communication processes while fostering more dysfunctional political behavior. C. C. Miller et al (1998) examined these possibilities by exploring more directly the link between cognitive diversity among executive leaders and the comprehensiveness and extensiveness of their strategic decision-making processes. Cognitive diversity was measured by assessing executive leaders' preferred organizational goals as well as their beliefs concerning cause-and-effect relationships. In three samples of executive leaders, they found that cognitive diversity was negatively associated with strategic comprehensiveness and extensiveness. Therefore, although cognitive diversity may have some positive benefits for TMTs, these benefits can be outweighed by ineffective communication among team members and other deleterious process effects that can be fostered by such diversity.

These studies demonstrated that individual executive leader characteristics as well as TMT demographics influence strategic decision-making processes and outcomes. They provide evidence for Hambrick and Mason's (1984) view that "top executives matter" (p. 194). However, these characteristics are likely to be markers of psychological constructs such as risk propensity, tolerance for ambiguity, and knowledge representations. For example, the effects of age and organizational tenure on strategic decision making often are attributable to the tendency of younger executive leaders to be less risk aversive and more willing to be innovative (Hambrick & Mason, 1984; Hitt & Tyler, 1991). Alternatively, SST posits that age is likely to be linked (with appropriate developmental experiences) to more complex cognitive skills, higher quality knowledge structures, and, therefore, to superior strategic analyses (Jaques, 1986; Lewis & Jacobs, 1992).

Unfortunately, however, few studies have associated demographic variables with such psychological constructs. Hambrick and Mason (1984) attributed this to three factors. First, psychological constructs often are not amenable to measurement. Second, some demographic variables do not have readily comparable psychological analogues. Third, objective characteristics would be more appropriate for the application of strategic models to executive leader selection and development. Regarding this last point, however, executive leader development typically targets psychological change. Also, because psychological characteristics are likely to be the most proximal determinants of an executive leader's influence on strategic decision-making processes, exclusive reliance on objective background data is not likely to provide a rich conceptual understanding of such processes. Accordingly, further research is necessary to link executive leader characteristics to psychological mediating constructs.

COGNITIVE ABILITIES

Only a few studies have examined executive leader cognitive abilities in relation to specific strategic decision-making processes and outcomes. Furthermore, the results of these studies are mixed. For example, Hitt and Tyler (1991) examined and found no support for the influence of executive leader cognitive complexity on simulated acquisition decisions made by 65 top executive leaders. Also, Dollinger (1984) found no effect of executive leader integrative complexity on an organization's financial performance. However, he did find that integrative complexity was associated with the amount of time executive leaders spent interacting outside of the organization's environment. In addition, higher integrative complexity resulted in stronger positive correlations between boundary-spanning activities and organizational performance. This suggests that cognitive abilities are necessary to organize and accurately interpret information acquired from boundary-spanning activities and to link such information to strategic actions to boost organizational performance. Finally, Lefebvre and Lefebvre (1992) reported that executive leader analytical abilities were associated with the degree of their organization's innovativeness.

The general trend of these studies is that cognitive abilities are related to some aspects of strategic decision making, but not others. Other studies described in chapter 3 link particular cognitive abilities to some broader executive leadership criteria (e.g., Baehr, 1992; Isenberg, 1984; Norburn, 1986; Rusmore, 1984; Rusmore & Baker, 1987). However, although the conceptual basis for a proposed link between cognitive abilities and strategic decision making is very strong, the empirical evidence remains scant. One constraint on such evidence is that the range of cognitive abilities is likely to be fairly restricted—few individuals are likely to reach top organizational levels without some of these abilities. Nonetheless, as suggested by SST, strategic leadership requires high-level conceptual capacities that go beyond intelligence and basic reasoning skills. Executive leaders are likely to differ regarding how much of such capacities they have and use. Unfortunately, measures of these capacities typically need further psychometric support and, in particular, additional construct validation (see chapter 3). This requirement inhibits their use at this time in investigating the role of cognitive capacities on various strategic decision-making processes.

EXPERTISE AND KNOWLEDGE

Several studies have examined the relationship between individual executive leader and TMT expertise and strategic decision making. In these studies, however, expertise often has been operationalized as the extent and breadth of an executive leader's (or TMT's) experience in different functional areas. Lefebvre and Lefebvre (1992) investigated the degree of functional experience possessed by the executive leaders of 74 manufacturing organizations. They found that functional experience in accounting and finance was negatively associated with firm innovativeness; expertise in engineering and production, however, was positively associated with innovativeness. Hoffman and Hegarty (1993) examined executive leader expertise in general management, marketing, production, research and development, and finance. They found that each form of expertise contributed significant variance to the degree of influence exerted by executive leaders on innovation decisions. These two studies suggest that the breadth of an executive leader's functional expertise positively influences the likelihood that he or she will be innovative in strategic decision making.

The studies mentioned previously examined individual strategic innovativeness. Bantel and Jackson (1989) investigated whether functional diversity among TMT members in the banking industry contributed to innovative decisions by the team as a whole. They found that the breadth of functional backgrounds of TMT members was related to innovative changes in banking administration, reflecting such areas as staffing, planning, personnel training, and compensation. Functional diversity was not related to technical innovation (e.g., innovation in services or products, delivery systems, and office automation), however, after controlling for other team characteristics (e.g., age, tenure, educational level, and heterogeneity in these three characteristics). Thus, TMT functional heterogeneity partially mirrored the findings reported regarding executive leader functional heterogeneity.

TMT functional heterogeneity can be beneficial because it increases the cognitive resources a team can devote to strategic analysis and decision making. The result should be more comprehensive environmental scanning and more accurate environmental perceptions. Sutcliffe (1994), however, found effects opposite these predictions. She examined team functional diversity, organizational scanning activities, performance monitoring activities, and accuracy of team members' perceptions of environment instability and environmental munificence. She reported that functional diversity exhibited a marginal negative relationship with organizational scanning and no association with performance monitoring (both arguably measures of comprehensiveness). She also found that diversity was not related to perceptual accuracy of environmental instability and negatively related to the accuracy of perceptions of environmental munificence. Thus, contrary to predictions, TMT functional diversity appears to impair some elements of strategic decision making.

This impairment may be a function of a byproduct of TMT functional diversity in internal conflict. The different perspectives brought by diversity may make it more difficult for the team to reach consensus regarding environmental perceptions, interpretations, and strategic choices. Some indirect support for this suggestion was offered by A. I. Murray (1989), who measured TMT efficiency in terms of short-term performance indices, arguing that such measures illustrate how quickly and efficiently a team responds to or exploits profit opportunities. He found that occupational heterogeneity within 26 oil company teams was negatively related to performance efficiency; this effect worsened under conditions of high industry competition. (He did not find these effects, however, in a corresponding sample of food industry teams.)

A. I. Murray's (1989) study assumed that short-term performance is an appropriate index of team efficiency in strategic decision making. K. G. Smith, Smith, Olian, Sims, O'Brannan, and Scully (1994) examined more directly the effects of team heterogeneity on two team processes—social integration and communication—as well as on team performance. They argued that heterogeneity would lead to more formal communication patterns among team members and therefore less social integration and cohesion. The result therefore should be lower organizational performance. They found support for this proposition in a sample of 67 technology-based organizations. Specifically, team heterogeneity impaired team communication, which in turn inhibited social integration. This consequently had negative effects on organization return on investments and sales growth.

These studies provide an interesting picture of the influences of executive leader and team functional expertise on strategic decision making. The research reported by Lefebvre and Lefebvre (1992), Hoffman and Hegarty (1993), and Bantel and Jackson (1989) indicated that breadth of executive leader expertise appears to be related to greater strategic innovativeness. However, studies of TMT expertise suggest that breadth of expertise within the TMT may impair team processes, thereby hindering other measures of organizational performance. Integrating these findings suggests that TMT functional heterogeneity (and, therefore, its breadth of expertise) can help organizational performance only if team conditions that facilitate the exchange of diverse strategic perspectives without sacrificing team processes and cohesion can be established. Amason (1996) illustrated differences between cognitive and affective conflict in TMTs and demonstrated that cognitive conflict was positively related to higher quality strategic decisions, whereas affective conflict impaired such decisions. He did not, however, examine whether team heterogeneity was more or less linked to either or both forms of conflict. Nonetheless, separating these forms of team conflict and demonstrating their opposing effects on team performance suggests an avenue for future investigations of team heterogeneity and strategic decision making.

MOTIVATIONAL AND PERSONALITY CHARACTERISTICS

Several studies have confirmed the importance of executive leader motivational and personality characteristics on strategic decision making. D. Miller, Kets de Vries, and Toulouse (1982) examined executive leader locus of control, strategy innovativeness, and other strategic process variables in a sample of 33 organizations representing a variety of industries. They found that executive leaders with an internal locus of control displayed more innovation in production and service methods, introduced more new products, and initiated more product research and development than executive leaders with an external locus of control. Executive leaders with an internal locus of control also were more proactive in their strategies, higher in risk taking, and more likely to engage in long-term planning and environmental scanning than executive leaders with an external locus of control.

D. Miller and Toulouse (1986) confirmed this effect of executive leader locus of control on strategy innovation in a sample of 97 organizations from a variety of industries. They also reported a significant correlation between locus of control and growth in organization sales over a 5-year period, with executive leaders with an internal locus of control linked to higher performance. Lefebvre and Lefebvre (1992) found similar effects of executive leader attitudes toward risk, proactive attitudes, and locus of control in executive leaders from 95 manufacturing organizations. Finally, Khan and Manopichetwattana (1989) divided 50 organizations into five groups, two groups representing innovative organizations and three noninnovative organizations. Of the three groups of noninnovative organizations, the one lowest on several indices of organizational competence included organizations headed by executive leaders who tended to have an external locus of control.

D. Miller and Toulouse (1986) also examined the relationship between executive leaders' achievement needs and flexibility and organizational strategy and performance. Executive leader flexibility was associated with less environmental analysis and long-term planning and proactive strategy formation. More flexible executive leaders also were more oriented toward taking risks, although flexibility was not associated with strategy innovation. Executive leader flexibility was correlated, however, with organizational sales and net income growth over a 5-year period. High achievement needs in executive leaders were associated with more environmental analysis and proactive strategy making. However, such needs were not associated with strategy innovation and organizational performance.

Howell and Higgins (1990) compared top executive leaders who were champions of technological innovation with those who did not champion new products or projects. They examined product innovation in 28 organizations and identified for each organization and innovation both a product champion and nonchampion. These groups of executive leaders were then compared on several personality measures. Howell and Higgins reported that champions differed from nonchampions by displaying higher risk-taking propensity, stronger achievement orientation, and more creativity. They did not differ on social skills or endurance.

These findings provide substantial support for Propositions 8 and 9 that motivational and personality characteristics would be associated with executive leader strategic decision-making processes and outcomes. The only characteristic that was proposed as an important executive leader characteristic but has received little support is executive leader self-efficacy. However, to date, this characteristic has not been investigated sufficiently in these kinds of settings. Future research may provide such evidence and justify its inclusion as an important determinant of executive leader decision-making ability.

SUMMARY

The research summarized on executive leader characteristics that facilitate strategic decision making provides support for all of the offered propositions. The qualities receiving the most support are demographic characteristics and personality constructs. Functional expertise appears to influence strategic innovation; however, it is necessary to disentangle the positive and negative effects of functional heterogeneity on cognitive and affective conflict, respectively, within TMTs. Finally, there are a handful of studies that support the proposed link between cognitive abilities and strategic decision making.

A caveat is that few studies have examined all of these personal qualities in a single multivariate study (although two studies, by Lefebvre & Lefebvre, 1992, and Hitt & Tyler, 1991, did examine a subset of these variables in a multivariate framework). A multivariate approach could provide data regarding three questions. First, what is the relative contribution of each set of executive leader characteristics to strategic decision making? One might argue that cognitive abilities should have the strongest influence. However, the evidence just cited seems to be most positive for personality characteristics. A multivariate study could likely resolve this issue. Second, do the effects of demographic characteristics on strategic decision-making processes and decisions actually reflect the influence of unmeasured psychological constructs? For example, is age a marker for risk taking propensity? And third, do the joint or multiplicative influences of these sets of variables explain significant variance in strategic outcomes beyond their additive effects? A multivariate approach could address whether both cognitive abilities and personality constructs are necessary (and neither alone is sufficient) for effective strategic decision making. The findings from such studies would prove invaluable for subsequent executive leader selection and development efforts.

Strategic Decision-Making Models: General Conclusions

This empirical review of strategic decision-making models of executive leadership has provided the following conclusions regarding the propositions presented in Figure 7-1:

- By their actions, and the personal qualities that maximize the effectiveness of those actions, executive leaders play a determining role in organizational performance and adaptation beyond the influences of environmental and organizational characteristics. That is, there is significant empirical support for the strategic choice or upper echelons models of executive leadership (e.g., Child, 1972; Hambrick & Mason, 1984).
- Environmental scanning, information interpretation, and the quality of strategies formed by executive leaders (and TMTs) are related to organizational performance. The strength of these relationships is moderated by environmental conditions.
- There is little empirical evidence regarding strategic decision implementation and actions on organizational performance. Some studies have shown, however, that the participation of lower-level managers in strategic decision making improves their understanding and acceptance of final strategic choices.
- Executive leader characteristics are related both to the nature of strategic decision-making processes and to the quality and innovativeness of strategic outcomes. Team heterogeneity, however, exerts mixed influences on TMT decision-making processes and outcomes.

These studies illustrate how executive leader cognitive processes are related to long-term planning and organizational strategic outcomes. The conceptual complexity theories discussed in chapters 2 and 3 describe how the causal maps and integrated understandings of the organization and its environment that are developed by the executive leader add value to the organization. The research described in this chapter is certainly compatible with those models. However, the strategic decision-making models of executive leadership provide a description of the decision-making processes that influence the formation and use of integrated organizational causal maps. They add a degree of conceptual richness to the conceptual complexity theories. Alternatively, the conceptual complexity theories are more explicit about changes in strategic decision making across organizational levels and the nature of requisite leader cognitive capacities. Thus, they, in turn, inform the various strategic decision-making perspectives.

Another contribution to understanding executive leadership made by the strategic decision-making models is their focus on TMTs. It is likely that strategic decisions in most types of organizations are made by a team of executive leaders. Even when a CEO or other top executive leader assumes significant responsibility for a decision, he or she is still likely to rely on a relatively small group of senior executive leaders for decision input. The conceptual complexity theories, particularly SST, have noted the actions of senior executive leaders in forming social networks and consensus building. These actions are not entirely analogous to TMT processes. The research reviewed in this chapter suggests a number of key issues regarding these processes that, when addressed, should provide significant advances in understanding the dynamics of executive leadership.

Research regarding executive leader strategic decision making has focused disproportionately on strategy formation. However, strategic implementation activities are equally important to the success of strategic change. Well-constructed long-term strategies are ineffectual if they are not successfully translated into equally well-constructed implementation plans and activities, the most important of which are (a) the translation of long-term strategies into short-term objectives and (b) the motivation of subordinates to implement strategic change. Furthermore, the specification of executive leader characteristics that facilitate strategic decision making appears to have been driven by strategy formation, not by the requirements of strategy implementation. Because strategy implementation requires intensive and often difficult social interactions, a variety of social competencies are likely to be necessary for executive leaders to be successful (Zaccaro, 1996; Zaccaro, Gilbert, Thor, & Mumford, 1991). However, such competencies are infrequently discussed in the strategic decision-making literature.

Instead, these particular issues have been raised and explored in the visionary and inspirational models of executive leadership. Such models emphasize the role of the executive leader in developing and, more importantly, selling an organizational vision to organizational constituencies and to his or her subordinates. Indeed, Bass (1985) argued that an essential role of the executive leader is to empower subordinates to "take over" the vision and assume responsibility for its implementation. Thus, perhaps such visionary and inspirational leadership models can fill the gap left by the strategic decision-making models in terms of operationalizing the long-term organizational directions established by executive leaders.

Visionary and Inspirational Models of Executive Leadership: Conceptual Review and Evaluation

8

Like the strategic decision-making models of executive leadership, the visionary and inspirational models emphasize the role of the executive leader in formulating direction for the organization and taking action within the organization to implement that direction. However, according to the visionary and inspirational models of executive leadership, the nature of what is formulated as a directional statement is different from that created from the strategic decision-making models. Unlike the rational, strategic decision-making evaluation of environment and organization, visionary and inspirational models of executive leadership suggest that direction is established through a visionary statement that is (a) more amorphous, (b) reflects a longer time perspective, and (c) is more value based than those of other leadership models and theories. Visions, however, do lead to strategies.

Nature of Organizational Vision

Visionary and inspirational theories and models of executive leadership argue that the formation and articulation of organizational vision is central to the activities of the executive leader. What, then, is vision compared with strategy? Table 8-1 contains several definitions offered by theorists who emphasize vision in their leadership models. A number of common characteristics can be discerned in these definitions. The first is that an organizational vision often represents an idealized image of what the organization should become. Thus, unlike strategies, visions are not necessarily derived from objective environmental criteria and organizational characteristics. In fact, visions often reject current dy-

TABLE 8-1

Definitions of *Vision*

Reference	Definition
Bennis & Nanus, 1985, p. 89	To choose a direction, a leader must first have developed a mental image of a possible and desirable future state of the organization. This image, which we call a vision, may be as vague as a dream or as precise as a goal or mission statement. The critical point is that a vision articulates a view of a realistic, credible, attractive future for the organization, a condition that is better in some important ways than what now exists.
Collins & Porras, 1991, p. 33	At the broadest level, vision consists of two major components: a Guiding Philosophy that, in the context of expected future environments, leads to a Tangible Image.
Kotter, 1990, p. 36	In the sense that it is used here, vision is not mystical or intangible, but means simply a description of something (an organization, a corporate culture, a business, a technology, an activity) in the future, often the distant future, in terms of the essence of what it should become. Typically, a vision is specific enough to provide real guidance to people, yet vague enough to encourage initiative and to remain relevant under a variety of conditions.
Kouzes & Posner, 1987, p. 85	Vision, first of all, . . . is a "see" word. It evokes images and pictures. Visual metaphors are very common when we are talking about the long-range plans of an organization. Second, vision suggests a future orientation—a vision is an image of the future. Third, a vision connotes a standard of excellence, an ideal. It implies a choice of values. Fourth, it also has the quality of uniqueness. Therefore, we define vision as *an ideal and unique image of the future*.
Nanus, 1992, pp. 25–26	A vision is a mental model of a future state of a process, a group, or an organization. As such, it deals with a world that exists only in the imagination, a world built upon plausible speculation, fabricated from what we hope are reasonable assumptions about the future, and heavily influenced by our own judgments of what is possible and worthwhile. A vision portrays a fictitious world that cannot be observed or verified in advance and that, in fact, may never become reality. It is a world whose very existence requires an act of faith.
Sashkin, 1986, p. 59	Visions vary infinitely in the specifics of their content. Vision that is to have a substantial impact on an organization. One of these elements is change. . . . Another basic element all visions must incorporate is a goal. . . . A final element of an effective vision: It centers on people, both customers and employees.

namics to propose a very different perspective of how the organization should fit with its environment.

This is not to say that visions are out of touch with environmental realities. Instead, they reflect an interpretation of some future environment. This is a second characteristic of visions. Visions often are projections of a longer-term organizational future than strategies. For example, Kotter (1990) suggested that visions reflect 3- to 20-year time spans, whereas strategies are designed to operate within 1- to 5-year time spans.

Also, visions are not rigid, static, or inflexible (Nanus, 1992). Instead, they are flexible to adapt to environmental contingencies (although effective executive leaders do not change the value-based core of their visions). Visionary and inspirational models of executive leadership recognize and reflect the importance of environmental forces and characteristics cited by the strategic contingency and strategic choice models of executive leadership.

Visions are statements of preference about what the organization should be. Accordingly, they reflect the primary value orientation of the visionary. Hambrick and Brandon (1988) proposed a role for executive leader values in strategic decision making. They suggested that values could dictate certain patterns of executive leader behavior (i.e., "behavior channeling"). However, they asserted that the more common effect of values is to create a screen for executive leader perceptions of environmental stimuli. Compared with visions, values have a more pervasive role in that they are the foundation for the desired state an executive leader constructs for the organization. Values influence what the executive leader decides is a desirable organizational state—that is, what the organization should be.

A final characteristic of visions is that they become symbols of change used by executive leaders to reorient the collective behavior of organizational members. Both strategies and visions are used to produce organizational change. However, a key difference is that strategies often are the basis for structural changes in organizational processes (e.g., changes in production methods, development of particular functional units), whereas visions may be used more often to enact changes in organizational culture and climate. In this way, visions become the means by which executive leaders inspire and give meaning to the actions of subordinates (Shamir, House, & Arthur, 1993).

Vision and strategy are not necessarily mutually exclusive, however. Visionary and inspirational models of executive leadership have noted that for executive leaders to be effective, visions must be translated into day-to-day operations and activities. Thus, for these models, the nature of executive leadership involves both the articulation of an organizational vision and the translation of that vision into purposeful and meaningful organizational actions. This entails operationalizing the vision into strategies, goals, and objectives. Figures 8-1 and 8-2 illustrate this process as described by Kelly (1993) and Kotter (1990), respectively. In characterizing the work of Jack Welch, chair and chief executive officer of General Electric, Kelly (1993) described how Welch's strategic visions lead to objectives; strategic plans; and, ultimately, organizational

FIGURE 8-1

Moving From Vision to Action

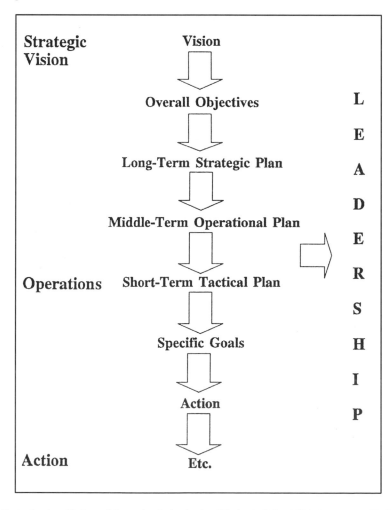

From *Facts Against Fiction of Executive Behavior* (p. 88), by J. Kelly, 1993, Westport, CT: Quorum Books (Greenwood Publishing Group). Copyright 1993 by J. Kelly. Reprinted with permission of Greenwood Publishing Group.

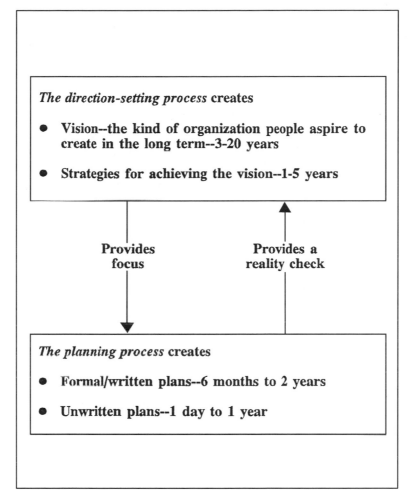

FIGURE 8-2

Direction-Setting and Planning Processes

The direction-setting process **creates**

- **Vision--the kind of organization people aspire to create in the long term--3-20 years**

- **Strategies for achieving the vision--1-5 years**

Provides
focus

Provides a
reality check

The planning process **creates**

- **Formal/written plans--6 months to 2 years**

- **Unwritten plans--1 day to 1 year**

Reprinted with the permission of The Free Press, a division of Simon & Schuster, Inc. From *How Leadership Differs From Management* (p. 39), by J. P. Kotter, 1990, New York: Free Press. Copyright © 1993.

action. Kotter (1990) outlined how visions of a long-term (3 to 20 years) future state are translated into a short-term (1 to 5 years) strategic plan that is then used to develop more specific plans of action having time spans ranging from 1 day to 2 years. Figures 8-1 and 8-2 illustrate the clear connection between vision as an idealized future organizational state and more operational strategic plans. Unlike the strategic decision-making models described in chapters 6 and 7, visionary and inspirational models of executive leadership suggest that strategies emerge from a combination of the executive leader's value-laden images of the future organization and his or her perception of the environmental contingencies needed to achieve that future state.

A critical role for executive leaders ascribed by visionary and inspirational models of executive leadership is to change and manage organizational processes in line with a formulated direction. This task is illustrated in Figures 8-1 and 8-2. Executive leaders are expected to translate their visions into operational organizational plans. Visionary and inspirational leadership and strategic decision-making models agree regarding the overall requirements of executive leadership. However, as noted previously, the implementation of direction in strategic decision-making models typically focuses on changes to organizational structure. Directive leadership in visionary and inspirational models generally takes the form of motivating, inspiring, and empowering subordinates such that they assume responsibility for structural change (Bass, 1985; Westley & Mintzberg, 1989). Thus, organizational climate change becomes the primary means of directive implementation used by executive leaders in visionary and inspirational models of executive leadership. Yukl and Van Fleet (1992) described one set of such models as follows:

> Transformational leadership refers to the process of influencing major changes in the attitudes and assumptions of organizational members (organizational culture) and building commitment for major changes in the organization's objectives and strategies. Transformational leadership involves influence by leaders on subordinates, but the effect is to empower subordinates who become *leaders and change agents also in the process of transforming the organization* [italics added]. (p. 174)

According to visionary and inspirational models of executive leadership, executive leaders implement visions or preferred organizational directions through four primary processes. The first is by enhancing subordinate motivation by associating follower self-concepts with organizational outcomes (Shamir et al., 1993). According to Shamir et al., charismatic leaders achieve this by (a) increasing the intrinsic value of subordinates' work-related efforts such that work becomes a more salient component of their self-concept; (b) empowering subordinates such that their self-esteem, and by extension their self-efficacy, is enhanced (see also Bass, 1990); (c) increasing the intrinsic value of goal accomplishment by clarifying the meaning of subordinate effort and associating daily efforts with the overall mission or vision; and (d) enhancing subordinate faith in a better future.

The second process through which visionary and inspirational executive leaders implement new organizational direction is modeling and teaching the behaviors suggested by new courses of action. House

(1977) noted that charismatic leaders "express, by their actions, a set of values and beliefs to which they want their followers to subscribe" (p. 194). Such leaders present a constant message that is consistent with their vision, and, more important, they link their daily actions to that message.

The third process is impression management and image building by the executive leader (Bass, 1990; House, 1977). For significant change to occur, executive leaders need the confidence and trust of their followers. Accordingly, they initiate actions that are likely to increase subordinate perceptions of their expertise and competence. Such actions bind subordinates more closely to the executive leader and enhance the likelihood that he or she can convince them of the need for change.

The fourth means by which visionary and inspirational executive leaders implement vision is through their manipulation of meaning and symbols (Bass, 1988, 1990; Schein, 1992; Siehl & Martin, 1984). A vision conveys beliefs and values that create meaning for organizational action. This meaning is instrumental in facilitating subordinate motivation because it develops a sense of purpose for their individual actions. Executive leaders need to manage the meaning imparted to critical events in a manner that is congruent with the articulated vision. In addition, symbols can provide a simple and coherent representation of meaning. For example, in the 1994 congressional elections, the Republican "Contract With America" was presented as a symbol of Republican philosophy and promise of governmental change. After the election, Republican legislators carried a laminated card listing the contract items, and they punched it each time a promised vote occurred. Thus, the contract became a visionary symbol. It also became a way of managing the meaning of the election and its implications for what Republicans called a revolutionary and cultural change in government.

All models and theories of visionary and inspirational leadership suggest one or more of these processes as key components of the work of executive leaders. Some emphasize the empowerment of subordinates and the development of a partnership between executive leaders and followers in creating organizational change (e.g., Bass, 1985; Tichy & Devanna, 1986b). Others focus on the executive leader as a somewhat mythical figure who inspires loyalty or worship in followers (House, 1977). All of these theories agree that the visionary or inspirational executive leader seeks to change subordinate attitudes and behaviors so that they are congruent with his or her articulated vision. Accordingly, the criteria for executive leader effectiveness include not only measures of overall organizational effectiveness, but also indices of subordinate performance, motivation, and satisfaction (House, 1977). This point distinguishes visionary and inspirational leadership theories from other conceptual perspectives of executive leadership.

A significant point of disagreement among visionary and inspirational leadership theorists is the degree to which crisis is necessary for charismatic leaders to emerge (Weber, 1947). An organizational crisis signals the need for a fundamental change and enhances the likelihood that organizational members will attend to the alternative perspective (or vision) offered by the charismatic leader (Bass, 1990). However, House (1977) and Boal and Bryson (1988) argued that it is the effective articulation of a vision and the definition of follower roles in ideological terms that lead to the emergence of charismatic leaders. Although a crisis can provide an opportunity for such articulation, it is not necessary that such leaders emerge.

Four leading theories of visionary and inspirational executive leadership are described in the following sections. These theories share many characteristics regarding the nature of executive leadership. Although other theories and models of visionary and inspirational leadership can be found in the literature (e.g., Bennis & Nanus, 1985; Boal & Bryson, 1988; Burns, 1978; Collins & Porras, 1991; Kouzes & Posner, 1987; Nanus, 1992; Tichy & Devanna, 1986a, 1986b; Trice & Beyer, 1986; Weber, 1947; Westley & Mintzberg, 1989), these four have received the most attention in terms of empirical testing and elaboration.

Nature of Organizational Leadership

These points suggest several aspects regarding the nature of leadership from the perspective of visionary and inspirational leadership models. Fundamental to these models is the establishment of a close bond between leader and follower that promotes strong and implicit trust. This trust becomes the basis for subsequent collective action. Thus the nature of leadership from this perspective derives from a relationship between leader and follower that is different from the ones described by the other perspectives in this book.

HOUSE'S THEORY OF CHARISMATIC LEADERSHIP

House's (1977) theory of charismatic leadership emphasizes the charismatic quality of effective leaders. Charismatic executive leaders produce organizational change by articulating a vision for the organization and establishing strong emotional attachment with followers that leads to their acceptance of that vision. This attachment develops from associating the leader's organizational vision with follower self-concept (Shamir et al., 1993). According to House, charismatic leaders promote strong identification with themselves in their followers. Through such personal identification, these leaders equate fealty to, and work on behalf of, the leader's vision with the followers' self-concept. The results are (a) personal commitment by followers to the leader, (b) more self-sacrificing and organizational citizen behavior by followers, and (c) stronger perceptions by followers of the meaningfulness of their work.

House (1977) identified several executive leader behaviors that result in stronger follower identification and loyalty. A primary executive leader behavior is the articulation of an ideological goal. This is the vision that is used to give meaning to organizational and subordinate actions. The ideological tone of the vision provides a moral basis for prescribed actions and is used to enhance followers' emotional attachment to the leader. A second executive leader behavior, role modeling of attitudes, values, and beliefs engendered by the leader's vision, also facilitates follower attachment. Such modeling increases the valence of these elements for followers.

Another important charismatic leader behavior is the management of his or her image to followers. To effect organizational change, an executive leader must garner the implicit trust of organizational members. To gain such trust, the charismatic leader engages in actions designed to demonstrate his or her competence and effectiveness.

Two other executive leader behaviors suggested by House (1977) are directed at enhancing follower self-efficacy regarding the work requirements of the prescribed organizational change. The executive leader enhances followers' self-efficacy by (a) setting high performance expectations and (b) communicating confidence in followers' ability to meet them. Setting high performance goals increases subordinates' motivation subordinates to meet those goals (Eden, 1984, 1990). Bandura (1986) also noted that persuasion by others of one's own competence was an effective determinant of self-efficacy.

House's (1977) theory of charismatic leadership emphasizes the development of trust and loyalty in subordinates that results in their acceptance of proposed organizational changes. However, the next theory of visionary and inspirational leadership to be reviewed, Bass's (1985) transformational leadership theory, emphasizes subordinate empowerment as the primary mechanism of organizational change.

BASS'S TRANSFORMATIONAL LEADERSHIP THEORY

Burns (1978) introduced transformational leadership as a mode of leader influence in which followers are motivated to act beyond their self-interest in the service of a larger community. This mode of influence is in contrast to transactional leadership, in which the exchange between leader and followers is based less on transcending ideals and more on the ability of the leader to provide for the personal gain of followers. Transactional leadership relies on legitimate and reward power as the basis for influence, whereas transformational leadership incorporates referent power. An interesting point made by Burns is that transformational leadership is not reserved solely for executive leaders. Instead, such leadership influence can occur at all organizational levels and also can include upward influence (i.e., subordinates to superior; Yukl & Van Fleet, 1992).

Following Burns (1978), Bass (1985, 1996) argued that effective executive leadership involves transforming the motivation of subordinates so that they endeavor on behalf of the organization for goals and ideals other than self-interest. Transformational leaders seek to activate higher order growth and self-actualizing needs (Maslow, 1954). Furthermore, transformational leaders clarify the importance of organizational tasks and actions beyond followers' personal perspectives. A significant difference between Burns's view of leadership and Bass's later perspective, however, is that Burns considered transformational and transactional leadership to be opposing styles. Bass argued that transactional leadership involves not only reward distribution and rule making, but also the clarification of goal paths. Thus, according to Bass, successful executive leaders use both modes of influence.

An important distinction between transformational leadership and charismatic leadership is that charismatic leaders bring about change by establishing emotional attachment in followers that leads to unquestioning trust in the leader's vision. Conversely, transformational leaders empower subordinates as co-agents of organizational change (Bass, 1985; Westley & Mintzberg, 1989; Yukl & Van Fleet, 1992). For example, Westley and Mintzberg suggested the following:

> Indeed, there are important instances when the "followers" stimulate the leader, as opposed to the other way around. In most cases, however, it would appear that leader and follower participate together in creating the vision. The specific content—the original idea or perception—may come from the leader . . . , but the form which it takes, the special excitement which marks, is co-created. (p. 21)

Bass (1985, 1990, 1996; Bass & Avolio, 1993) proposed several behavioral characteristics of transformational leaders. One is that transformational leaders provide an organizational vision and mission. This vision elicits an emotional attachment from subordinates and is the basis for strong identification with the leader. Another characteristic is that they communicate strong performance expectations and use symbols to manage the meaning of critical information and components of the vision. These two characteristics link transformational leadership with House's (1977) notion of charismatic leadership. However, Bass argued that charisma alone is insufficient for effective executive leadership. To empower followers and create a partnership for organizational change, transformational leaders must provide intellectual stimulation and individualized consideration to subordinates. Such leaders encourage subordinates to think autonomously and examine problems from different perspectives. They also provide individual and focused attention to subordinates, often in the role of mentor or adviser. Bass (1990) noted that these qualities, particularly intellectual stimulation, prevent the "habitual followership" (p. 216) and blind obedience that can be engendered by purely charismatic leadership styles.

An important consequence of these activities is that transformational leadership cascades through organizational levels (Bass, Waldman, & Avolio, 1987). If executive leaders are successful in empowering their subordinates, then they too will demonstrate a transformational approach to their subordinates, and so on. This suggests that Bass's theory does not clearly distinguish between the activities of effective lower-level and executive leaders. Tichy and Ulrich (1984; see also Tichy & Devanna, 1986a, 1986b) offered a dissenting voice. They argued that the vision necessary for effective transformational leadership is developed at the top of the organization. Subordinates and lower-level leaders focus on the implementation of this vision and, thus, are likely to display a more directive leadership style. Bass suggested that transformational leadership occurs at multiple levels, although he concurred that it is more likely to be evident at higher organizational levels. Along these lines, Bass and Avolio (1993) wrote,

> Although much that has been written about transformational leadership (Burns, 1978; Bennis & Nanus, 1985; Tichy & Devanna, 1985) has concentrated on leaders at the top of the organizations and movements, we have been able to observe and measure transformational leadership at all levels, even at the lowest levels of supervision and among nonsupervisory projects leaders, as well as among student leaders. However, even though transformational leadership behavior has been observed at lower organizational levels, it is likely to occur more frequently at the highest organizational levels. (p. 54)

CONGER AND KANUNGO'S THEORY OF CHARISMATIC LEADERSHIP

Bass's transformational leadership theory incorporated and expanded on House's (1977) theory of charismatic leadership (see House & Shamir, 1993, for their integration of these different perspectives). However, these theories differ fundamentally regarding the role of followers in the process of organizational change. Conger and Kanungo's (1987) theory of charismatic leadership extended the role of followers in visionary and inspirational executive leadership by highlighting their significance in legitimizing such leaders.

Conger and Kanungo (1987, 1992; Kanungo & Conger, 1992) described charisma as a quality that is attributed by followers to a leader based on his or her behavior. They proposed that the attribution of charisma results from the executive leader's demonstration of three specific cognitive and behavioral patterns. The first is the executive leader's evaluation of the organization and its environment to determine the need for change and the organization's capacity to effect such change. The leader assesses existing organizational shortcomings, environmental constraints, and organizational members' abilities and needs.

This assessment leads to the second behavioral pattern, the articulation of a vision that is discrepant with the status quo. To be successful, the executive leader's articulation of his or her vision to subordinates must be logical, cogent, and persuasive. Accordingly, the leader's presentation of his or her vision should include descriptions of the following: (a) the problems in the current organizational state; (b) the nature of the vision; (c) how the vision resolves or improves the organizational problems; and (d) the strategic plans needed to implement the vision (Kanungo & Conger, 1992).

The third pattern leading to the attribution of leader charisma is the use of unconventional and innovative behaviors to implement the vision. Conger and Kanungo (1987) argued that because such behaviors are counternormative, they entail considerable personal risk for the executive leader. A behavior pattern that is personally risky and highly costly is perceived as selfless and therefore inspires admiration and credibility in followers.

Conger and Kanungo's (1987, 1992; Kanungo & Conger, 1992) theory of charismatic leadership is different in two ways from the theories described earlier. According to Conger and Kanungo, for leaders to emerge followers need to perceive a crisis confronting the organization that requires significant change. Alternatively, executive leaders need to create a compelling need for change. Thus, the task for charismatic executive leaders is to convince potential followers of the critical situation that needs to be faced or to at least persuade them of the advantages of an alternate organizational direction. Also, in contrast to the other models, Conger and Kanungo emphasized the need for charismatic leaders to display behaviors denoting significant personal risk. Such behaviors contribute to the development of the emotional attachment required of followers for successful charismatic leadership.

Conger and Kanungo's (1987, 1992; Kanungo & Conger, 1992) notion of the attribution of charisma suggests the importance of followers in legitimizing the charismatic leader (Hollander & Julian, 1970). This point is implicitly part of House's (1997) theory of charismatic leadership in that such leaders are not effective unless followers accept and trust their vision of the organization's future. However, by positing an attributional framework, Conger and Kanungo placed particular emphasis on the critical behavioral patterns that must be displayed in some combination by executive leaders attempting to bring about organizational change.

SASHKIN'S VISIONARY LEADERSHIP THEORY

Sashkin's (1988; Sashkin & Fulmer, 1988) visionary leadership theory focuses on the content of the executive leader's vision and the process of visioning. Sashkin noted that visions have three themes: (a) change, (b) ideal goals, and (c) social orientation. Visions address change in the environment and what is necessary for organizational adaptation. They posit ideal goals that raise organizational standards. They also convey an emphasis or focus on people within the organization and/or its customers. This last quality means that visions provide images of new roles for organizational members as well as of the centrality of consumers of organizational products or services.

Sashkin (1988) characterized *visioning* as involving the expression of the vision, explaining the vision to others, extending the vision across a variety of organizational situations, and expanding the vision by "applying it in many different ways, in a wide range of circumstances, and to a broader context" (p. 130). Sashkin noted that each of these visioning behaviors can take place at all organizational levels. However, after Jaques (1986; Jacobs & Jaques, 1987), he argued that at successively higher organizational levels, the time span for visioning becomes progressively longer until executive leaders are establishing 5- to 15-plus-year visions. Executive leaders also have a broader systems perspective than leaders at lower organizational levels.

Sashkin (1988) described several executive leader behaviors that are linked to visionary and inspirational leadership. One is focusing subordinate attention on the critical points and key issues of the vision. Another is developing two-way communication that provides an open forum for the transmission of the vision and information on how followers receive and respond to it. A third critical behavior is the executive leader demonstrating consistency and trustworthiness. Such behavior conveys the sincerity and value-based core of the executive leader's vision. A fourth behavior is displaying respect for subordinates. As suggested by House (1977) and Bass (1985), such executive leader behaviors build followers' self-esteem and increase their empowerment. Finally, visionary and inspirational executive leaders take personal risks for the purpose of expressing their commitment to the vision. According to Sashkin, these behaviors contribute to the charismatic effect of the executive leader.

One quality that distinguishes Sashkin's (1988) theory from other theories and models of visionary and inspirational leadership (House & Shamir, 1993) is his notion that executive leaders need to show versatility in their operational leadership actions (Sashkin & Fulmer, 1988). Executive leaders must evaluate what a situation requires and be able to respond accordingly. The implementation of a vision requires a range of both task- and relationship-oriented behaviors. Therefore, effective executive leaders need to have the versatility to act in multiple and different ways according to situation specifics and subordinate needs.

Although Sashkin's (1988) theory includes elements found in both other charismatic leadership and transformational leadership theories, his approach is more centered on the nature and consequences of effective visions. And, although all theories and models of visionary and inspirational leadership obviously emphasize the organizational visions of top executive leaders, insufficient attention has been paid to the critical components of this construct. Sashkin's theory and other more recent contributions (e.g., Larword, Falbe, Kriger, & Miesing, 1995; Nanus, 1992; Zaccaro, Marks, O'Connor-Boes, & Costanza, 1995) have begun to address this issue.

OTHER MODELS OF VISIONARY AND INSPIRATIONAL LEADERSHIP

As noted earlier, there are other models and theories of visionary and inspirational leadership that describe the behavior of executive leaders in developing and implementing an organizational vision. These models and theories have in common several of the elements associated with the theories discussed in this chapter. Therefore, a description of these models and theories would be redundant. However, a summary of these models and theories developed by House and Shamir (1993) is presented in Table 8-2. They are compared according to the behaviors ascribed to executive leaders attempting to effect changes in organizational culture through the articulation of vision and the empowerment of subordinates.

Requisite Executive Leader Characteristics

The role requirements of the executive leader prescribed by vision-based models and theories of executive leadership suggest a number of key

T A B L E 8 - 2

Behaviors Specified in Charismatic, Transformational, and Visionary Theories of Executive Leadership

Behavior	Weber (1947)	House (1977)	Burns (1978)	Bass (1985)	Bennis & Nanus (1985)	Conger & Kanungo (1987)	Sashkin (1988)	Shamir, House, & Arthur (1991)
Vision development	X	X	X	X	X	X	X	X
Frame alignment								X
Empowerment: Showing confidence in and respect for followers		X	X	X	X	X	X	X
Empowerment: Setting challenging expectations	X							X
Role modeling: Setting personal example	X	X		X		X	X	X
Role modeling: Showing self-confidence	X	X		X			X	X
Image building: Establishing trustworthiness		X				X	X	X
Image building: Displaying competence	X	X				X	X	X
Demonstrating exceptional behavior					X	X	X	X
Risk taking	X					X	X	X
Support: Showing consideration and concern				X			X	
Adaptation: Showing versatility							X	
Demonstrating environmental sensitivity						X	X	
Providing intellectual stimulation				X				X

Note. From "Toward the Integration of Transformational, Charismatic, and Visionary Theories," by R. J. House and B. Shamir, in *Leadership Theory and Research: Perspectives and Directions* (p. 85), by M. M. Chemers and R. Ayman (Eds.), 1993, San Diego, CA: Academic Press. Copyright 1993 by Academic Press. Adapted with permission.

executive leader characteristics that facilitate visionary and inspirational leadership. Specifically, qualities that enhance executive leadership include those that promote the development of an effective vision, as well as those that enhance the executive leader's ability to elicit trust, emotional attachment, and strong organizational commitment from followers.

COGNITIVE ABILITIES

The development of an effective vision requires that the executive leader be able to derive an adaptive and appropriate fit between the organization and its environment at some future time. This time can be as much as 15 to 20 years in the future for executive leaders at the top of the organization (Jacobs & Jaques, 1987; Lewis & Jacobs, 1992; Sashkin, 1988). Thus, executive leaders are required to create a logical framework from highly ambiguous and complex data. Furthermore, they need to understand the complexity of the organization and its congruence with the emerging vision. This suggests that several cognitive abilities, such as creativity, reasoning skills, and intelligence, are necessary for effective visionary leadership (Atwater, Penn, & Rucker, 1991; Sashkin, 1988; Tichy & Devanna, 1986a, 1986b).

Sashkin (1988, 1992) argued that the ambiguity of both the organization and its environment, particularly because they must correspond at some point in the distant future, requires cognitive complexity in the visionary executive leader. Like Jaques (1986), Sashkin (1988) identified four necessary executive leader cognitive skills: (a) expression, (b) explanation, (c) extension, and (d) expansion of his or her vision. Kanungo and Conger (1992) agreed, emphasizing the communication requirements of successful charismatic leadership and skill in vision articulation. Vision articulation is the first step in successfully implementing the vision within the organization. This contribution suggests that crystallized cognitive skills such as verbal expression are critical competencies of successful visionary and inspirational leaders.

SELF-CONFIDENCE

Several researchers have argued that to be effective visionary and inspirational executive leaders need high self-confidence (Atwater et al., 1991; Bass, 1985; Boal & Bryson, 1988; House, 1977; House & Howell, 1992). High self-confidence helps executive leaders develop an innovative vision and confront the difficult challenges they may face in implementing it. By displaying a strong sense of confidence, executive leaders convey to followers a positive message about the vision's feasibility and workability. Self-confidence also encourages the trust necessary for successful vision implementation.

Related to self-confidence is a strong sense of personal control. Sash-kin (1992) argued that a successful visionary leader needs high self-efficacy, or the belief that he or she can effectively confront difficult challenges. Likewise, Howell and Avolio (1993) proposed that transformational leadership requires an internal locus of control. Executive leaders with an internal locus of control act from the belief that they can have significant control over the direction and nature of organizational events. House and Howell (1992) suggested that self-efficacy, self-confidence, and an internal locus of control would affect the influence tactics selected by an executive leader. When an executive leader is self-confident, he or she is more likely to select supportive and rational modes of influence (i.e., such as those related to transformational leadership). Low self-confidence leads to the use of more reward-based or coercive modes of executive leader influence.

SOCIALIZED POWER MOTIVE

History is replete with examples of constructive and destructive charismatic leaders. A major distinction between these types of charismatic leaders is that constructive charismatic leaders are more likely to be operating from high power needs but with a socialized orientation, or what McClelland (1985) termed "activity inhibition." House and Howell (1992) posited activity inhibition as a key characteristic of effective (i.e., constructive) charismatic leaders. Like McClelland, they defined this characteristic as "an unconscious motive to use social influence, or to satisfy the power need, in socially desirable ways, for the betterment of the collective rather than for personal self-interest" (p. 95). Sashkin (1988) also noted that socialized power motives lead to the executive leader's predisposition to empower subordinates. Personalized power motives engender the opposite behavior pattern, that is, all power is retained by the executive leader.

RISK PROPENSITY

Conger and Kanungo (1987, 1992; Kanungo & Conger, 1992) argued that the attribution of charisma results from the executive leader's articulation of a vision that is unconventional and counter to the status quo. Furthermore, this attribution occurs when the executive leader takes personal risks in the service of this vision. Thus, a strong propensity for risk taking appears to be a critical aspect of the personality of successful visionary and inspirational executive leaders.

Tichy and Devanna's (1986a, 1986b) theory of transformational leadership makes a similar point. They argued that such executive leaders are intellectually and emotionally courageous. Such leaders are able to discern when it is possible to confront a painful reality and when the risk in doing so is too strong to pursue. They also are able to resist conformity and risk saying potentially unpalatable things to subordinates.

SOCIAL SKILLS

Conger and Kanungo (1987) argued that effective charismatic leaders are sensitive to and acutely aware of environmental contingencies and realities. They also noted that such leaders are "sensitive to both the abilities and emotional needs of followers, and they understand the resources and constraints of the physical and social environments in which they operate" (p. 643). Thus, another critical competency for successful visionary and inspirational leadership is social perceptiveness and sensitivity (Zaccaro, Gilbert, Thor, & Mumford, 1991). Furthermore, that such executive leaders must articulate and "sell" a vision to subordinates means they need to have strong persuasion and negotiation skills.

NURTURANCE

The focus of transformational leaders on empowering and developing subordinates requires that they have an orientation toward helping others and being concerned with their progress. Accordingly, some theorists have associated successful leadership with a nurturant and empathetic personality (House & Howell, 1992; Ross & Offerman, 1991). This characteristic is associated with Bass's (1985) individualized consideration aspect of transformational leadership. For example, Bass noted that personal counseling is an important dimension of successful military leadership, although its focus changes across ranks. That is, at lower levels (e.g., lieutenant and captain), personal counseling skills involve the ability to listen, identify personal problems, and encourage subordinates to express the emotional aspects of their problems to fully understand them. At upper ranks (e.g., colonel and general officers), these skills more often involve reinforcing a better fit between subordinate needs and job requirements. In such situations, the executive leader is attuned to signs of distress that are engendered by a poor fit. These differences in the nature of counseling skill requirements by rank, however, may be attributed to differences in the age and emotional maturity of the subordinates at upper versus lower military ranks.

Measurement

The key dimensions of visionary and inspirational leadership reflect a variety of influences on subordinate commitment, attitudes, and work effort. The most systematic attempt to assess these dimensions is Bass's Multi-Factor Leadership Questionnaire (MLQ). This survey instrument assesses seven leadership factors subsumed under the categories of transformational, transactional, and laissez-faire leadership. These factors have emerged from several factor analyses of early scales (Bass, 1985; Hater & Bass, 1988; Waldman, Bass, & Einstein, 1987). The four factors of transformational leadership described by Bass and Avolio (1993, pp. 51–52) are summarized as follows:

- *Charisma or idealized influence*: Executive leaders are trusted and seen as having an attainable mission and vision. Sample item: "Has my trust in his or her ability to overcome any obstacle."
- *Inspirational motivation*: Executive leaders provide symbols and simplified emotional appeals to increase awareness and understanding of mutually desired goals. Sample item: "Uses symbols and images to focus our efforts."
- *Intellectual stimulation*: Executive leaders encourage followers to question their ways of doing things or to break with the past. Followers are supported for questioning their values, beliefs, and expectations and for thinking on their own and addressing challenges. Sample item: "Enables me to think about old problems in new ways."
- *Individualized consideration*: Followers are treated differently but equitably on a one-to-one basis. They also are provided with learning opportunities. Sample item: "Coaches me if I need it."

These factors reflect transformational leadership as a process of changing follower attitudes, beliefs, and motivation to reflect stronger commitment to the executive leader's articulated vision. These factors define the essential components of subordinate empowerment.

Bass and Avolio (1993, p. 52) identified the following as transactional leadership factors:

- *Contingent reward*: Involves positively reinforcing interactions between executive leaders and followers that emphasize exchange (e.g., the executive leader provides appropriate rewards when followers meet agreed-on objectives). Sample item: "Makes sure there is close agreement between what he or she expects me to do and what I can get from him or her for my effort."
- *Management by exception*: Executive leaders intervene only when things go wrong. They may remain passive until problems develop, or they may arrange to monitor the performance of followers more actively to intervene when mistakes are made. Sample item: "Takes action only when a mistake has occurred."

These factors reflect an exchange or transaction whereby subordinates provide work effort and executive leaders structure and facilitate subordinate goal attainment. Executive leaders provide rewards and support for subordinates' acceptance of work structure, rules, and procedures. Deviations are met with punishment and discipline. The description of management by exception includes both an active and passive mode (Bass, 1996). The active mode refers to the establishment of procedures to monitor subordinate compliance with work procedures and to detect problems in a timely manner. The passive mode refers to executive leaders' intervention only when problems are apparent. This passivity is noted more strongly in the last factor, which was defined by Bass and Avolio (1993, p. 53) as *nonleadership*:

■ *Laissez-faire*: Leadership is absent. Intervention by the nominal executive leader is avoided. Decisions often are delayed; feedback, rewards, and involvement are absent; and there are no attempts to motivate followers or to recognize and satisfy their needs. Sample item: "Doesn't tell me where he or she stands on issues."

The MLQ reflects the major dimensions of transformational leadership as well as items assessing transactional leadership and nonleadership. The transformational leadership characteristics include charisma, effectively subsuming the work of House (1977) and Conger and Kanungo (1987, 1992). This factor reflects the vision-setting role of executive leaders. One of the behavioral indicators of this construct is that the leader "transmits a sense of joint mission and ownership" (Bass & Avolio, 1983, p. 56). The factor Inspirational Motivation also contains vision-setting behaviors. One such behavioral indicator that reflects this factor is that the executive leader "presents an optimistic and attainable view of the future" (Bass & Avolio, 1983, p. 56). Thus, the MLQ appears to be applicable to multiple theories of visionary or inspirational leadership.

The MLQ has been administered to many samples of leaders at all organizational levels. These samples have been gathered worldwide, from a diverse number of groups, organizations (for profit and nonprofit), and institutions. The MLQ has demonstrated strong psychometric properties. The evidence regarding these properties is presented in chapter 9.

Executive Leader Development

Several researchers have described approaches to training and developing visionary and inspirational leadership (e.g., Avolio & Gibbons, 1988; Bass, 1996; Conger & Kanungo, 1988; Kouzes & Posner, 1987).

A central issue that has emerged is how much of such leadership can be trained.

LIFE HISTORY INFLUENCES

Most likely, the personal qualities that promote effective visionary and inspirational leadership emerge from a constellation of life experiences. Several of them, however, may also be amenable to focused training interventions. These points are covered next. Avolio and Gibbons (see also Gibbons, 1986) argued that transformational leadership emerges from a pattern of life history events that contribute to an individual's sense of leadership as a transforming process. They described seven key background elements that were derived by Gibbons (1986) from her administration of the MLQ to top corporate executive leaders followed by extensive interviews to gain some understanding of their life histories. These elements are as follows:

- An individual develops a predisposition to set high standards for achievement as a result of parental encouragement and expectations, which extends to many areas of his or her life.
- An individual's family situation, conditions, and circumstances may be difficult and often demanding, but sufficient resources, both individual and systematic, are available to enable the individual to avoid being overwhelmed.
- An individual learns how to deal with his or her emotions, including conflict and disappointment and their effects.
- An executive leader has had many previous leadership opportunities and experiences in a variety of settings.
- An executive leader has a strong desire to engage in developmental work, especially with adults. Such work is undertaken in a conscious and deliberate way, and it becomes so much a part of transformational leadership that it appears automatic.
- Workshops; events; other more formal, structured developmental activities; and relationships with influential individuals who also may have been role models are used to augment and enhance the developmental process.
- The executive leader views all experiences as learning experiences and demonstrates a strong tendency to be self-reflective and to integrate experiences positively. (Avolio & Gibbons, 1988, pp. 289–290)

This research, as well as other studies by Avolio (1994) and Bass and Avolio (undated, cited in Bass, 1996, pp. 108–111), suggests that transformational (and inspirational) leadership is in part grounded in a life-spanning developmental orientation. This does not mean, however, that such forms of leadership are immutable to targeted developmental efforts. Avolio and Gibbons (1988) provided several recommendations for developing executive leaders in organizations, including the use of focused workshops and interventions.

FULL-RANGE LEADERSHIP PROGRAM

Avolio and Bass (1991; described also in Bass, 1996) developed a training program called the Full-Range Leadership Program (FRLP) to develop transformational leaders. The FRLP involves two workshops, the first basic and the second advanced, into 13 modules. The program begins with the administration of the MLQ and a presentation of the principles of transformational and transactional leadership. The intention is to have participants learn to display both forms of leadership and to identify their own weaknesses regarding each form. They then learn new approaches to leadership that reflect less management by exception and a more transformational orientation.

The basic workshop consists of eight modules (Bass, 1996). The first module has participants explore their own implicit theories of leadership. They are asked to describe an executive leader from their own experiences. The ensuing discussion is intended to illustrate how the defining elements of these executive leaders reflect transformational principles. The second and third modules are designed to educate participants regarding the components and key behaviors associated with transformational leadership. The fourth module involves the administration of the MLQ and exploration of participants' leadership profiles. The product of this module is a self-development plan that is intended to foster growth in particular areas of weakness identified in the leadership profile.

The remaining 4 modules are intended to facilitate the learning and development of transformational leadership behaviors. Module 5 involves videotaped role-playing and discussion. Module 6 is designed to foster the effective delegation of responsibility, a key element of subordinate empowerment. Module 7 is a follow-up discussion of each participant's leadership profile as displayed during previous modules, exercises, and interactions. Finally, Module 8 focuses on organizational constraints and blocks to each participant's self-development plan.

The basic workshop is followed by a 3-month interval during which participants are expected to practice and refine learned skills. They are assigned readings and case studies and asked to identify an organizational problem to be the focus of the advanced workshop. This workshop consists of 5 modules, the first of which is a progress review and discussion of participants' leadership development plans. The next module examines the role of values in executive leader decision making, particularly regarding resource allocation decisions. Module 11 involves group discussions of the various organizational problems presented by participants. The groups are encouraged to use creative and intellectually stimulating strategies to resolve these problems. Module 12 focuses on organizational climate and culture issues. Participants explore desired changes in their organization and ways of facilitating these changes from a transformational perspective. The final module concerns the development of organizational vision. Participants are encouraged to complete a follow-up workshop 6 months after completing the advanced workshop.

Bass (1996) reported that more than 1500 executive leaders had completed the FRLP program. He described several evaluations of the program that are reviewed in chapter 9. This program differs from others described in earlier chapters in that development occurs primarily through targeted instruction. However, three other elements are more consistent with other developmental perspectives. First, as indicated by Avolio and Gibbons (1988), an orientation toward transformational leadership emerges from certain life history patterns; thus, executive leader developmental plans

> should have a life span orientation with respect to how the individual leader will build on his or her strengths while reducing his or her weaknesses. The plan must be individually oriented, keyed to earlier life events . . . and flexible enough to accommodate changes in the individual and in the context in which he or she operates. (pp. 302–303)

The second element is that the FRLP involves several components that foster the generalization of learned skills into the workplace. Thus, participants are encouraged to consider transformational leadership in the context of their own organizations. And third, the FRLP incorporates the notion of pushing leaders to the limits of their current ways of thinking and behaving, a developmental practice that is recommended by theorists from both the conceptual and behavioral complexity perspectives of executive leadership. Executive leaders are encouraged to think creatively and in novel ways about their work situations. What is missing, however, is an on-the-job mentor or facilitator who can encourage such thinking.

In summary, Bass and his colleagues (1996) created an executive leader development program that is designed to foster important transformational leadership competencies. This program makes effective use of an assessment instrument keyed to those competencies. The program incorporates a number of elements related to the envisioning process as well as to facilitating subordinate empowerment. Thus, although it was developed from the conceptual framework of transformational leadership theory, it is congruent with several other visionary and inspirational models of executive leadership.

Summary

In the 1980s and 1990s, the visionary and inspirational models of executive leadership were among the most prominent leadership perspectives. However, although these theories arguably are the most visible of recent theories, they are perhaps directed the least explicitly to executive-level leadership. And. whereas several visionary leadership models focus on executive leadership, one of the most prominent, Bass's (1985) transformational leadership theory, does not suggest that qualitative differences exist in the performance requirements of leaders across organizational levels. Instead, leaders at all levels can be transformational or inspirational in relation to their subordinates.

Like the behavioral complexity theories and the strategic decision-making models, but for different reasons, the visionary and inspirational theories of executive leadership do not reflect all of Day and Lord's (1988) suggestions for a systematic theory of executive leadership. These theories, particularly transformational leadership, considerably blur the distinction between upper- and lower-level leadership requirements. Some of these theories, such as those describing charismatic leadership, consider subordinates to be passive recipients of overwhelming leadership influence. According to such theories, top executive leaders exert charismatic influence on the organization as a whole, with other, lower-level executive leaders and managers contributing little to this influence except to maintain it. There is not a systematic attempt, such as that offered by stratified systems theory (SST), to articulate differences in leader contributions and requirements across organizational levels. Thus, there is not a basis for specifying requisite leader performance requirements that change across organizational levels.

Another difference between visionary and inspirational models and theories of executive leadership, again transformational leadership in particular, and other theories and models discussed in this book, is the general lack of specification of the executive leader's boundary management or external systemic role. Much of the conceptual focus is on the internal dynamics of organizational leadership and organizational change. Although Sashkin (1988) and Nanus (1992) discussed vision development as reflecting in part an external awareness, the major focus of these and most other visionary and inspirational theories and models of executive leadership is on facilitating organizational and subordinate acceptance of and commitment to an articulated vision.

Alternatively, the visionary and inspirational theories and models of executive leadership add useful information to the other perspectives discussed in this book by delineating the ingredients and determinants of the process of subordinate influence. These theories and models describe in greater detail some of the roles prescribed by the behavioral complexity theories (e.g., visionary/innovator; mentor). They also provide a framework regarding strategic and vision implementation that is lacking in the strategic decision-making models. Finally, the internal systemic perspective of executive leaders is articulated more forcefully in the visionary and inspirational theories and models of executive leadership than in SST, which focuses predominantly on the executive leader's external systemic perspective.

Two other significant contributions of transformational leadership theory are (a) its measurement of such leadership and (b) an executive leader developmental intervention that is grounded in Bass's (1985) theory as well as in other developmental theories (see Avolio & Gibbons, 1988, for a discussion of these theories). Thus, more than other perspectives, this approach provides a well-researched assessment tool that is integrated in a leader-training program. The Career Path Appreciation technique based on SST (Stamp, 1988) holds similar promise, but it requires additional validation research. Furthermore, the work of Avolio and Gibbons (1988) and Gibbons (1986) provides a life history perspective of transformational leadership as well as a context for executive leader development. This perspective is generally missing from other theories and models of executive leader development.

To summarize, Bass's (1985) transformational leadership theory does not articulate clear cross-level differences in organizational leadership requirements, but it does assign essential characteristics of executive leadership to lower-level managers. This raises significant questions, in particular whether lower-level managers develop visions that become operative within the organizational context. Most other theories and models, such as the theories of charismatic leadership and the theories and models described in previous chapters, assign individuals at lower organizational levels the role of operationalizing and implementing organizational directions established by upper-level executive leaders. Nonetheless, the internal systemic focus of these theories and models and their focus on subordinate empowerment add a conceptual understanding of executive leadership that is lacking in other systematic approaches. Indeed, a full and comprehensive understanding of executive leadership is likely to emerge from integration of the conceptual perspectives described thus far in this book, especially if this integration reflects the bulk of empirical research also reviewed.

Visionary and Inspirational Models of Executive Leadership: Empirical Review and Evaluation

9

Research Model

The research model illustrated in Figure 9-1, which is based primarily on Bass's (1985, 1996; Bass & Avolio, 1993) transformational leadership theory, provides a starting point for review of empirical research investigating visionary and inspirational theories and models of executive leadership. This particular theory was chosen for two reasons. First, most, if not all, of the visionary and inspirational theories and models of executive leadership are fairly compatible with this approach. Bass's theory includes the charismatic influence cited by House (1977) as well as the subordinate empowerment dimension that is part of other visionary and inspirational theories and models of executive leadership. Second, Bass's transformational leadership theory is perhaps the most comprehensive and the most researched theory, and it is the only one that provides a systematic measurement and executive leader development system.

Although the diagram in Figure 9-1 indicates that executive leader assessment and development are based on executive leader characteristics from several visionary and inspirational theories and models of executive leadership, Bass's (1985) measure, the Multi-Factor Leadership Questionnaire (MLQ), and his Full-Range Leadership Program (FRLP; Avolio & Bass, 1991; Bass, 1996) reflect more directly the dimensions of transformational leadership. The model indicates paths from executive leader characteristics and models and theories of executive leadership directly to executive leader assessment and development.

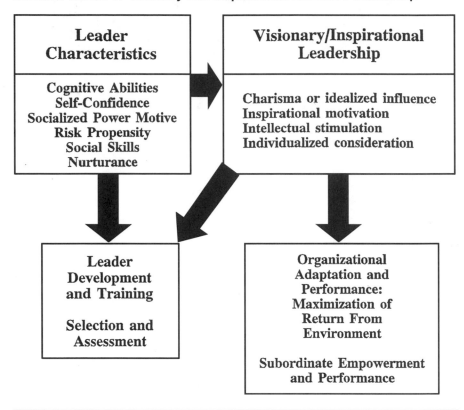

FIGURE 9-1

Research Model of Visionary and Inspirational Executive Leadership

Nature of Organizational Leadership

An essential feature of executive work offered by visionary and inspirational leadership theories is the development of organizational vision. A key empirical question, then, is what are the characteristics of executive vision? The act of translating this vision into collective action links visionary leadership to organizational performance. These themes are examined in the next sections.

CHARACTERISTICS OF VISION

Until recently, there were few, if any, systematic attempts to examine empirically the content of organizational visions. In one study, however,

Larwood, Falbe, Kriger, and Miesing (1995) asked 331 top executive leaders from organizations across the United States to provide a short description of their organizational vision and then to rate their vision using a set of descriptors (e.g., action-oriented, responsive to competition, long-term, changing, directs effort, formalized, risky). Responses to these descriptors were then factor analyzed to determine the content dimensions characterizing the visions of these executive leaders. Study participants were also asked to provide information regarding personal characteristics (e.g., tenure, functional background, time span of their visions) and organizational and environmental characteristics (e.g., rapidity of change in the organization and environment; importance of vision in the organization; degree to which the vision is shared within the organization).

Larwood et al. (1995) reported that seven factors related to vision content were derived from their factor analysis. The first factor was labeled *vision formulation*. This factor referred to whether the vision reflected a long-term, strategic perspective. The second factor was termed *implementation*; it reflected the degree to which the vision was widely understood and communicated throughout the organization. Factor 3 was described as *innovative realism*. This factor referred to the innovativeness of the vision and its flexible responsiveness to environmental changes. The remaining factors had fewer items loading on them and were termed *general* (or "difficult to describe"), *detailed, risk-taking*, and *profit-oriented*. Scores on the various factors were associated with organizational and environmental characteristics. For example, executive leaders who scored high on Factor 1 were likely to report that their vision was important for their organization. Those with high scores on Factor 2 were likely to report that the organizational environment was rapidly changing and that their visions were accepted within the organization.

The vision content reported by Larwood et al. (1995) mirrors the definitions offered by several other researchers (e.g., Kotter, 1990; Nanus, 1992; Sashkin, 1987). These visions have a long-term focus; they are innovative (i.e., different from the status quo); and they reflect environmental and organizational dynamics. What is missing, though, is a value orientation. According to most definitions, visions reflect the executive leader's idealized representation of what the organization should become (see Table 8-1). Accordingly, visions reflect the primary value orientation of the visionary. Values provide the passion and persuasiveness effective executive leaders use to convey to subordinates and others their desired organizational image. Hence, values are the basis for the role of vision in facilitating organizationwide executive leader influence (Senge, 1990).

Senge (1990) argued that effective visions are grounded in positive values that reflect an aspiration for growth and long-term change. Negative visions are based on maintaining the status quo in the face of environmental changes. Regarding this distinction, Senge noted the following:

> Negative visions are limiting for three reasons. First, energy that could build something new is diverted to "preventing" something we don't want to happen. Second, negative visions carry a subtle yet unmistakable message of powerlessness: our people really don't care. They can pull together only when there is sufficient threat. Lastly, negative visions are inevitably short term. The organization is motivated so long as the threat persists. Once it leaves so does the organization's vision and energy. (p. 225)

Zaccaro, Marks, O'Connor-Boes, and Costanza (1995) investigated the role of values in the contents of executive leader visions. They presented Army officers ranging in rank from first and second lieutenant to colonel with a scenario requiring them to construct a vision monograph for the Army. They were asked to rate the importance of 78 items for inclusion in the monograph. The items contained both growth-oriented (or positive) and status-quo-focused (or negative) statements. Officers also were to select the 10 most important items characterizing their vision. These represented the essence of their vision, defined as their *vision core*. The premise was that senior officers would rate growth-oriented values higher and status-quo values-focused lower than junior officers. It also was expected that the vision cores of senior officers would reflect a more growth-oriented value orientation than those of junior officers.

Analyses of statement ratings and item selections supported this premise. For example, colonels reported more growth-oriented (vs. status-quo-focused) values as part of their organizational visions than did lieutenants. Furthermore, an analysis was performed to determine the percentage of each group of participants (i.e., lieutenants, majors, and colonels) who (a) selected no values as part of their vision core (i.e., "valueless visions") or (b) selected only status-quo-based values as the basis for their vision. The results indicated that this percentage was much higher for undergraduates and lieutenants than for majors and colonels, with no colonels reporting a valueless vision and only 4% presenting a status-quo vision. Officers were also asked to provide responses to complex problem-solving exercises. Analyses of these responses indicated that officers with more growth-oriented visions developed higher quality solutions to exercise problems. These results indicate the importance of values as a component of effective visions.

Both of these studies provide information on the content of visions. However, they represent only preliminary investigations. Additional research is necessary to identify the components of vision that (a) are most important for organizational action and (b) facilitate acceptance of, and commitment to, the vision within the organization. Furthermore, the content of executive leader visions needs to be associated with the process of envisioning. Such efforts should enhance understanding of the role of vision in executive leader and organizational effectiveness.

TRANSFORMATIONAL LEADERSHIP AND ORGANIZATIONAL PERFORMANCE

Bass (1985) contended that the modeling of transformational leadership behaviors by upper-level executive leaders would increase the probability that lower-level leaders would also display such behaviors, creating a cascading effect (see also Avolio & Bass, 1988, 1995; Bass & Avolio, 1990; Bass, Waldman, Avolio, & Bebb, 1987). Thus, according to Bass, transformational leadership can generalize across organizational levels. Other theorists have argued that visionary and inspirational leadership behaviors are more likely to be displayed by upper-level executive leaders than by individuals at lower organizational levels (Tichy & Devanna, 1986b). Finally, Bass argued that both transformational and transactional leadership are necessary for effective executive leader and organizational performance, whereas Burns (1978) stated that these leadership styles are opposing and mutually exclusive.

These arguments suggest the following propositions regarding transformational leadership and organizational outcomes:

1. The display of charismatic influence, inspirational motivation, intellectual stimulation, and individualized consideration by upper-level executive leaders will be positively associated with the display of these qualities by lower-level leaders.
2. The display of transformational leadership qualities by executive leaders will be positively associated with subordinate commitment and empowerment.
3. The display of transformational leadership qualities by executive leaders will be positively associated with overall organizational effectiveness.
4. Transformational leadership qualities will contribute to subordinate commitment and organizational effectiveness beyond the influence of transactional leadership qualities.

Cascading Influence of Transformational Leadership

Bass et al. (1987) examined the cascading premise of transformational leadership. They administered the MLQ (Bass, 1985) to 56 first-level supervisors who worked for the New Zealand government. Participants rated their second-level supervisors, and five subordinates of each participant also rated the supervisors using the MLQ. Bass et al. predicted that the transformational leadership displayed at the higher organizational level would be positively associated with the amount of transformational leadership displayed at the lower level. They found that, indeed, ratings of charismatic influence, individualized consideration, and intellectual stimulation assigned by second-level supervisors were correlated with the same ratings of first-line supervisors. One of the two transactional leadership factors, contingent reward, also yielded a significant cross-level correlation.

These data indicate that transformational leadership has a cascading effect and provide support for Proposition 1. Second-level supervisors who were rated highly on transformational leadership characteristics had subordinates who also were rated as displaying transformational leadership. However, as Bass et al. (1997) noted, this effect may not be a socialization one whereby the second-level supervisors fostered the emergence of a transformational orientation in their subordinates. Instead, selection processes may have operated to create matches between supervisors. That is, organizations and second-level supervisors may have selected compatible first-level supervisors, or the latter may have self-selected into their assignments. Thus, appropriate testing of Proposition 1 would require a longitudinal design examining changes in lower-level leadership patterns as a function of transformational leadership modeling by upper-level executive leaders.

Outcomes of Transformational Leadership

Hater and Bass (1988) examined the association between two elements of transformational leadership, charisma and intellectual stimulation, and the performance ratings of 54 managers by their superiors. Each manager was rated on (a) judgment and decision making, (b) financial management, (c) communication, (d) persuasiveness, and (e) risk taking. Subordinates of each manager provided ratings of both dimensions of transformational leadership and the manager's use of contingent reward. The results indicated significant correlations between display of charisma and all of the performance ratings. Intellectual stimulation of subordinates was correlated with financial management and communication. Use of contingent reward was not correlated with any of the rated effectiveness measures. Hater and Bass's results support the proposed link between transformational leadership behaviors and individual executive leader effectiveness. They also suggest the superiority of vision-based leadership over more conventional leadership styles that are based on reward exchange.

Yammarino, Spangler, and Bass (1993) also investigated the effects of displayed transformational leadership on individual leader performance. Yammarino et al. studied junior naval officers. Senior subordinates provided ratings of each junior officer's display of charisma, individualized consideration, intellectual stimulation, and inspirational leadership as well as display of transactional leadership. They also provided ratings of subordinate satisfaction and officer effectiveness in meeting the job-related needs of subordinates. These items were combined into a measure of attributed performance. Yammarino et al. also collected performance ratings from each officer's superior as well as recommendations for early promotion. These ratings were combined into a measure of appraised performance. Yammarino et al. found that transformational leadership, but not transactional leadership, was significantly associated with both measures of officer performance.

Both of these studies (Hater & Bass, 1988; Yammarino et al., 1993) examined the link between transformational leadership and individual performance in junior leaders. Two studies by House and his colleagues (House, Spangler, & Woycke, 1991; House, Woycke, & Fodor, 1988) examined charisma and performance in U.S presidents. House et al. (1988) asked nine political historians to rate each U.S president using a measure of displayed charisma. Presidents clearly rated as charismatic or noncharismatic were selected for further analyses. Other raters coded the biographies of two cabinet members for each president according to whether presidents rated as charismatic (a) displayed proposed charismatic behaviors and (b) had a positive effect on their cabinet members. House et al. (1988) also associated rated charisma with five independent rankings of presidential performance. They found that effective, charismatic presidents rated higher in the frequency of displayed charismatic behaviors and positive influence on their cabinet members than ineffective, noncharismatic presidents. However, effective, charismatic presidents did not differ from effective, noncharismatic presidents on these measures. Because of the very low sample size (i.e., effective, noncharismatic presidents = 3), the power of this test was small. In the rankings of presidential performance, all but one of the charismatic presidents were rated as great or near great for each ranking. Most of the noncharismatic presidents were rated at the bottom of the rankings.

House et al. (1991) followed this study with one that used ratings of presidential charisma from coded editorials and coded biographies by cabinet members and ratings provided by Simonton (1988). Presidential performance was assessed using a number of measures, including two separate surveys of historians who rated presidents on several performance dimensions (Maranell, 1970; Murray & Blessing, 1983), citations of "great decisions" (Winter, 1987) for each president, and performance ratings based on presidential biographies. House et al.'s analyses indicated that presidential charisma was associated with most of the various performance measures.

Together, these four studies support the premise that vision-based leadership, operationalized as display of charisma or transformational leadership behavior, is associated with the performance of the individual executive leader. In addition, these studies suggest an association with organizational performance as well. Howell and Avolio (1993) assessed this relationship more directly by measuring transformational and transactional leadership in 78 managers from the top four organizational levels of a single organization. They also acquired measures of the performance of each manager's consolidated unit. These measures were based on the achievement of targeted goals 1 year after the measures of leadership were obtained. The results indicated that "leaders who displayed less management by exception and less contingent reward and more individualized consideration, intellectual stimulation, and charisma positively contributed to the achievement of business-unit goals" (p. 899). These findings confirm those of other studies (see Bass & Avolio, 1993, for a review) that transformational leadership appears to more strongly influence leader effectiveness than transactional leadership. This study also provided evidence for the influence of visionary leadership on organizational performance.

Table 9-1 is a summary by Bass and Avolio (1993) of other studies that administered the MLQ (Bass, 1985) to leaders and assessed the effects of transformational and transactional leadership on various indices of performance. This table indicates correlations between dimensions of transformational leadership and the measure of rated performance that is also part of the MLQ. These correlations are uniformly high. A noteworthy aspect of this review by Bass and Avolio is that it included leaders at all organizational levels. It must also be noted, however, that these correlations are inflated by same-source or method bias. For example, Bass and Avolio reported that studies that included different measures of transformational leadership and performance also reported significant, albeit lower, correlations (e.g., Avolio, Waldman, & Einstein, 1988).

The strength or magnitude of correlations between transformational leadership predictors and outcomes has varied widely across studies. Lowe, Kroeck, and Sivasubramaniam (1995) completed a meta-analysis of these correlations to determine the average magnitude adjusted for statistical and methodological artifacts. They examined several moderators of these correlations, including the organizational level of the leaders (upper or lower), the type of organization (public or private), and the nature of the criterion (subordinate perceptions or organizational measures). They also contrasted published and unpublished studies of transformational leadership. Based on five selection criteria, Lowe et al. identified 39 published and 17 unpublished studies of transformational leadership for inclusion in their meta-analysis.

TABLE 9-1

Correlations Between Dimensions of Transformational Leadership and Rated Organizational Effectiveness

Sample	n	Transformational leadership score			
		CH	IL	IS	IC
U.S. Army officers	104	.85		.47	.70
New Zealand professionals and managers	45	.56		.52	.62
World-class leaders; student raters	67	.58		.34	.40
New Zealand educational administrators	23	.76		.66	.63
Division heads, *Fortune* 500 high-tech firm	49	.72		.44	.47
Indian professionals and managers	58	.59	.56	.54	.46
Project leaders, *Fortune* 500 high-tech firm	75	.66	.44	.55	.55
Religious ministers, parishioners	28	.61		.52	.54
Vice presidents, *Fortune* 500 high-tech firm	9	.71		.59	.53
Middle-level managers, *Fortune* 500 high-tech firm	38	.75		.60	.66
Middle-level managers, Federal Express	26	.88	.79	.79	.79
U.S. Navy junior officers	186	.87	.73	.74	.73
U.S. Navy senior officers	318	.83		.72	.73
U.S. Army officers (NATO)	341	.72		.61	.56
Canadian Army field-grade officers	226	.53		.38	.53
German Army field-grade officers	167	.40		.41	.38
Japanese middle-level managers	132	.62		.50	.51

Note. CH = charisma; IL = inspirational leadership; IS = intellectual stimulation; IC = individualized consideration. Reproduced by special permission of the Distributor, Mind Garden, Inc., 1690 Woodside Road 202, Redwood City, CA 94061 (650) 261-3500 from the *Multifactor Leadership Questionnaire* by Bernard M. Bass and Bruce J. Avolio. Copyright 1997 by Bernard M. Bass and Bruce J. Avolio. All rights reserved. Further reproduction is prohibited without the Distributor's written consent.

Lowe et al. (1995) found a highly similar pattern of results in published and unpublished studies and therefore combined the two samples. They also found that the transformational factors of charismatic influence (raw $r = .62$); individualized consideration (raw $r = .53$); and intellectual stimulation (raw $r = .51$) were all more strongly related to outcomes than the transactional factors of contingent reward (raw $r = .34$) and management by exception (raw $r = .04$), with charismatic influence demonstrating the strongest association (inspirational motivation was not measured in many of these studies). The range of correlations for each of the transformational leadership factors suggested the presence of moderators. Accordingly, Lowe et al. found that the effects of transformational leadership were stronger in public than private organizations and when subordinate perceptions were used as criteria. The magnitude of the correlations with subordinate perceptions was on average about 40 points higher (mean $r = .71$) than the correlations with organizational measures (mean $r = 30$). However, Lowe et al. also noted that the latter correlations were still statistically significant. This study demonstrated not only the strength of transformational leadership effects but also at least two moderators of these effects.

All of the studies described thus far were based on the MLQ (Bass, 1985). Using a different operationalization, Podsakoff, MacKenzie, Moorman, and Fetter (1990) examined the effects of transformational leadership on subordinate attitudes and commitment. This influence is critical to visionary and inspirational models of executive leadership because a fundamental mechanism of organizational change used by such leaders is empowering subordinates and garnering their commitment on behalf of the organization. Podsakoff et al. had subordinates in a diversified petrochemical company provide ratings of their manager on six behaviors: (a) identifying and articulating a vision, (b) serving as an appropriate model, (c) fostering the acceptance of group goals, (d) establishing high performance expectations, and (e) providing individualized support, and providing intellectual stimulation. Followers also rated their own satisfaction, their trust in their leader, and their organizational citizenship behavior. Podsakoff et al. found that visionary leadership behavior was associated with both greater follower trust and satisfaction and greater organizational citizenship behavior. Furthermore, the influence of transformational leadership behavior on organizational citizenship was mediated entirely by follower trust. That is, executive leaders engender follower commitment to the organization by increasing their trust. These results held even when same-source bias was controlled.

The central premise of visionary and inspirational theories and models of executive leadership is that executive organizational leaders, if not leaders at other organizational levels, are required to provide a vision to followers that inspires them to work hard on behalf of organization and to support necessary organizational change. If the vision is appropriate and followers provide effort and commitment, the result should be stronger organizational performance. The studies discussed in this chapter show demonstrate significant support for this premise. Likewise, Shamir, House, and Arthur (1993) provided the following summary of 35 empirical studies of charismatic leadership:

> Collectively, these findings indicate that leaders who engage in the theoretical charismatic behaviors produce the theoretical effects. In addition, they receive higher performance ratings, have more satisfied and more highly motivated followers, and are

viewed as more effective leaders by their superiors and followers than others in positions of leadership. Further, the effect size of charismatic leader behavior on follower satisfaction and performance is consistently higher than prior field study findings concerning other leader behavior, generally, ranging well below 0.01 probability of error due to chance, with correlations frequently ranging in the neighborhood of .50 or better. (pp. 578–579)

Together, these studies provide significant support for Propositions 2 and 3. They demonstrate that the components of transformational leadership, as measured by the MLQ (Bass, 1996), are related to (a) organizational effectiveness and overall performance; (b) the leader's unit's effectiveness; (c) ratings of the individual leader's performance; and (d) ratings of subordinates' satisfaction and commitment. These influences have been identified, not only with the MLQ but also through other operationalizations of visionary and inspirational leadership. However, the question remains whether transformational leadership adds more positive influence than transactional leadership.

Augmentation Effects

The positive correlations between transformational and transactional leadership behaviors and performance found in the meta-analysis by Lowe et al. (1995) and in the review by Bass and Avolio (1993), respectively, suggest that both forms of leadership improve executive leader effectiveness. Bass (1985) proposed that transformational leadership would augment the influence of transactional leadership on organizational outcomes. Burns (1978), however, suggested that they are alternate forms of leadership. Several studies have provided evidence for the augmentation effect proposed by Bass (Avolio & Howell, 1992; Hater & Bass, 1988; Seltzer & Bass, 1987; Waldman, Bass, & Yammarino, 1990). Across these studies, this effect was examined using hierarchical regression analysis in which transactional behaviors were entered at the first step, followed by transformational behaviors. The results were similar transformational leadership adds significantly to the prediction of executive leader effectiveness beyond the influence of transactional leadership. These findings support Proposition 4.

Summary

Studies of visionary and transformational leadership have provided strong support for the premise that such leadership significantly enhances executive leader effectiveness and organizational performance. This connection has been identified in a variety of samples, using both different operationalizations of visionary leadership and a range of organizational-related criteria. An interesting point is that visionary leadership has been demonstrated to exist at all organizational levels. In fact, Lowe et al. (1995) reported in their meta-analysis that mean transformational leadership scores were actually higher for lower-level organizational leaders than for upper-level leaders, although the magnitude of correlations between these scores and organizational outcomes did not differ by organizational level. Thus, in general, the data do not support the premise that transformational and inspirational leadership are exclusively the province of top executive leaders.

It should be noted that transformational leadership has been predominantly assessed as a subordinate interaction style. The four transformational leadership behaviors assessed by the MLQ (Bass, 1985), for example, refer to patterns of leader interaction with and influence of followers. The emphasis is on gaining follower support and commitment, with attendant consequences for organizational effectiveness. The MLQ does not systematically measure the long-term or strategic focus of visionary or inspirational leadership. Although leaders at multiple organizational levels may display a transformational orientation with their subordinates, the vision that should be the foundation of such influence most likely emerge from upper-level leaders. Alternatively, the subordinate empowerment that is intended as the product of transformational leadership means that subordinates should have considerable input regarding the future direction of the organization. Although this notion contradicts other visionary and inspirational models and theories of executive leadership described elsewhere in this book, it does suggest that vision may not necessarily cascade solely from the top of the organization. Nonetheless, future research on transformational leadership needs to incorporate the concept of vision, and particularly its content (Larwood et al., 1995), into the process of such leadership.

Requisite Leader Characteristics

The conceptual theories and models described in chapter 8 and the research model illustrated in Figure 9-1 proposed several personal characteristics as fostering the effective display of visionary and inspirational (i.e., transformational) executive leadership. The following propositions summarize the relationships among these personal characteristics and effective executive leadership:

5. Executive leaders' cognitive abilities will be positively associated with the effective display of charismatic influence, inspirational

motivation, intellectual stimulation, and individualized consideration.

6. Executive leaders' self-confidence will be positively associated with the effective display of charismatic influence, inspirational motivation, intellectual stimulation, and individualized consideration.

7. Executive leaders' socialized power motives will be positively associated with the effective display of charismatic influence, inspirational motivation, intellectual stimulation, and individualized consideration.

8. Executive leaders' risk propensity will be positively associated with the effective display of charismatic influence, inspirational motivation, intellectual stimulation, and individualized consideration.

9. Executive leaders' social skills will be positively associated with the effective display of charismatic influence, inspirational motivation, intellectual stimulation, and individualized consideration.

10. Executive leaders' nurturing orientation will be positively associated with the effective display of charismatic influence, inspirational motivation, intellectual stimulation, and individualized consideration.

Much of the research on executive leader qualities and effective visionary and inspirational leadership has focused on motivational and personality characteristics. In their examination of presidential charisma, for example, House et al. (1991) assessed the motive patterns of each president by coding the content of (a) presidents' inaugural addresses (Winter, 1987); (b) their letters and speeches; (c) their autobiographies; and (d) biographies written by others. Motives measured were affiliation, power, achievement, and activity inhibition. Presidential charisma was assessed from coded editorials, coded biographies by cabinet members, and ratings provided by Simonton (1988). House et al. found that, as predicted, charisma was positively related to need for power and activity inhibition. According to McClelland (1985) and House and Howell (1992), this combination of motives represents an orientation toward using power on behalf of others. House et al. also found that charismatic presidents scored low on achievement motives and that charisma was not significantly related to affiliation needs.

B. J. Smith (1982) compared two groups of effective executive leaders who were considered to be either high or low in charisma. Participants were asked to identify leaders from their work environment who were (a) effective and charismatic or (b) effective but not charismatic. Questionnaires were then distributed to other followers of each leader assessing their perceptions of the leader's self-confidence, their trust in the leader, their departmental identification, and their job involvement. The leaders were also interviewed to assess their developmental propensity. According to the results of analyses of these data, charismatic leaders were perceived as more self-confident than noncharismatic leaders. Charismatic leaders also were found to be more concerned about the professional growth and development of subordinates than noncharismatic leaders. Followers of charismatic leaders expressed greater trust, loyalty, and commitment to their leaders than followers of noncharismatic leaders. These data provide evidence of self-confidence and nurturance as characteristics of visionary and inspirational leaders. Likewise, this study also confirmed some proposed effects of charisma on follower attitudes.

Ross and Offerman (1991) also found support for nurturance as a quality of visionary and inspirational leaders. They measured nurturance, self-confidence, dominance, pragmatism, need for change, and other personality characteristics in mid-career Air Force commissioned officers. MLQ (Bass, 1985) ratings were also collected to calculate transformational leadership scores for each officer. Ross and Offerman's results indicated that the strongest personality correlates of transformational leadership were pragmatism (.69), nurturance (.67), and self-confidence (.63).

Atwater, Penn, and Rucker (1991) asked participants from a range of jobs and occupations in the military and civilian sectors to select both a charismatic and noncharismatic leader to evaluate. Participants then completed an extensive personality inventory for each leader. Charismatic leaders were perceived as more insightful, confident, and determined than noncharismatic leaders. They also were more likely to be perceived as risk takers and rated as low on conformity.

Howell and Avolio (1993) examined locus of control as a characteristic of transformational leaders. In this study, 78 managers from the top four levels of a financial institution completed Rotter's I-E scale; followers provided ratings of transformational leadership behaviors from the MLQ (Bass, 1985). The results indicated that managers with an internal locus of control had higher scores on intellectual stimulation and individualized consideration, but not charisma, than managers with an external locus of control. These results are the only ones to date to connect an executive leader's sense of personal control with his or her display of visionary and inspirational leadership.

Together, these studies demonstrate support for some of the personal executive leader characteristics that are proposed as determinants of visionary and inspirational leadership. Specifically, self-confidence, socialized power motives, risk propensity, and nurturance have been associated with one or more factors of transformational leadership. Thus, support has been demonstrated for Propositions 6, 7, 8, and 10. Few, if any, studies have examined the link between cognitive and social abilities, respectively, and transformational leadership. Thus, evidence is lacking to support of Propositions 5 and 9. This is surprising given the strong intellectual and social demands required of transformational leadership. For example, the intellectual stimulation of others would presumably require that the executive leader possess significant cognitive abilities and intelligence. Also, the communication and implementation of an organizational vision that is at the heart of visionary and inspirational leadership influence would indicate the importance of social skills and competencies. Further research specifically targeting these skill sets as determinants of effective visionary and inspirational leadership is necessary.

In addition, it should be noted that many of the studies reviewed in this chapter reported bivariate correlations that could represent spurious effects. Furthermore, few, if any, studies have examined the association between proposed executive leader characteristics and such activities as the development of an effective vision and the implementation of this vision in a complex social domain. Some (although not all) of the studies suffer from same-source bias in that followers provide estimates of both charisma and assessments of personality (e.g., Atwater et al., 1991). Again, further research, particularly multivariate research, is necessary to validate proposed individual determinants of visionary and inspirational leadership (see Atwater & Yammarino, 1993, as an example).

Measurement

The MLQ was developed by Bass (1985) to assess the components of transformational, transactional, and laissez-faire leadership. The following proposition regarding the MLQ is examined in this section:

11. The MLQ will exhibit acceptable levels of reliability, construct validity, and criterion-related validity.

The structure of the MLQ has emerged from several factor analyses of its items. The first such analysis by Bass (1985) was completed with 176 U.S. Army colonels and yielded the following five factors: Charismatic Influence, Contingent Reward, Individualized Consideration, Management by Exception, and Intellectual Stimulation. Hater and Bass (1988) completed another factor analysis of the MLQ and reported a similar structure, except that they divided Management by Exception into active and passive modes. Howell and Avolio (1993) used a more stringent confirmatory analysis strategy (i.e., they adopted a partial least squares analysis and used only factor loadings mostly greater than seven) and reported the same factor structure. These studies support six of the components of transformational leadership. Items reflecting Inspirational Motivation loaded on Charismatic Influence. Despite this result, Bass (1996) continued to argue for a conceptual distinction between these two factors.

Internal consistency estimates have proved strong for all of the factors except Management by Exception. Lowe et al.'s (1995) meta-analysis of 56 studies indicated the following mean Cronbach alphas: charisma = .92; individualized consideration = .88; intellectual stimulation = .86; contingent reward = .82; and management by exception = .65. However, the active and passive modes of Management by Exception were combined in the studies reviewed by Lowe et al. Howell and Avolio (1993) examined them separately and reported internal consistency estimates of .86 and .72 for the active and passive modes, respectively. The three transformational leadership factors and three transactional leadership factors (including both the passive and active modes of Management by Exception) have exhibited acceptable levels of internal consistency. The meta-analysis by Lowe et al. and reviews by Bass (1990, 1996) and Bass and Avolio (1993), however, did not report any studies providing test–retest reliabilities.

As indicated in Table 9-1 and in reviews by Bass (1990, 1996), the criterion validity of the transformational leadership factors has been amply demonstrated for subordinate satisfaction and leader performance. Questions remain regarding the construct validity of the MLQ (Bass, 1985) transformational leadership factors. The factor analyses suggest six distinct factors. However, although Bass (1996) argued for the conceptual divergence of inspirational motivation, no empirical evidence has supported this distinction. Bass and Avolio (1993) also argued that individualized consideration is conceptually different from the consideration construct measured by the Leader Behavior Description Questionnaire. However, Seltzer and Bass (1990) reported a correlation of .69 between these two measures, a magnitude that is too high for discriminant validity. These reviews, as well as that of Bass (1990), did not report any attempt to validate the remaining constructs assessed by the MLQ using, for example, a multimethod-multitrait approach (Campbell & Fiske, 1959). Additional research is necessary to determine the construct validity of these measures.

To summarize, studies of the psychometric properties of the MLQ (Bass, 1985) have yielded mixed support for Proposition 11. The internal consistencies and criterion-related validities of the transformational leadership factors have been demonstrated to be fairly strong. Factor analyses completed by several researchers have supported the proposed distinctiveness among the measured constructs. However, additional evidence is need to fully determine the convergent and discriminant validity of these constructs

Leader Development

Avolio and Bass (1991; also reported in Bass, 1996) designed the Full Range Leadership Program (FRLP) as a training intervention to develop transformational leadership skills in both individuals in leadership positions and potential leaders. The FRLP consists of 13 modules that are designed to (a) teach the principles of transformational and transactional leadership; (b) assist participants in understanding their own leadership profile and develop a plan to improve weaknesses; (c) have participants learn and practice the skills of transformational leadership; and (d) confront and resolve issues connected with the transfer and practice of these skills in participants' organizations. The first, or basic, workshop consists of eight modules; the remaining five modules are presented in an advanced workshop that is completed 3 months after the basic workshop.

Bass (1996) reported two unpublished studies that evaluated the effectiveness of the FRLP. The first, by Crookall (1989), used a Solomon four-group design that contrasted the FRLP with the Hershey-Blanchard situational leadership development program and with two control groups. The sample was supervisors of inmates working in prison shops. Criteria included productivity, absenteeism, and prosocial behavior. In describing the results of this evaluation, Bass reported the following:

> Significant training effects were obtained on such outcomes as productivity, absenteeism, and the prosocial behavior of the inmates who worked for the trained supervisors. Specifically, compared with untrained supervisors, trained supervisors were found to be more effective leaders on a variety of specific measures of organizational and individual level outcomes. More dramatic effects were reported for the FRLP than for situational leadership although both forms of training were found to the shop supervisor's performance.
>
> The performances of both trained samples improved, but in comparison to the three other groups of supervisors, those who were trained in transformational leadership did as well or better at improving productivity, absenteeism, and "citizenship" behavior among the inmates; they also won more respect from the inmates. (p. 123)

These outcomes reflect Kirkpatrick's (1959) behavioral and results-oriented training criteria and indicate a considerable level of success regarding the FRLP. Another evaluation study by Avolio and Bass (1994) that was described in Bass (1996) also provided evidence for the FRLP's success in developing transformational leadership skills. This study evaluated 66 participants from several organizations who completed both the basic and advanced workshops as well as a follow-up module 6 months to 2 years after the advanced workshop. The data from these participants were derived from (a) pre- and post-test self-ratings, (b) ratings by followers, (c) questionnaires, and (d) structured interviews. The results indicated a significant increase in rated transformational behaviors (except for individualized consideration) as well as a significant decrease in management by exception. Participants also reported positive affective reactions to the program.

Combined, these two evaluations provide evidence for the effectiveness of the FRLP. Participants reported high levels of satisfaction with the program. And, as reported by their subordinates, they appeared to learn the skills of transformational leadership and transfer them to their work settings. Finally, the data indicating reduced absenteeism and higher performance reported by Crookall (1989) suggests significant gains in organizational results. The use of subordinate respect and performance as criteria in this study is particularly important because they reflect significant intended outcomes of transformational leadership. Thus, the FRLP appears to improve the work behavior and attitudes of the subordinates of participants as well as the skills of participants themselves.

Visionary and Inspirational Models of Executive Leadership: General Conclusions

This empirical review of visionary, inspirational, and transformational theories and models of executive leadership suggests the following conclusions regarding the relationships depicted in Figure 9-1:

- Three characteristics of transformational leadership—charismatic influence, individualized consideration, and intellectual stimulation—have consistently been associated with subordinate attitudes and commitment, leader performance, and unit or organizational effectiveness. These associations have been found in leaders at all organizational levels.
- Transformational leadership behaviors displayed by upper-level leaders generally are associated with the display of similar behavior patterns by lower-level leaders.

- Transformational leadership behaviors augment the effects of transactional leadership behaviors on both leader and organizational effectiveness.
- Leader characteristics related to self-confidence, socialized power motives, nurturance, and risk propensity have been associated with the display of transformational and charismatic leadership. However, there is little evidence linking cognitive and social skills to the display of such leadership.
- The MLQ has demonstrated acceptable internal consistency and criterion-related validity. It also has yielded a stable factor structure. However, the construct validity of its components has not been amply demonstrated.
- A leader development program based on transformational leadership theory has demonstrated effectiveness in terms of enhancing participants' transformational leadership skills and improving subordinates' attitudes and performance.

This review illustrates the importance of visionary and inspirational leadership for organizational effectiveness. Such leadership facilitates the implementation of the long-range strategies and visions developed by top organizational leaders. The conceptual complexity theories and strategic decision-making models of executive leadership examined in earlier chapters provide more extensive descriptions of strategy-formation processes than of strategic implementation. Behavioral complexity theories highlight the executive leader's role in implementation, but they do not describe the processes connected with that role. The models, theories, and research reviewed in this chapter and chapter 8 define the nature of such processes in terms of requisite leadership patterns. Furthermore, they specify the executive leadership characteristics that facilitate vision and strategic implementation. Thus, the visionary and inspirational theories and models of executive leadership provide an important complement to the other approaches to executive leadership.

A number of studies cited by Bass and Avolio (1993) and in the meta-analysis by Lowe et al. (1995) reported significant levels of transformational leadership behaviors in lower-level leaders. In fact, Lowe et al. found that the mean rating of such behaviors was actually higher for lower-level leaders than for upper-level leaders. Thus, this empirical research, and the conceptual models and theories that underlie this research, do not support the notion explicit in the other models and theories described that there are qualitative differences in leadership requirements across organizational levels. The nature of effective leadership, defined in terms of transformational influence of subordinates in line with an organizational vision, appears to be the same for leaders at all organizational levels. However, the vision that is the basis for this influence is more likely to emerge from individuals in top executive leadership positions. If the effectiveness of transformational leadership influence is at all grounded in the content and quality of the leader's vision, and the development and promulgation of this vision is more likely the province of the executive leader, then further research is necessary to define more clearly the basis of leader vision and its association with the process of transformational leadership. Such efforts should lead to more explicit specification of cross-level differences in the nature of visionary and transformational leadership in organizations.

As noted earlier, transformational leadership theory provides a conceptualization of vision and strategic-implementation processes that generally is lacking in other models and theories of executive leadership. This suggests that a full understanding of such leadership is likely to emerge only from an approach that synthesizes and integrates the various conceptual perspectives described in this book and the empirical research derived from those perspectives. Such an approach, with accompanying recommendations for future research on executive leadership, is presented in the last chapter of this book.

Executive Leadership: An Integrated Model $\Big|$ 10

Although the various conceptual models and theories of executive leadership described in this book illustrate different features associated with executive leadership, there is significant value in synthesizing and integrating them into a single framework. As summarized in Table 10-1, each model or theory emphasizes a different dimension of executive leadership while ignoring other important aspects. Therefore, each perspective presents only an incomplete description of executive leadership. Despite their somewhat fundamental differences, however, these conceptual perspectives share a number of common elements. For example, in line with Katz and Kahn (1967, 1978), each describes executive organizational leaders as boundary spanners. Each perspective also emphasizes the executive leader's role in defining organizational direction and managing the organization in keeping with this direction. Thus, each perspective reflects Barnard's (1938) executive leader functions, as mentioned in chapter 1, of establishing organizational purpose and facilitating organizationwide coordination. In addition, the four conceptual models or theories imply that leadership requirements change across organizational levels. Although only stratified systems theory (SST) specifies the nature of these differences in clear and operational terms, leadership work generally becomes increasingly more complex at upper organizational levels. Finally, although the relative emphasis on particular individual qualities varies according to the theory or model being considered, these different conceptual approaches provide a relatively common core of personal characteristics that facilitate the effective accomplishment of executive leadership requirements. Thus, although the conceptual frameworks described in this book present different notions of executive leadership, their similarities reflect the fundamental executive roles specified by Barnard and Katz and Kahn.

TABLE 10-1

Executive Leadership Perspectives

Perspective	Focus of executive leadership	Executive leader performance requirements	Changes in performance requirements across organizational levels	Requisite executive leader characteristics	Developmental prescription
Conceptual complexity theories	To provide conceptual frame of reference for organizational complexity	Long-term planning and strategy making; boundary management and environmental engagement; acquisition of organizational resources; network development and consensus building	Work and planning reflect longer future time span; boundary spanning increasingly occurs with constituencies outside the organization; leadership influence within the organization becomes increasingly indirect as leaders have charge of multiple organizational units	Conceptual capacity, flexible integrative complexity, interpersonal skills, knowledge of organizational operating environment, temperamental proclivity for reflective thinking and mental model building	Potential executive leaders should be given challenging work assignments (i.e., stretch assignments), under the guidance of a mentor, that promote emergence of more complex and comprehensive frames of reference
Behavioral complexity theories	To balance and effectively enact multiple organizational roles with competing performance requirements	Balancing of the following roles: mentor, facilitator, innovator, broker, director, producer, coordinator, and monitor	Demands and requirements from greater variety of constituencies need to be balanced; broader spectrum of organizational roles must be enacted	Conceptual complexity, need for power, social intelligence, behavioral flexibility	Potential executive leaders should be encouraged to break from habitual work roles and provided opportunities to learn new roles
Strategic decision-making models	To create and manage co-alignment between organizational and environmental elements through the development of long-term strategy	Environmental and organizational scanning; information interpretation and sense making; strategy formation and imlementation	No clear differences articulated; however, executive leaders more likely to be responsible for strategy formation, whereas more junior leaders may be more responsible for day-to-day strategy implementation	Cognitive abilities, knowledge of operating environment, functional expertise, need for achievement, locus of control, self-efficacy, risk propensity, flexibility	No clear perscriptions; importance of functional expertise suggests potential executive leaders should be provided with work opportunities in many functional organizational domains
Visionary and inspirational models of executive leadership	To change and manage organizational process in line with an articulated vision; to inspire, motivate, and empower subordinates so that they assume responsibility for organizational change	Charismatic or idealized influence of subordinates; provision of inspirational motivation, intellectual stimulation, and individualized consideration to subordinates	No differences articulated; transformational leadership can occur at all organizational levels; some models suggest guiding organizational visions more likely to be articulated by executive leaders	Cognitive abilities, self-confidence, socialized power motives, social skills, nurturance skills, risk propensity	Potential executive leaders should be provided opportunities for self-understanding regarding leadership styles and training to learn both transformational and transactional leadership behaviors

An Integrated Model of Executive Leadership

Ultimately, then, an integrated model of executive leadership that combines the various perspectives of executive leadership would capitalize on the contributions of each to provide a more comprehensive framework for future research. Hunt (1991) proposed a single integrated framework, the extended multiple-level-organizational level model. Hunt's model is patterned closely after SST, but it also combines elements of Streufert's interactive complexity theory as well as other models and theories (e.g., behavioral complexity theories, transformational leadership theory). It also describes performance requirements at three organizational levels, requisite individual capabilities at each level, and the influential and moderating role of environmental factors. The model presented in this section is similar to Hunt's in that it outlines executive leader performance requirements at multiple levels and includes similar individual capabilities. However, it differs in several details from Hunt's model and extends it by describing the relationships among external and internal executive functions and by addressing the interdependency among multiple executive leader qualities. Furthermore, it identifies the reciprocal influences of leader functions within and among organizational levels. Compared with Hunt's primarily categorical description of executive leadership, these model parameters provide a more process-oriented description of executive leadership.

Figure 10-1 displays a model of multilevel organizational leadership performance requirements, which integrates several key themes of this book. Figure 10-2 illustrates only the executive leader requirements but adds the influence of environmental characteristics on executive leader performance as well as the notion that executive leadership is a direct determinant of organizational effectiveness and adaptation. Similar moderating influences and leadership consequences are likely to be applicable at lower organizational levels as well. However, for the sake of brevity and because the focus of this book is executive leadership, these particular relationships are discussed only in terms of top organizational levels.

The leadership performance requirements model is described in more detail in the following sections. Specifically reviewed are (a) the basic premises of the model, (b) how performance requirements change across organizational levels, (c) how informational and social complexity drive these changes, and (d) the basic leadership tasks of direction setting and operational management as they occur at different organizational levels. The remaining sections of this chapter discuss the requisite

FIGURE 10-1

Model of Multilevel Organizational Leadership Performance Requirements

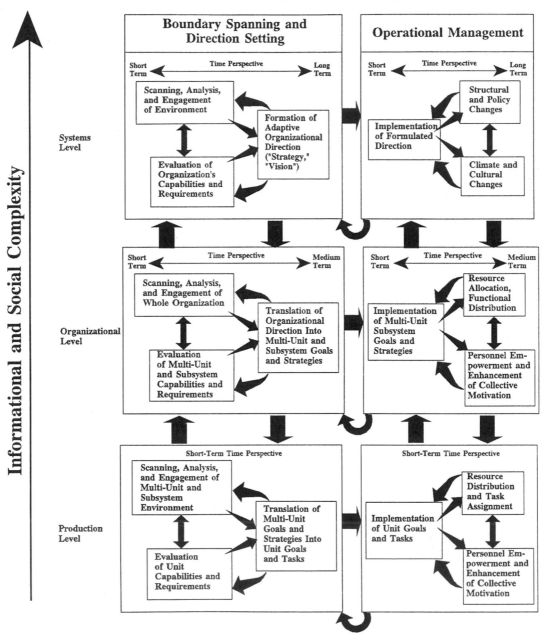

Reprinted from S. J. Zaccaro, Social Complexity and the Competencies Required for Effective Leadership. In J. G. Hunt, G. Dodge, and L. Ward, *Out-of-the-Box Leadership: Transforming the Twenty-First Century Army and Other Top-Performing Organizations*, p. 142. Copyright 1999, with permission from Elsevier Science.

FIGURE 10-2

Executive Leader Performance Requirements

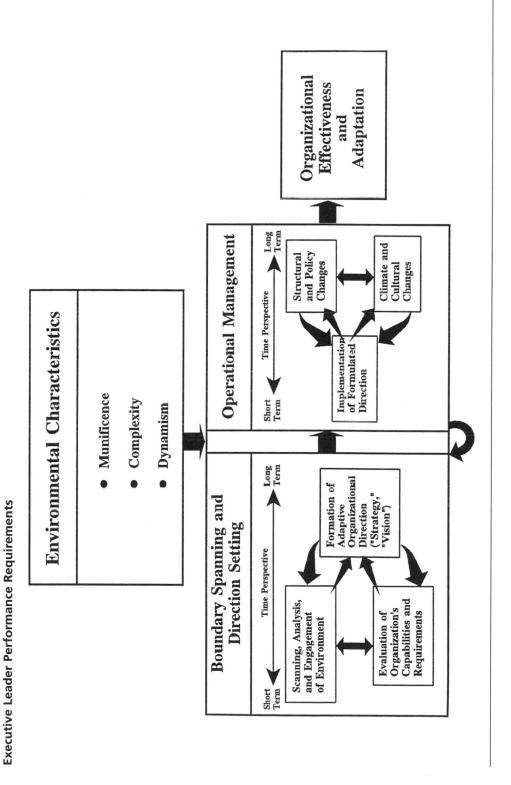

executive leader characteristics suggested by this model and provide recommendations for future research on executive leadership.

BASIC PROPOSITIONS

The leadership performance requirements model is synthesized from the four conceptual perspectives presented in this book as well as from the empirical findings reviewed in previous chapters. Six general propositions that have received substantial empirical support from analyses of executive leader performance requirements provided the bases for this model. They are as follows:

1. Leader performance requirements can be described in terms of three distinct organizational levels (i.e., production level, organizational level, and systems level).
2. All organizational leaders engage in direction setting (e.g., goal setting, planning, strategy making, envisioning) for their constituent units. Such direction setting incorporates increasingly longer time spans at higher organizational levels.
3. All organizational leaders engage in boundary-spanning activities that link their constituent units with their environments. At lower organizational levels, this environment is the broader organization. At upper levels, boundary spanning and environmental analysis increasingly occur within the organization's external environment.
4. All organizational leaders are responsible for operational coordination and maintenance within the organization. At upper levels, operational influence becomes increasingly indirect.
5. The effective accomplishment of executive leader performance functions facilitates organizational performance and success.
6. Characteristics of the operating environment influence the nature and quality of executive leader performance requirements.

The first proposition is indicated by the identification of three levels of organizational leadership in Figure 10-1: (a) production level, (b) organizational level, and (c) systems level. Although some models and theories (e.g., SST) articulate more gradations, empirical evidence has supported three general strata. Propositions 2 to 4 are supported by the delineation of executive leader functions at each of the three levels. For example, at each level, executive leaders engage in boundary management and organizational (or unit) and environmental analysis. They also engage in operational management. Boundary management and organizational analysis contribute to formulating a direction that serves as the basis of operational activities.

The last two propositions are indicated explicitly in Figure 10-2. The executive leader performance requirements of boundary spanning, direction setting, and operational management are linked directly to organizational effectiveness and environmental adaptation. Environmental characteristics, however, determine the scope and extent of requisite boundary spanning as well as the nature of direction setting and operational management. Several strategic decision-making models also suggest that the environment influences the extent to which executive leader performance requirements determine organizational performance (Bourgeois, 1984, 1985; Hitt & Tyler, 1991; Pfeffer & Salancik, 1978).

ORGANIZATIONAL STRATIFICATION OF EXECUTIVE LEADERSHIP REQUIREMENTS

Day and Lord (1988) argued that a theory of executive leadership should define the qualitative differences in leadership requirements across organizational levels. Accordingly, the executive leadership performance requirements model illustrated in Figure 10-1 specifies two qualitative shifts in requirements to produce three distinct levels of organizational leadership. This specification is similar to those offered by Hunt (1991) and Katz and Kahn (1978). It also reflects the three superordinate domains of SST. However, the finer distinctions offered by SST (i.e., seven strata) or by Mumford, Zaccaro, Harding, Fleishman, and Reiter-Palmon (1993; i.e., four levels) are not included because the available evidence cited in earlier chapters supports no more than three levels of organizational requirements.

The lowest level, the production level, involves direct leadership of single organizational units in which leaders define and translate short-term unit tasks and goals within the context of objectives established at higher levels. Problems confronting the leader at this level are fairly concrete and reflect a short time span (Jacobs & Jaques, 1987). At the next level, the organizational level, leadership becomes increasingly more indirect, as leaders manage multiple units, or subsystems of the organization, each with its own supervisor (Jacobs & Jaques, 1987). Problems at this level are more complex, with multiple components and a longer time horizon, but they are still fairly well-defined. One of the central roles of middle-level managers is to translate the even longer-term perspectives, strategies, and objectives established at top organizational levels into concrete, short-term objectives for lower-level managers. They also must allocate organizational resources among functional units in accordance with organizational objectives.

At the systems level, which incorporates executive-level leadership, the executive leader manages the organization as a whole, typically within the context of a complex environment. This level of management is characterized more than others by external boundary-spanning activities (managers at lower levels span the boundaries of their units or subsystems within the internal organizational environment). Executive leaders are required to scan and analyze the organization's environment to determine (a) the nature of changes in that environment, (b) organizational requirements to enable it to adapt to environmental changes, and (c) the resources available to the organization to meet these requirements. Finally, part of executive leader boundary spanning includes attempts by top executive leaders to influence and change the environmental conditions within which the organization must operate. Effective executive leaders are not passive recipients of environmental contingencies. Instead, they seek to engage the environment and shape the contingencies affecting the organization.

The time span of systems leadership planning and action includes a long-term perspective. Note, however, that the executive leadership performance requirements model indicates that time perspectives for top executive leaders will vary from short term to long term (Judge & Spitzfaden, 1995). Long time horizons and diversity among strategic plans mean that organizational problems at the systems level become increasingly ill defined. Accordingly, executive leaders confronting such problems need to construct their parameters, search for acceptable solution paths, and specify a goal state that may not generate universal consensus among organizational stakeholders regarding its appropriateness. Furthermore, many of these problems will have elements that are substantially unfamiliar to even the most knowledgeable executive leader, and they often will require the generation of novel frames of reference and solutions (Mumford, Zaccaro, et al., 1993). These problem characteristics contribute to the complexity of leadership at higher organizational levels.

INFORMATIONAL AND SOCIAL COMPLEXITY

Informational complexity and social complexity are central dynamics within the leadership performance requirements model: The operating environment for organizational leaders becomes increasingly complex at higher levels. This complexity results from greater task- or information-processing demands as well as increased social demands. Executive leader information processing is considered complex regarding the information content that must be assimilated, the problems that must be confronted, and the cognitive structures required for a fully integrated representation of diverse organization-related stimuli (Campbell, 1988; Schroder, Driver, & Streufert, 1967).

The greater social complexity results from the responsibility that executive leaders have to coordinate and supervise the activities of different departments and subsystems within the organization. Each subsystem presents the executive leader with different and often conflicting demands, goals, and agendas. In developing an overall organizational direction, the executive leader must consider and reconcile the requirements of each of these organizational subsystems. The executive leader also is responsible to a variety of different internal and external stakeholders. Implementation of an organizational vision may require that an executive leader fundamentally change the social dynamics of the organization. This requires careful negotiation as executive leaders try to balance myriad social demands. At lower organizational levels, leaders are responsible for fewer organizational units, and their superiors are likely to have completed much of the social integration work. Thus, the level of social complexity is less at lower organizational levels.

EXECUTIVE LEADER DIRECTION SETTING AND OPERATIONAL MANAGEMENT

The leadership performance requirements model of executive leadership depicts two fundamental requirements for leaders at all organizational levels, including executive leaders. The first is to provide a direction for collective action. The second is to manage the day-to-day operations of the organization (or unit or units within the organization). These requirements are consistent with all of the theoretical perspectives presented in this book. For example, in SST, Jacobs and Jaques (1990) offered a definition of leadership that applied across organizational levels: "Leadership is a process of giving purpose [meaningful direction] to collective effort, and causing willing effort to be expended to achieve purpose" (p. 282). Thus, leaders define and articulate a direction in accordance with external or environmental conditions for their subordinate unit or units and create the internal conditions to accomplish the tasks specified by this direction.

At the top of the organization, executive leader direction setting generally takes the form of a vision. An organizational vision is a desired image of the organization at some future point in time. As suggested by several theories of visionary and inspirational leadership, leader values are a defining element of such visions (Bennis & Nanus, 1985; Nanus, 1992; Senge, 1990). This vision becomes operationalized in terms of an organizational strategy that becomes shared at lower organizational levels.

Once a vision and strategy are formulated, they become the guides for organizational and environmental analyses. After an executive leader develops a vision or strategy, further evaluations of organizational capabilities are made in light of the formulated direction to determine the increasing (or decreasing) alignment of the organization and its environment. When environmental or organizational conditions change significantly such that they become seriously inconsistent with the formulated direction, then the executive leader must adapt his or her vision to the changed conditions or fail.

As these points suggest, the leadership performance requirements model includes feedback loops, or reciprocal influences, by which leader visions shape the subsequent organizational and environmental information acquisition of executive leaders. This information then serves in the ongoing evaluation of organizational progress regarding attainment of formulated objectives. Similar processes operate at lower organizational levels, where a manager's evaluation of unit progress and unit capabilities as a function of direction setting becomes a basis for adjustments to unit goals, tasks, and objectives. However, this evaluation and these adjustments occur within the structures created by upper-level leaders. Alternatively, goal adjustments at lower levels contribute to the reevaluation of organizational capabilities and requirements at upper levels.

The operational management activities defined by the leadership performance requirements model represent the internal perspective of executive leaders prescribed by Katz and Kahn (1978). The second major performance requirement of executive leadership is implementing the formulated direction by coordinating the necessary organizational elements. The process of implementation is integral to the operationalization of the leader's vision. When an executive leader translates her or his vision into strategy, objectives, goals, plans, and tasks, implementation has begun. The next critical step is the coordination of organizational elements. Katz and Kahn noted the following:

> Every organization, itself a system, consists in turn of subsystems. These subsystems have different needs and the people in them manifest characteristically different kinds of strivings. It is an unavoidable function of leadership to integrate and harmonize these subsystem differences; indeed, coordination and control of subsystems are essential functions of the managerial subsystem. . . . To perform these functions requires awareness and perceptiveness of the changing requirements of the subsystems and their populations. (p. 541)

Guiding this coordination is the vision provided by the executive leader.

The implementation process takes two forms. The first involves planned change in the structure and policies of the organization. This change process is the unique responsibility of senior executive leaders. The second process involves changing the climate and culture of the organization and altering the basis for the connection between leader and followers. This change involves (a) greater emotional attachment based on the contents of the leader's vision and (b) empowerment of subordinates through the enhancement of their work-related self-esteem. This empowerment results in their participation in the change process.

Changes in either structure and policies or climate and culture influence each other. For example, when organizational structures are decentralized, the result can be greater assignment of responsibilities to, and therefore stronger empowerment of, subordinates. Likewise, changing the psychological climate of an organization may result in social pressures for alternate structural arrangements that are congruent with the new climate. Thus, each change process is seen as reciprocally determined.

Changes in organizational structures, policies, climate, and culture can provoke the executive leader to reevaluate his or her implementation strategies. Furthermore, as implementation proceeds, changes in the organization become information for subsequent environmental scanning and evidence of whether the original formulated direction is effective. Thus, as shown in Figure 10-1, feedback loops or reciprocal influences exist between the executive leader's direction-setting and implementation activities.

EXECUTIVE LEADER PERFORMANCE REQUIREMENTS

Figure 10-2 displays the same systems-level performance requirements shown in Figure 10-1, but with two components added to make other critical points about executive leadership. First, the consequences of accomplishing executive leader performance requirements are organizational effectiveness and environmental adaptation. Day and Lord (1988) specified several potential ways executive leaders influence organizational performance. These methods of influence, shown in Table 10-2, reflect several of the activities specified in the integrated model of executive leadership as executive leader performance requirements. The second component is the moderating role of environmental contingencies on executive leader performance requirements. If executive leadership is focused on creating a co-alignment or adaptive fit between the organization and its environment, then characteristics of the external environment should determine the nature of requisite executive leader performance requirements as well as the strategic decisions made by executive leaders (Bluedorn, Johnson, Cartwright, & Barringer, 1994; Hambrick, 1989; Hambrick & Mason, 1984; Rajagopalan, Rasheed, & Datta, 1993). Three environmental dimensions are indicated: munificence, complexity, and dynamism (Hall, 1991). *Munificence* refers to the richness or scarcity of resources within the environment. Executive leader decisions are less risky in a resource-rich or munificent environ-

TABLE 10-2

Methods by Which Executive Leaders Can Affect Organizational Performance

Target	Objective	Tactic	
		Direct	Indirect
Influencing external environments			
Government policy (e.g., regulation, taxation, trade)	Change policy to reduce uncertainty or increase resources	Direct political influence	Political influence through other groups (e.g., unions, suppliers)
Acquiring resources and maintaining boundaries	Increase stability Reduce competition	Horizontal or vertical integration Promote entry barriers and noncompetitive pricing	Create favorable public image or opinion Enhance image of organization or product
Adapting to external environments			
Choice of markets or environments	Increased stability and munificence	Strategic planning	Influence top management's schemas; select those with similar schemas
Management and production system	Fit with environment and strategy	Organizational design	Guide top management's labeling of environments
Exerting internal influence and encouraging adaptation			
Subsystem organization and management	Rationalization and integration Coordination and appraisal	Definition and functional specification of roles Design and implementation of management information systems	Shape top management's schemas of organizing; select those with similar schemas Use information as sign and symbol
Productivity	Increase organizational efficiency	Reduce capital or personnel costs	Strengthen productivity norms
Quality	Increase product quality	Increase quality control	Strengthen quality norms
Organizational climate and culture	Increase motivation and commitment of employees	Determine or influence organizational politics	Enhance participative decision-making norms, symbolism of chief executive officer

Note. For each objective there are additional tactics; however, space limitations prohibit their inclusion. From "Executive Leadership and Organizational Performance: Suggestions for a New Theory and Methodology," by D. V. Day and R. G. Lord, 1988, *Journal of Management, 14,* p. 461. Copyright 1988 by the Southern Management Association. Adapted with permission.

ment because resources lost as a result of bad decisions often can easily be replenished (provided the organization still retains sufficient assets). *Complexity* is environmental diversity in terms of resource suppliers, clients and customers, markets, and geographical locations. Environmental complexity presents more alternatives, options, and solution paths to strategic decision makers, increasing the information-processing demands of executive leaders. *Dynamism* reflects the rapidity and unpredictability of change in the environment and the degree of interconnections among environmental elements. High environmental dynamism requires more analysis and strategic planning by executive leaders than organizational environments that are relatively stable and predictable (Ansoff, 1979; Glick, Miller, & Huber, 1993; C. C. Miller & Cardinal, 1994; C. C. Miller & Frieson, 1984).

The leadership performance requirements model presents an elaborate conceptualization of executive leader work. The model advances the perspectives described in this book by combining their overall themes into a single integrative framework. The usefulness of the model or theory lies not only in its specification of the elements of executive leadership, but also in its provision of the basis for delineating the executive leader characteristics required to successfully complete such work.

Requisite Executive Leader Characteristics

The individual qualities necessary for executive leader success are grounded in the high information-processing demands and social complexity that define the operating environment of executive leaders. These characteristics, as distilled from the conceptual perspectives and empirical research described in this book, are displayed in Table 10-3. There are five sets of characteristics: (a) cognitive capacities, (b) social capacities, (c) personality, (d) motivation, and (e) knowledge and expertise.

COGNITIVE CAPACITIES

The following cognitive capacities are associated with successful executive leadership: (a) intelligence, (b) analytical reasoning, (c) flexible integrative complexity, (d) metacognitive skills, (e) verbal/writing skills (or crystallized cognitive skills), and (f) creativity (see Table 10-2). Given the high level of information-processing demands and task complexity that confront executive leaders, all of the conceptual frameworks de-

TABLE 10-3

Requisite Executive Leader Characteristics

Category	Skill
Cognitive capacities	Intelligence
	Analytical reasoning
	Flexible integrative complexity
	Metacognitive skills
	Verbal/writing skills
	Creativity
Social capacities	Behavioral flexibility
	Negotiation skills
	Conflict management skills
	Persuasion skills
	Social reasoning skills
Personality	Openness
	Flexibility
	Adaptability
	Risk propensity
	Locus of control
	Self-discipline
	Curiosity
Motivation	Need for achievement
	Self-efficacy
	Need for socialized power
Knowledge and expertise	Functional expertise
	Social expertise
	Knowledge of environmental elements

scribed in this book propose some of these cognitive skills and capacities as necessary prerequisites for effective executive leadership. Katz and Kahn (1978) noted that although technical, interpersonal, and conceptual skills are required for successful organizational leadership, "in the upper managerial levels the conceptual abilities of the manager considerably overshadow in importance technical skills and skills in human relations" (p. 541). Lewis and Jacobs (1992) concurred, arguing as follows:

> The fundamental individual difference variable that most often distinguishes successful strategic leaders from unsuccessful ones is the extent to which leaders' conceptual capacity meets or exceeds the conceptual demands inherent in their work. Those promoted to strategic leadership typically already possess the requisite interpersonal and technical skills needed to be successful. These skills and the motivation to lead will usually already have been amply demonstrated at lower managerial levels. (p. 541)

A number of studies on executive leadership have proposed that metacognitive problem-solving skills are important executive leader qualities (Geiwitz, 1993; Laskey, Leddo, & Bresnick, 1990; Markessini, 1991). *Metacognitive capacities* are defined in terms of the skill application of superordinate cognitive functions that control the application and operation of cognitive abilities and skills (Brown, 1978; Sternberg, 1985, 1988). Problem solvers use cognitive abilities and skills such as inductive reasoning, deductive reasoning, divergent thinking, information-processing skills, and verbal reasoning to derive effective solutions. However, metacognitive skills regulate and monitor the application of these skills in three general ways (Brown, 1978; Davidson, Deuser, & Sternberg, 1994; Geiwitz, 1993):

1. They facilitate an understanding of the problem itself and its critical parameters.
2. They promote the search for and specification of effective solutions.
3. They are used in monitoring solution implementation, generating feedback regarding implementation, and adapting solutions to changing conditions.

SOCIAL CAPACITIES

The high level of social complexity that characterizes the operating environment of executive leaders argues for social capacities as critical executive competencies. Social capacities include two sets of skills: (a) those related to interactional competencies and (b) those related to social reasoning competencies. Interactional competencies include behavioral flexibility, negotiation skills, conflict management skills, and persuasion skills. Because organizational environments are complex and dynamic, a solution that works in one problem scenario may be inappropriate or even counter-productive in another. Thus, executive leaders require behavioral flexibility to respond effectively in significantly different ways to different organizational scenarios and in accordance with different, sometimes conflicting, organizational goals (Bray, 1982; Howard & Bray, 1988; Zaccaro, Gilbert, Thor, & Mumford, 1991). Behavioral flexibility involves the ability to respond equally well to very different situational demands. As suggested in chapter 4, this ability is necessary for the effective display of behavioral complexity by executive leaders.

The role of executive leaders as representatives of organizational systems containing multiple, sometimes conflicting, constituencies illustrates the importance of negotiation skills, conflict management skills, and persuasion skills as key interactional competencies. The activities fostered by these skills have long been recognized as critical aspects of organizational leadership, often comprising about 25% of a manager's total work time (K. W. Thomas & Schmidt, 1976). Conflict management typically involves the application of one or more resolution strategies to interacting parties (K. W. Thomas, 1992). Negotiation skills are used to develop consensus among conflicting individuals or units. Both sets of skills reflect the importance of behavioral flexibility, as executive leaders must be able to respond in different ways to multiple conflicts.

Zaccaro, Gilbert, et al. (1991) argued that to be effective these interactional competencies and their behavioral manifestations must be applied in accordance with situational cues and requirements. This suggests that interactional competencies are necessary, but not sufficient, for effective executive leadership; social reasoning skills are also required. One basis for effective social reasoning is social perceptiveness, that is, the capacity to be insightful regarding the needs, goals, demands, and problems of multiple organizational constituencies (Zaccaro, Gilbert, et al., 1991). This insight extends to individual organizational members, relations among members, relations among organizational units, and interactions among an executive leader's organization and other organizations. Previous research on social perceptiveness and leadership has focused primarily on recognizing the needs and problems of individual organizational personnel (e.g., Bass, 1990, pp. 117–120). This represents skill in interpersonal perceptiveness and interpretation. However, the social insightfulness of successful leaders, particularly executive leaders, also includes awareness of the needs and goals of teams and organizations as a whole as well as sensitivity to opportunities in the larger environment that can advance organizational goals. This reflects skill in system perceptiveness and judgment.

PERSONALITY AND MOTIVATIONAL QUALITIES

The complexity of executive leader operating environments suggests that certain temperament and motivational qualities are associated with executive leader performance. Because of the high levels of uncertainty and ambiguity characteristic of such environments, executive leaders who thrive are likely to be those whose dispositions include an orientation toward openness, flexibility, and adaptability. These qualities are also important because a significant portion of executive leader work requires creativity and the ability to solve novel, ill-defined problems (Mumford & Connelly, 1991; Mumford, Zaccaro, et al., 1993). Openness and flexibility foster an executive leader's willingness to work with new ideas and consider changes (Barrick & Mount, 1991; Bray, Campbell, & Grant, 1974; Howard & Bray, 1988; Keller, 1986; McCrae & Costa, 1987).

The exploration of new and uncharted areas by executive leaders significantly increases the possibility of subsequent failure. Personality characteristics such as risk propensity, ego resiliency, and self-discipline therefore are important for successful executive leadership because they promote boldness and a strong sense of self-assurance. Executive leaders low in ego resiliency and risk taking (or, alternatively, exhibiting defensive rigidity and anxiety) perform poorly in creative problem-solving situations because their dispositions interfere with the effective application of cognitive resources (Mumford, Baughman, Threlfall, Costanza, & Uhlman, 1993; Mumford, Costanza, Baughman, Threlfall, & Fleishman, 1994). They also are more threatened by instability and therefore less motivated in such situations. Executive leaders with high self-confidence and ego resiliency thrive under the challenge of uncertainty and high-risk ventures.

Motivational characteristics contribute to effective executive leadership for several reasons. First, executive leadership requires a significant amount of energy and personal commitment. Second, the tasks of top executive leaders include the accomplishment of large-scale organizational change and the creation of new business units within the organization (Jacobs & Jaques, 1987). Such efforts are facilitated by high achievement needs and self-efficacy. Third, the creation of an innovative organizational product requires significant social influence by the executive leader, as he or she may need to move the entire organization in a different strategic direction. Thus, executive leaders also need to possess a strong need or desire for dominance and socialized power (House & Howell, 1992; McClelland, 1985; Sashkin, 1988).

KNOWLEDGE AND EXPERTISE

Several of the conceptual models and theories described in this book have emphasized the importance of executive leader knowledge and expertise. Jacobs and Jaques (1987) argued fundamentally that executive leaders add value to the organization by developing a framework of understanding, or a causal map of the organization within its environment, that is used to provide meaning for the activities and efforts of organizational members and units. Strategic choice models and behavioral complexity theories also propose functional knowledge and expertise as critical executive leadership competencies. For example, Hambrick and Mason (1984) noted that knowledge of different functional areas was related to the quality of executive leader decision making (see also Hambrick, 1981). Some researchers have argued that executive leaders tend to bring their own functional perspective to strategic decision making (Dearborn & Simon, 1958). However, Hitt and Tyler (1991) noted that executive leaders typically have a range of functional experiences. Their beliefs and knowledge structures represent an integration of those experiences. Similarly, Hoffman and Hegarty (1993) proposed that a range of expertise was associated with innovative decision making, including expertise in (a) general management; (b) marketing and product research and development; and (c) finance, personnel management, and production.

There has been growing attention given to the kinds of mental models and knowledge structures that executive leaders develop and apply to organizational problem solving (Huff, 1990; Zaccaro, Marks, O'Connor-Boes, and Costanza, 1995). The most generic executive leader mental models are likely to be those that organize information about the nature and role of leadership in organizations (Mumford, Baugham, Threlfall, et al., 1993). Alternatively, the most specific mental models used by executive leaders are those that pertain to particular tasks and problem domains (Cannon-Bowers, Salas, & Converse, 1993; Holyoak, 1984). Situational assessment models are specific to certain problem scenarios. They facilitate the interpretation of these scenarios and the selection of appropriate responses to them. Zaccaro, Marks, et al. (1995) described two forms of executive leader mental models that are specific enough to have significant applicability in particular problem domains while at the same time encoding information that is generalizable across most organizational problems. These are mental models that encode knowledge about the executive leader's teams and about the organization within which the executive leader and his or her team or teams operate. Team mental models include organized knowledge about the elements, characteristics, and dynamics that influence how individuals work interdependently to perform collective tasks. Information encoded in team mental models includes such concepts as team and subordinate resources, team role structure and assignments, team cohesion and morale, team communication and social influence patterns, team tenure, team size, and specific team performance protocols and norms (cf. Fleishman & Zaccaro, 1992). Such models, when shared among team members, were described by Cannon-Bowers et al. (1993) as critical for successful team performance. Executive leaders use team mental models to help them understand the relationships among the components that influence team processes and accordingly predict how well a team may perform in particular circumstances. Thus, executive leaders use these mental models to determine the team and subordinate factors they need to consider and possibly change when facilitating team performance.

Because many teams are embedded within organizations and team leader responsibilities include boundary-spanning activities (Ancona, 1987, 1990; Ancona & Caldwell, 1992), executive leaders also need to understand organizational parameters and dynamics. This understanding is encoded in an organization mental model. Organizational mental models contain organized knowledge about key components, events, and operations of an executive leader's organization that bear possible relevance to his or her problem-solving efforts. Elements of these models include (a) role, communication, and decision-making structures within the organization; (b) personnel, material, and financial resources of the organization; (c) relations among subsystems within the organization; and (d) organizational climate and culture. These models also may include information and procedures for assessing the risks and benefits associated with particular solution paths. Mental models of organizational characteristics and dynamics often are used in executive leader problem solving to evaluate the feasibility of alternate solutions. That is, executive leaders will use their understanding of organizational variables and dynamics gained from prior experiences to evaluate the constraints, restrictions, and demands associated with different problem solutions in a particular organizational domain. Such knowledge facilitates the selection of organizationally appropriate problem solutions.

A third type of mental model that is important for executive leader action encodes an individual's structured understanding of the elements and entities that comprise the organizational environment. Such models are called environmental mental models. These models include the social dynamics of other organizations and external constituencies that influence the executive leader's organization and therefore must be considered in strategic thinking and planning. Conceptual elements of such models include consumer or client demands and requirements, market forces, regulatory considerations, and short- and long-term resource availability. For example, the environmental mental models of military executive leaders would encode information about political institutions and current political dynamics, organizations within both the public and private sectors that have importance for military affairs, and national and international institutions with which the executive leader must interact.

The development of team, organizational, and environmental mental models requires social reasoning and conceptual skills. Executive leaders must be able to perceive the dynamics of whole social systems and understand those dynamics within a broad context. For this reason, system perceptiveness and interpretation are critical competencies, particularly for executive leaders. Furthermore, executive leaders use their team, organizational, and environmental mental models to construct a representation of where the organization should be at some future point in time. That is, the executive leader mental models described are necessary components of strategic planning and the development of organizational vision.

These mental models are defined both as the result of social and cognitive capacities based on experience and as important executive leader attributes in their own right. Research directed at the measurement of these mental models and the specification of other knowledge structures that foster effective executive leadership is needed, however.

EXECUTIVE FLEXIBILITY

A recurrent theme in research on executive leadership qualities is the notion of flexibility. For example, Streufert and Swezey (1986) contrasted hierarchical integrative complexity with flexible integrative complexity in terms of the structure of cognition. Hierarchical complexity reflected fixed relationships among conceptual elements in a cognitive space, whereas flexible complexity resulted in dynamic and fluid relationships among conceptual elements that varied according to changes in environmental stimuli. Streufert and Swezey noted "where *flexible* integration can be responsive to anticipated changes in the environment that would require reconceptualizations of event relationships, hierarchical integration cannot" (p. 17). For this reason, executive leaders who exhibit flexible integrative complexity are hypothesized to perform better than those executive leaders who display hierarchical integrative complexity, particularly in a fluid and complex environment.

Zaccaro, Gilbert, Thor, and Mumford (1991) argued for the importance of behavioral flexibility to successful executive leadership. Because the social situations confronting executive leaders require diverse responses, executive leaders need to be able to discern what responses are required in particular situations and respond accordingly. Other researchers have characterized this flexibility as *self-monitoring*, which was described by Snyder (1974, 1979; see also Briggs, Cheek, & Buss, 1980) as having three components: (a) concern for social appropriateness, (b) sensitivity to social cues, and (c) ability to control one's behavior in response to those cues. Several studies have associated a measure of this construct with various indices of leadership (Dobbins, Long, Dedrick, & Clemons, 1990; Ellis, 1988; Ellis, Adamson. Deszca, & Cawsay, 1988; Foti & Cohen, 1986; Garland & Beard, 1979; Rueb & Foti, 1990; Zaccaro, Foti, & Kenny, 1991). Others have linked behavioral flexibility to required executive leader attributes such as adaptiveness to new situations (Gangestad & Synder, 1985; Synder, 1979); boundary-spanning effectiveness (Caldwell & O'Reilly, 1982); and communication effectiveness and persuasiveness (Sypher & Sypher, 1983). Two studies, one in a military sample (Gilbert & Zaccaro, 1995) and the other in an industrial one (Howard & Bray, 1988), reported significant correlations between measures of behavioral flexibility and career advancement.

Zaccaro, Gilbert, et al. (1991) argued that behavioral flexibility is grounded in social reasoning skills that provide the foundation for an executive leader's ability to make appropriate responses in diverse social situations. This suggests that behavioral flexibility depends in part on skill in differentiating and integrating social domain knowledge (i.e., integrative cognitive complexity). Flexibility also requires, however, that leaders display openness and tolerance when faced with social uncertainty and ambiguity. This quality, defined in terms of openness to experience, has been recognized as a major personality dimension distinguishing individuals (McCrae & Costa, 1987, 1991).However, behavioral flexibility can become behavioral vacillation under conditions of uncertainty unless the executive leader possesses a degree of self-discipline that forces closure on a behavioral action even when social cues do not point clearly to a particular appropriate response. These observations have led several researchers to argue that flexibility, and related personal qualities (e.g., adaptability, openness), are important executive personality characteristics (Howard & Bray, 1988; Miller & Toulouse, 1986; Mumford, Baughman, Threlfall, et al., 1993).

These various perspectives suggest that executive leader flexibility develops from an integrated constellation of cognitive, social, and dispositional qualities. This constellation of qualities is illustrated in Figure 10-3. Three general sets of individual qualities are portrayed: (a) social, behavioral flexibility; (b) flexible integrative complexity; and (c) dispositional orientation toward flexibility. The overlapping circles represent the premise that effective executive leadership results in part from the combined influence of these qualities. That is, these characteristics are not additive or independent in their influence on executive leadership. For example, integrative complexity allows the executive leader to develop the elaborate response models required in complex social domains, whereas behavioral flexibility reflects the mechanism of translating executive leader thought and reflection to appropriate action across diverse organizational scenarios. Boal and Whitehead (1992) described individuals who are high on both of these dimensions as "informed flexibles" who have "both a wide array of cognitive maps with which to interpret the situation and a wide array of behavioral responses" (p. 239). Their approach, however, assumes independence between these two qualities. The illustration in Figure 10-3 emphasizes their interdependence in terms of successful executive leadership.

Both cognitive and behavioral flexibility are facilitated by a disposition toward flexibility. Because individuals who can be characterized as high in these qualities display adaptiveness instead of rigidity in dynamic social domains, they are more likely to be behaviorally flexible in such situations. Likewise, conceptual capacity and the construction of elaborate frames of reference, as described by SST, require a degree of openness and curiosity on the part of the executive leader. Without these qualities and a high tolerance for ambiguity, executive leaders could not cope with the dynamic and complex environment within

FIGURE 10-3

Components of Executive Leader Flexibility

Reprinted from S. J. Zaccaro, Social Complexity and the Competencies Required for Effective Leadership. In J. G. Hunt, G. Dodge, and L. Ward, *Out-of-the-Box Leadership: Transforming the Twenty-First Century Army and Other Top-Performing Organizations*, p. 134. Copyright 1999, with permission from Elsevier Science.

which they need to operate. Another aspect of this dimension, however, is self-discipline, which brings an executive leader to closure in a conceptual domain. Streufert and Swezey (1986) noted a negative aspect of flexible integrative complexity in that "the higher the level of integration and the more flexible the integrative style, the more likely an inability to close for decision making may emerge." Self-discipline minimizes the likelihood that a conceptually complex executive leader will cycle through too many decision iterations without reaching a functional level of conceptual understanding. In addition, the openness to new experiences that is part of disposition-based flexibility prevents such understandings from becoming rigid.

Effective executive leadership lies at the nexus of these three interdependent qualities. Successful leadership is not likely to emerge from just one, or even two, of these qualities, particularly in turbulent or dynamic organizational environments. More fundamentally, social or behavioral flexibility will not be displayed unless executive leaders also possess the disposition to be flexible as well as the conceptual skills to develop and distinguish among different situationally appropriate response scripts. Therefore, research on executive leadership that assesses one or more of these qualities to the exclusion of others will result in an incomplete or even misdirected picture of executive leadership.

Recommendations for Research on Executive Leadership

As the integrated model of executive leader performance requirements illustrates, there is emerging consensus about the general nature of executive leadership work and the personal qualities necessary to accomplish it well. However, conceptual research on executive leadership has far outpaced confirmatory empirical research. A proposed model for research on executive leadership is presented in Figure 10-4. A central element of this model is executive leader characteristics. These are the personal qualities that facilitate the successful accomplishment of executive leader performance requirements. These characteristics provide a framework for the construction of (a) measures and tools that can be used for executive leader selection and assessment and (b) training and development programs that target one or more of the necessary executive leader competencies, skills, or personality characteristics.

The construction of executive leader assessment tools that can be used in organizational settings requires the demonstration of their ability to measure the executive leader competencies, skills, and dispositional qualities they are intended to capture (i.e., they must demonstrate construct validity). Executive leader characteristics also need to be linked with the accomplishment of executive leader performance requirements and, indirectly, with organizational performance before they are made the focus of expensive development programs. Thus far, there has been little quality research with top executive leaders demonstrating that proposed executive leader qualities such as conceptual capacity actually promote successful executive-level leadership or unit effectiveness. Also, those few studies that have examined executive leader characteristics have rarely examined them as constellations of characteristics that are jointly necessary to influence effectiveness. Therefore, despite a strong conceptual foundation, there is insufficient empirical evidence to con-

---

FIGURE 10-4

Recommended Model for Research on Military Executive Leadership

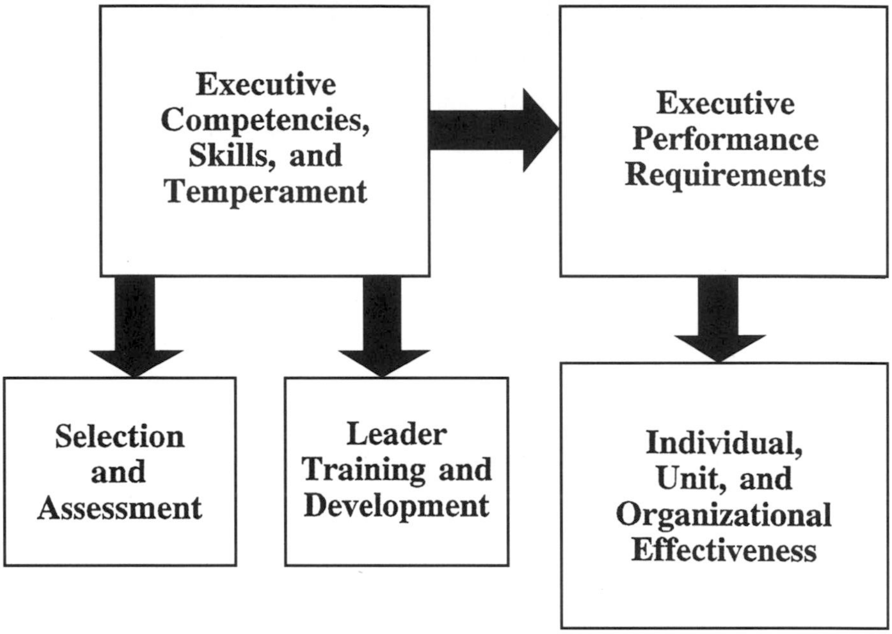

---

firm that particular sets of attributes should be the focus of executive leader assessment and development.

Thus, a fundamental recommendation for future research on executive leadership is that any program of research be conducted within the systematic framework illustrated in Figure 10-4. This model is a basic one that has driven most research on personnel selection and assessment (e.g., Dunnette, 1963); measurement validation (Ghiselli, Campbell, & Zedeck, 1981); and developmental intervention validation (Goldstein, 1986, 1991). It represents a more complete and comprehensive approach others that have driven earlier research on executive leadership because it specifically links (a) executive leader characteristics with performance requirements and (b) executive leader performance with organizational success. Executive leader characteristics also are the foundation for executive leader assessment and development. Using such a model as the basis for research will result in a more systematic and coherent body of knowledge regarding the determinants and effective development of successful executive leadership.

The remaining recommendations are grouped according to three themes: (a) research topics, (b) methodological approaches, and (c) developmental guidelines. These themes represent the major components of the integrated executive leadership performance requirements model as well as elements of the research model shown in Figure 10-4. Given this, the recommendations offered in this section are consistent with the above admonition that future executive leadership research follow the latter model.

RESEARCH TOPICS

The research topics offered for further consideration emphasize the personal attributes that contribute to executive leader effectiveness. Key leadership and top management team processes are also included as critical concerns for further study.

Social Complexity and Social Capacities

Research on executive leadership has been predicated on the premise that the information-processing demands that must be addressed by leaders increase as they ascend the organizational hierarchy. At the same time, technical and interpersonal skills have been considered to be proportionately less important for executive leader performance. This perspective, as depicted in Figure 10-5(A), has been widely advocated by many leadership theorists (e.g., Katz, 1955; Katz & Kahn, 1967, 1978; Lawrence & Lorsch, 1967; Yukl, 1994).

However, the integrated model of executive leadership performance requirements presented in Figure 10-1 indicates that in addition to information-processing demands, social complexity increases as a leader ascends the organizational hierarchy. Thus, social skills and capacities also become more important at higher organizational levels. This perspective is illustrated in Figure 10-5(B).

Several theorists have suggested the increased importance of social skills for executive leaders. However, systematic research on these qualities has lagged behind research on the cognitive capacities of executive leaders. Accordingly, the following recommendation is offered:

> Research on executive leadership should focus on (a) the identification of particular social competencies that facilitate the successful accomplishment of executive leader performance requirements; (b) the development of validated measures that assess these competencies; and (c) the construction and validation of executive leader developmental and training interventions that target these competencies.

Executive Leader Cognitive Models

Jacobs and Jaques (1987) argued that executive leaders add value to the organization by building integrated causal maps and frames of ref-

FIGURE 10-5

Two Perspectives of Organizational-Level and Requisite Leader Competencies

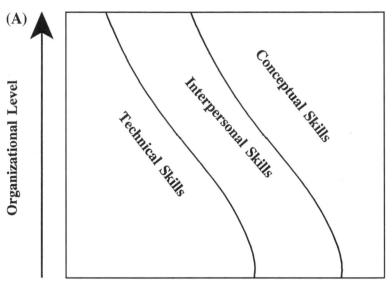

Traditional view of organizational level
and requisite leader competencies

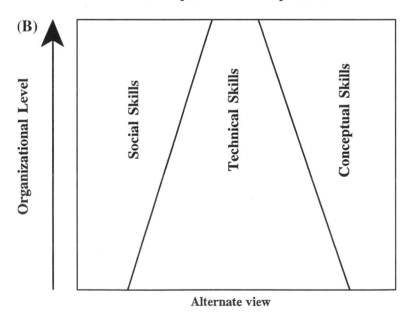

Alternate view

(A) Traditional view of organizational level and requisite leader competencies. From U.S. Army Pamphlet 600-80, 1987. (B) Alternate view.

erence that are used to give meaning to and guide organizational action. The mental models executive leaders form of the organization and its environment arguably may be the most proximal or direct cause of executive leader action and performance. That is, other capacities and skills affect performance through their influences on the formation and quality of these models. This cognitive perspective has become increasingly prominent in strategic management research (Huff, 1990; Schwenk, 1984; J. B. Thomas, Clark, & Gioia, 1993; Walsh & Fahey, 1986). However, although some researchers have begun to examine the role of executive mental models in organizational leadership empirically, more research is necessary to fully understand how executive leaders add value to the organization through cognitive framing processes. The growing body of research on this topic has provided sufficient methodological frameworks for conducting such studies. Accordingly, the following are recommended:

> Research should be directed at the measurement of the mental models and cognitive maps developed by executive leaders. Such research efforts also should examine how these cognitive structures are related to executive leader action and organizational performance.

Leader Direction Setting

One of the earliest conceptualizations of executive leadership functions (Barnard, 1938) emphasized the executive leader's role in setting organizational direction. This function is also an integral part of each of the conceptual models or theories described in this book. Furthermore, as suggested both by Jacobs and Jaques (1990) and the integrated model of executive leadership depicted in Figure 10-1, this requirement exists at all organizational levels, although its accomplishment becomes significantly more complex at higher organizational levels.

Despite the ubiquity of this concept in executive leadership theory, there is insufficient empirical research on the nature of executive direction setting and how an articulated direction influences subsequent collective action. In particular, there is little understanding developed from empirical evidence of what elements of visions or strategies are most important for galvanizing collective behavior. How correspondence between long-term vision and subsequent collective action is established and, more important, how that correspondence is monitored and changed when circumstances warrant such change needs to be investigated. Along these lines, a 1992 review by Yukl and Van Fleet (p. 179) raised the following questions regarding issues requiring additional research:

▪ How do leaders develop a vision that will appeal to followers?

▪ How do leaders obtain the commitment of followers to a new vision, especially in a large organization in which there are competing visions?

▪ How do leaders empower followers, and what aspects of that process are most important?

These are important questions that require research attention. In addition, there are several other questions that also deserve to be investigated:

▪ What is the amount of gain in performance at different organization levels that can be attributed to leader direction setting?

▪ What is the role of leader values in the development of vision or long-term strategies?

▪ How do leader values influence the process of strategic implementation?

▪ How does the nature and process of leader direction setting change at different organizational levels?

▪ What is the strength of association between leader conceptual and social competencies and the formation and implementation of leader direction?

Resolution of these questions should contribute to a better understanding of the process of leadership, not only at executive levels, but at other organizational levels as well. Accordingly, the following recommendation is made:

Research should be directed at (a) the nature of leader direction setting; (b) how such direction setting changes at multiple organizational levels; and (c) how leader direction is translated into effective collective action.

Chief Executive Officers and Top Management Teams

Although top management teams (TMTs) have been a major research focus in the strategic management literature, little research has been directed at understanding their processes (see exceptions by Hambrick, 1994, 1995; Siegel & Hambrick, 1996) and particularly at how chief executive officers (CEOs) can foster TMT effectiveness. Much of the research on TMTs has focused on team demographics and their effects on strategic decision making and organizational performance. However, team processes are likely to mediate the effects of demographics on team outcomes. Likewise, effective CEOs are likely to be those who manage the demographic mix of the TMT (through staffing decisions) and team processes so that team heterogeneity does not result in dysfunctional forms of conflict. Accordingly, the following research theme is recommended:

Research on executive leadership should include an examination of (a) the processes and systems that characterize effective TMTs and (b) the processes CEOs use to manage and lead TMTs.

METHODOLOGICAL RECOMMENDATIONS

The specification of multiple social and cognitive capacities as key leader attributes requires certain methodological adjustments in executive leadership research. Two of these are discussed in this section.

Multivariate Research Strategies

A problem with previous research on executive leadership is that although the questions raised by various conceptual approaches called for a multivariate research strategy, the strategy selected by the researcher or researchers typically was a bivariate one. In addition, sample size or methodology (e.g., interviews) often constrains the use of multivariate approaches. For example, SST suggests several executive leader performance requirements. These include building frames of reference for the organization, long-term planning, consensus building, and network development. A pertinent question is which executive leader performance requirement is most important, or do they all make unique contributions to the organization? SST also argues for the primacy of conceptual capacities and cognitive skills over technical and interpersonal skills as requisite executive leader competencies. Testing these questions and assumptions requires a multivariate research strategy in which more than one predictor is examined in relation to targeted criteria and data are analyzed using multiple regression techniques. Covariate analyses are necessary to isolate the influences of particular determinants of executive leadership. Structural equation modeling techniques should be applied to assess the validity of theoretical models of the determinants and consequences of executive leadership. These and other multivariate strategies would provide more sophisticated examinations of executive leadership. Although a number of excellent examples of such research exist in the literature (e.g., Bourgeois, 1985; Calori, Johnson, & Sarnin, 1994; Dollinger, 1984; Hitt & Tyler, 1991; House, Spangler, & Woycke, 1991; Howell & Avoilo, 1993; Judge & Spitzfaden, 1995; Miller & Toulouse, 1986), more of these kinds of studies are necessary for significant advances to be made in understanding executive leadership. Accordingly, the following is recommended:

A greater proportion of executive leadership research should be completed using multivariate methodological strategies.

Development of Constructed-Response Measures of Executive Leader Competencies

This book has documented significant support for the premise that high-level conceptual capacities and cognitive skills are significant determinants of effective executive leadership. Further validation of this premise requires the measurement of such capacities and skills. Several researchers have argued that cognitive skill assessment should not rely on the use of multiple-choice inventories; instead, such measures should be based on constructed-response tasks (Ackerman & Smith, 1988; Birenbaum & Tatsuoka, 1987; Sebrechts, Bennett, & Rock, 1994: Ward, Frederickson, & Carlson, 1980). A *constructed-response task* is defined as "any task for which the space of examinee responses is not limited to a small set of presented options. As such, the examinee is forced to formulate, rather than recognize, an answer" (Bennett, 1993b, p. 100). Such measures have been cited as more closely resembling the kinds of tasks completed in actual performance settings (Bennett, 1993b; Bennett et al., 1990; Sebrechts et al., 1991). Constructed-response measures can vary in format from multiple choice, in which some construction is required before response selection, to an aggregation of multiple constructed responses selected over time and organized into a portfolio (Bennett, 1993a; Snow, 1993). The Career Path Appreciation technique (CPA), developed to measure conceptual capacity, is one form of a constructed-response measure (Lewis, 1993, 1995; McIntyre, Jordan, Mergen, Hamill, & Jacobs, 1993; Stamp, 1988). Mumford et al. (1993) and Zaccaro, Marks, et al. (1995) described other constructed-response measures that were used to assess problem-solving skills in military officers ranging in rank from second lieutenant to colonel.

Preliminary evidence regarding these measures has indicated considerable success in assessing qualities related to military leadership. Stamp (1988) reported predicted validity coefficients for the CPA in the range of .70 to .92. Lewis (1995) found significant correlations between the CPA and ratings of strategic thinking skill and general officer potential. Zaccaro, Marks, et al. (1995) reported that their constructed-response measures of complex problem-solving skills explained a significant proportion of variance in officer career achievement indices; these measures also differed across Army officer grades in that upper-level officers scored higher than lower-level officers. These findings support the value of developing measures using a constructed-response format to assess executive leadership competencies. Accordingly, the following recommendation is offered:

> Research should be directed to the development of constructed-response tasks that can be used to assess executive leadership competencies, particularly cognitive capacities and skills.

DEVELOPMENTAL GUIDELINES

A central focus of leader development is the provision to potential leaders of challenging work assignments to potential executive leaders that push them to new understandings of more complex operating environment. For example, based on SST, Lewis and Jacobs (1992) argued the following:

> Slow and progressive changes in the way a person constructs experience occur not primarily as a result of being taught better ways of making sense of the world but, instead, in response to directly experiencing the limitations of one's current way of making sense of experience (Kegan, 1982). . . . The heart of managerial development, therefore, should be the planned assignment of high-potential leaders and managers to successively more challenging work roles where a mentor is present who can help the individual better understand the new, more complicated world in which the new manager must now operate. (pp. 135–136)

The role of work challenge in leader development was also addressed by Hooijberg and Quinn (1992), who spoke from the behavioral complexity theory perspective (i.e., Quinn's competing values framework):

> We propose . . . that having to deal with challenges to the work role will elicit the enactment of new leadership roles and/or the rebalancing of leadership roles. This change, in turn, we propose, will lead to more behavioral complexity. It is the interaction between the individual and his or her environment that stimulates development.

McCauley, Eastman, and Ohlott (1995) identified several job components, called *stretch assignments*, that pose challenging developmental experiences for position incumbents. These components are listed in Table 10-4. The five categories of developmental experiences are (a) transitions, (b) creating change, (c) high level of responsibility, (d) nonauthority relationships, and (e) obstacles. *Transitions* are leaders moving to a new position or being assigned new functional responsibilities. *Creating change* involves leaders being given responsibility for decisions that could entail changes in current organizational policies or components. *High level of responsibility* means assigning to leaders tasks and projects having significant consequences for the organization. These tasks involve the resolution of complex problems that may require more boundary management than tasks with less responsibility. *Nonauthority relationships* refers to placing leaders in situations in which they must cultivate new forms of social influence that are likely to be more operative at the executive level. Finally, *obstacles* are difficulties engendered by circumstances faced by leaders with which they must learn to cope

---

TABLE 10-4

Leader Development Job Components

Category	Job component
Transitions	*Unfamiliar responsibilities*: The leader must handle responsibilities that are new, very different, or much broader than previous ones.
	Proving oneself: The leader has added pressure to show others he or she can handle the job.
Creating change	*Developing new directions*: The leader is responsible for starting something new in the organization, making strategic changes in the organization, carrying out a reorganization, or responding to changes in the organizational environment.
	Inherited problems: The leader has to fix problems created by a former incumbent or take over problem employees.
	Reduction decisions: Decisions about shutting down operations or staff reductions have to be made.
	Problems with employees: Employees lack adequate experience, are incompetent, or are resistant.
High level of responsibility	*High stakes*: Clear deadlines, pressure from executive leaders, high visibility, and responsibility for key decisions make success or failure in this position clearly evident.
	Managing organizational diversity: The scope of this position is broad, with responsibilities for multiple functions, groups, products, customers, or markets.
	Job overload: The sheer size of the job requires a large investment of time and energy.
	Handling external pressure: External factors that affect the organization (e.g., negotiating with unions or government agencies, working in a foreign culture, coping with serious community problems) must be addressed.
Nonauthority relationships	*Influencing without authority*: Getting the job done requires influencing peers, upper management, external parties, or other key people over whom the leader has no direct authority.
Obstacles	*Adverse organizational conditions*: The business unit or product line faces financial problems or difficult economic conditions.
	Lack of upper-level support: Upper-level management is reluctant to provide direction, support, or resources for current work or new projects.
	Lack of personal support: The leader is excluded from key networks and gets little support and encouragement from others.
	Difficult superior: The leader's opinions or management style differs from those of his or her superior, or the superior has major shortcomings.

These components correspond to the 15 scales on the Development Challenge Profile. From "Linking Management Selection and Development Through Stretch Assignments," by C. D. McCauley, L. J. Eastman, and P. J. Ohlott, in *Human Resource Management, 34*, 1995. Copyright © 1995 by John Wiley & Sons, Inc. Adapted with permission.

successfully. McCauley et al. noted, "successfully dealing with obstacles deepens the manager's understanding of problematic situations and can increase confidence in facing such challenges again" (p. 98).

McCauley et al.'s (1995) work highlights the importance of challenging work assignments as developmental tools. Future research on work-based development needs to be considered within the context of a work-experience model. Tesluk and Jacobs (1998) offered such a model in which they described three core components of work experience. The first is a quantitative component that refers to both time-based (e.g., job and organizational tenure) and amount-based (e.g., number of experiences and times work has been completed) aspects of work experience. The second is a qualitative component that reflects the nature of the experience (e.g., degree of autonomy or challenge in the assignment). McCauley's research on stretch assignments refers to this aspect of work experiences. The third component of Tesluk and Jacobs' model is the timing of experiences. This refers to when an assignment or experience occurs during an individual's career or developmental program.

Tesluk and Jacobs (1998) also described several ways individual variables influence the role of work experiences as developmental interventions. First, individuals with high levels of certain characteristics or abilities are more likely to receive certain assignments and experiences. Second, individuals can select, shape, or define the nature of their work experiences, thereby increasing or decreasing their developmental potential. Finally, according to their cognitive capacities, different individuals will draw different lessons from the same experience. These conceptual arguments suggest that more research is needed to link work-experience models with theories of executive leader development requirements to understand why (a) some executive development interventions succeed and others fail and (b) some executive leaders thrive in a development program and others derail.

The development of executive leaders also needs to be considered as a career-long systematic intervention process that integrates formal instruction with carefully structured work experiences. Mumford and Marks (1994) offered a model of corresponding instructional and work assignments to reflect the kinds of conceptual gains required at successively higher levels of leadership in the U.S. Army. An adaptation of this model is presented in Figure 10-6. It assumes four levels of leadership through which an officer proceeds, from technical-based training and socialization to the acquisition and application of complex problem-solving skills and conceptualization of the systems within which he or she must operate. Each level of instruction is followed by a series of assignments to stretch the officer's skills and capabilities at that level of development. Mumford and Marks indicated in their model (a) the de-

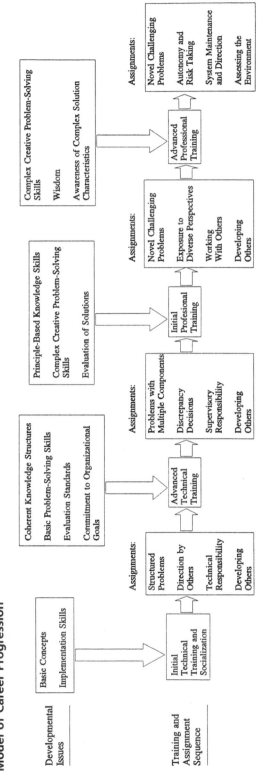

FIGURE 10-6

Model of Career Progression

Reprinted from *Leadership Quarterly, 11*, M. D. Mumford, M. A. Marks, S. J. Zaccaro, M. S. Connelly, and R. Reiter-Palmon, Development of Leadership Skills. Experience, Timing, and Growth, pp. 115–133. Copyright 2000, with permission from Elsevier Science.

velopment issues (i.e., knowledge, skills, and capacities) that need to emerge at each level of organizational leadership; (b) the primary focus of instruction at each career point; and (c) the characteristics of challenging or stretch assignments at each career point. Work assignments occur under the guidance of superiors who understand their responsibilities to provide the degree of work challenge that fosters leader growth and to facilitate the development of more adaptive ways of thinking and behaving. Mumford and Marks suggested, however, that mentoring experiences "may not prove especially beneficial until leaders have progressed far enough in their careers and have the expertise, problem-solving skills, and social appraisal skills that make mentoring a useful experience" (p. 60). Although this model emerged from data gathered from military officers regarding the kinds of experiences they found rewarding at various career stages, it should be applicable to other organizations as well.

These observations and Mumford and Marks's (1994) model suggest that executive leader development efforts should (a) emphasize work and job challenges that provide stretch experiences for emerging executive leaders (b) integrate formal instruction and unit assignments into a more cohesive framework in which one experience builds on the next. It is worth noting that Mumford and Marks's model was developed analysis of leader development within the U.S. Army, in which leaders are part of a single system for their entire careers. This is rarely the case in private industry. Nonetheless, an integrative and systems perspective of executive development is both applicable and necessary.

A recent text from the Center for Creative Leadership (McCauley, Moxley, & Van Velsor, 1998) described several elements of such integrative leader development programs, including feedback, skill-based training, job assignments, and developmental relationships. Regarding a systems perspective, Moxley and Wilson noted that today's organizations are more likely to be integrating developmental experiences into a budding leader's typical work. They emphasized the linking of several developmental experiences into a *leadership development system*, which they defined as the "confluence of interdependent organizational and management processes that work together to provide maximum impact for leadership development experiences" (p. 222).

These are fairly new ideas in executive development. They deserve further research attention to determine their quality. Accordingly, the following actions are recommended:

> ▪ Research on executive leader development should explore more fully the validity and usefulness of stretch assignments in fostering growth in requisite executive leader competencies. This research should be embedded within and derived from work-experience models.

▪ Research should identify the key features and principles of integrated executive leader development models, such as career progression programs and leadership development systems. Research also should be directed at the validity and usefulness of such models.

Summary

Kimmel's 1981 review of executive leadership research identified a significant body of research on such leadership. However, the amount of this research was quite small compared with the research on leadership in general. This book and its reviews of conceptual and empirical research illustrate the tremendous burgeoning interest in executive leadership. There are now multiple conceptual models and theories of executive leadership as well as a growing empirical research base supporting several theoretical postulates derived from these models and theories. Promising assessment strategies used to measure requisite executive leader characteristics are being developed and validated. Finally, several conceptual perspectives of executive leader development are beginning to converge on a common framework. All of these efforts portend significant advancements in the study of executive leadership in the near future.

Existing and emerging theories of executive leadership reflect several of the prescriptions for an executive leadership theory outlined by Day and Lord (1988). The various conceptual approaches presented in this book provide alternate perspectives of executive leadership, each offering elements lacking in the others. However, each framework is limited in scope. Greater progress in understanding executive leadership is likely to occur through an integration of these different models and theories. The integrated leader performance requirements model, the list of executive leader competencies and temperamental qualities, and the constellation of characteristics contributing to executive flexibility that were presented in this chapter reflect one such integration attempt.

The advancement of executive leadership research also will likely occur through the adoption of a research framework like the one in Figure 10-4, in which (a) the accomplishment of executive leader performance requirements is linked to unit and organizational effectiveness; (b) executive leader competencies and personal characteristics are examined as determinants of such accomplishments; and (c) validated competencies and qualities become the bases for measuring development and the evaluation of potential executive leader development programs. Such research programs should be grounded in multivariate methodologies instead of the bivariate ones that have characterized most existing research. Such a program should include the development of multiple assessment strategies that reflect a wider range of executive leader characteristics. Finally, this program should incorporate both qualitative and quantitative methodologies, reflecting idiographic and nomothetic approaches to the study of executive leadership.

The incorporation of these and other recommendations offered in this book is likely to fuel growth in executive leadership research even greater than that experienced recently. The results should provide a better and more thorough understanding of the dynamics, processes, and products of executive leadership and its development.

References

Ackerman, P. L. (1986). Individual differences in information processing: An investigation of intellectual abilities and task performance during practice. *Intelligence, 10,* 101–139.

Ackerman, P. L. (1987). Individual differences in skill learning: An integration of psychometric and information processing perspectives. *Psychological Bulletin, 102,* 3–27.

Ackerman, T. A., & Smith, P. L. (1988). A comparison of the information provided by essay, multiple choice, and free-response writing tests. *Applied Psychological Measurement, 12,* 117–128.

Aldrich, H. E. (1979). *Organizations and environments.* Englewood Cliffs, NJ: Prentice Hall.

Alexander, L. D. (1979). The effect level in the hierarchy and functional area have on the extent Mintzberg's roles are required by managerial jobs. *Proceedings of the Academy of Management* (pp. 186–189). Atlanta: Academy of Management.

Alliger, G. M., & Janak, E. A. (1989). Kirkpatrick's levels of training criteria: Thirty years later. *Personnel Psychology, 42,* 331–341.

Amason, A. C. (1996). Distinguishing the effects of functional and dysfunctional conflict on strategic decision making: Resolving a paradox for top management teams. *Academy of Management Journal, 39,* 123–148.

Amason, A. C., & Sapienza, H. J. (1997). The effects of top management team size and interaction norms on cognitive and affective conflict. *Journal of Management, 23,* 495–516.

Ancona, D. G. (1987). Groups in organizations: Extending laboratory models. In C. Hendrick (Ed.), *Group processes and intergroup relations.* Newbury Park, CA: Sage.

Ancona, D. G. (1990). Outward Bound: Strategies for team survival in the organization. *Academy of Management Journal, 33,* 334–365.

Ancona, D. G., & Caldwell, D. F. (1992). Bridging the boundary: External process and performance in organizational teams. *Administrative Science Quarterly, 37,* 527–548.

Anderson, J. R. (1990). *Cognitive psychology and its implications* (3rd ed.). New York: Freeman.

Anderson, J. R. (1993). Problem solving and learning. *American Psychologist, 48,* 35–44.

Ansoff, H. I. (1979). *Strategic management.* London: Macmillan.

Anstey, E. (1977). A thirty-year follow-up of the CSSB procedure with implications for the future. *Journal of Occupational Psychology, 50,* 149–159.

Asch, S. (1946). Forming impressions of personality. *Journal of Abnormal and Social Psychology, 41,* 1230–1240.

Ashby, W. (1952). *Design for a brain.* New York: Wiley.

Atwater, L., & Yammarino, F. J. (1993). Personal attributes as predictors of superiors' and subordinates' perceptions of military academy leadership. *Human Relations, 46,* 645–668.

Atwater, L., Penn, R., & Rucker, L. (1991). Personal qualities of charismatic leaders. *Leadership and Organizational Development Journal, 12,* 7–10.

Avolio, B. J. (1994). The "natural": Some antecedents to transformational leadership. *International Journal of Public Administration, 17,* 1559–1581.

Avolio, B. J., & Bass, B. M. (1988). Charisma and beyond. In J. G. Hunt, B. R. Baliga, H. P. Dachler, & C. A. Schriesheim (Eds.), *Emerging leadership vistas* (pp. 29–49). Lexington, MA: Heath.

Avolio, B. J., & Bass, B. M. (1991). *The full range of leadership development: Basic and advanced manuals.* Binghamton, NY: Haworth.

Avolio, B. J., & Bass, B. M. (1994). *Evaluate the impact of transformational leadership training at individual, group, organizational and community levels* (Final report to the W. K. Kellogg Foundation). Binghamton, NY: State University of New York at Binghamton.

Avolio, B. J., & Bass, B. M. (1995). Individual consideration viewed at multiple levels of analysis: A multi-level framework for examining the diffusion of transformational leadership. *Leadership Quarterly, 6,* 199–218.

Avolio, B. J., & Gibbons, T. C. (1988). Developing transformational leaders: A lifespan approach. In J. A. Conger & R. N. Kanungo (Eds.), *Charismatic leadership: The elusive factor in organizational effectiveness* (pp. 276–308). San Francisco: Jossey-Bass.

Avolio, B. J., & Howell, J. M. (1992). The impact of leader behavior and leader-personality match on satisfaction and unit performance. In K. E. Clark, M. B. Clark, & D. R. Campbell (Eds.), *Impact of leadership.* Greensboro, NC: Center for Creative Leadership.

Avolio, B. J., Waldman, D. A., & Einstein, W. O. (1988). Transformational leadership in management game simulation. *Group and Organization Studies, 13,* 59–80.

Baehr, M. E. (1992). *Predicting success in higher level positions: A guide to the system for testing and evaluation of potential.* Westport, CT: Quorum.

Baird, I. S., & Thomas, H. (1985). Toward a contingency model of risk taking. *Academy of Management Review, 10,* 230–243.

Bandura, A. (1986). *Social foundations of thought and action: A social cognitive theory.* Englewood Cliffs, NJ: Prentice Hall.

Bantel, K. A. (1993). Strategic clarity in banking: Role of top management team demography. *Psychological Reports, 73,* 1187–1201.

Bantel, K. A., & Jackson, S. E. (1989). Top management and innovations in banking: Does the composition of the top team make a difference? *Strategic Management Journal, 10,* 107–124.

Barber, H. F. (1990). Some personality characteristics of senior military officers. In K. E. Clark & M. B. Clark (Eds.), *Measures of leadership.* Greensboro, NC: Center for Creative Leadership. Barnard, C. I. (1938). *The functions of the executive.* Cambridge, MA: Harvard University Press.

Barnard, C. I. (1938). *The functions of the executive.* Cambridge, MA: Harvard University Press.

Barr, P., Stimpert, L., & Huff, A. (1992). Cognitive change, strategic action, and organizational renewal. *Strategic Management Journal, 13,* 15–36.

Barrick, M. R., Day, D. V., Lord, R. G., & Alexander, R. A. (1991). Assessing the utility of executive leadership. *Leadership Quarterly, 2,* 9–22.

Barrick, M. R., & Mount, M. K. (1991). The big five personality dimensions and job performance: A meta-analysis. *Personnel Psychology, 44,* 1–26.

Bartunek, J. M., & Loius, M. R. (1988). The design of work environments that stretch managers' capacities for complex thinking. *Human Resources Planning, 11,* 13–22.

Bass, B. M. (1985). *Leadership and performance beyond expectations.* New York: Free Press.

Bass, B. M. (1988). The inspirational process of leadership. *Journal of Management Development, 75,* 21–31.

Bass, B. M. (1990). *Bass and Stogdill's handbook of leadership: Theory, research and managerial applications* (3rd ed.). New York: Free Press.

Bass, B. M. (1996). *A new paradigm of leadership: An inquiry into transformational leadership*. Alexandria, VA: U.S. Army Research Institute for the Behavioral and Social Sciences.

Bass, B. M., & Avolio., B. J. (n.d.). *Intuitive-empirical approach to biodata analysis*. Binghamton: Center for Leadership Studies, State University of New York at Binghamton.

Bass, B. M., & Avolio, B. J. (1990). The implications of transactional and transformational leadership for individual, team, and organizational development. In R. W. Woodman & W. A. Passmore (Eds.), *Research in organizational change and development*. Greenwich, CT: JAI Press.

Bass, B. M., & Avolio, B. J. (1993). Transformational leadership: A response to critiques. In M. M. Chemers & R. Ayman (Eds.), *Leadership theory and research*. San Diego, CA: Academic Press.

Bass, B. M., Waldman, D. A., Avolio, B. J., & Bebb, M. (1987). Transformational leadership: The falling dominoes effect. *Group and Organization Studies, 12,* 73–87.

Bell, G. B., & Hall, H. E. (1954). The relationship between leadership and empathy. *Journal of Abnormal and Social Psychology, 49,* 156–157.

Bennett, R. E. (1993a). On the meanings of constructed response. In R. E. Bennett & W. C. Ward (Eds.), *Construction versus choice in cognitive measurement* (pp. 1–28). Hillsdale, NJ: Erlbaum.

Bennett, R. E. (1993b). Toward intelligent assessment: An integration of constructed response testing, artificial intelligence, and model based measurement. In N. Frederiksen, R. J. Mislevy & I. I. Bejar (Eds.), *Test theory for a new generation of tests* (pp. 99–124). Hillsdale, NJ: Erlbaum.

Bennett, R. E., Rock, D. A., Braun, H. I., Frye, D., Spohrer, J. C., & Soloway, E. (1990). The relationship of constrained free-response items to multiple choice and open-ended items. *Applied Psychological Measurement, 14,* 151–162.

Bennis, W., & Nanus, B. (1985). *Leaders: The strategies for taking charge*. New York: Harper & Row.

Bentz, V. J. (1987). *Explorations of scope and scale: The critical determinant of high-level effectiveness* (Tech. Rep. No. 31). Greensboro, NC: Center for Creative Leadership.

Birenbaum, M., & Tatsuoka, K. K. (1987). Open-ended versus multiple-choice response formats: It does make a difference for diagnostic purposes. *Applied Psychological Measurement, 11,* 385–395.

Bluedorn, A. C., Johnson, R. A., Cartwright, D. K., & Barringer, B. R. (1994). The interface and convergence of the strategic management and the organizational environment domains. *Journal of Management, 20,* 201–262.

Boal, K. B., & Bryson, J. M. (1988). Charismatic leadership: A phenomenological and structural approach. In J. G. Hunt, B. R. Baliga, H. P. Dachler, & C. A. Schriesheim (Eds.), *Emerging leadership vistas*. Lexington, MA: Heath.

Boal, K. B., & Whitehead, C. J. (1992). A critique and extension of the stratified systems theory perspective. In R. L. Phillips & J. G. Hunt (Eds.), *Strategic leadership: A multiorganizational-level perspective*. Westport, CT: Quorum.

Bobko, P., & Shwartz, J. P. (1984). A metric for integrating theoretically related but statistically unrelated constructs. *Journal of Personality Assessment, 48,* 281–320.

Boeker, W. (1997). Strategic change: The influence of managerial characteristics and organizational growth. *Academy of Management Journal, 40,* 152–170.

Bourgeois, L. J., III. (1984). Strategic management and determinism. *Academy of Management Review, 9,* 586–596.

Bourgeois, L. J., III. (1985). Strategic goals, perceived uncertainty, and economic performance in volatile environments. *Academy of Management Journal, 28,* 548–573.

Bourgeois, L. J., III, & Eisenhardt, K. M. (1988). Strategic decision processes in high velocity environments: Four cases in the microcomputer industry. *Management Science, 34,* 816–835.

Boyatzis, R. R. (1982). *The competent manager: A model for effective performance.* New York: Wiley.

Boyd, B. K. (1991). Strategic planning and financial performance. *Journal of Management Studies, 28,* 353–374.

Brass, D. J., & Krackhardt, D. (1999). The social capital of the 21st century leaders. In J. G. Hunt, R. L. Phillips, & L. Wong (Eds.), *Out-of-the-box leadership: Transforming the 21st century Army and other top performing organizations.* Greenwich, CT: JAI Press.

Braun, H. I. (1988). Understanding scoring reliability: Experiments in calibrating essay readers. *Journal of Educational Statistics, 13,* 1–18.

Bray, D. W. (1982). The assessment center and the study of lives. *American Psychologist, 37,* 180–189.

Bray, D. W., Campbell, R. J., & Grant, D. L. (1974). *Formative years in business: A long term AT&T study of managerial lives.* New York: Wiley.

Briggs, S. R., Cheek, J. M., & Buss, A. H. (1980). An analysis of the self-monitoring scale. *Journal of Personality and Social Psychology, 38,* 679–686.

Briggs Myers, I. & McCauley, M. H. (1985). *Manual: A guide to the development of the Myers-Briggs Type Indicator.* Palo Alto, CA: Consulting Psychologists Press.

Brown, A. L. (1978). Knowing when, where, and how to remember: The problem of metacognition. In R. Glaser (Ed.), *Advances in instructional psychology.* New York: Halsted Press.

Bruner, J. (1966). *Toward a theory of instruction.* New York: Norton.

Bryant, C. D. (1994). *Strategies for augmentation initiatives for leadership self-development program* (ARI Research Note No. 94-29). Alexandria, VA: U.S. Army Research Institute for the Behavioral and Social Sciences.

Burns, J. M. (1978). *Leadership.* New York: Harper & Row.

Byars, L. L. (1984). The strategic management process: A model and terminology. *Managerial Planning, 32,* 38–44.

Calder, B. J. (1977). An attributional theory of leadership. In B. Staw & G. Salancik (Eds.), *New directions in organizational behavior.* Chicago: St. Clair Press.

Caldwell, D. F., & O'Reilly, C. A., III. (1982). Boundary spanning and individual performance: The impact of self-monitoring. *Journal of Applied Psychology, 67,* 124–127.

Calori, R., Johnson, G., & Sarnin, P. (1994). CEOs' cognitive maps and the scope of the organization. *Strategic Management Journal, 15,* 437–457.

Cameron, K. (1986). Effectiveness as paradox. *Management Science, 32,* 539–553.

Cameron, K., & Whetton, D. A. (1983). *Organizational effectiveness: A comparison of multiple models.* New York: Academic Press.

Campbell, D. T. (1955). An error in some demonstrations of the superior social perceptiveness of leaders. *Journal of Abnormal and Social Psychology, 51,* 694–695.

Campbell, D. T. (1988). Task complexity: A review and analysis. *Academy of Management Review, 13,* 40–52.

Campbell, D. T., & Fiske, D. W. (1959). Convergent and discriminant validation by the multitrait–multimethod matrix. *Psychological Bulletin, 56,* 81–105.

Campbell, J. P., Dunnette, M. D., Lawler, E. E., & Weick, K. E. (1970). *Managerial behavior, performance and effectiveness.* New York: McGraw Hill.

Cannon-Bowers, J. A., Salas, E., & Converse, S. A. (1990). Cognitive psychology and team training: Shared mental models in complex systems. *Human Factors Society Bulletin, 33,* 1–4.

Cannon-Bowers, J. A., Salas, E., & Converse, S. (1993). Shared mental models in expert team decision making. In N. J. Castellan, Jr. (Ed.), *Individual and group decision making.* Hillsdale, NJ: Erlbaum.

Cantor, N., & Kihlstrom, J. F. (1987). *Personality and social intelligence.* Englewood Cliffs, NJ: Prentice Hall.

Carlson, S. (1951). *Executive behavior: A study of the work load and training methods of managing directors.* Stockholm: Strombergs.

Carroll, S. J., & Gillen, D. J. (1987). Are the classical management functions useful in describing managerial work? *Academy of Management Review, 12,* 38–51.

Child, J. (1972). Organization structure, environment and performance: The role of strategic choice. *Sociology, 6*, 2–22.

Chowdhry, K., & Newcomb, T. W. (1952). The relative abilities of leaders and nonleaders to estimate opinions of their own groups. *Journal of Abnormal and Social Psychology, 47*, 51–57.

Church, L. M., & Alie, R. E. (1986). Relationships between managers' personality characteristics and their management levels and job foci. *Akron Business and Economic Review, 4*, 29–45.

Chusmir, L. H., & Koberg, C. S. (1986). Creativity differences among managers. *Journal of Vocational Behavior, 29*, 240–253.

Clement, S. D., & Ayres, D. B. (1976). *The matrix of organizational leadership dimensions.* Washington, DC: U.S. Army Administration Center.

Cohen, M. S., Adelman, L., Tolcott, M. A., Bresnick, T. A., & Marvin, F. F. (1994). *A cognitive framework for battlefield commanders' situation assessment* (ARI Tech. Rep. No. 1002). Alexandria, VA: U.S. Army Research Institute for the Behavioral and Social Sciences.

Cohen, S. A. (1993). Defining and measuring effectiveness in public management. *Public Productivity and Management Review, 25*, 45–57.

Collins, J. C., & Porras, J. I. (1991, Fall). Organizational vision and visionary organizations. *California Management Review*, 30–82.

Conger, J. A., & Kanungo, R. N. (1987). Toward a behavioral theory of charismatic leadership in organizational settings. *Academy of Management Review, 12*, 637–647.

Conger, J. A., & Kanungo, R. N. (1988). Behavioral dimensions of charismatic leadership. In J. A. Conger & R. N. Kanungo (Eds.), *Charismatic leadership: The elusive factor in organizational effectiveness* (pp. 78–97). San Francisco: Jossey-Bass.

Conger, J. A., & Kanungo, R. N. (1992). Perceived behavioural attributes of charismatic leadership. *Canadian Journal of Behavioural Science, 24*(1), 86–102.

Copeman, G., Luijk, H., & Hanika, F. (1963). *How the executive spends his time.* London: Business Publications Limited.

Cowan, D. A., Fiol, C. M., & Walsh, J. P. (1992). A midrange theory of strategic choice processes. In R. L. Phillips & J. G. Hunt (Eds.), *Strategic leadership: A multiorganizational-level perspective.* Westport, CT: Quorum.

Crookall, P. (1989). *Management of inmate workers: A field test of transformational and situational leadership.* Unpublished doctoral dissertation, University of Western Ontario, London, Ontario, Canada.

Cyert, R. M., & March, J. G. (1963). *A behavioral theory of the firm.* Englewood Cliffs, NJ: Prentice Hall.

Daboub, A. J., Rasheed, A. M. A., Preim, R. L., & Gray, D. (1995). Top management team characteristics and corporate illegal activity. *Academy of Management Review, 20*, 138–170.

Daft, R. L., Sormunen, J., & Parks, D. (1988). Chief executive scanning, environmental characteristics, and company performance: An empirical study. *Strategic Management Journal, 9*, 123–139.

Daft, R. L., & Weick, K. E. (1984). Toward a model of organizations as interpretation systems. *Academy of Management Review, 9*, 284–295.

Dalton, D. R., & Kesner, I. F. (1985). Organizational performance as an antecedent of inside/outside chief executive succession: An empirical assessment. *Academy of Management Journal, 28*, 749–762.

Davidson, J. E., Deuser, R., & Sternberg, R. J. (1994). The role of metacognition in problem solving. In J. Metcalf & A. P. Shimamura (Eds.), *Metacognition: Knowing about knowing.* Cambridge, MA: MIT Press.

Davies, J., & Easterby-Smith, M. (1984). Learning and developing from managerial work experiences. *Journal of Management Studies, 2*, 169–183.

Day, D. V., & Lord, R. G. (1988). Executive leadership and organizational performance: Suggestions for a new theory and methodology. *Journal of Management, 14*, 453–464.

Dean, J. W., Jr., & Sharfman, M. P. (1996). Does decision process matter? A study of strategic decision-making effectiveness. *Academy of Management Journal, 39*, 368–396.

Dearborn, D. C., & Simon, H. A. (1958). Selective perception: A note on the departmental identifications of executives. *Sociometry, 21,* 140–144.

Deckert, J. C., Entin, E. B., Entin, E. E., MacMillan, J., & Serfaty, D. (1994). *Military command decisionmaking expertise.* Burlington, MA: Alphatech, Inc.

Denison, D. R., Hooijberg, R., & Quinn, R. E. (1995). Paradox and performance: Toward a theory of behavioral complexity in managerial leadership. *Organization Science, 6,* 524–540.

Dobbins, G. H., Long, W. S., Dedrick, E. J., & Clemons, T. C. (1990). The role of self-monitoring and gender on leader emergence: A laboratory and field study. *Journal of Management, 16,* 493–502.

Dollinger, M. J. (1984). Environmental boundary spanning and information processing effects on organizational performance. *Academy of Management Journal, 27,* 351–368.

Donaldson, G., & Lorsch, J. (1983). *Decision making at the top.* New York: Basic Books.

Drenth, P., & Koopman, P. (1992). Duration and complexity in strategic decision-making. In F. Heller (Ed.), *Decision making and leadership.* Cambridge, MA: Cambridge University Press.

Driver, M. J., & Streufert, S. (1966). *The general incongruity adaption level (GIAL) hypothesis: An analysis and integration of cognitive approaches to motivation* (Publication No. 114). Lafayette, IN: Purdue University, Institute for Research in the Behavioral, Economic, and Management Sciences.

Driver, M. J., & Streufert, S. (1966). *Group composition, input load, and group information processing* (Institute Paper No. 142). Lafayette, IN: Purdue University, Herman C. Kraennert Graduate School of Industrial Administration, Institute for Research in the Behavioral, Economic and Management Sciences.

Dunnette, M. D. (1963). A modified model for selection research. *Journal of Applied Psychology, 47,* 317–323.

Dunnette, M. D. (1972). *Validity study results for jobs relevant to the petroleum refining industry.* Washington, DC: American Petroleum Institute.

Dutton, J. E., & Jackson, S. E. (1987). Categorizing strategic issues: Links to organizational action. *Academy of Management Review, 12,* 76–90.

Eden, D. (1984). Self-fulfilling prophecy as a management tool: Harnessing Pygmalion. *Academy of Management Review, 9,* 64–73.

Eden, D. (1990). *Pygmalion in management: Productivity as a self-fulfilling prophecy.* Lexington, MA: Lexington Books.

Ellis, R. J. (1988). Self-monitoring and leadership emergence in groups. *Personality and Social Psychology Bulletin, 14,* 681–693.

Ellis, R. J., Adamson, R. S., Deszca, G., & Cawsay, T. F. (1988). Self-monitoring and leadership emergence. *Small Group Behavior, 19,* 312–324.

Elron, E. (1997). Top management teams within multinational corporations: Effects of cultural heterogeneity. *Leadership Quarterly, 8,* 393–412.

Emery, F. E., & Trist, E. L. (1965). The causal texture of organizational environments. *Human Relations, 18,* 21–32.

Fahey, L., & Narayanan, V. (1989). Linking changes in revealed causal maps and environmental change: An empirical study. *Journal of Management Studies, 25,* 361–378.

Faraquhar, K. W. (1995). Not just understudies: The dynamics of short-term leadership. *Human Resource Management, 34,* 51–70.

Farh, J. L., Hoffman, R. C., & Hegarty, W. H. (1984). Assessing environmental scanning at the subunit level: A multitrait–multimethod analysis. *Decision Sciences, 15,* 197–220.

Ferentinos, C. (1996). *Linking social intelligence and leadership: An investigation of leaders' situational responsiveness under condition of changing group tasks and membership.* Unpublished doctoral dissertation, George Mason University, Fairfax, VA.

Feuerstein, R. (1980). *Instrumental enrichment: An intervention program for cognitive modifyability.* Baltimore, MD: University Park Press.

Fiedler, F. E. (1964). A contingency model of leadership effectiveness. In L. Berkowitz (Ed.), *Advances in experimental social psychology* (Vol. 1, pp. 149–190). New York: Academic Press.

Finkelstein, S. (1992). Power in top management teams: Dimensions, measurement and validation. *Academy of Management Journal, 35*, 505–538.

Finkelstein, S., & Hambrick, D. C. (1990). Top-management tenure and organizational outcomes: The moderating role of managerial discretion. *Administrative Science Quarterly, 25*, 484–503.

Flanagan, J. C. (1954). The critical incident technique. *Psychological Bulletin, 51*, 327–358.

Flavell, J. H. (1979). Metacognition and cognitive monitoring: A new area of cognitive developmental inquiry. *American Psychologist, 34*, 906–911.

Fleishman, E. A. (1975). Toward a taxonomy of human performance. *American Psychologist, 30*, 1127–1149.

Fleishman, E. A., & Friedman, L. (1994). *Cognitive competencies related to management performance requirements in R&D organizations.* Fairfax, VA: Center for Behavioral and Cognitive Studies, George Mason University.

Fleishman, E. A., & Mumford, M. D. (1989a). Abilities as causes of individual differences in skill acquisition. *Human Performance, 2*, 201–222.

Fleishman, E. A., & Mumford, M. D. (1989b). Individual attributes and training performance: Applications of ability taxonomies in instructional systems design. In I. L. Goldstein & Associates (Eds.), *Training and development in organizations.* San Francisco: Jossey-Bass.

Fleishman, E. A., & Zaccaro, S. J. (1992). Toward a taxonomy of team performance functions. In R. W. Swezey & E. Salas (Eds.), *Teams: Their training and performance.* Norwood, NJ: Ablex.

Fleishman, E. A., & Quaintance, M. K. (1984). *Taxonomies of human performance: The description of human tasks.* Orlando, FL: Academic Press.

Fleishman, E. A., & Salter, J. A. (1963). Relation between the leader's behavior and his empathy toward subordinates. *Journal of Industrial Psychology, 1*, 79–84.

Fleishman, E. A., Mumford, M. D., Zaccaro, S. J., Levin, K. Y., Korotkin, A. L., & Hein, M. B. (1991). Taxonomic efforts in the description of leader behavior: A synthesis and functional interpretation. *Leadership Quarterly, 2*, 245–287.

Ford, M. E., & Tisak, M. S. (1983). A further search for social intelligence. *Journal of Educational Psychology, 75*, 196–206.

Forsyth, D. R. (1990). *Group dynamics* (2nd ed). Pacific Grove, CA: Brooks/Cole.

Foti, R. J., & Cohen, B. A. (1986). *Self-monitoring and leadership emergence.* Unpublished manuscript.

Frederickson, J. W. (1984). The comprehensiveness of strategic decision processes: Extension, observation, future directions. *Academy of Management Journal, 27*, 445–466.

Frederickson, J. W., & Iaquinto, A. (1989). Inertia and creeping rationality in strategic decision processes. *Academy of Management Journal, 32*, 526–542.

Frederickson, J. W., & Mitchell, T. R. (1984). Strategic decision processes: Comprehensiveness and performance in an industry with an unstable environment. *Academy of Management Journal, 27*, 399–423.

Gage, N. L., & Exline, R. V. (1953). Social perception and effectiveness in discussion groups. *Human Relations, 6*, 381–396.

Gagné, R. M. (1985). *The conditions of learning and theory of instruction.* Philadelphia: Holt, Rinehart & Winston.

Gangestad, S. W., & Snyder, M. (1985). On the nature of self-monitoring: An examination of a latent causal structure. In P. Shaver (Ed.), *Review of personality and social psychology* (Vol. 6, pp. 65–85). Beverly Hills, CA: Sage.

Garafolo, J., & Lester, F. K. (1985). Metacognition, cognitive monitoring, and mathematical performance. *Journal for Research in Mathematics Education, 16*, 163–176.

Gardner, W. L., III, & Schermerhorn, J. R., Jr. (1992). Strategic operational leadership and the management of supportive work environments. In R. L. Phillips & J. G. Hunt (Eds.), *Strategic leadership: A multiorganizational-level perspective.* Westport, CT: Quorum.

Garland, H., & Beard, J. F. (1979). Relationship between self-monitoring and leader emergence across two task situations. *Journal of Applied Psychology, 64*, 72–76.

Geiwitz, J. (1993). *A conceptual model of metacognitive skills* (ARI Tech. Rep. No. 51-1, Contract No. MDA903-93-C-0109). Alexandria, VA: U.S. Army Research Institute for the Behavioral and Social Sciences.

Georgopoulos, B. S., & Tannenbaum, A. S. (1957). A study of organization effectiveness. *American Sociological Review, 22,* 534–540.

Ghiselli, E. E., Campbell, J. P., & Zedeck, S. (1981). *Measurement theory for the behavioral sciences.* New York: Freeman.

Gibbons, T. C. (1986). *Revisiting: The question of born vs. made: Toward a theory a theory of development of transformational leaders.* Unpublished doctoral dissertation, Fielding Institute, Santa Barbara, CA.

Gibbs, B. (1994). The effects of environment and technology on managerial roles. *Journal of Management, 20,* 581–604.

Gilbert, J. A., & Zaccaro, S. J. (1995, August). *Social intelligence and organizational leadership.* Paper presented at the 103rd annual convention of the American Psychological Association, New York.

Gilmore, T. N. (1982). Leadership and boundary management. *Journal of Applied Behavioral Science, 18,* 343–356.

Gladstein, D. (1984). Groups in context: A model of task group effectiveness. *Administrative Science Quarterly, 29,* 499–517.

Glick, W. H., Miller, C. C., & Huber, G. P. (1993). Upper-level diversity in organizations: Demographic, structural, and cognitive influences on organizational effectiveness. In G. P. Huber & W. H. Glick (Eds.), *Organizational change and redesign: Ideas and insights for improving performance* (pp. 176–214). New York: Oxford University Press.

Glueck, W. F. (1980). *Strategic management and business policy.* New York: McGraw Hill.

Goldstein, I. L. (1986). *Training in organizations: Needs assessment, development and evaluation* (2nd ed.). Pacific Grove, CA: Brooks/Cole.

Goldstein, I. L. (1991). Training in work organizations. In M. D. Dunnette & L. M. Hough (Eds.), *Handbook of industrial and organizational psychology* (Vol. 2, pp. 506–620). Palo Alto, CA: Consulting Psychologists Press.

Goodacre, D. M. (1951). The use of a sociometric test as a predictor of combat unit effectiveness. *Sociometry, 14,* 148–152.

Goodman, P. S. (1967). An empirical examination of Elliott Jacques' concept of time span. *Human Relations, 20,* 155–170.

Goodman, P., & Penning, J. (1977). *New perspectives on organizations' effectiveness.* San Francisco: Jossey-Bass.

Govindarajan, V. (1988). A contingency approach to strategy implementation at the business unit level: Integrating administrative mechanisms with strategy. *Academy of Management Journal, 31,* 828–853.

Greening, D. W., & Johnson, R. A. (1997). Managing industrial and environmental crises: The role of heterogeneous top management teams. *Business and Society, 36,* 334–361.

Greer, F. L., Galanter, E. H., & Nordlie, P. G. (1954). Interpersonal knowledge and individual and group effectiveness. *Journal of Abnormal and Social Psychology, 49,* 411–414.

Grimm, C. M., & Smith, K. G. (1991). Management and organizational change: A note on the railroad industry. *Strategic Management Journal, 12,* 557–562.

Gualtieri, J. W., Parker, C. W., & Zaccaro, S. J. (1995). *Group decision making: An examination of decision processes and performance.* Paper presented at the 10th annual meeting of the Society for Industrial and Organizational Psychology, Orlando, FL.

Gupta, A. K. (1984). Contingency linkages between strategy and general managerial characteristics: A conceptual examination. *Academy of Management Review, 9,* 399–412.

Gupta, A. K. (1987). SBU strategies, corporate–SBU relations, and SBU effectiveness in strategy implementation. *Academy of Management Journal, 30,* 477–500.

Gupta, A. K. (1988). Contingency perspectives on strategic leadership: Current knowledge and future research directions. In D. C. Hambrick (Ed.), *The executive effect: Concepts and methods for studying top managers.* Greenwich, CT: JAI Press.

Gupta, A. K., & Govindarajan, V. (1984). Business unit strategy, managerial characteristics, and business unit effectiveness at strategy implementation. *Academy of Management Journal, 27,* 25–41.

Haas, J. A., Porat, A. M., & Vaughan, J. A. (1969). Actual versus ideal time allocations reported by managers: A study of managerial behavior. *Personnel Psychology, 22*, 61–75.

Hackman, J. R., & Walton, R. E. (1986). Leading groups in organizations. In P. S. Goodman & Associates (Eds.), *Designing effective work groups*. San Francisco: Jossey-Bass.

Halebian, J., & Finkelstein, S. (1993). Top management team size, CEO dominance, and firm performance: The moderating roles of environmental turbulence and discretion. *Academy of Management Journal, 36*, 844–863.

Hales, C. P. (1986). What do managers do? A critical review of the evidence. *Journal of Management Studies, 23*, 88–115.

Hall, R. H. (1987). *Organizations: Structures, processes and outcomes* (4th ed.). Englewood Cliffs, NJ: Prentice Hall.

Hall, R. H. (1991). *Organizations: Structures, processes and outcomes* (5th ed.). Englewood Cliffs, NJ: Prentice Hall.

Hambrick, D. C. (1981a). Environment, strategy, and power within top management teams. *Administrative Science Quarterly, 26*, 253–275.

Hambrick, D. C. (1981b). Specialization of environmental scanning activities among upper-level executives. *Journal of Management Studies, 18*, 299–320.

Hambrick, D. C. (1989). Guest editor's introduction: Putting top managers back in the strategy picture. *Strategic Management Journal, 10*, 5–15.

Hambrick, D. C. (1982). Environmental scanning and organizational strategy. *Strategic Management Journal, 3*, 159–174.

Hambrick, D. C. (1994). Top management groups: A conceptual integration and reconsideration of the "team" label. In *Research in organizational behavior* (Vol. 16, pp. 171–213). Greenwich, CT: JAI Press.

Hambrick, D. C. (1995). Fragmentation and other problems CEOs have with their top management teams. *California Management Review, 37*, 110–127.

Hambrick, D. C., & Brandon, G. (1988). Executive values. In D. C. Hambrick (Ed.), *The executive effect: Concepts and methods for studying top managers*. Greenwich, CT: JAI Press.

Hambrick, D. C., Geletkanycz, M. A., & Frederickson, J. W. (1993). Top executive commitment to the status quo: Some tests of its determinants. *Strategic Management Journal, 14*, 401–418.

Hambrick, D. C., & Mason, P. A. (1984). Upper echelons: The organization as a reflection of its top managers. *Academy of Management Review, 9*, 195–206.

Hannan, M. T., & Freeman, J. (1977). The population ecology of organizations. *American Journal of Sociology, 82*, 926–963.

Harmon, J., Tremble, T. R., Jr., & Goodwin, G. F. (1993). *Junior leader development in Army units* (ARI Study Rep. No. 93-01). Alexandria, VA: U.S. Army Research Institute for the Behavioral and Social Sciences.

Harrell, A. M., & Stahl, M. J. (1981). A behavioral decision theory approach to measuring McClelland's trichotomy of needs. *Journal of Applied Psychology, 66*, 242–244.

Harris, P., & Lucas, K. W. (1991). *Executive leadership: Requisite skills and developmental processes for three- and four-star assignments*. Alexandria, VA: U.S. Army Research Institute for the Behavioral and Social Sciences.

Hart, S. L., & Quinn, R. E. (1993). Roles executives play: CEOs, behavioral complexity, and firm performance. *Human Relations, 46*, 543–574.

Hater, J. J., & Bass, B. M. (1988). Supervisors' evaluations and subordinates' perceptions of transformational leadership. *Journal of Applied Psychology, 73*, 695–702.

Havron, M. D., & McGrath, J. E. (1961). The contribution of the leader to the effectiveness of small military groups. In L. Petrullo & B. M. Bass (Eds.), *Leadership and interpersonal behavior*. New York: Holt, Rinehart & Winston.

Haythorn, W. W., Kimmel, M. J., & Steinberg, A. G. (1985). *Leadership on the future battlefield*. McLean, VA: Pergamon–Brassey's.

Heller, F. A. (1972). *Managerial decision making: A study of leadership styles and power sharing among senior managers*. New York: Harper & Row.

Hemphill, J. K. (1950). Relations between the size of the group and the behavior of "superior" leaders. *Journal of Social Psychology, 32,* 11–22.

Hemphill, J. K. (1959). Job descriptions for executives. *Harvard Business Review, 37,* 55–67.

Hemphill, J. K. (1960). *Dimensions of executive positions.* Columbus: Ohio State University, Bureau of Business Research.

Herriot, P. (1987). Graduate recruitment— Getting it right. *Employment Gazette, 95,* 78–83. London: Department of Employment.

Hinsz, V. B., Tindale, R. S., & Vollrath, D. A. (1997). The emerging conceptualization of groups as information processors. *Psychological Bulletin, 121,* 43–64.

Hites, R. W., & Campbel, D. T. (1950). A test of the ability of fraternity leaders to estimate group opinion. *Journal of Social Psychology, 32,* 95–100.

Hitt, M. A., Hoskisson, R. E., Johnson, R. A., & Moesel, D. D. (1993). *The market for corporate control and managerial commitment to innovation.* Paper presented at the annual meeting of the Academy of Management, Atlanta.

Hitt, M. A., & Tyler, B. B. (1991). Strategic decision models: Integrating different perspectives. *Strategic Management Journal, 12,* 327–351.

Hoffman, R. C., & Hegarty, W. H. (1993). Top management influence on innovations: Effects of executive characteristics and social culture. *Journal of Management, 19,* 549–574.

Hogan, R., Raskin, R., & Fazzini, D. (1990). The dark side of charisma. In K. E. Clark & M. B. Clark (Eds.), *Measures of leadership* (pp. 343–354). West Orange, NJ: Leadership Library of America.

Hollander, E. P., & Julian, J. W. (1970). Studies in leader legitimacy, influence, and innovation. In L. Berkowitz (Ed.), *Advances in experimental social psychology* (Vol. 5). New York: Academic Press.

Holyoak, K. J. (1984). Mental models in problem solving. In J. R. Anderson & K. M. Kosslyn (Eds.), *Tutorials in learning and memory* (pp. 193–210). New York: Freeman.

Hooijberg, R. (1996). A multidirectional approach toward leadership: An extension of the concept of behavioral complexity. *Human Relations, 49,* 917–946.

Hooijberg, R., & Quinn, R. E. (1992). Behavioral complexity and the development of effective managers. In R. L. Phillips & J. G. Hunt (Eds.), *Strategic leadership: A multiorganizational-level perspective.* Westport, CT: Quorum.

Horne, J. H., & Lupton, T. (1965). The work activities of "middle managers": An exploratory study. *Journal of Management Studies, 2,* 14–33.

Horvath, J. A., Forsyth, G. B., Sweeney, P. J., McNally, R., Wattendorf, J., Williams, W. M., & Sternberg, R. J. (1994). *Tacit knowledge in military leadership: Evidence from officer interviews* (ARI Tech. Rep. No. TR1018). Alexandria, VA: U.S. Army Research Institute for the Behavioral and Social Sciences.

House, R. J. (1977). A 1976 theory of charismatic leadership. In J. G. Hunt & L. Larson (Eds.), *Leadership: The cutting edge.* Carbondale: Southern Illinois University Press.

House, R. J. (1992). Afterword: Stratified systems theory and leadership: Where do we go from here? In R. L. Phillips & J. G. Hunt (Eds.), *Strategic leadership: A multiorganizational-level perspective.* Wesport, CT: Quorum.

House, R. J., & Avolio, B. J. (1993). Transformational leadership, transactional leadership, locus of control, support for innovation: Key predictors of consolidated business unit performance. *Journal of Applied Psychology, 78,* 891–902.

House, R. J., & Howell, J. M. (1992). Personality and charismatic leadership. *Leadership Quarterly, 3,* 81–108.

House, R. J., & Shamir, B. (1993). Toward the integration of transformational, charismatic and visionary leadership theories. In M. Chemers & R. Ayman (Eds.), *Leadership theory and research: Perspectives and directions.* New York: Academic Press.

House, R. J., Spangler, W. D., & Woycke, J. (1991). Personality and charisma in the U.S. presidency: A psychological theory of leader effectiveness. *Administrative Science Quarterly, 36,* 364–396.

House, R. J., Woycke, J., & Fodor, E. M. (1988). Charismatic and noncharismatic leaders: Differences in behaviour and effectiveness. In J. A. Conger & R. N. Kanungo (Eds.), *Charismatic leadership* (pp. 98–121). San Francisco: Jossey-Bass.

Howard, A., & Bray, D. W. (1988). *Managerial lives in transition: Advancing age and changing times*. New York: Guilford Press.

Howell, J. M., & Avolio, B. J. (1993). Transformational leadership, transactional leadership, locus of control, and support for innovation: Key predictors of consolidated-business-unit performance. *Journal of Applied Psychology, 78*, 891–902.

Howell, J. M., & Higgins, C. A. (1990). Champions of technological innovation. *Administrative Science Quarterly, 35*, 317–341.

Hrebiniak, L. G., & Joyce, W. F. (1984). *Implementing strategy*. New York: Macmillan.

Huff, A. S. (1990). *Mapping strategic thought*. Chichester, England: Wiley.

Huff, A. S., & Fletcher, K. E. (1990). Conclusion: Key mapping decisions. In A. S. Huff (Ed.), *Mapping strategic thought*. Chichester, England: Wiley.

Hunt, J. G. (1991). *Leadership: A new synthesis*. Newbury Park, CA: Sage.

Hunt, J. G., Osborn, R. N., & Martin, H. J. (1981). *A multiple influence model of leadership* (ARI Tech. Rep. No. 520). Alexandria, VA: U.S. Army Research Institute for the Behavioral and Social Sciences.

Hunter, J. E., & Hunter, R. F. (1984) Validity and utility of alternate predictors of job performance. *Psychological Bulletin, 96*, 72–98.

Iaquinto, A. L., & Frederickson, J. W. (1997). Top management team agreement about the strategic decision process: A test of some of its determinants and consequences. *Strategic Management Journal, 18*, 63–75.

Ickes, W. J., & Barnes, R. D. (1977). The role of sex and self-monitoring in unstructured dyadic interactions. *Journal of Personality and Social Psychology, 35*, 315–330.

Industrial College of the Armed Forces (1994). *A guide to the Strategic Leader Development Inventory*. Washington, DC: National Defense University, Industrial College of the Armed Forces.

Isenberg, D. J. (1984). How senior managers think. *Harvard Business Review, 62*, 81–90.

Jackson, S. E., & Dutton, J. E. (1988). Discerning threats and opportunities. *Administrative Science Quarterly, 33*, 370–387.

Jacobs, T. O. (1983). Cognitive behavior and information processing under conditions of uncertainty. In R. F. Williams & R. D. Abeyta (Eds.), *Management of risk and uncertainty in systems acquisition: Proceedings of the Defense Risk and uncertainty Workshop*. Fort Belvoir, VA: Army Procurement Research Office.

Jacobs, T. O. (1985). The air–land battle and leadership requirements. In J. G. Hunt & J. D. Blair (Eds.), *Leadership on the future battlefield*. Washington DC: Pergamon–Brassey's.

Jacobs, T. O., & Jaques, E. (1987). Leadership in complex systems. In J. Zeidner (Ed.), *Human productivity enhancement*. New York: Praeger.

Jacobs, T. O., & Jaques, E. (1990). Military executive leadership. In K. E. Clark & M. B. Clark (Eds.), *Measures of leadership*. Greensboro, NC: Center for Creative Leadership.

Jacobs, T. O., & Jaques, E. (1991). Executive leadership. In R. Gal & A. D. Manglesdorff (Eds.), *Handbook of military psychology*, Chichester, England: Wiley.

Jacobs, T. O., & Lewis, P. (1992). Leadership requirements in stratified systems. In R. L. Phillips & J. G. Hunt (Eds.), *Strategic leadership: A multiorganizational-level perspective*. Westport, CT: Quorum.

Jaques, E. (1956). *Measurement of responsibility*. Cambridge, MA: Harvard University Press.

Jaques, E. (1964). *Time span handbook*. London: Heinemann.

Jaques, E. (1978). *A general theory of bureaucracy*. Exeter, NH: Heinemann.

Jaques, E. (1986). The development of intellectual capability: A discussion of stratified systems theory. *Journal of Applied Behavioral Science, 22*, 361–384.

Jaques, E. (1989). *Requisite organization*. Arlington, VA: Cason Hall.

Jaques, E. (1990a). Cognitive complexity. In G. H. Pollack (Ed.), *Creativity and work* (pp. 81–100). Madison, CT: International Universities Press.

Jaques, E. (1990b). Maturation of cognitive power. In G. H. Pollack (Ed.), *Creativity and work* (pp. 101–124). Madison, CT: International Universities Press.

Jaques, E. (1990c). Task complexity. In G. H. Pollack (Ed.), *Creativity and work* (pp. 43–80). Madison, CT: International Universities Press.

Jaques, E., & Clement, S. D. (1991). *Executive leadership: A practical guide to managing complexity*. Arlington, VA: Cason Hall.

Jaques, E., Clement, S. D., Rigby, C., & Jacobs, T. O. (1986). *Senior leadership requirements at the executive level* (ARI Research Rep. No. 1420). Alexandria, VA: U.S. Army Research Institute for the Behavioral and Social Sciences.

Jausovec, N. (1994a). *Flexible thinking: An explanation for individual differences in ability*. Cresskill, NJ: Hampton Press.

Jausovec, N. (1994b). Metacognition in creative problem solving. In M. A. Runco (Ed.), *Problem finding, problem solving, and creativity*. Norwood, NJ: Ablex.

Javidan, M., & Dastmalchian, A. (1993). Assessing senior executives: The impact of context on their roles. *Journal of Applied Behavioral Science, 29*, 328–342.

Johnson, E. M. (1987).Foreword. In S. R. Stewart & J. M. Hicks, *Leader development training assessment of U.S. Army Training and Doctrine Command (TRADOC) brigadier commanders* (ARI Research Rep. No. 1454). Alexandria, VA: U.S. Army Research Institute for the Behavioral and Social Sciences.

Jonas, H. S., Fry, R. E., & Srivasta, S. (1990). The office of the CEO: Understanding the executive experience. *Academy of Management Executive, 4*, 36–67.

Judge, W. Q., & Spitzfaden, M. (1995). The management of strategic time horizons within biotechnology firms. *Journal of Management Inquiry, 4*, 179–196.

Kanungo, R., & Conger, J. A. (1992). Charisma: Exploring new dimensions of leadership behaviour. *Psychology and Developing Societies, 4*, 21–38.

Kaplan, R. E. (1986). The warp and woof of the general manager's job. In B.

Schneider & D. Schoorman (Eds.), *Facilitating work effectiveness*. Lexington, MA: Lexington Books.

Katz, D., & Kahn, R. L. (1967). *The social psychology of organizations*. New York: Wiley.

Katz, D., & Kahn, R. L. (1978). *The social psychology of organizations* (2nd ed.). New York: Wiley.

Katz, R. (1982). The effects of group longevity on group communication and performance. *Administrative Science Quarterly, 27*, 81–104.

Katz, R. L. (1955, January–February). Skills of an effective administrator. *Harvard Business Review*, 33–42.

Keck, S. L., & Tushman, M. L. (1993). Environmental and organizational context and executive team structure. *Academy of Management Journal, 36*, 1314–1344.

Kegan, R. (1982). *The evolving self: Problem and process in human development*. Cambridge, MA: Harvard University Press.

Keller, R. T. (1986). Predictors of the performance of project groups in R&D organizations. *Academy of Management Journal, 29*, 715–726.

Kelly, J. (1993). *Facts against fictions of executive behavior: A critical analysis of what managers do*. Westport, CT: Quorum.

Kenny, D. A., & Zaccaro, S. J. (1983). An estimate of variance due to traits in leadership. *Journal of Applied Psychology, 68*, 678–685.

Kerr, S., & Jermier, J. M. (1978). Substitutes for leadership. *Organizational Behavior and Human Performance, 22*, 375–403.

Kerr, S., Schriesheim, C. A., Murphy, C. J., & Stogdill, R. M. (1974). Toward a theory of leadership based upon the consideration and initiating structure literature. *Organizational Behavior and Human Performance, 12*, 62–82.

Kesner, I. F., & Sebora, T. C. (1994). Executive succession: Past, present, and future. *Journal of Management, 20*, 327–372.

Khan, A. M., & Manapichetwattana, V. (1989). Innovative and noninnovative small firms: Types and characteristics. *Management Science, 35*, 597–606.

Kiesler, S., & Sproull, L. (1982). Managerial response to changing environments:

Perspectives on problem sensing from social cognition. *Administrative Science Quarterly, 27,* 548–570.

Kimmel, M. J. (1981). *Senior leadership: An annotated bibliography of the military and nonmilitary literature.* Alexandria, VA: U.S. Army Research Institute for the Behavioral and Social Sciences.

Kirchoff, B. A. (1977). Organizational effectiveness measurement and policy research. *Academy of Management Review, 2,* 346–355.

Kirkpatrick, D. L. (1959). Techniques for evaluating training programs. *Journal of the American Society of Training Directors, 13,* 3–9, 21–26.

Klein, G. (1989). Recognition-primed decisions. In W. B. Rouse (Ed.), *Advances in man–machine system research* (Vol. 5, pp. 47–92). Greenwich, CT: JAI Press.

Klimoski, R., & Mohammed, S. (1994). Team mental model: Construct or metaphor? *Journal of Management, 20,* 403–437.

Knowlton, W., & McGee, M. (1994). *Strategic leadership and personality: Making the MBTI relevant.* Washington, DC: National Defense University, Industrial College of the Armed Forces.

Kogan, N., & Wallach, M. A. (1964). *Risk taking: A study in cognition and personality.* New York: Holt, Rinehardt & Winston.

Korsgaard, M. A., Schweiger, D. M., & Sapienza, H. J. (1995). Building commitment, attachment, and trust in strategic decision-making teams: The role of procedural justice. *Academy of Management Journal, 38,* 60–84.

Kotter, J. P. (1982a). *The general managers.* New York: Free Press.

Kotter, J. P. (1982b). What effective general managers really do. *Harvard Business Review, 60*(6), 156–167.

Kotter, J. P. (1990). *A force for change: How leadership differs from management.* New York: Free Press.

Kouzes, J. M., & Pozner, B. Z. (1987). *The leadership challenge: How to get extraordinary things done in organizations.* San Francisco: Jossey-Bass.

Kozlowski, S. W. J., Gully, S. M., Salas, E., & Cannon-Bowers, J. A. (1996). *Team leadership and development: Theory, principles, and guidelines for training leaders and teams.* In M. M. Beyerlein, D. Johnson, & S. T. Beyerlein (Eds.), *Interdisciplinary studies of work teams: Vol. 3. Team leadership.* Greenwich, CT: JAI Press.

Kraut, A. I., Pedigo, P. R., McKenna, D. D., & Dunnette, M. D. (1989). The role of the manager: What's really important in different management jobs. *Academy of Management Executive, 3,* 286–293.

Kretch, D., & Crutchfield, R. S. (1948). *Theory and problems of social psychology.* New York: McGraw-Hill.

Kurke, L. B., & Aldrich, H. E. (1983). Mintzberg was right!: A replication and extension of *The nature of managerial work. Management Science, 29,* 975–984.

Lant, T. K., Milliken, F. J., & Batra, B. (1992). The role of managerial learning and interpretation in strategic persistence and reorientation: An empirical exploration. *Strategic Management Journal, 13,* 585–608.

Larwood, L., Falbe, C. M., Kriger, M. P., & Miesing, P. (1995). Structure and meaning of organizational vision. *Academy of Management Journal, 38,* 740–769.

Laskey, K. B., Leddo, J. M., & Bresnick, T. A. (1990). *Executive thinking and decision skills: A characterization and implications for training* (ARI Research Note 91-07). Alexandria, VA: U.S. Army Research Institute for the Behavioral and Social Sciences.

Lau, A. W., Newman, A. R., & Broedling, L. A. (1980). The nature of managerial work in the public sector. *Public Administration Review, 40,* 513–520.

Lawrence, P., & Lorsch, J. (1967). *Organization and environment.* Boston: Harvard University Business School, Division of Research.

Lefebvre, E., & Lefebvre, L. A. (1992). Firm innovativeness and CEO characteristics in small manufacturing firms. *Journal of Engineering and Technology Management, 9,* 243–277.

Leidecker, J. K., Bruno, A. V., & Yanow, A. (1988). A delicate balance: The two functions of the CEO. *Management Review,* 18–22.

Levine, J. M., & Moreland, R. L. (1990). Progress in small group research. *American Review of Psychology, 41,* 585–614.

Levinson, H. (1994). Why the behemoths fell: Psychological roots of corporate failure. *American Psychologist, 49,* 428–436.

Levinson, H., & Rosenthal, S. (1984). *CEO: Corporate leadership in action.* New York: Basic Books.

Lewicki, R. J., & Sheppard, B. H. (1985). Choosing how to intervene: Factors affecting the use of process and outcome control in third party dispute resolution. *Journal of Occupational Behavior, 6,* 49–64.

Lewis, P. M. (1993). *Career Path Appreciation (CPA) data reduction and analysis.* Alexandria, VA: U.S. Army Research Institute for the Behavioral and Social Sciences.

Lewis, P. M. (1995). *Conceptual capacity and officer effectiveness.* Alexandria, VA: U.S. Army Research Institute for the Behavioral and Social Sciences.

Lewis, P. M., & Jacobs, T. O. (1992). Individual differences in strategic leadership capacity: A constructive/development view. In R. L. Phillips & J. G. Hunt (Eds.), *Strategic leadership: A multiorganizational-level perspective.* Westport, CT: Quorum.

Lieberson, S., & O'Connor, J. F. (1972). Leadership and organizational performance: A study of large corporations. *American Sociological Review, 37,* 117–130.

Locke, E. A., & Latham, G. (1990). *A theory of goal setting and task performance.* Englewood Cliffs, NJ: Prentice Hall.

Lombardo, M. M., & McCauley, C. D. (1988). *The dynamics of managerial derailment* (Tech. Rep. No. 34). Greensboro, NC: Center for Creative Leadership.

Lombardo, M. M., Ruderman, M. N., & McCauley, C. D. (1987). *Explanations of success and derailment in upper-level management positions.* Paper, Academy of Management, New York.

Lord, R. G., & Maher, K. J. (1993). *Leadership and information processing.* London: Routledge.

Lowe, K. B., Kroeck, K. G., & Sivasubramaniam, N. (1995, May). *Effectiveness correlates of transformational and transactional leadership: A meta-analytic review.* Paper presented at the 10th annual meeting of the Society for Industrial and Organizational Psychology, Orlando, FL.

Lubatkin, M. H., Chung, K. H., Rogers, R. C., & Owers, J. E. (1989). Stockholder reactions to CEO changes in large corporations. *Academy of Management Journal, 32,* 47–68.

Lucas, K. W., Harris, P. & Stewart, S. R. (1988). *Training technology for the operational level of war.* Alexandria, VA: U.S. Army Research Institute for the Behavioral and Social Sciences.

Lucas, K. W., & Markessini, J. (1993). *Senior leadership in a changing world order: Requisite skills for U.S. Army one- and two-star generals* (ARI Tech. Rep. No. 976). Alexandria, VA: U.S. Army Research Institute for the Behavioral and Social Sciences.

Luthans, F. (1988). Successful vs. effective real managers. *Academy of Management Executive, 2,* 127–132.

Luthans, F., & Lockwood, D. L. (1984). Toward an observation system for measuring leader behavior in natural settings. In J. G. Hunt, D. Hosking, C. A. Schriesheim, & R. Stewart (Eds.), *Leaders and managers: International perspectives on managerial behavior and leadership.* New York: Pergamon Press.

Luthans, F., Rosenkrantz, S. A., & Hennessey, H. W. (1985). What do successful managers really do? An observational study of managerial activities. *Journal of Applied Behavioral Science, 21,* 255–270.

MacDaid, G. P., McCaulley, M. H., & Kainz, R. I. (1987). *Myers-Briggs Type Indicator Atlas of Type Tables.* Gainesville, FL: Center for the Application of Psychological Type.

Maggiotto, M. A., & McKenna, F., Jr. (1992). Assessing productivity and management in local government. *Public Productivity and Management Review, 15,* 309–313.

Mahoney, T. A., Jerdee, T. H., & Carroll, S. I. (1965). The job(s) of management. *Industrial Relations, 4,* 97–110.

Mahoney, T. A., & Weitzel, W. (1969). Managerial models of organizational effectiveness. *Administrative Science Quarterly, 18,* 77–88.

Mann, F. C. (1965). Toward an understanding of the leadership role in formal organizations. In R. Dubin, G. C. Homans, F. C. Mann, & D. C. Miller (Eds.), *Leadership and productivity.* San Francisco: Chandler.

Maranell, G. M. (1970). The evaluation of presidents: An extension of the job Schiesinger polls. *Journal of American History, 57*, 104–113.

March, J. G., & Simon, H. A. (1958). *Organizations.* New York: Wiley.

Markessini, J. (1991). *Executive leadership in a changing world order: Requisite cognitive skills. A taxonomy of cognitive capabilities for executives.* Alexandria, VA: U.S. Army Research Institute for the Behavioral and Social Sciences.

Markessini, J., Lucas, K. W., Chandler, N., & Jacobs, T. O. (1994). *Executive leadership: Requisite skills and developmental processes for the U.S. Army's civilian executives* (ARI Research Note No. 94-26). Alexandria, VA: U.S. Army Research Institute for the Behavioral and Social Sciences.

Marks, M. A., & Zaccaro, S. J. (1997). *Leader–team dynamics in hierarchical decision making teams.* Paper presented at the 1997 meeting of the Academy of Management, Boston.

Maslow, A. (1954). *Motivation and personality.* New York: Harper.

McCall, M. W., & Lombardo, M. M. (1983). *Off the track: Why and how successful executives get derailed.* Greensboro, NC: Center for Creative Leadership.

McCall, M. W., & Segrist, C. A. (1980). *In pursuit of the manager's job: Building on Mintzberg* (Tech. Rep. No. 14) Greensboro, NC: Center for Creative Leadership.

McCauley, C. D., Eastman, L. J., & Ohlott, P. J. (1995). Linking management selection and development through stretch assignments. *Human Resource Management, 34*, 93–115.

McCauley, C. D., Moxley, R. S., & Van Velsor, E. (Eds.). (1998). *Handbook of leadership development.* San Francisco: Jossey-Bass.

McCauley, C. D., Ruderman, M. N., Ohlott, P. J., & Morrow, J. E. (1994). Assessing the developmental components of managerial jobs. *Journal of Applied Psychology, 37*, 46–67.

McCaulley, M. H. (1990). The Myers-Briggs Type Indicator and leadership. In K. E. Clark & M. B. Clark (Eds.), *Measures of leadership.* West Orange, NJ: Leadership Library of America.

McClelland, D. C. (1961). *The achieving society.* Princeton, NJ: Van Nostrand.

McClelland, D. C. (1985). *Human motivation.* Chicago: Scott, Foresman.

McCrae, R. R., & Costa, P. T. (1987). Validation of the five-factor model of personality across instruments and observers. *Journal of Personality and Social Psychology, 52*, 81–90.

McCrae, R. R., & Costa, P. T. (1991). Adding Liebe und Arbeit: The full five-factor model and well-being. *Personality and Social Psychology Bulletin, 17*, 227–232.

McGrath, J. (1984). *Groups: Interaction and performance.* Englewood Cliffs, NJ: Prentice Hall.

McIntyre, R. M., Jordan, P., Mergen, C., Hamill, L., & Jacobs, T. O. (1993). *The construct validity of the CPA: Report on three investigations* (ARI Tech. Rep. No. TCN 92-017). Alexandria, VA: U.S. Army Research Institute for the Behavioral and Social Sciences.

McIntyre, R. M., & Salas, E. (1995). Measuring and managing for team performance: Lessons from complex environments. In R. A. Guzzo & E. Salas (Eds.), *Teams' effectiveness and decision making in organizations.* San Francisco: Jossey-Bass.

Meindl, J. R. (1990). On leadership: An alternative to the conventional wisdom. In B. M. Staw & L. L. Cummings (Eds.), *Research in organizational behavior* (Vol. 12, pp. 159–203). Greenwich, CT: JAI Press.

Meindl, J. R., & Ehrlich, S. B. (1987). The romance of leadership and the evaluation of organizational performance. *Academy of Management Journal, 30*, 91–109.

Meindel, J. R., Ehrlich, S. B., & Dukerich, J. M. (1985). The romance of leadership. *Administrative Science Quarterly, 30*, 78–102.

Merton, R. K. (1957). *Social theory and social structure.* Glencoe, IL: Free Press.

Merz, G. R., & Sauber, M. H. (1995). Profiles of managerial activities in small firms. *Strategic Management Journal, 16*, 551–564.

Meyer, A. (1982). Adapting to environmental jolts. *Administrative Science Quarterly, 27*, 515–538.

Miles, R. E., & Snow, C. C. (1978). *Organizational strategy, structure, and process.* New York: McGraw Hill.

Miller, C. C., Burke, L. M., & Glick, W. H. (1998). Cognitive diversity among upper-echelon executives: Implications for strategic decision processes. *Strategic Management Journal, 19,* 39–58.

Miller, C. C., & Cardinal, L. B. (1994). Strategic planning and firm performance: A synthesis of more than two decades of research. *Academy of Management Journal, 37,* 1649–1665.

Miller, C. C., & Frieson, P. H. (1984). *Organizations: A quantum view.* Englewood Cliffs, NJ: Prentice Hall.

Miller, D. (1991). Stale in the saddle: CEO tenure and the match between the organization and environment. *Management Science, 37,* 34–52

Miller, D. (1993). Some organizational consequences of CEO succession. *Academy of Management Journal, 36,* 644–659.

Miller, D., & Toulouse, J. M. (1986). Chief executive personality and corporate strategy and structure in small firms. *Management Science, 32,* 1389–1409.

Miller, D., Kets de Vries, M. F., & Toulouse, J. M. (1982). Top executive locus of control and its relationship to strategy-making, structure, and environment. *Academy of Management Journal, 25,* 237–253.

Milliken, F. (1990). Perceiving and interpreting environmental change: An examination of college administrators' interpretation of changing demographics. *Academy of Management Journal, 33,* 42–63.

Minionis, D. P., Zaccaro, S. J., & Perez, R. (1995, May). *Shared mental models, team coordination, and team performance.* Paper presented at the 10th annual meeting of the Society for Industrial and Organizational Psychology, Orlando, FL.

Mintzberg, H. (1973). *The nature of managerial work.* New York: Harper & Row.

Mintzberg, H. (1975). The manager's job: Folklore and fact. *Harvard Business Review, 53,* 49–61.

Mintzberg, H. (1987). Crafting strategy. *Harvard Business Review, 65,* 66–75.

Mintzberg, H. (1990). The design school: Reconsidering the basic premises of strategic management. *Strategic Management Journal, 11,* 171–195.

Mintzberg, H. (1994). *The rise and fall of strategic planning.* New York: Free Press.

Morgan, B. B., Jr., Glickman, A. S., Woodard, E. A., Blaiwes, A., & Salas, E. (1986). *Measurement of team behaviors in a Navy environment* (NTSC Tech. Rep. No. 86-014). Orlando, FL: Naval Training Systems Center.

Morrow, P. C. (1981). Environmental uncertainty and subunit effectiveness: A second look at the information processing approach to subunit communication. *Academy of Management Journal, 24,* 851–858.

Morse, J. J., & Wagner, F. R. (1978). Measuring the process of managerial effectiveness. *Academy of Management Journal, 21,* 23–35.

Mumford, M. D. (1986). Leadership in the organizational context: Conceptual approach and its application. *Journal of Applied Social Psychology, 16,* 212–226.

Mumford, M. D, Baughman, W. A., Supinski, E. P., Costanza, D. P., & Threlfall, K. V. (1993). *Cognitive and metacognitive skill development: Alternative measures for predicting leadership potential* (ARI Tech. Rep. No. MRI 93-2 for the U.S. Army Research Institute for Behavioral and Social Sciences). Bethesda, MD: Management Research Institute.

Mumford, M. D., Baughman, W. A., Threlfall, K. V., Costanza, D. P., & Uhlman, C. E. (1993). Personality, adaptability, and performance: Performance on well-defined and ill-defined problem-solving tasks. *Human Performance, 6,* 245–285.

Mumford, M. D., Baughman, W. A., Uhlman, C. E., Costanza, D. P., & Threlfall, K. V. (1993). Personality variables and skill acquisition: Performance at different stages of practice on a complex task. *Human Performance, 6,* 345–381.

Mumford, M. D., & Connelly, M. S. (1991). Leaders as creators: Leader performance and problem solving in ill-defined domains. *Leadership Quarterly, 2,* 289–316.

Mumford, M. D., Costanza, D. P., Baughman, W. A., Threlfall, K. V., & Fleishman, E. A. (1994). The influence of abilities on performance during practice: Effects of massed and distributed practice. *Journal of Educational Psychology, 86,* 1–11.

Mumford, M. D., & Marks, M. (1994). Leader development. In M. D. Mumford, S. J. Zaccaro, E. A. Fleishman, & F. D. Harding (Eds.), *The thinking leader: Developing leaders for a more complex world*. Alexandria, VA: U.S. Army Research Institute for the Behavioral and Social Sciences.

Mumford, M. D., Yarkin-Levin, K., Korotkin, A. L., Wallis, M. R., & Marshall-Mies, J. (1986). *Characteristics relevant to performance as an army leader: Knowledges, skills, abilities, other characteristics and generic skills* (ARI Research Note No. RN86-24). Alexandria, VA: U.S. Army Research Institute for the Behavioral and Social Sciences.

Mumford, M. D., Zaccaro, S. J., Fleishman, E. A., & Harding, F. D. (1995). *The thinking leader: Developing leaders for a more complex world*. Alexandria, VA: U.S. Army Research Institute for the Behavioral and Social Sciences.

Mumford, M. D., Zaccaro, S. J., Harding, F. D., Fleishman, E. A., & Reiter-Palmon, R. (1993). *Cognitive and temperament predictors of executive ability: Principles for developing leadership capacity*. Alexandria, VA: U.S. Army Research Institute for the Behavioral and Social Sciences.

Murray, A. I. (1989). Top management group heterogeneity and firm performance. *Strategic Management Journal, 10*, 125–141.

Murray, R. K., & Blessing, T. H. (1983). The presidential performance study: A progress report. *Journal of American History, 70*, 535–555.

Myers, I. B., & McCaulley, M. H. (1985). *Manual: A guide to the development and use of the Myers-Briggs Type Indicator*. Palo Alto, CA: Consulting Psychologists Press.

Nagle, B. F. (1954). Productivity, employee attitude, and supervisor sensitivity. *Personnel Psychology, 7*, 219–232.

Nanus, B. (1992). *Visionary leadership*. San Francisco: Jossey-Bass.

Newell, A., & Simon, H. A. (1972). *Human problem solving*. Englewood Cliffs, NJ: Prentice Hall.

Noble, D. (1993). A model to support development of situation assessment aids. In G. Klein, J. Orasanu, R. Calderwood, & C. E. Zsambok (Eds.), *De-cision making in action: Models and methods*. Norwood, NJ: Ablex.

Norburn, D. (1986). GOGO's, YOYO's, and DODO's: Company directors and industry performance. *Strategic Management Journal, 7*, 101–117.

O'Bannon, D. P., & Gupta, A. K. (1992). *The utility of homogeneity versus heterogeneity within top management teams: Alternate resolutions of the emerging conundrum*. Paper presented at the annual Academy of Management meeting, Las Vegas, NV.

O'Reilly, C. A., III, Synder, R. C., & Boothe, J. N. (1993). Executive team demography and organizational change. In G. P. Huber & W. H. Glick (Eds.), *Organizational change and redesign: Ideas and insights for improving performance* (pp. 147–175). New York: Oxford.

Page, R. C., & Tornow, W. W. (1987). *Managerial job analysis: Are we further along?* Paper presented at the annual meeting of the Society for Industrial and Organizational Psychology, Atlanta.

Paolillo, J. G. (1981). Managers' self-assessments of managerial roles: The influence of hierarchical level. *Journal of Management, 7*, 43–52.

Paulus, D. L., & Martin, C. L. (1988). Functional flexibility: A new conception. *Journal of Personality and Social Psychology, 84*, 55, 88–101.

Pavett, C. M., & Lau, A. W. (1982). Managerial work: The influence of hierarchical level and functional specialty. *Academy of Management Journal, 26*, 170–177.

Pearce, J. A., II, Freeman, E. B., & Robinson, R. B., III. (1987). The tenuous link between formal strategic planning and financial performance. *Academy of Management Review, 12*, 658–675.

Pearce, J. A., II, Robbins, D. K., & Robinson, R. B., Jr. (1987). The impact of grand strategy and planning formality on financial performance. *Strategic Management Journal, 8*, 125–134.

Pearce, J. A., II, & Robinson, R. B. (1995). *Strategic management: Formulation, implementation, and control*. Chicago: Irwin.

Pearce, J. A., III. (1981). An executive-level perspective on the strategic management process. *California Management Review, 24*, 39–48.

Pence, E. C., Welp, R. L., & Stenstrom, D. J. (1990). *A measurement concept for assessing corps performance* (ARI Research Note No. RN 90-138). Alexandria, VA: U.S. Army Research Institute for the Behavioral and Social Sciences.

Peters, T. J., & Waterman, R. H. (1982). *In search of excellence.* New York: Harper & Row.

Pfeffer, J. (1977). The ambiguity of leadership. *Academy of Management Review, 2,* 104–112.

Pfeffer, J. (1981). *Power in organizations.* Boston: Pitman

Pfeffer, J., & Salancik G. R. (1978). *The external control of organizations: A resource dependence perspective.* New York: Harper & Row.

Phillips, R. L., & Hunt, J. G. (1992). *Strategic leadership: A multiorganizational-level perspective.* Westport, CT: Quorom.

Pinchot, J., III. (1985). *Intrapreneuring.* New York: Harper & Row.

Podsakoff, P. M., MacKenzie, S. B., Moorman, R. H., & Fetter, R. (1990). Transformational leader behaviors and their effects on followers' trust in leader, satisfaction, and organizational citizenship behaviors. *Leadership Quarterly, 1,* 107–142.

Price, J. L. (1972). *Handbook of organizational measurement.* Lexington, MA: Heath.

Priem, R. L. (1990). Top management team group factors, consensus, and firm performance. *Strategic Management Journal, 11,* 469–478.

Quinn, J. B. (1980). Formulating strategy one step at a time. *Journal of Business Strategy, 1,* 42–63.

Quinn, R. E. (1984). Applying the competing values approach to leadership: Towards an integrative framework. In J. G. Hunt, D. Hosking, C. A. Schriesheim, & R. Stewart (Eds.), *Leaders and managers: International perspectives on managerial behavior and leadership.* New York: Pergamon Press.

Quinn, R. E. (1988). *Beyond rational management: Mastering paradoxes and competing demands of high performance.* San Francisco: Jossey-Bass.

Quinn, R. E., Faerman, S. R., & Dixit, N. (1987). *Perceived performance: Some archetypes of managerial effectiveness and ineffectiveness* (Working paper). Albany: Institute for Government and Policy Studies, Department of Public Administration, State University of New York at Albany.

Quinn, R. E., Faerman, S. R., Thompson, M. P., & McGrath, M. R. (1990). *Becoming a master manager.* New York: Wiley.

Quinn, R. E., & Rohrbaugh, J. (1981). A competing values approach to organizational effectiveness. *Public Productivity Review, 5,* 122–140.

Quinn, R. E., Spreitzer, G. M., & Hart, S. (1991). Challenging the assumptions of bipolarity: Interpenetration and managerial effectiveness. In S. Srivastva & R. Fry (Eds.), *Executive continuity.* San Francisco: Jossey-Bass.

Rajagopalan, N., Rasheed, A. M. A., & Datta, D. K. (1993). Strategic decision processes: Critical review and future directions. *Journal of Management, 19,* 349–384.

Reynierse, J. H. (1991). The psychological types of outplaced executives. *Journal of Psychological Type, 22,* 27–32.

Rigby, C. K., & Harris, P. (1987). *Program management offices: Structural modeling through applications of stratified systems theory* (ARI Tech. Rep. No. 736). Alexandria, VA: U.S. Army Research Institute for the Behavioral and Social Sciences.

Ringle, P. M., & Savickas, M. L. (1983). Administrative leadership: Planning and time perspective. *Journal of Higher Education, 54,* 649–661.

Ritchie, R. J. (1994). Using the assessment center method to predict senior management potential. [Special issue: Issues in the assessment of managerial and executive leadership]. *Consulting Psychology Journal: Practice and Research, 46,* 16–23.

Roach, B. (1986). Organizational decision-makers: Different types for different levels. *Journal of Psychological Type, 12,* 16–24.

Rohrbaugh, J. (1981). Operationalizing the competing values approach: Measuring performance in the employment service. *Public Productivity Review, 5,* 141–159.

Romanelli, E., & Tushman, M. L. (1986). Inertia, environments, and strategic choice: A quasi-experimental design for comparative-longitudinal research. *Management Science, 32,* 608–621.

Ross, S. M., & Offermann, L. R. (1991). *Transformational leaders: Measurement of personality attributes and work group performance.* Paper presented at the 2nd annual meeting of the Society for Industrial and Organizational Psychology, St. Louis, MO.

Rotter, J. B. (1966). Generalized expectancies for internal versus external control of reinforcement. *Psychological Monographs, 90,* No. 609.

Rouse, W. B., & Morris, N. M. (1986). On looking into the black box: Prospects and limits in the search for mental models. *Psychological Bulletin, 100,* 359–363.

Rueb, J. D., & Foti, R. J. (1990, April). *Traits, self-monitoring and leadership emergence.* Paper presented at the 5th annual meeting of the Society for Industrial and Organizational Psychology, Miami.

Rumelt, R. (1982). Diversification strategy and performance. *Strategic Management Journal, 3,* 359–369.

Rusmore, J. T. (1984). *Executive performance and intellectual ability in organizational levels.* San Jose, CA: San Jose State University, Advanced Human Systems Institution.

Rusmore, J. T., & Baker, H. (1987). *Executive performance in four organizational levels and two kinds of intellectual ability.* Paper presented at the annual meeting of the Society for Industrial and Organizational Psychology, Atlanta.

Salancik, G. R., & Pfeffer, J. (1977). Constraints on administrator discretion: The limited influence of mayors on city budgets. *Urban Affairs Quarterly, 12,* 475–498.

Salas, E., Dickinson, T. L., Converse, S., & Tannenbaum, S. I. (1992). Toward an understanding of team performance and training. In R. W. Swezey & E. Salas (Eds.), *Teams: Their training and performance.* Norwood, NJ: Ablex.

Sashkin, M. (1987). A new vision of leadership. *Journal of Management Development, 6,* 19–28.

Sashkin, M. (1988). The visionary leader. In J. A. Conger & R. N. Kanungo (Eds.), *Charismatic leadership: The elusive factor in organizational effectiveness.* San Francisco: Jossey-Bass.

Sashkin, M. (1992). Strategic leadership competencies. In R. L. Phillips & J. G. Hunt (Eds.), *Strategic leadership: A multiorganizational-level perspective.* Westport, CT: Quorum.

Sashkin, M., & Fulmer, R. M. (1988). Toward an organizational leadership theory. In J. G. Hunt, B. R. Baliga, H. P. Dachler, & C. A. Schriesheim (Eds.), *Emerging leadership vistas.* Lexington, MA: Lexington Books.

Savell, J. M., Tremble, T. R., Jr., & Teague, R. C. (1993). *Some lessons learned about leadership in operation Desert Storm/Shield* (ARI Study Rep. No. 93-05). Alexandria, VA: U.S. Army Research Institute for the Behavioral and Social Sciences.

Sawyerr, O. O. (1993). Environmental uncertainty and environmental scanning activities of Nigerian manufacturing executives: A comparative analysis. *Strategic Management Journal, 14,* 287–299.

Schein, E. H. (1992). *Organizational culture and leadership* (2nd ed.). San Francisco: Jossey-Bass.

Schneir, C. E. (1979). Measuring cognitive complexity: Developing reliability, validity, and norm tables for a personality instrument. *Educational and Psychological Measurement, 39,* 599–612.

Schreyogg, G., & Steinmann, H. (1987). Strategic control: A new perspective. *Academy of Management Review, 12,* 91–103

Schroder, H. M., Driver, M. J., & Streufert, S. (1967). *Human information processing.* New York: Holt, Rinehart & Winston.

Schroder, H. M., & Streufert, S. (1962). *The measurement of four systems of personality structure varying in level of abstractness: Sentence completion method* (ONR Tech. Rep. No. 11). Princeton, NJ: Princeton University.

Schwenk, C. R. (1984). Cognitive simplification processes in strategic decision-making. *Strategic Management Journal, 5,* 111–128.

Schwenk, C. R. (1988). Effects of devil's advocacy on escalating commitment. *Human Relations, 41,* 769–782.

Seashore, S. E., Cammann, C., Fichman, M., Ford, L., Ross, G., & Rousseau (1982). *Organizational effectiveness: De-*

velopment and validation of integrated models. *Report I: Development of an integrated multivariate model of organizational effectiveness.* Alexandria, VA: U.S. Army Research Institute for the Behavioral and Social Sciences.

Seashore, S. E., Fichman, M., Fakhouri, J., Ford, L., Rousseau, & Sutton, R. I. (1982). *Organizational effectiveness: Development and validation of integrated models. Report II: Empirical studies of organizational effectiveness using multivariate models* (ARI Tech. Rep. No. 83-24). Alexandria, VA: U.S. Army Research Institute for the Behavioral and Social Sciences.

Sebrechts, M. M., Bennett, R. E., & Rock, D. A. (1991). Agreement between expert-system and human raters' scores on complex constructed-response quantitative items. *Journal of Applied Psychology, 76,* 856–862.

Seltzer, J., & Bass, B. M. (1990). Transformational leadership: Beyond initiation and consideration. *Journal of Management, 16,* 693–703.

Selznick, P. (1957). *Leadership in administration: A sociological interpretation.* Evanston, IL: Row, Peterson.

Senge, P. M. (1990). *The fifth discipline: The art and practice of the learning organization.* New York: Doubleday.

Shamir, B., House, R. J., & Arthur, M. (1993). The motivational effects of charismatic leadership: A self-concept based theory. *Organization Science, 4,* 577–594.

Shartle, C. L., Stogdill, R. M., & Campbell, D. T. (1949). *Studies in naval leadership.* Columbus: Ohio State University, Bureau of Business Research.

Shrader, C. B., Taylor, L., & Dalton, D. R. (1984). Strategic planning and organizational performance: A critical appraisal. *Journal of Management, 10,* 149–171.

Siegel, P. A., & Hambrick, D. C. (1996). Business strategy and the social psychology of top management teams. *Advances in Strategic Management, 13,* 91–119.

Simon, H. A. (1957). *Models of man.* New York: Wiley.

Simonton, D. K. (1988). Presidential style: Personality, biography, and performance. *Journal of Personality and Social Psychology, 55,* 928–936.

Smith, B. J. (1982). *An initial test of a theory of charismatic leadership based on the responses of subordinates.* Unpublished doctoral dissertation, University of Toronto, Ontario, Canada.

Smith, J. E., Carson, K. P., & Alexander, R. A. (1984). Leadership: It can make a difference. *Academy of Management Journal, 27,* 765–776.

Smith, K. G., Smith, K. A., Olian, J. D., Sims, H. P., O'Brannan, O. P., & Scully, J. A. (1994). Top management team demography and process: The role of social integration and communication. *Administrative Science Quarterly, 39,* 412–438.

Snow, R. E. (1993). Construct validity and constructed-response tests. In R. E. Bennett & W. C. Ward (Eds.), *Construction versus choice in cognitive measurement* (pp. 45–60). Hillsdale, NJ: Erlbaum.

Snyder, M. (1974). The self-monitoring of expressive behavior. *Journal of Personality and Social Psychology, 30,* 526–537.

Snyder, M. (1979). Self-monitoring processes. In L. Berkowitz (Ed.), *Advances in experimental social psychology, 12,* 86–128. New York: Academic Press.

Stahl, M. J. (1983). Achievement, power and managerial motivation: Selecting managerial talent with the job choice exercise. *Personnel Psychology, 36,* 775–789.

Stamp, G. P. (1986). Some observations on the career paths of women. *Journal of Applied Behavioral Science, 22,* 385–396.

Stamp, G. P. (1988). *Longitudinal research into methods of assessing managerial potential* (ARI Tech. Rep. No. DAJA45-86-c-0009). Alexandria, VA: U.S. Army Research Institute for the Behavioral and Social Sciences.

Starbuck, W. H. (1983). Organizations as action generators. *American Sociological Review, 48,* 91–102.

Starbuck, W. H. (1985).

Starbuck, W. H., & Milliken, F. J. (1988). Executives' perceptual filters: What they notice and how they make sense. In D. C. Hambrick (Ed.), *The executive effect: Concepts and methods for studying top managers.* Greenwich, CT: JAI Press.

Steinberg, A. G., & Leaman, J. A. (1990a). *The Army leader requirements tasks* analysis: Commissioned officer results (ARI Tech. Rep No. 898). Alexandria, VA: U. S. Army Research Institute for the Behavioral and Social Sciences.

Steinberg, A. G., & Leaman, J. A. (1990b). *Dimensions of Army commissioned and noncommissioned officer leadership* (ARI Tech. Rep. No. RT 879). Alexandria, VA: U.S. Army Research Institute for the Behavioral and Social Sciences.

Steiner, I. D. (1972). *Group process and productivity*. New York: Academic Press.

Sternberg, R. J. (1985). Implicit theories of intelligence, creativity, and wisdom. *Journal of Personality and Social Psychology, 49*, 606–627.

Sternberg, R. J. (1988). A three-faceted model of creativity. In R. J. Sternberg (Ed.), *The nature of creativity: Contemporary psychological perspectives* (pp. 125–147). Cambridge, MA: Cambridge University Press.

Sternberg, R. J. (1994). Experimental approaches to human intelligence. *European Journal of Psychological Assessment, 10*, 153–161.

Stewart, R. (1967). *Managers and their jobs: A study of the similarities and differences in the way managers spend their time*. London: Macmillan.

Stewart, S. R. (1992). *Leader development training needs assessment of U.S. Army battalion commanders*. Alexandria, VA: U.S. Army Research Institute for the Behavioral and Social Sciences.

Stewart, S. R. (1994). Strategic leader competencies/senior service college experiences. *Strategic Leadership Conference Proceedings*. Carlisle Barricks, PA: U.S. Army War College.

Stewart, S. R., & Angle, D. C. (1992). *Correlates of creative problem solving*. Alexandria, VA: U.S. Army Research Institute for the Behavioral and Social Sciences.

Stewart, S. R., & Hicks, J. M. (1987). *Leader development training assessment of U.S. Army Training and Doctrine Command (TRADOC) brigadier commanders* (ARI Research Rep. No. 1454). Alexandria, VA: U.S. Army Research Institute for the Behavioral and Social Sciences.

Stewart, S. R., Kilcullen, R., & Hopkins, J. E. (1993). *Strategic Leader Development Inventory (SLDI)*. Paper presented at the annual meeting of the Military Testing Association, Williamsburg, VA.

Stogdill, R. M. (1948). Personal factors associated with leadership: A survey of the literature. *Journal of Psychology, 25*, 35–71.

Stogdill, R. M. (1963). *Manual for the Leader Behavior Description Questionnaire Form-XII*. Columbus: Ohio State University, Bureau of Business Research.

Stogdill, R. M. (1971). *Handbook of leadership: A survey of the literature*. New York: Free Press.

Stogdill, R. M., & Shartle, C. L. (1958). *Manual for the Work Analysis Forms*. Columbus: Ohio State University, Bureau of Business Research.

Stogdill, R. M., Shartle, C. L., Wherry, R. J., & Jaynes, W. E. (1955). A factorial study of administrative behavior. *Personnel Psychology, 8*, 165–180.

Streufert, S. (1983). The stress of excellence. *Across the Board, 20*, 8–11.

Streufert, S. (1984). The dilemma of excellence: How strategic decision making can kill you. *International Management, 39*, 36–40.

Streufert, S., & Driver, M. J. (1967). Impression formation as a measure of the complexity of conceptual structure. *Education and Psychological Measurement, 27*, 1025–1039.

Streufert, S., & Nogami, G. (1989). Cognitive style and complexity: Implications for I/O psychology. In C. L. Cooper & I. Robertson (Eds.), *International review of industrial and organizational psychology* (pp. 93–143). Chichester, England: Wiley.

Streufert, S., Nogami, G., Swezey, R. W., Pogash, R. M., & Piasecki (1988). Computer assisted training on complex managerial performance [Special issue: Dialogue on the relationship of learning theory to instructional theory]. *Computers in Human Behavior, 4*, 77–88.

Streufert, S., & Streufert, S. C. (1978). *Behavior in the complex environment*. New York: Wiley.

Streufert, S., Streufert, S. C., & Castore, C. H. (1968). Leadership in negotiations and the complexity of conceptual structure. *Journal of Applied Psychology, 52*, 218–223.

Streufert, S., & Swezey, R. W. (1986). *Complexity, managers, and organizations*. Orlando, FL: Academic Press.

Stumpf, S. A. (1989). Work experiences that stretch managers' capacities for strategic thinking. *Journal of Management Development, 8,* 31–39.

Suedfeld, P., Corteen, R. S., & McCormick, C. (1986). The role of integrative complexity in military leadership: Robert E. Lee and his opponents. [Special issue: Applications of social psychology to military issues]. *Journal of Applied Social Psychology, 16,* 498–507.

Suedfeld, P., & Rank, A. D. (1976). Revolutionary leaders: Long-term success as a function of changes in conceptual complexity. *Journal of Personality and Social Psychology, 34,* 169–178.

Sutcliffe, K. M. (1994). What executives notice: Accurate perceptions in top management teams. *Academy of Management Journal, 5,* 1360–1378.

Swezey, R. W., Streufert, S., & Mietus, J. (1983). Development of an empirically derived taxonomy of organizational systems. *Journal of the Washington Academy of Sciences, 73,* 27–42.

Swezey, R. W., Streufert, S., Criswell, E. L., Unger, K. W., & van Rijn, P. (1984). *Development of a computer simulation for assessing decision-making style using cognitive complexity theory* (SAI Report No. SAI84-04-178). McLean, VA: Science Applications, Inc.

Sypher, B. O., & Sypher, H. E. (1993). Perceptions of communication ability: Self monitoring in an organizational setting. *Personality and Social Psychology Bulletin, 9,* 297–304.

Szilagyi, A. D., Jr., & Schweiger, D. M. (1984). Matching managers to strategies: A review and suggested framework. *Academy of Management Review, 9,* 626–637.

Taylor, R. (1975). Age and experience as determinants of managerial information processing and decision making performance. *Academy of Management Journal, 18,* 74–81.

Tesluk, P. E., & Jacobs, R. R. (1998). Toward an integrated model of work experience. *Personnel Psychology, 51,* 321–355.

Thomas, J. B., Clark, S. B., & Gioia, D. A. (1993). Strategic sensemaking and organizational performance: Linkages among scanning, interpretation, action and outcomes. *Academy of Management Journal, 36,* 239–270.

Thomas, J. B., & McDaniel, R. R., Jr. (1990). Interpreting strategic issues: Effects of strategy and the information processing structure of top management teams. *Academy of Management Journal, 33,* 286–306.

Thomas, J. B., Shankster, L. J., & Mathieu, J. E. (1994). Antecedents to organizational issue interpretation: The roles of single-level, cross-level, and content cues. *Academy of Management, 37,* 1252–1284.

Thomas, K. W. (1992). Conflict and negotiation processes in organizations. In M. D. Dunnette & L. M. Hough (Eds.), *Handbook of industrial and organizational psychology* (Vol. 3). Palo Alto, CA: Consulting Psychologists Press.

Thomas, K. W., & Schmidt, W. H. (1976). A survey of managerial interests with respect to conflict. *Academy of Management Journal, 19,* 315–318.

Thomas, P., & Greenberger, D. B. (1995). The relationship between leadership and time orientation. *Journal of Management Inquiry, 4,* 272–292.

Thompson, J. D. (1967). *Organizations in action.* New York: McGraw-Hill.

Thordsen, M. L., Galushka, J., Klein, G. A., Young, S., & Brezovic, C. P. (1990). *A knowledge elicitation study of military planning* (ARI Tech. Rep. No. 876). Alexandria, VA: U.S. Army Research Institute for the Behavioral and Social Sciences.

Thune, S. S., & House, R. J. (1970). Where long-range planning pays off—Findings of a survey of formal and informal planners. *Business Horizons, 13,* 81–87.

Thurstone, T. G., & Mellinger, J. J. (1985). *Cree Questionnaire.* Park Ridge, IL: London House. (Original work published 1957)

Tichy, N., & Devanna, M. A. (1986a). The transformational leader. *Training and Development Journal, 40,* 27–32.

Tichy, N., & Devanna, M. A. (1986b). *Transformational leadership.* New York: Wiley.

Tichy, N., & Ulrich, D. O. (1984). SMR forum: The leadership challenge—A call for the transformational leader. *Sloan Management Review, 26*(1), 59–68.

Tornow, W. W., & Pinto, P. R. (1976). The development of a managerial job taxonomy: A system for describing, classifying, and evaluating executive positions. *Journal of Applied Psychology, 61*, 410–418.

Trapp, E. P. (1955). Leadership and popularity as a function of behavioral predictions. *Journal of Abnormal and Social Psychology, 51*, 452–457.

Tremble, T. R., Jr. (1992). *Relationships of leadership competence with leader and unit performance effectiveness* (ARI Research Rep. No. RR1625). Alexandria, VA: U.S. Army Research Institute for the Behavioral and Social Sciences.

Tremble, T. R., Jr., & Alderks, C. E. (1991). *Measures for research on small unit preparedness for combat effectiveness* (ARI Research Note No. RN92-03). Alexandria, VA: U.S. Army Research Institute for the Behavioral and Social Sciences.

Trice, H. M., & Beyer, J. M. (1986). Charisma and its routinization in two social movement organizations. In B. M. Staw & L. L. Cummings (Eds.), *Research in organizational behavior: An annual series of analytical essays and critical reviews* (pp. 113–164). Greenwich, CT: JAI Press

Tsui, A. S. (1984a). A multiple constituency framework of managerial reputational effectiveness. In J. G. Hunt, D. Hosking, C. Schriesheim, & R. Stewart (Eds.), *Leaders and managers: International perspectives on managerial behavior and leadership* (pp. 28–44). New York: Pergamon Press.

Tsui, A. S. (1984b). A role set analysis of managerial reputation. *Organizational Behavior and Human Performance, 34*, 64–96.

Twohig, P. T., Rachford, D. L., Savell, J. M., & Rigby, C. K. (1987). *Implementation of a cognitive skills training program in ROTC: The leadership enrichment program* (ARI Res. Rep. No. 1436). Alexandria, VA: U.S. Army Research Institute for the Behavioral and Social Sciences.

Twohig, P. T., & Tremble, T. R., Jr. (1987). Methodological issues in measuring leader performance. *Proceedings of the 29th Annual Conference of the Military Testing Association*, 130–135.

Twohig, P. T., & Tremble, T. R., Jr. (1991). *Leadership performance in a tactical environment* (ARI Research Rep. No.

RR1580). Alexandria, VA: U.S. Army Research Institute for the Behavioral and Social Sciences.

U.S. Army War College. (1994). *Strategic leadership conference: Proceedings.* Carlisle Barracks, PA: Author.

U.S. Department of the Army. (1987). *Executive leadership* (Department of the Army Pamphlet 600-80). Washington, DC: HQDA.

U.S. Department of the Army (1993). *Leadership at senior and strategic levels* (Working draft, Field Manual 22-103). Carlisle Barracks, PA: U.S. Army War College.

U.S. Department of the Army (1995). *Force XXI: Meeting the 21st century challenge.* Fort Monroe, VA: Office of the Chief of Staff, U.S. Army.

Van Zelst, R. H. (1952). Empathy test scores of union leaders. *Journal of Applied Psychology, 36*, 293–295.

Virany, B., Tushman, M., & Romanelli, E. (1985). Executive succession and organizational outcomes in turbulent environments: An organizational learning approach. *Organization Science, 3*, 72–91.

Wagner, R. K., & Sternberg, R. J. (1985). Practical intelligence in real-world pursuits: The role of tacit knowledge. *Journal of Personality and Social Psychology, 48*, 436–458.

Wagner, R. K., & Sternberg, R. J. (1986). Tacit knowledge and intelligence in the everyday world. In R. J. Sternberg & R. K. Wagner (Eds.), *Practical intelligence: Nature and origins of competence in the everyday world.* Cambridge, MA: Cambridge University Press.

Waldman, D. A., Bass, B. M., & Einstein, W. E. (1987). Leadership and outcomes of the performance appraisal process. *Journal of Occupational Psychology, 60*, 177–186.

Waldman, D. A., Bass, B. M., & Yammarino, F. J. (1990). Adding to contingent-reward behavior: The augmenting effect of charismatic leadership. *Group and Organization Studies, 15*, 381–394.

Walsh, J. P., & Fahey, L. (1986). The role of negotiated belief structures in strategy making. *Journal of Management, 12*, 325–338.

Ward, W. C., Friedericksen, N., & Carlson, S. B. (1980). Construct validity of free-response and machine-scorable forms of a test. *Journal of Educational Measurement, 17*, 11–29.

Weber, M. (1947). *The theory of social and economic organization* (T. Parsons, Trans.). New York: Free Press.

Weick, K. E. (1979). *The social psychology of organizations* (2nd ed.). Reading, MA: Addison-Wesley.

Weiner, N., & Mahoney, T. A. (1981). A model of corporate performance as a function of environmental, organizational, and leadership influences. *Academy of Management Journal, 24*, 453–470.

Westley, F., & Mintzberg, H. (1989). Visionary leadership and strategic management. *Strategic Management Journal, 10*, 17–32.

Wiersema, M. F., & Bantel, K. A. (1992). Top management team demography and corporate strategic change. *Academy of Management Journal, 35*, 91–121.

Williams, L. K. (1965). Some correlates of risk taking. *Personnel Psychology, 18*, 297–310.

Winter, D. G. (1987). Leader appeal, leader performance, and the motives profile of leaders and followers: A study of American presidents and elections. *Journal of Personality and Social Psychology, 52*, 96–102.

Wood, R., & Bandura. A. (1989). Social cognitive theory of organizational management. *Academy of Management Review, 14*, 361–384.

Woolridge, S. W., & Floyd, B. (1990). The strategy process, middle management involvement, and organizational performance. *Strategic Management Journal, 11*, 231–241.

Wortman, M. S. (1982). Strategic management and changing leader–follower roles. *Journal of Applied Behavioral Science, 18*, 371–383.

Yammarino, F. J., Spangler, W. D., & Bass, B. M. (1993). Transformational leadership and performance: A longitudinal investigation. *Leadership Quarterly, 4*, 81–102.

Yukl, G. A., (1989). *Leadership in organizations* (2nd ed.). Englewood Cliffs, NJ: Prentice Hall.

Yukl, G. A. (1994). *Leadership in organizations* (3rd ed.). Englewood Cliffs, NJ: Prentice Hall.

Yukl, G. A., & Van Fleet, D. D. (1992). Theory and research on leadership in organizations. In M. Dunnette & L. Hough (Eds.), *Handbook of industrial and organizational psychology* (Vol. 3). Palo Alto, CA: Consulting Psychologists Press.

Yukl, G. A., Wall, S., & Lepsinger, R. (1990). Preliminary report on the validation of the management practices survey. In K. E. Clark & M. B. Clark (Eds.), *Measures of leadership*. West Orange, NJ: Leadership Library of America.

Zaccaro, S. J. (1994). *Senior leadership: An annotated bibliography of research supported by the Army Research Institute*. Alexandria, VA: U.S. Army Research Institute for the Behavioral and Social Sciences.

Zaccaro, S. J. (1996, March). *Social complexity and the competencies required for effective military leadership*. Paper presented at the Army Leadership Conference, Chicago.

Zaccaro, S. J., Foti, R. J., & Kenny, D. A. (1991). Self-monitoring and trait-based variance in leadership: An investigation of leader flexibility across multiple group situations. *Journal of Applied Psychology, 76*, 308–315.

Zaccaro, S. J., Gilbert, J. A., Thor, K. K., & Mumford, M. D. (1991). Leadership and social intelligence: Linking social perceptiveness and behavioral flexibility to leader effectiveness. *Leadership Quarterly, 2*, 317–331.

Zaccaro, S. J., Marks, M., O'Connor-Boes, J., & Costanza, D. (1995). *The nature and assessment of leader mental models* (MRI Rep. No. 95-3). Bethesda, MD: Management Research Institute.

Zaccaro, S. J., Mumford, M. D., Marks, M., Connelly, M. S., Threlfall, K. V., Gilbert, J., & Fleishman, E. A. (1995). *Cognitive and temperament determinants of Army leadership* (MRI Tech. Rep. for the U.S. Army Research Institute for the Behavioral and Social Sciences). Bethesda, MD: Management Research Institute.

Zaccaro, S. J., Zazanis, M. M., Diana, M., & Gilbert, J. A. (1994). *Investigation of a background data measure of social intelligence* (ARI Tech. Rep. No. 1024). Alexandria, VA: U.S. Army Research Institute for the Behavioral and Social Sciences.

Zajac, E. J. (1990). CEO selection, compensation, and firm performance: A theoretical integration and empirical analysis. *Strategic Management Journal, 11,* 217–230.

Zenger, T. R., & Lawrence, B. S. (1989). Organizational demography: The differential effects of age and tenure distributions on technical communication. *Academy of Management Journal, 32,* 353–376.

Zsambok, C. E. (1993a). *Advanced team decision making: A model and training implications.* Alexandria, VA: U.S. Army Research Institute for the Behavioral and Social Sciences.

Zsambok, C. E. (1993b). Advanced team decision making in C^2 settings. *JDL Proceeding.*

Zukin, L. (1996). *Conceptual and empirical research on top management teams: An annotated bibliography.* Fairfax, VA: George Mason University, Center for Behavioral and Cognitive Studies.

Zukin, L. B., Cooke, A. E., & McGee, M. (1996, March). *Using MBTI preferences to predict strategic leadership performance.* Paper presented at the 17th annual Industrial/Organizational and Organizational Behavior Conference, Toledo, OH.

Author Index

Numbers in italics refer to listings in reference sections.

Subject Index

About the Author

Stephen J. Zaccaro received his MA (1980) and PhD (1981) from the University of Connecticut, specializing in social psychology. He is currently an associate professor of psychology at George Mason University, Fairfax, Virginia, and has also held positions on the faculties of Virginia Technical and Holy Cross College. He has been studying and teaching about leadership for almost 20 years and has written numerous articles, book chapters, and technical reports on leadership, group dynamics, team performance, and work attitudes. He has coedited two other books, *Occupational Stress and Organizational Effectiveness* (1987) and *The Nature of Organizational Leadership* (2001). He has also coedited three special issues of *Leadership Quarterly* on individual differences and leadership and is on the journal's editorial board. In addition, he has directed funded projects in the areas of team performance and shared mental models, leadership training, cognitive and metacognitive leadership capacities, and executive leadership.